THE BONDS WE SHARE

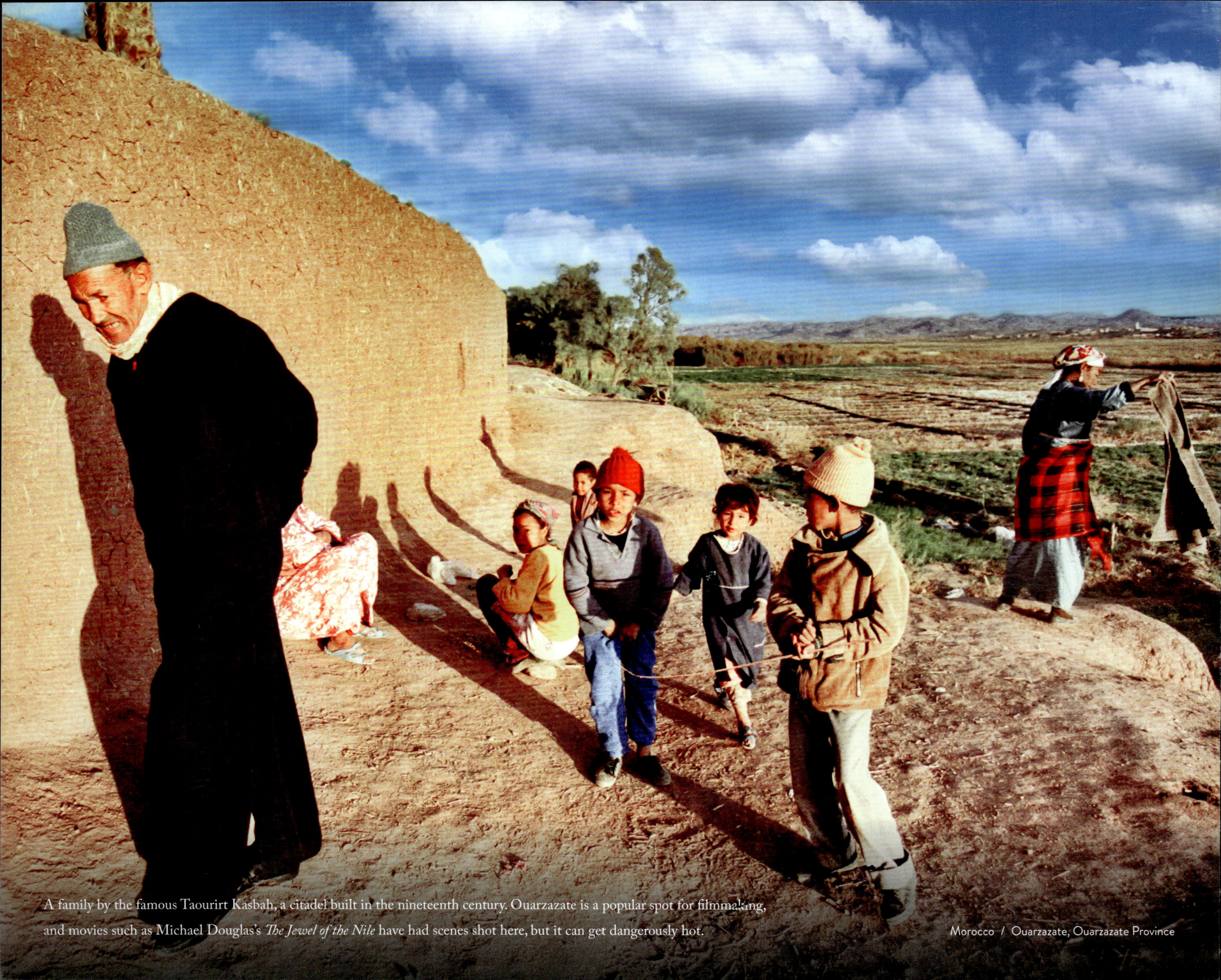

A family by the famous Taourirt Kasbah, a citadel built in the nineteenth century. Ouarzazate is a popular spot for filmmaking, and movies such as Michael Douglas's *The Jewel of the Nile* have had scenes shot here, but it can get dangerously hot.

Morocco / Ouarzazate, Ouarzazate Province

DR. GLENN LOSACK

THE BONDS WE SHARE

Images of Humanity, 40 Years Around the Globe

APOLLO
PUBLISHERS

The Bonds We Share: Images of Humanity, 40 Years Around the Globe

Published in compliance with California's Proposition 65.

Library of Congress Control Number: 2020936300

Print ISBN: 978-1-948062-41-1

Ebook ISBN: 978-1-948062-45-9

Printed in China.

This book is dedicated to the impoverished, the infirm, the voiceless, those whose suffering is ignored, those whose pain is never quelled, and those in the millions who motivate me to continue my mission in life, which is to share their plight so that hearts will open and lives will improve.

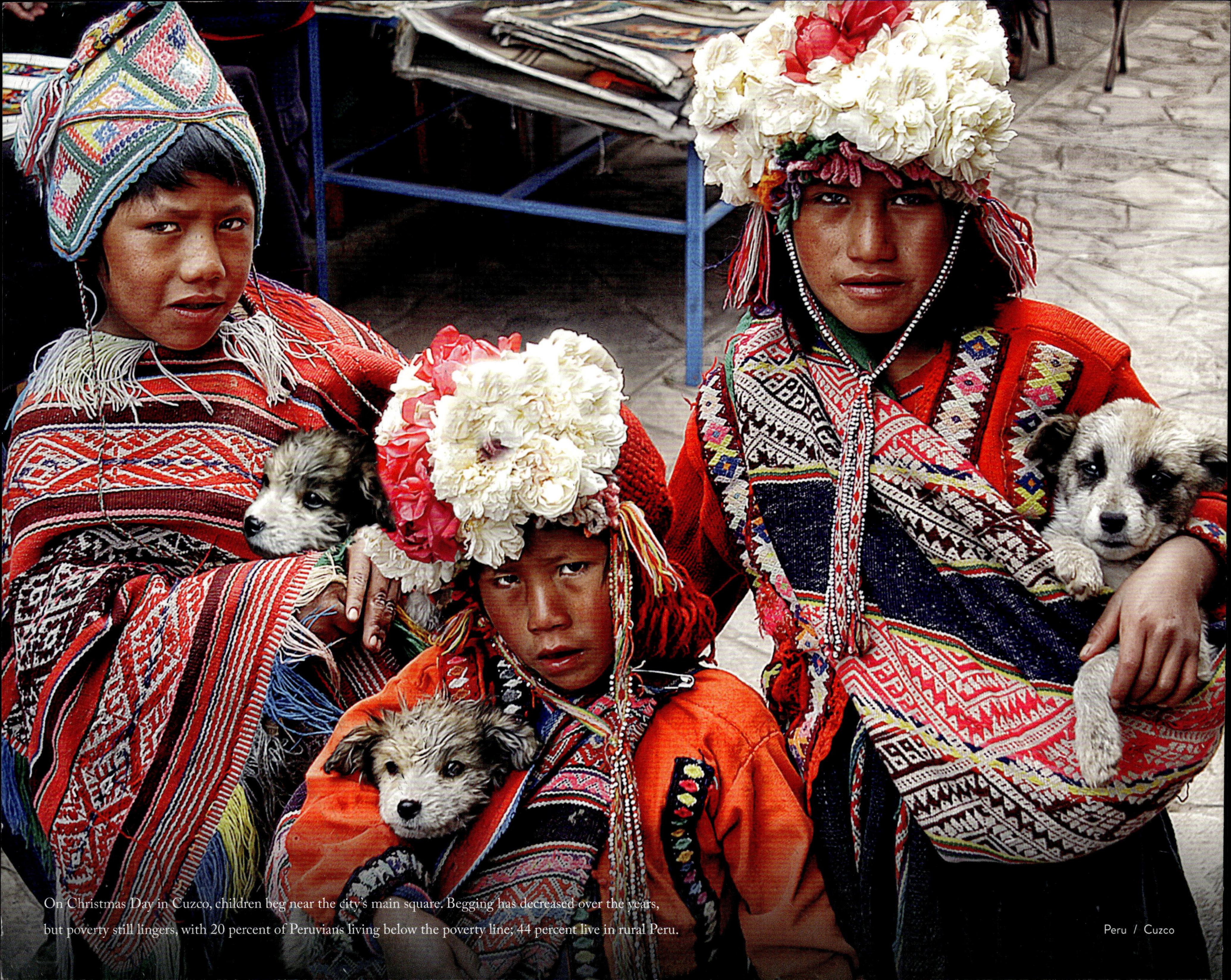

On Christmas Day in Cuzco, children beg near the city's main square. Begging has decreased over the years, but poverty still lingers, with 20 percent of Peruvians living below the poverty line; 44 percent live in rural Peru.

Contents

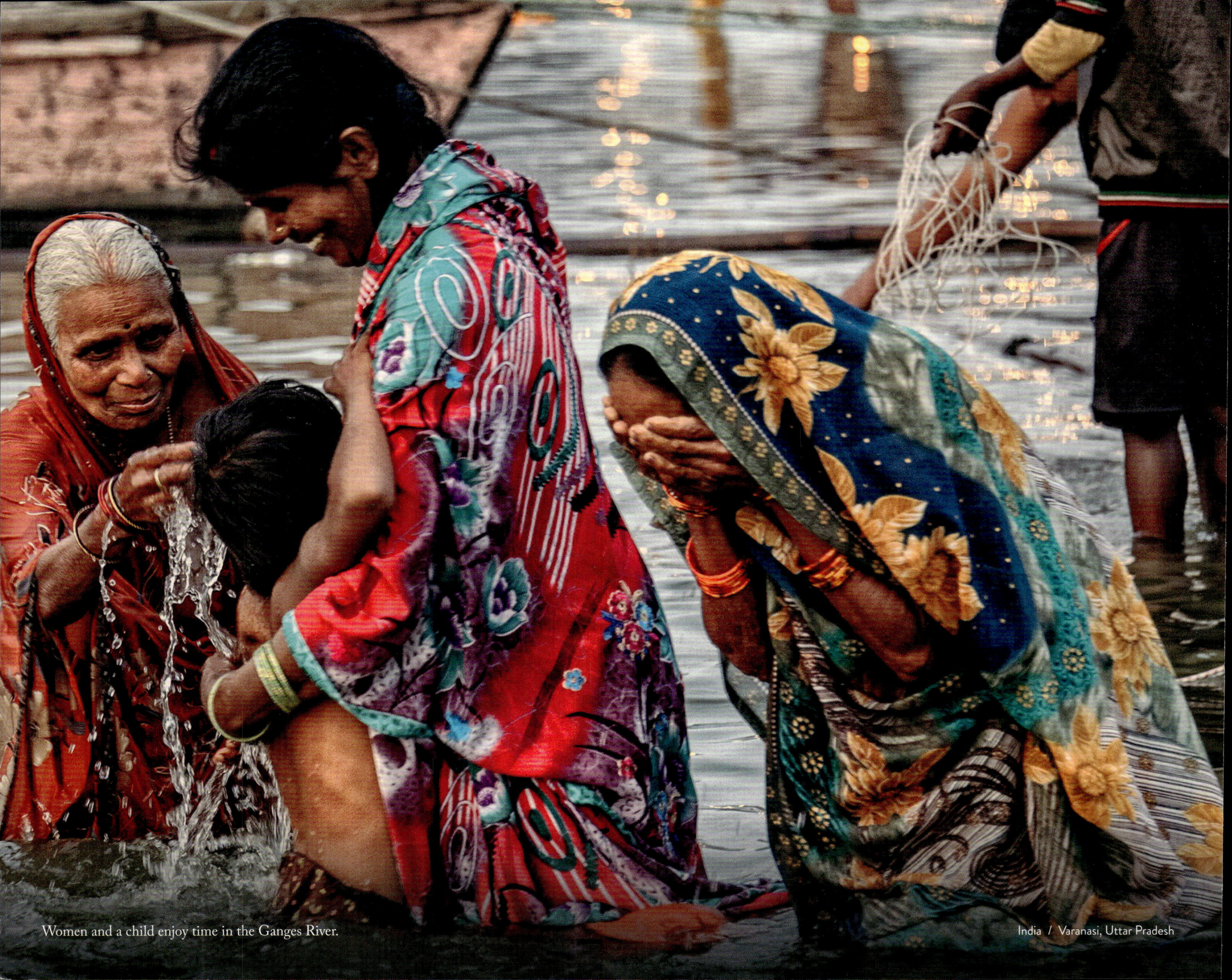

Women and a child enjoy time in the Ganges River.

India / Varanasi, Uttar Pradesh

FOREWORD
BY DR. ROBI LUDWIG

Every picture tells a story, especially when Dr. Glenn Losack is the photographer. In this uplifting book, *The Bonds We Share*, his street photography keenly documents the universality and commonality of the human condition.

Glenn captures foreign cultures with an emotive awareness and quite successfully involves his audience in this endeavor. His audience is moved emotionally—not just passively—by the photographs. He has an amazing knack for capturing his subject with respect, dignity, and elegance without being overbearing or intrusive. Every photograph is depicted with care and grace.

In this photo essay, we gain a more powerful understanding of the world's people. Dr. Losack's work is massive and exquisite, covering so many of life's more meaningful and evocative themes. In a world so divided and divisive, this book teaches us that we are more similar than different—a powerful and necessary message for our times.

I have learned so much about life from knowing Glenn. He is one of the most insightful artistic voices of our time—it is impossible not to be a huge fan.

PREFACE

What do the people of the West have in common with the people of India, Bangladesh, the Dominican Republic, Cambodia, Haiti, or Vietnam, to name a few? Some of those who live in the West think of the aforementioned nations as poor, always in dire straits. Some documentaries, in an attempt to show how the world's poorest live, contribute to the West's sense of separation and superiority and to a perception that Westerners are better off because they have more material things, higher standards of living, and little in common with the poorest of the poor. This can lead to derision, prejudice, misconceptions, and an inevitable ignorance.

Much of the photojournalism that exists of impoverished nations focuses on destitution, hardship, paucity, beggary, and despondency. Yet this is only half of the picture that I have found in my forty years trekking around the globe, mostly in developing nations, as a photographer, physician, and social activist. I have become quite intimate with places that most tourists avoid—the slums, alleys, shanties, and ghettos of these nations. I call myself a "traveler," not a tourist.

Through my lens I have penetrated the soul of these nations and found what I believe most foreigners visiting these places often overlook or plainly fail to recognize: Regardless of our geographic, cultural, and socioeconomic differences, there are bonds that link us all. Though we may look different, speak in different tongues, wear different clothes, have different standards and ways of living, and pray to different gods, we share a common humanity. This is the main thrust and core of *The Bonds We Share.*

In *The Bonds We Share*, I present hundreds of photographs of people, curated from tens of thousands of images taken over the last forty years from around the world, that speak to shared worldwide phenomena: the mother-child bond, children at play, love of animals, religious devotion, work, travel, joy, and sorrow. The photos are organized into seven sections, each based on a universal theme and the ligaments that connect all humans, regardless of our differences. These chapters are Devotion, Inheritance, Journey, Pastime, Connection, Resilience, and Community.

In my travels I have marveled at how people who live without clean water, proper medical care, electricity, in intense heat with little or no education or material things that we in the West take for granted, survive with joy, laughter, tenderness, compassion, celebration, and, above all, hope in spite of all of these adversities. It is crystal clear that money and materialism certainly do not lead to happiness, and the ostentatious display and gratification of one's wealth are certainly ephemeral. I have learned from my work as a psychiatrist and over four decades of photographing in developing nations that we are all born with a self-worth and a dignity intact that need to be respected.

I have encountered many people living in such countries who, despite abysmal poverty, declare that they are happy because of their families and their faith. To my surprise they appear to be satisfied with their lot in life. In my experiences, I have witnessed an optimism in many impoverished people that things will improve and their god will provide and take care of them. These amazing people who live without the materialism and government handouts we have in Western society certainly have the capacity to love one another and live life to the fullest.

In this photo-essay, I try to capture the humanity in the faces of people, both at home and abroad, from those who live in poverty and have no social advocacy, depending on the generosity of others to survive by begging, to those who live in well-to-do nations. Educated or uneducated, wealthy or impoverished, from the United States or Bangladesh, practicing Hinduism or Judaism, we each want happiness instead of suffering and a brighter future for our children. The only difference is the circumstances that lead us to where we are in life.

At a time when certain rhetoric fuels fears of immigrants, refugees, and those who look, sound, dress, love, and worship in ways that are different from our own subjective sense of what's "normal," *The Bonds We Share* shines a luminous spotlight on the qualities and experiences that bind us all together as members of the human race and proves that we are more alike than different in so many ways.

While historically much emphasis has been placed on one's continent, nation, and religion, communities can no longer afford to think of themselves as separate and even exist in isolation. The unprecedented Covid-19 pandemic that began in 2019 is sheer evidence of how people in every nation of the world are susceptible to a common invisible enemy and comprise one family—all experiencing fear, grief, anger, economic loss, sickness, distrust, and the horrific consequences of death in our families.

This global pandemic requires a sense of mutual accountability for almost all of the planet's eight billion people. As members of one family, we must care instead of disparage, help and not ignore, and support those in need rather than repel them. We can no longer put up fences, shun our neighbors, or fight for oil and natural resources. We must consider the interests of others.

The vision of a peaceful world laid out in the lyrics of John Lennon's "Imagine" might be a faraway dream, but it's a hopeful and compassionate blueprint for mankind to start realizing that we are more similar than different. Cooperation, love, and compassion will, I believe, lead to a more stable and civilized future, or, in the words of John Lennon, "a brotherhood of man."

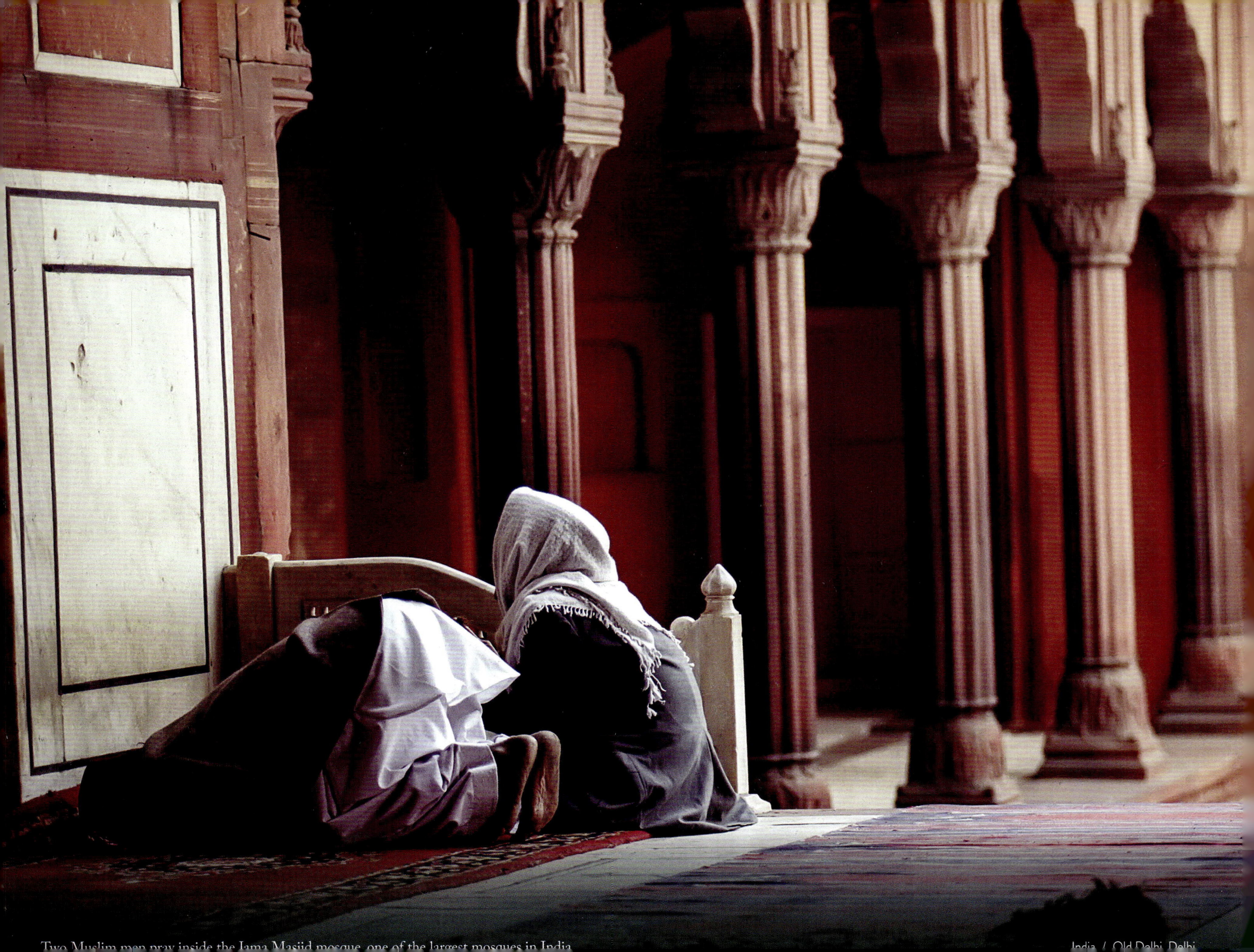

Two Muslim men pray inside the Jama Masjid mosque, one of the largest mosques in India.

India / Old Delhi, Delhi

DEVOTION

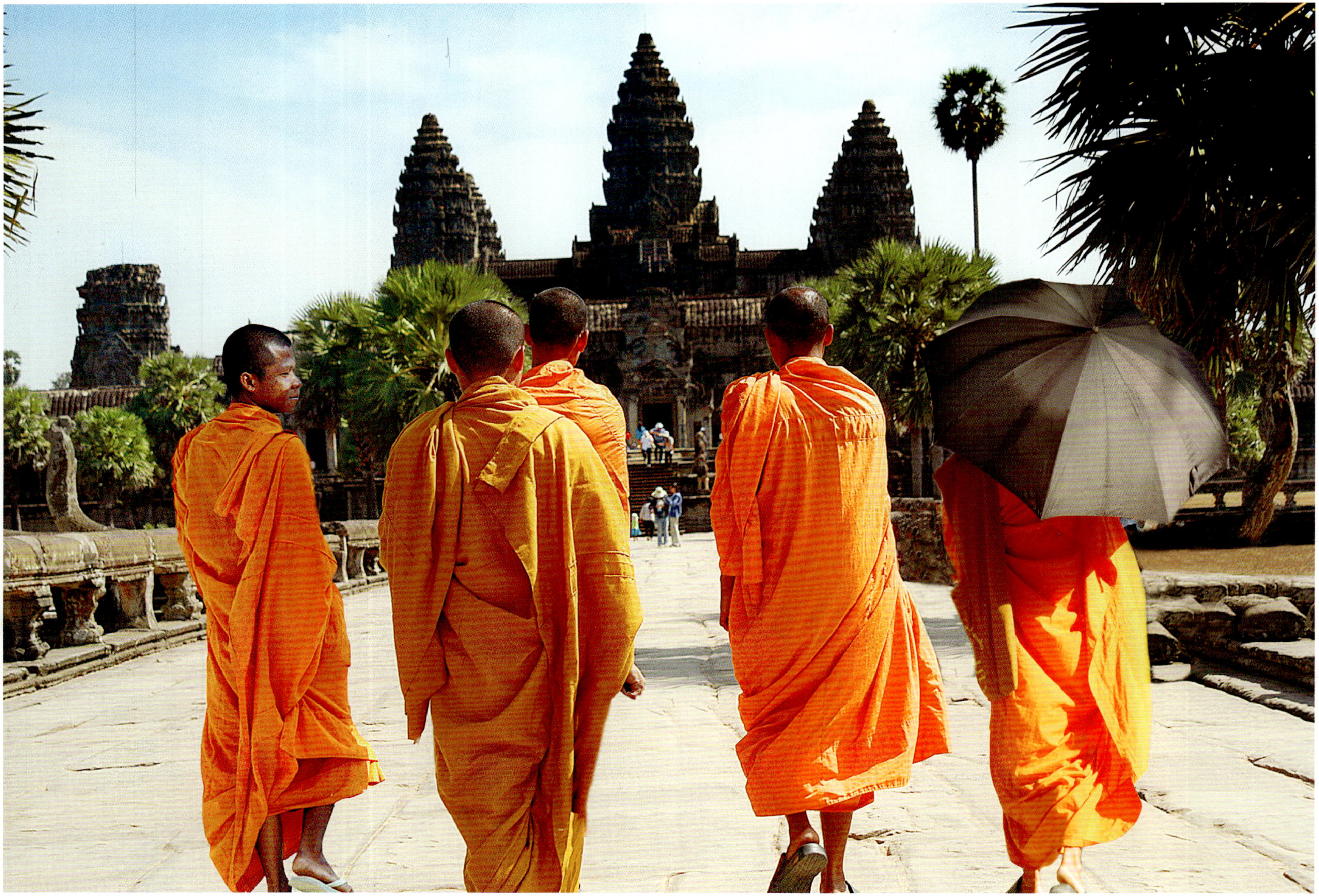

Cambodian monks walk toward Angkor Wat, a Hindu-Buddhist temple. Angkor Wat is the largest religious monument in the world and visited by millions of people each year.

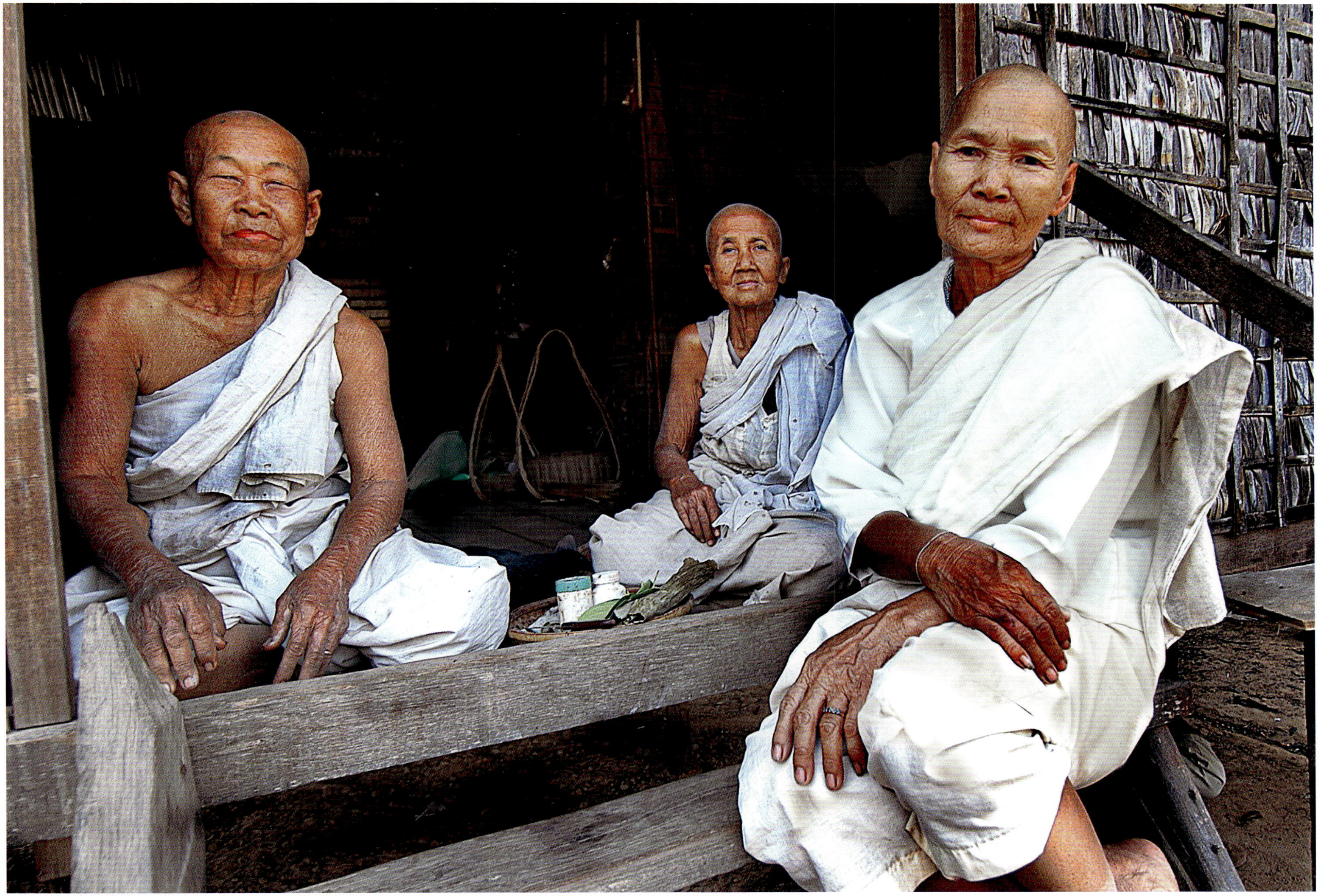

The Cambodian constitution enshrines Buddhism as the official religion of the nation. Monks like these perform ceremonies and minister to people's social and emotional needs. In the mornings, monks leave their temple and walk the streets for almsgiving. People stop the monks and give them food, and the monks give them a blessing in return.

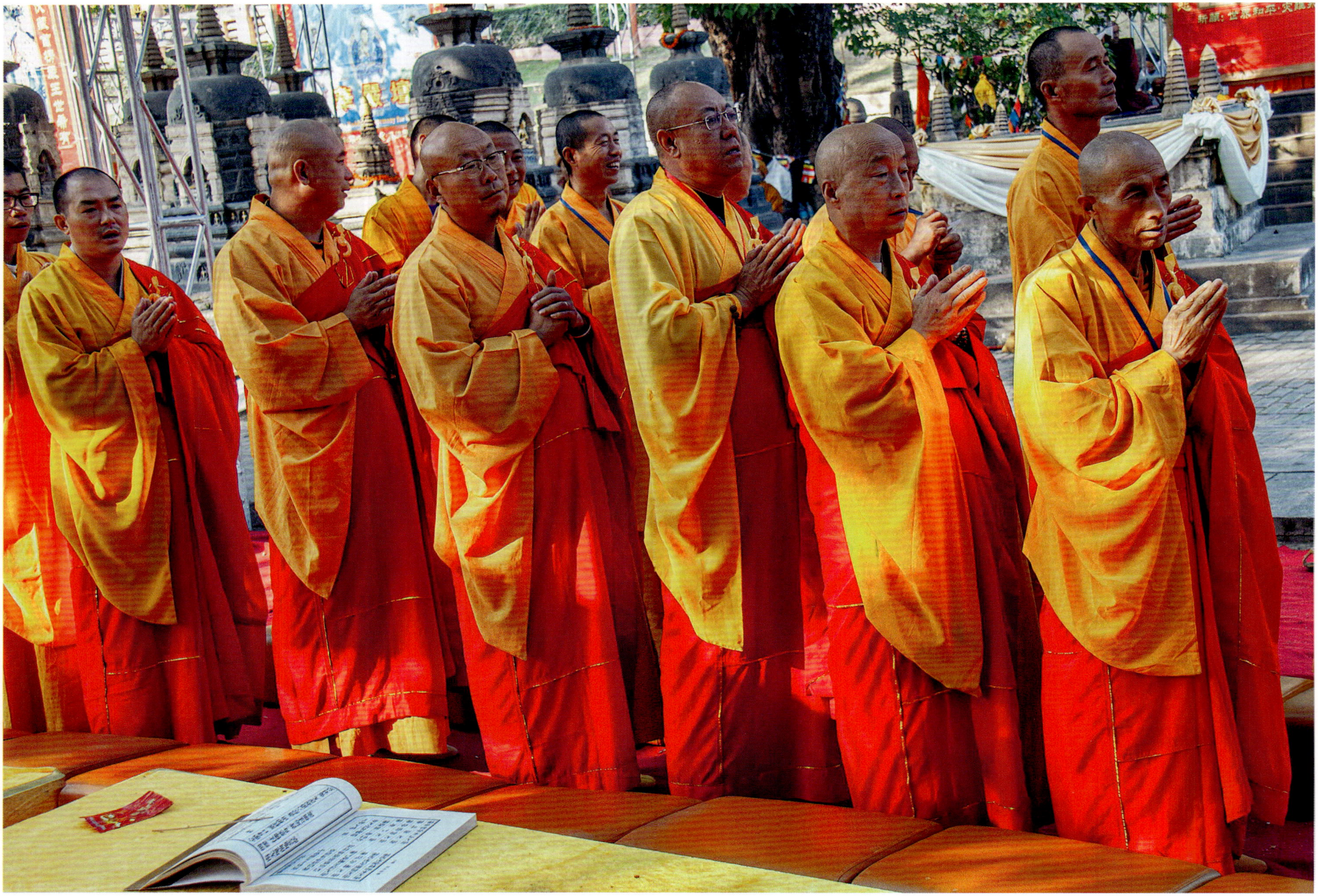

Monks pray in Bodh Gaya, the place where Buddha reached enlightenment.

With the border open, Thai monks cross the Sai River, going from Mae Sai in northern Thailand to Tachileik in eastern Myanmar. Buddhism is the official religion of both countries. A young boy is positioned on the bridge to ask passersby for money.

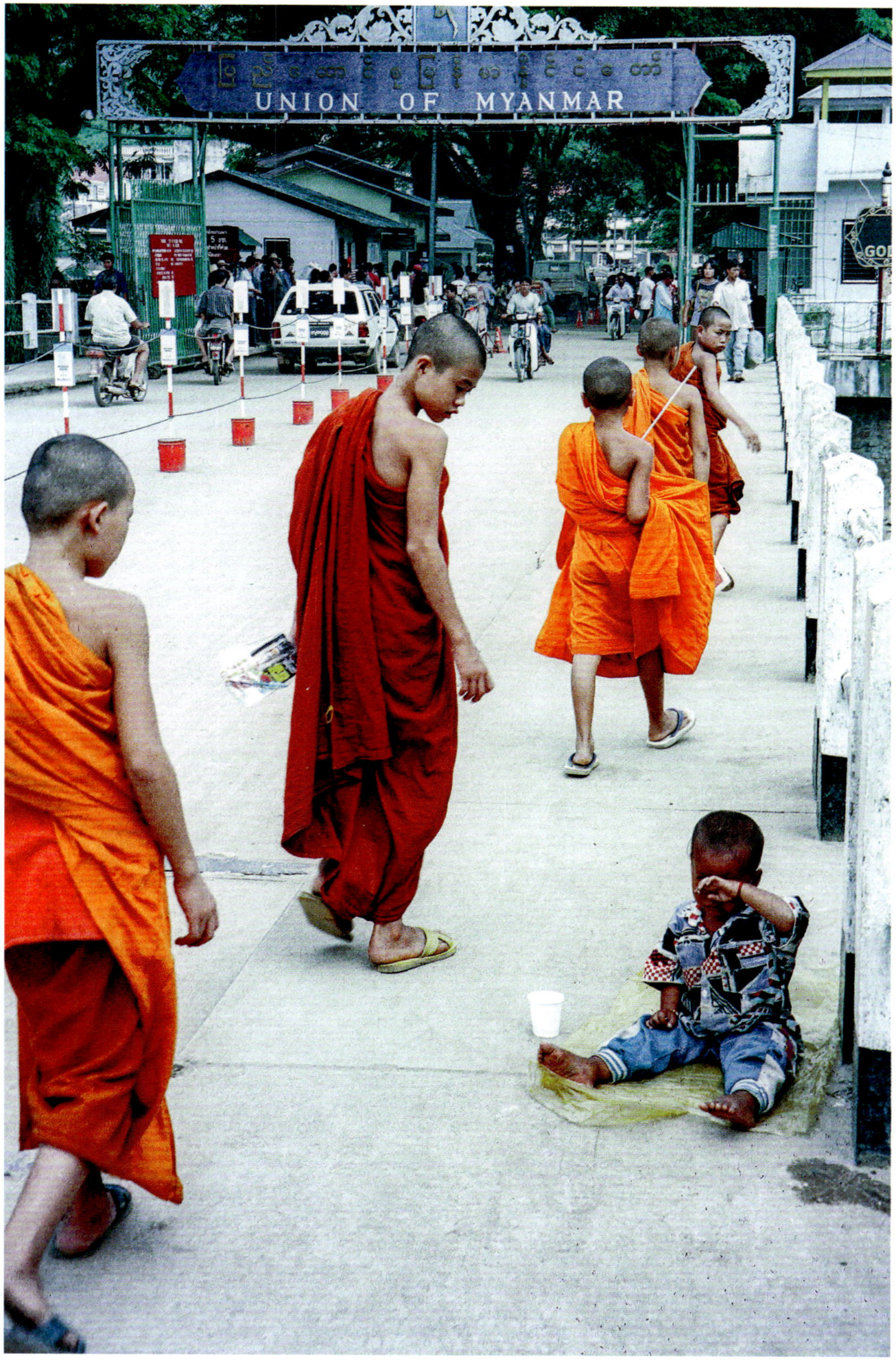

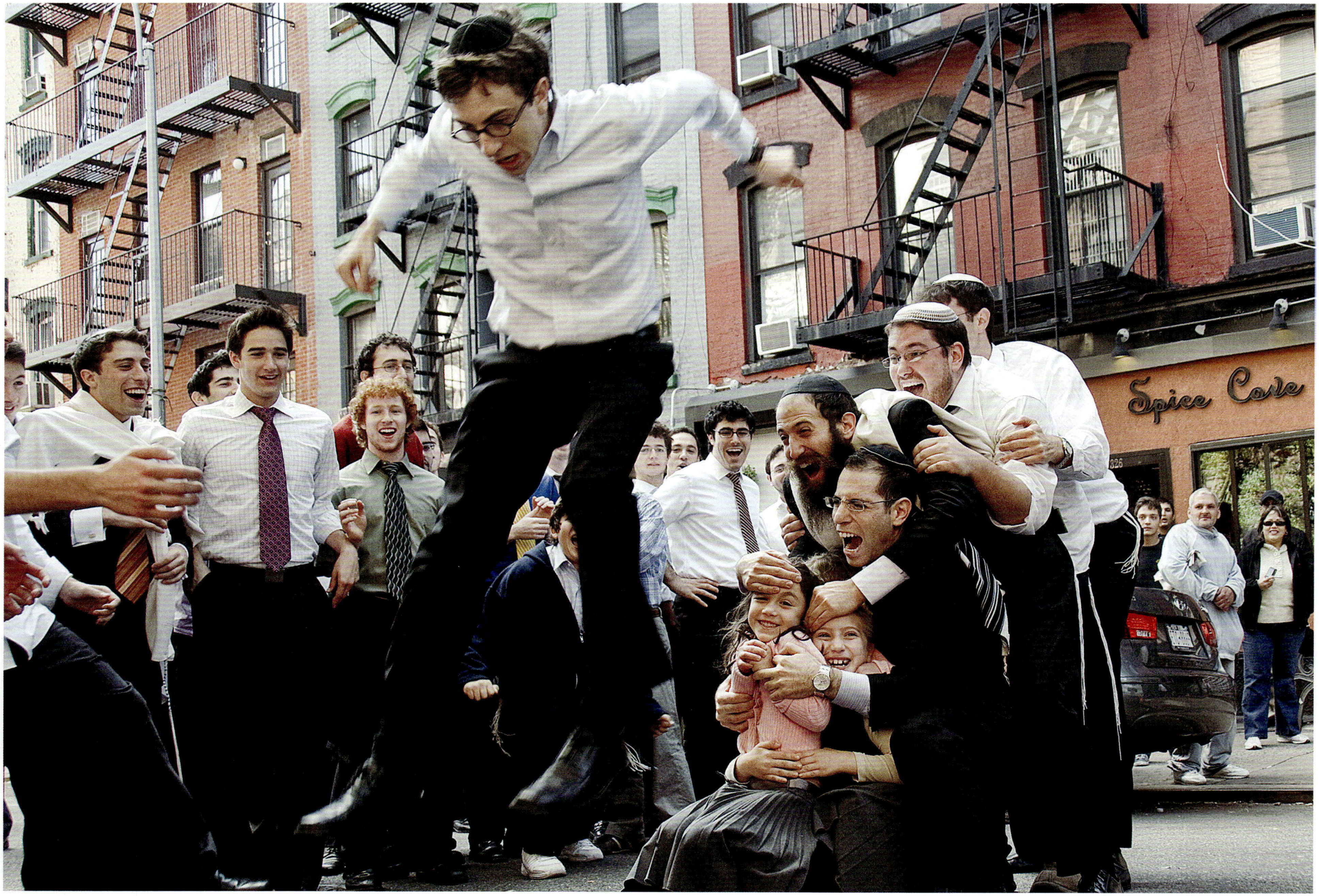

In Manhattan's East Village, a group of Orthodox Jews play leapfrog during the holiday of Simchat Torah. It is a day of celebration, and they have just left services at Sixth Street Community Synagogue.

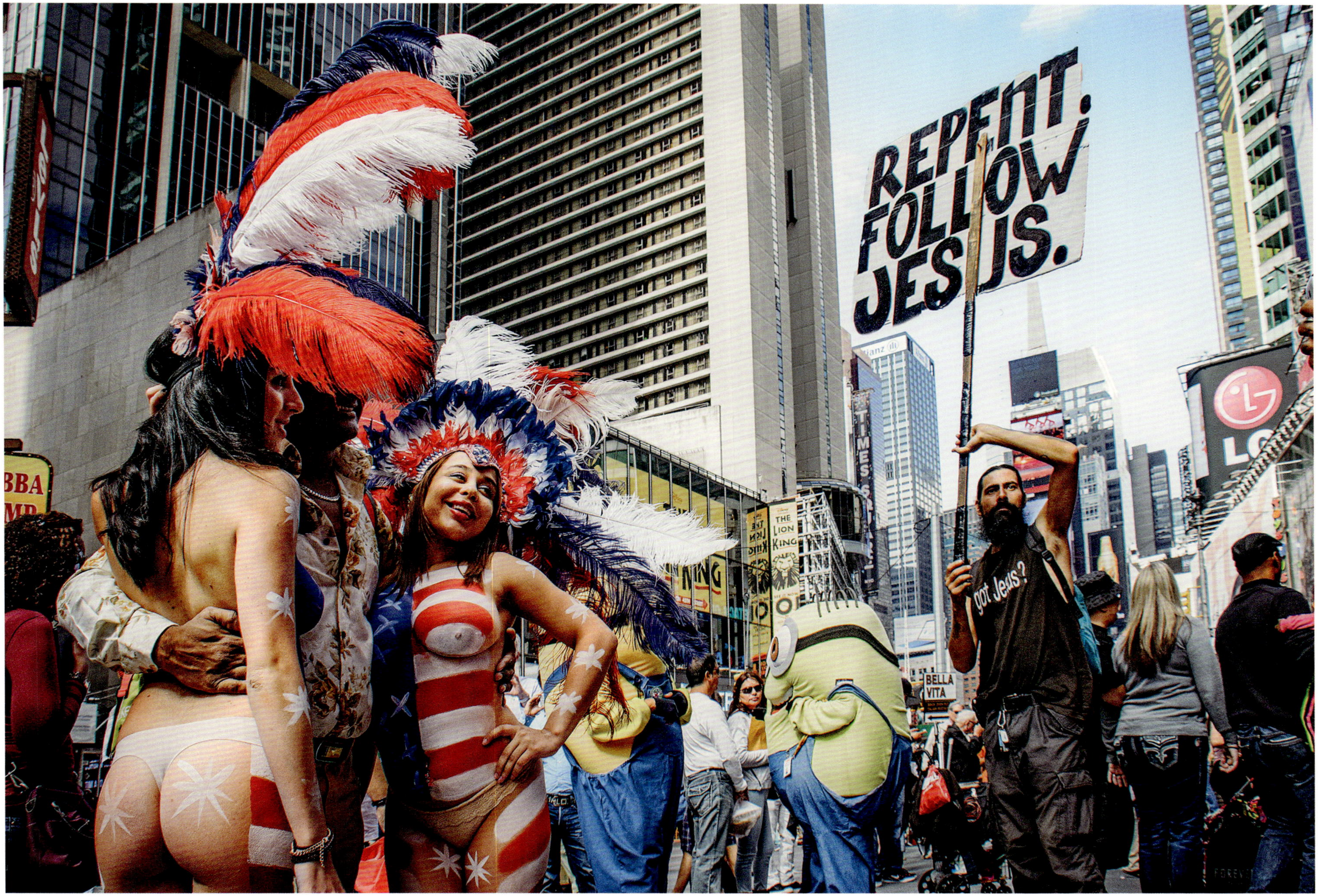

A man holds a sign imploring repentance as tourists and performers fill Manhattan's Times Square.

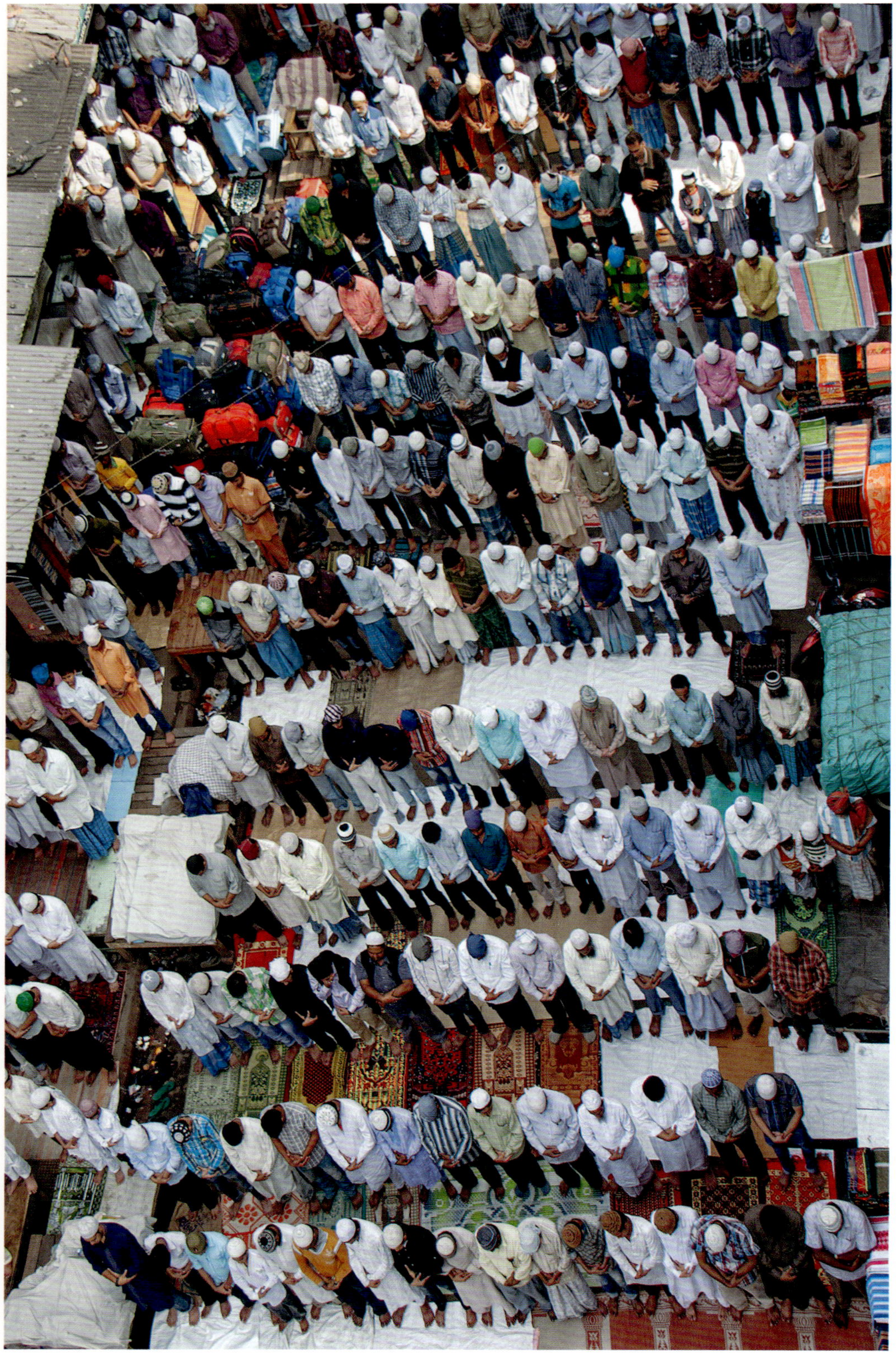

Men participating in ju‘mah,
Islam's Friday prayer.

India / Kolkata, West Bengal

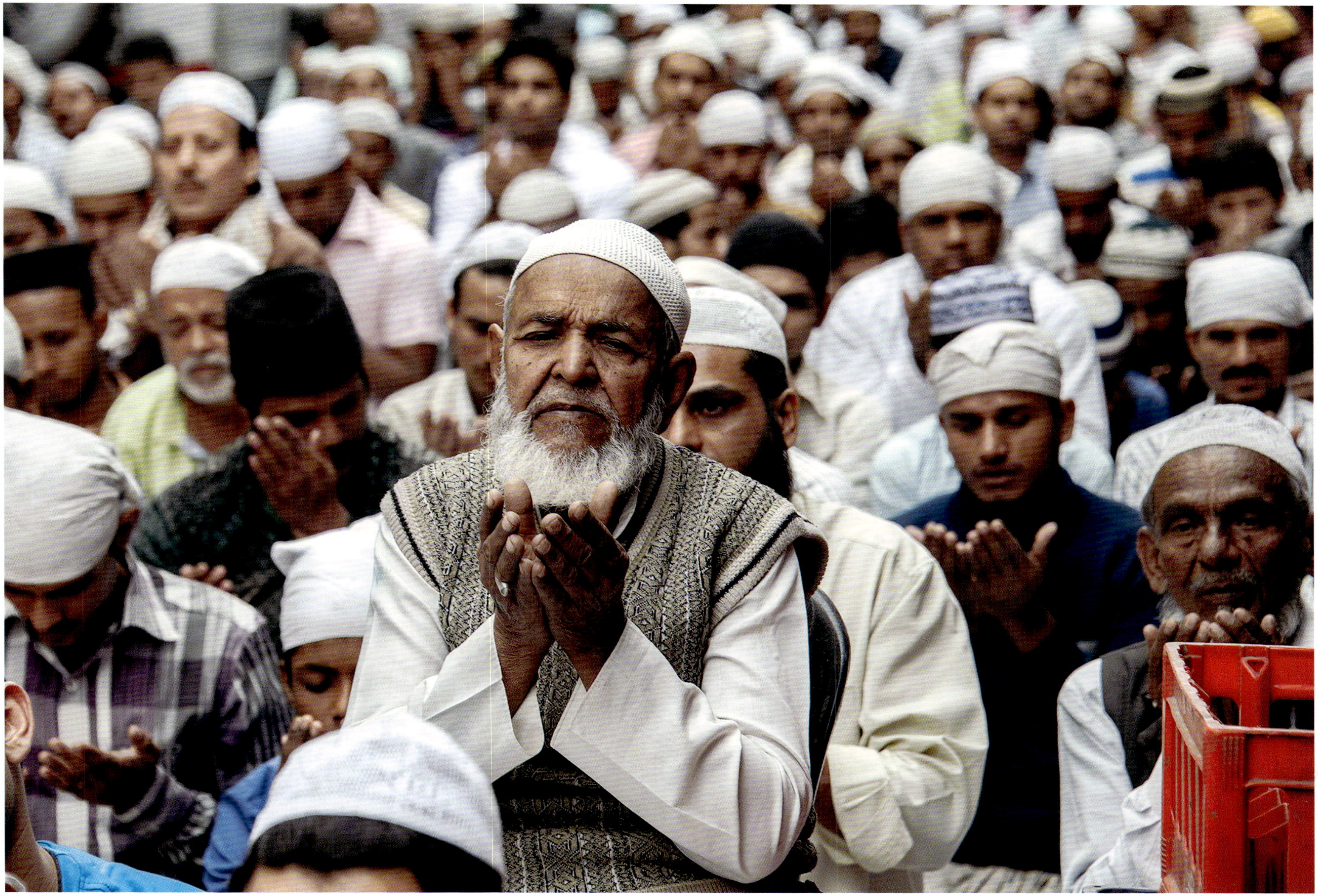

Praying with open palms is a part of Shiite Islam.

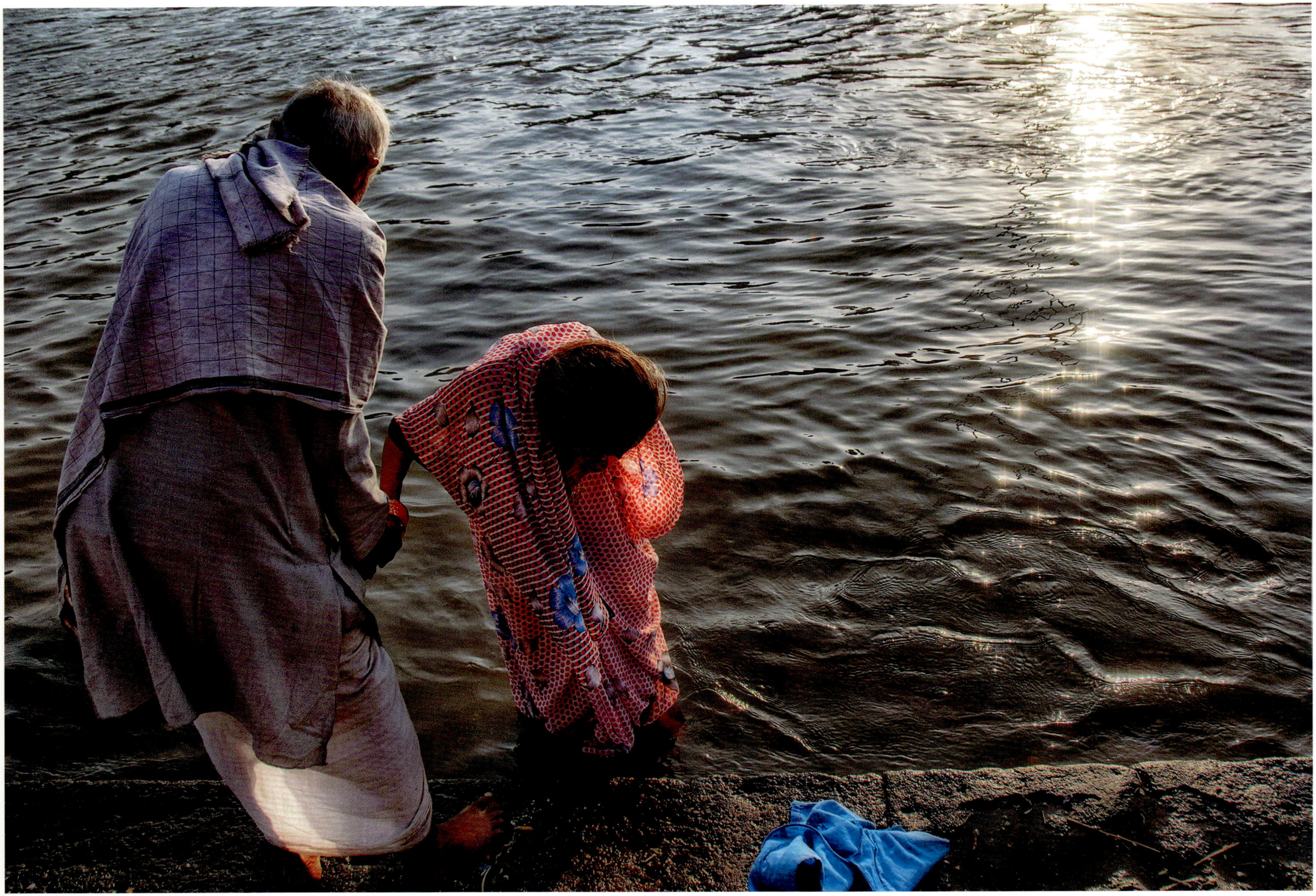

A couple perform puja, a prayer ritual, in the Godavari River, India's second longest river.

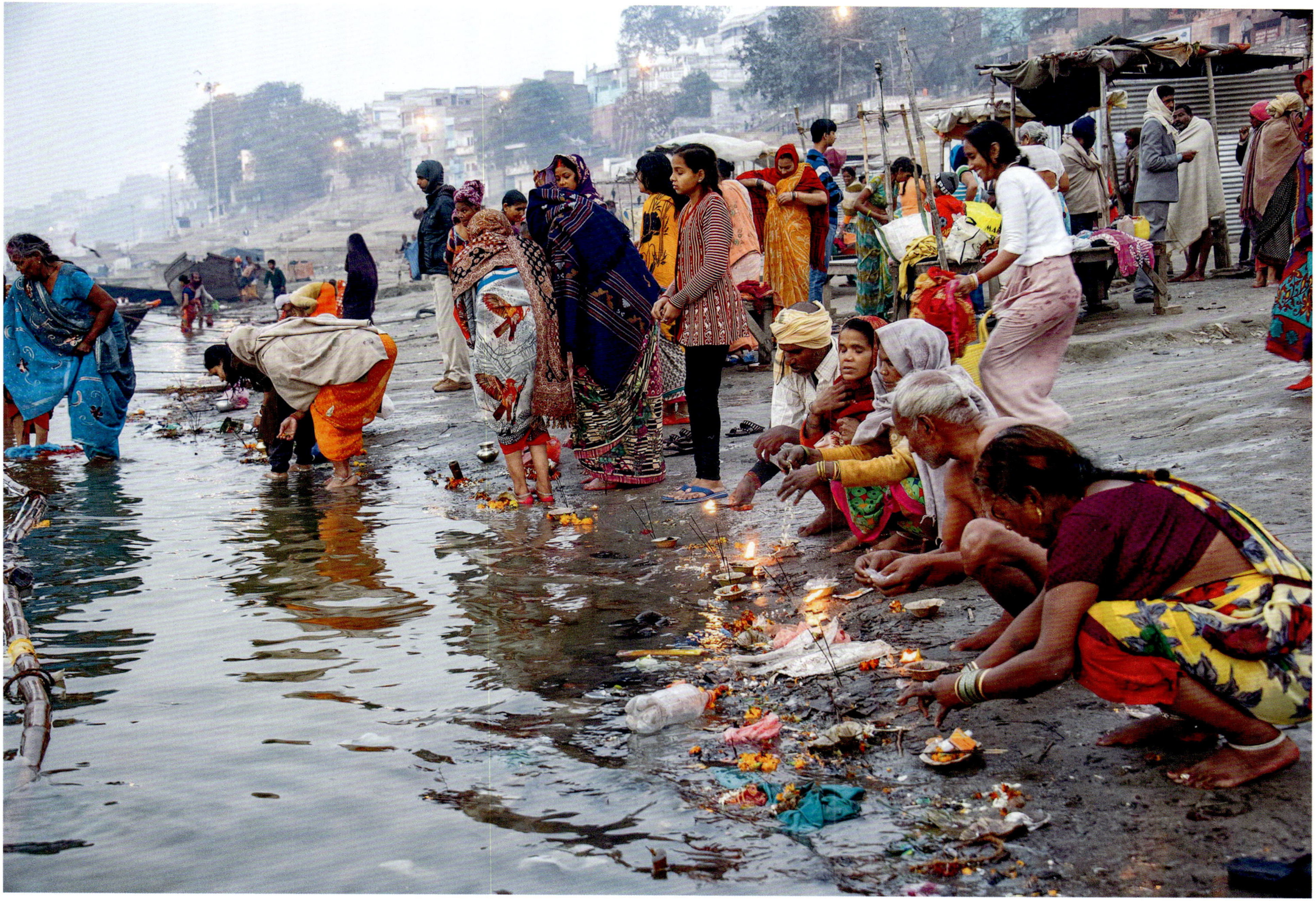

In the early morning in Varanasi, considered by Hindus to be India's holiest city, people perform puja in the Ganges River, India's longest river.

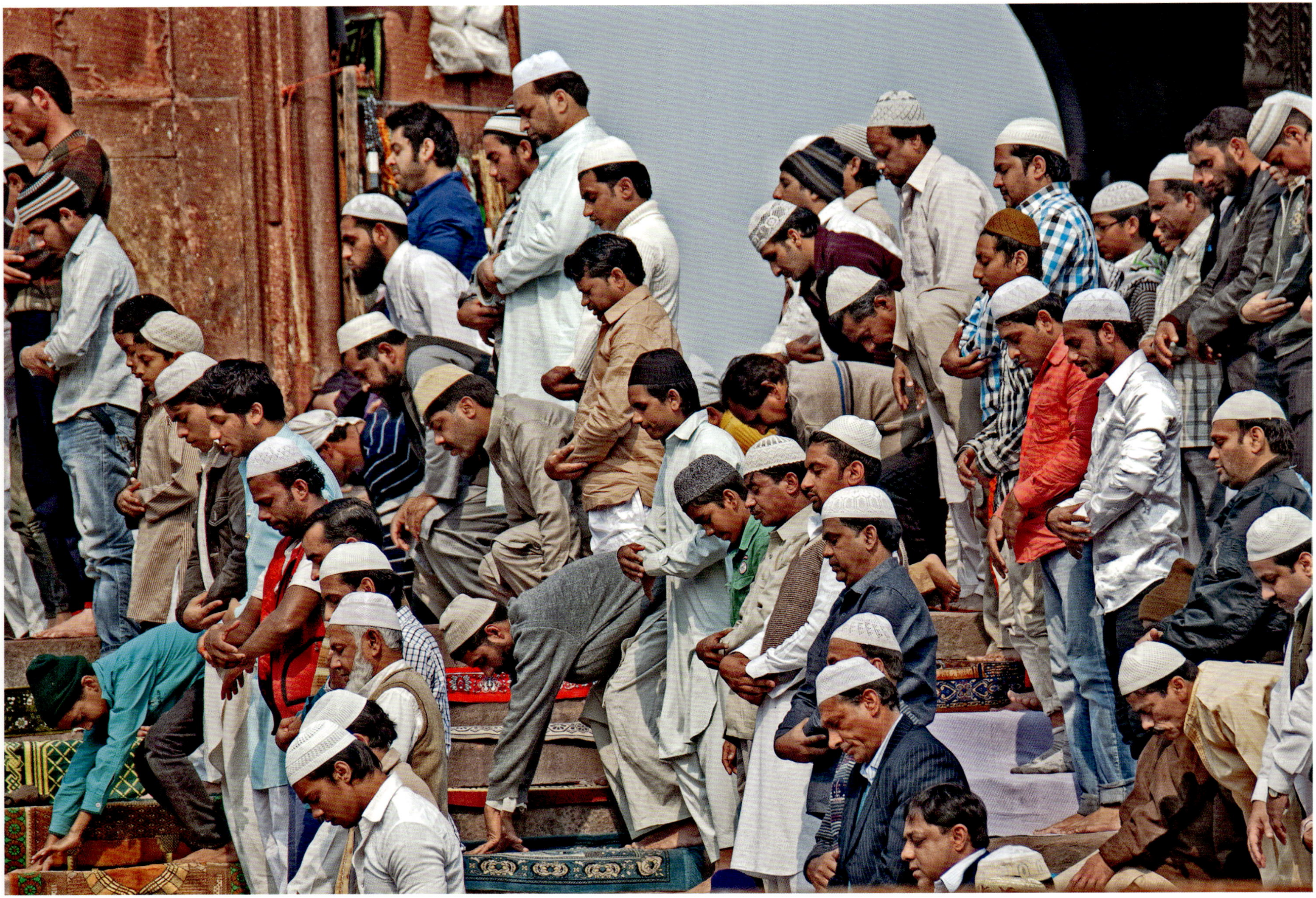

Men bow in prayer during jum'ah at Jama Masjid.

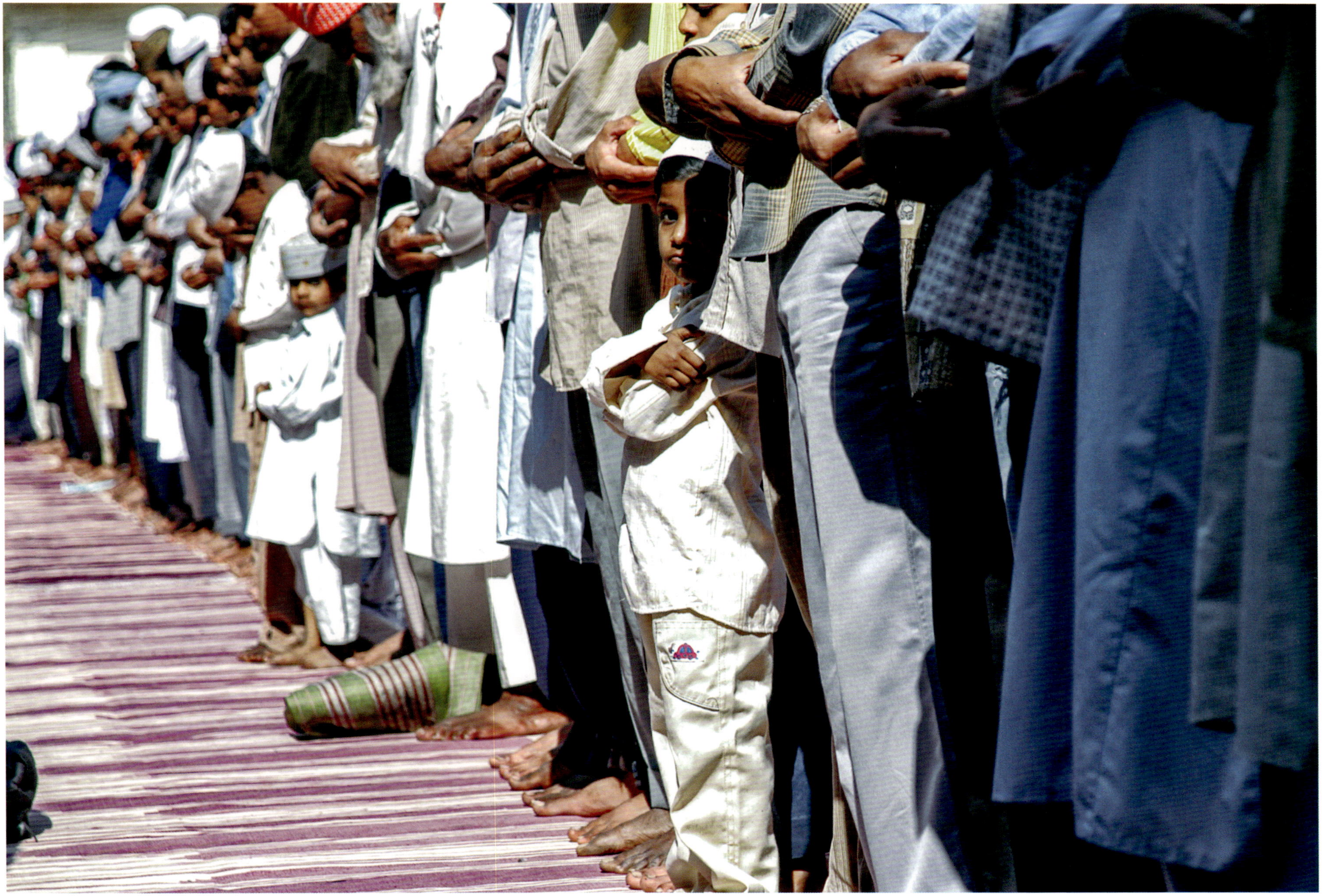

Men pray together in a line.

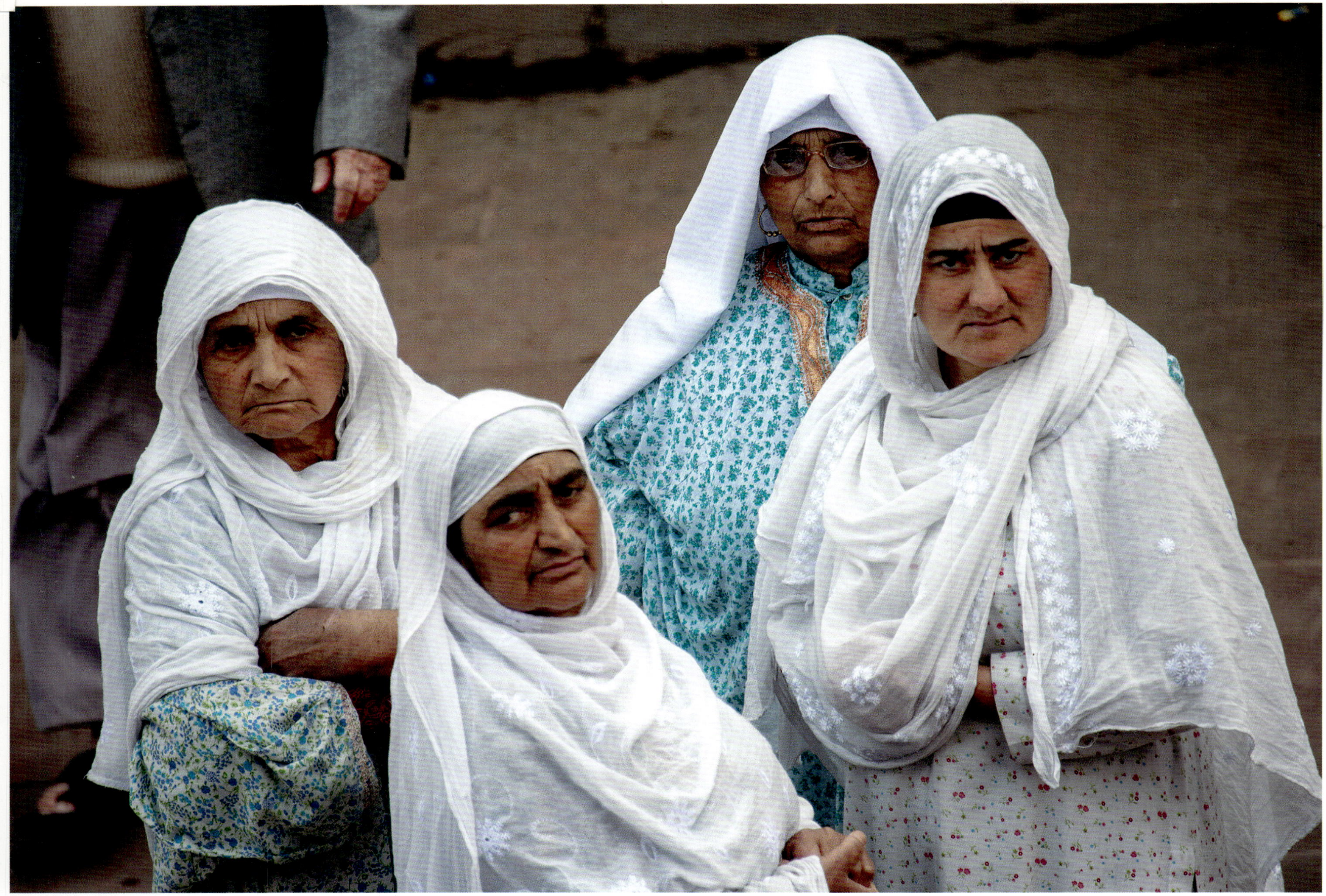

Muslim women wait to pray in Jama Masjid. They will be allowed in to pray only after the men have finished.

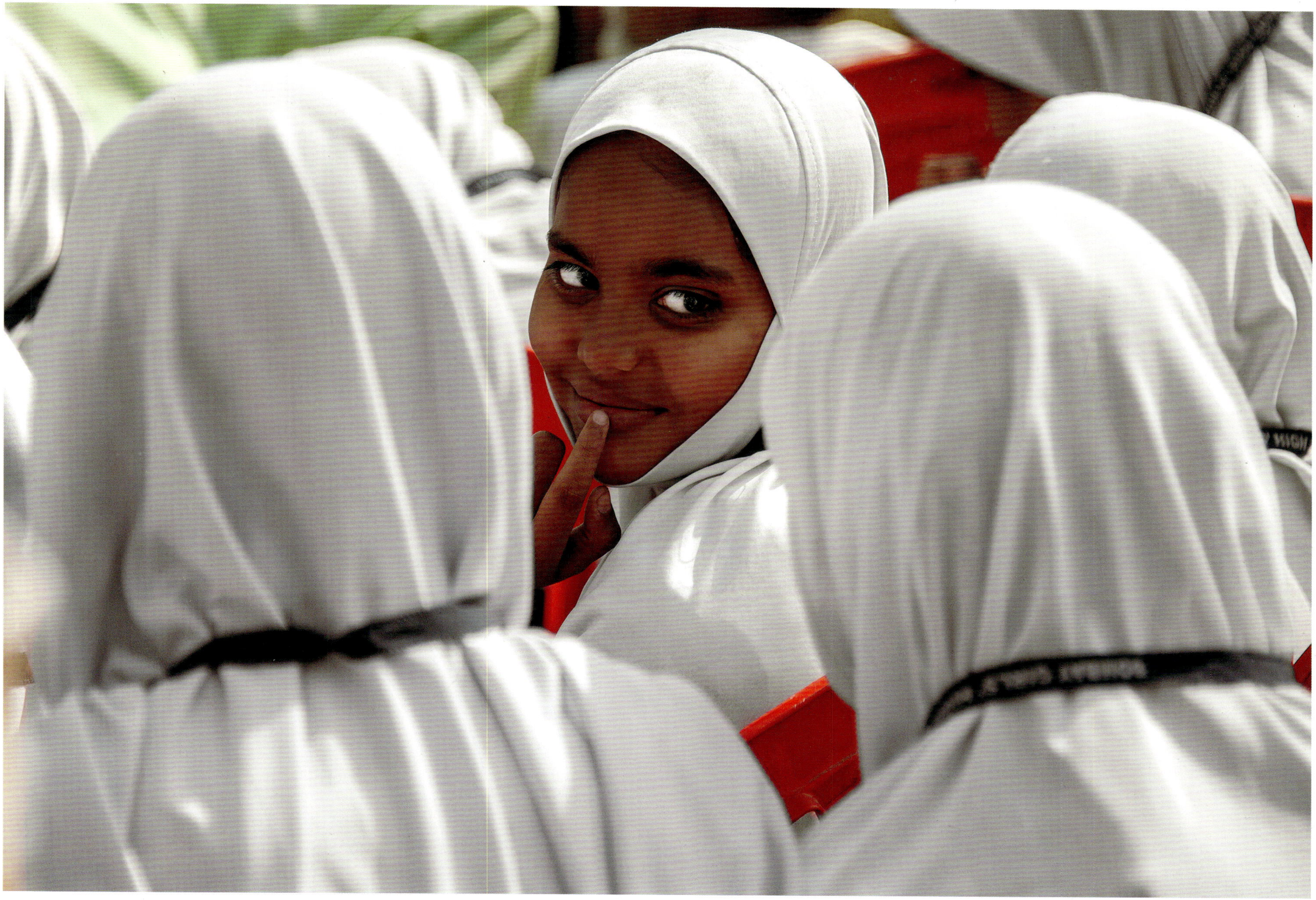

A girl smiles at her friends during a religious meeting. They wear hijabs for modesty.

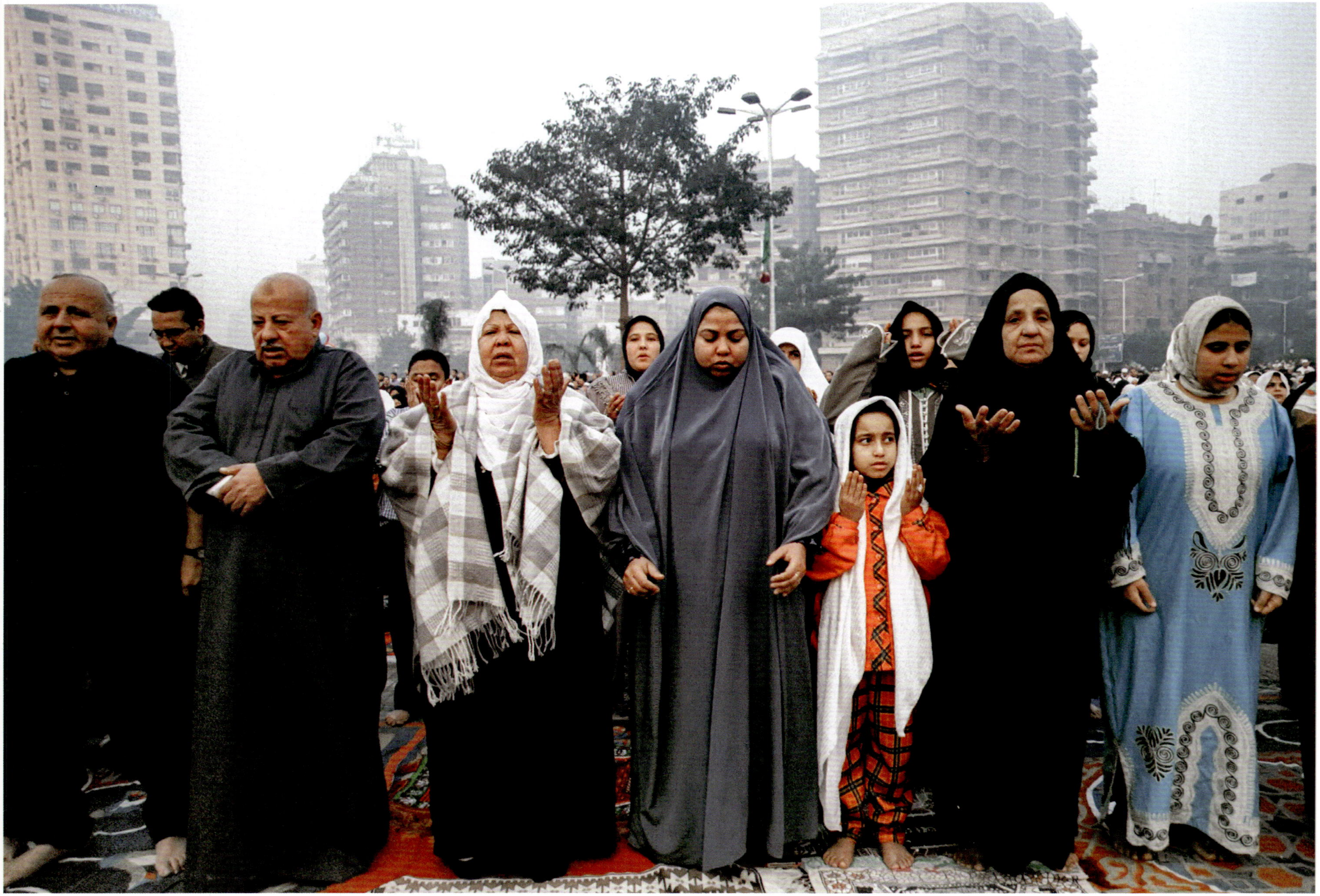

Muslims pray on Eid al-Fitr, the Festival of Breaking the Fast. The holiday marks the end of their monthlong fast during Ramadan.

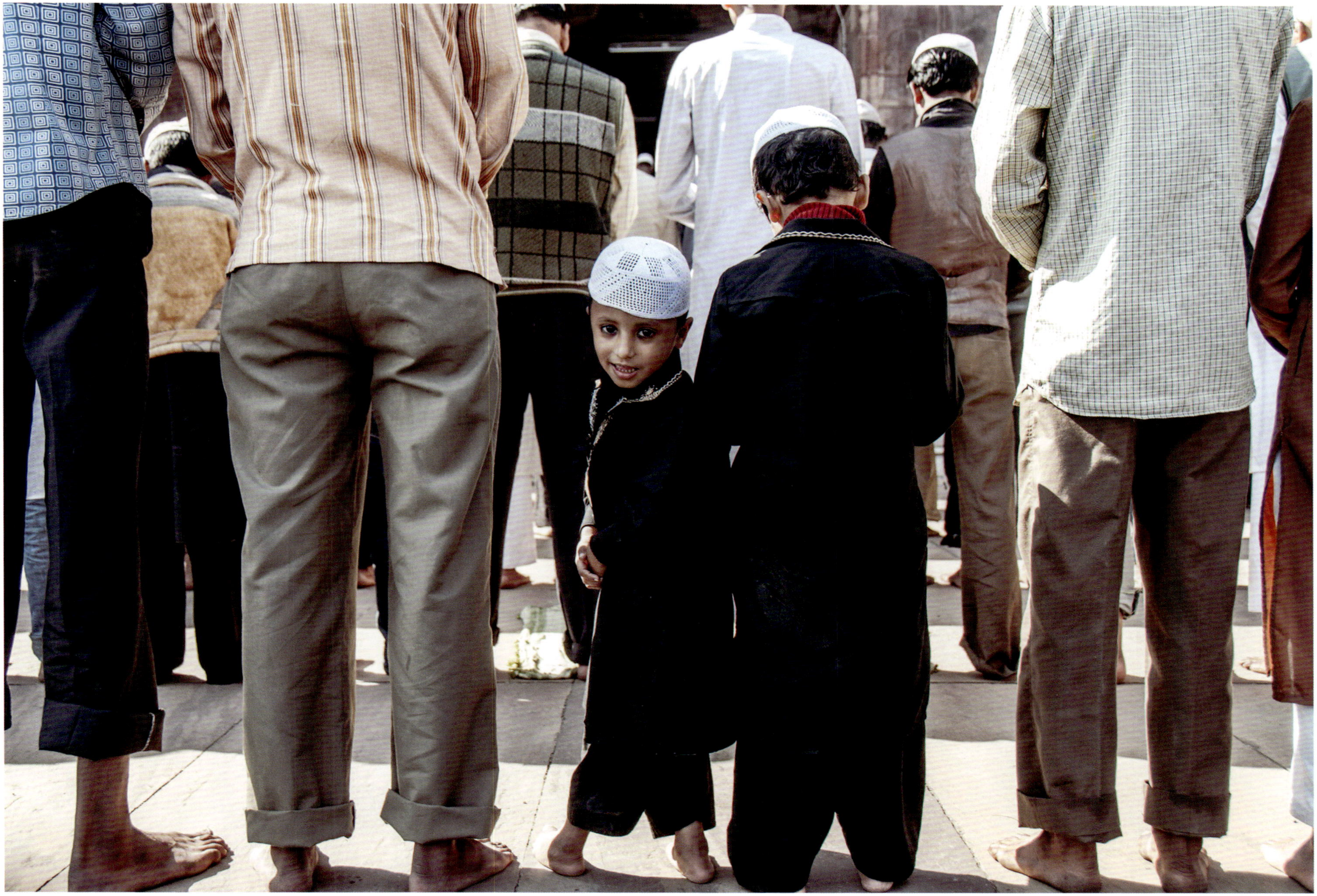

Muslims pray toward Mecca, but this young boy steals a quick look behind him.

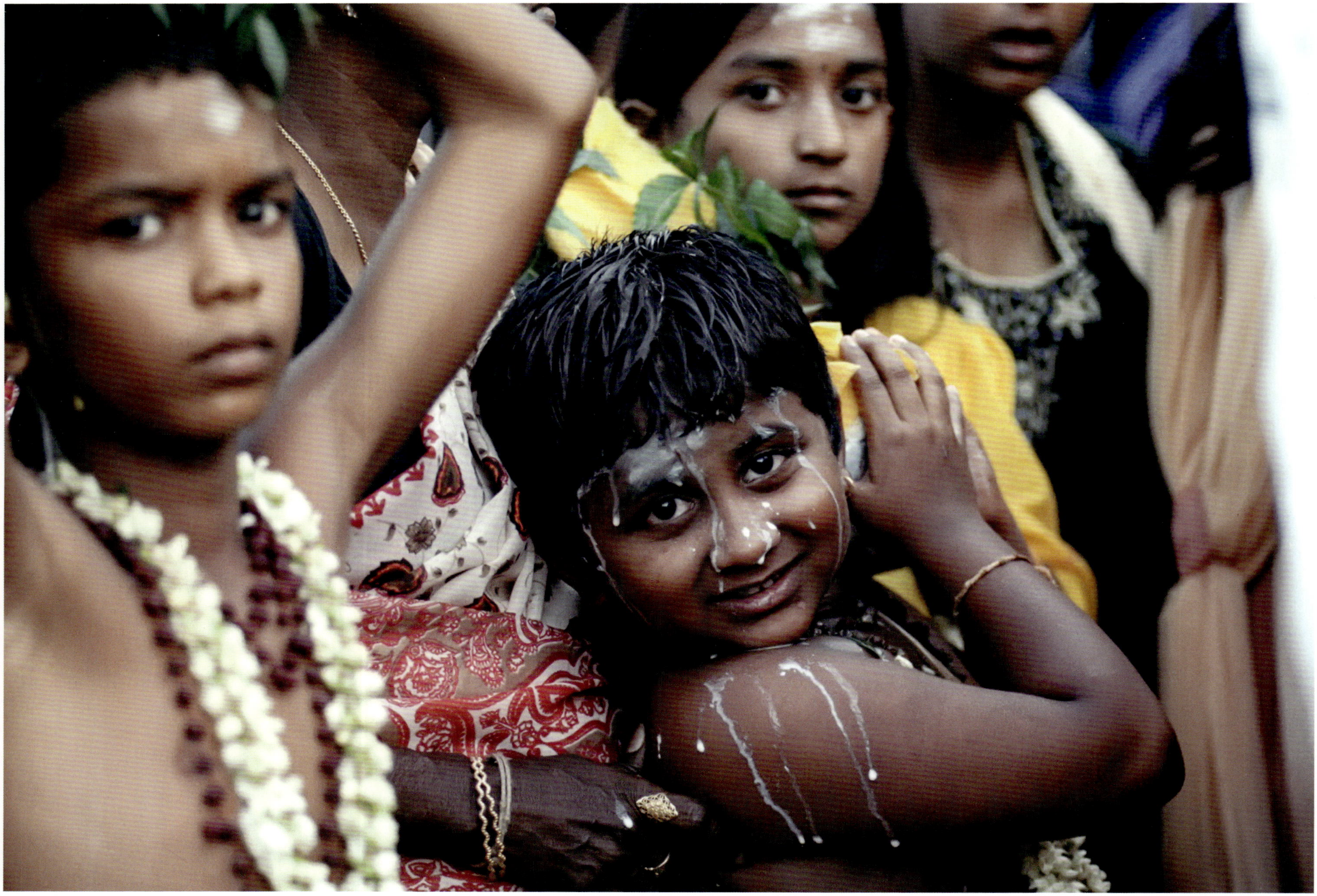

At the Batu Caves, a Hindu shrine, members of the Tamil community celebrate the festival of Thaipusam. During the festival, devotees often pierce their face or body and drag heavy sleds and carry pitchers of milk—offerings to the gods—on their heads. These people have done so on their pilgrimage to the Batu Caves.

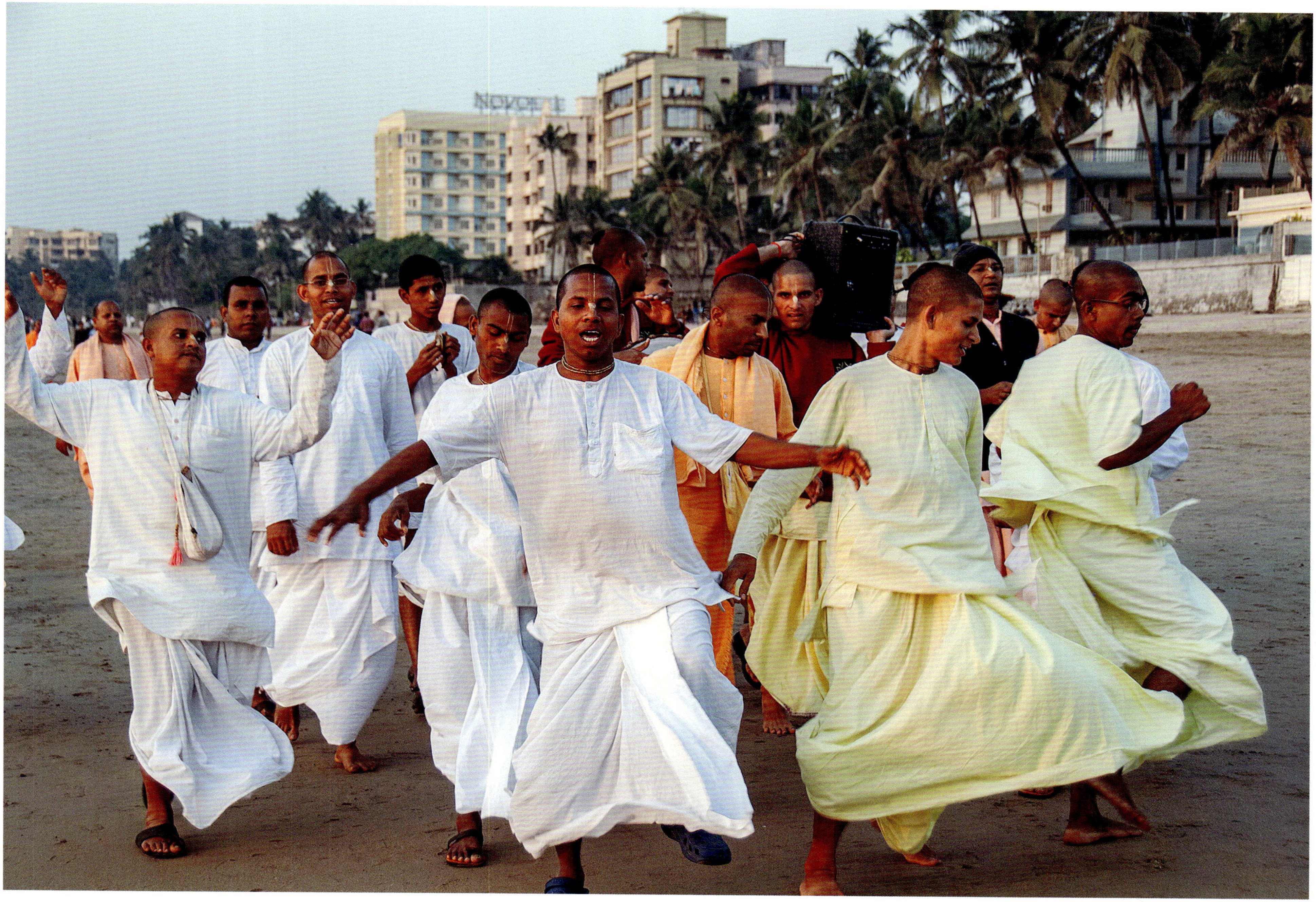

Members of the Hare Krishna faith sing on Juhu Beach.

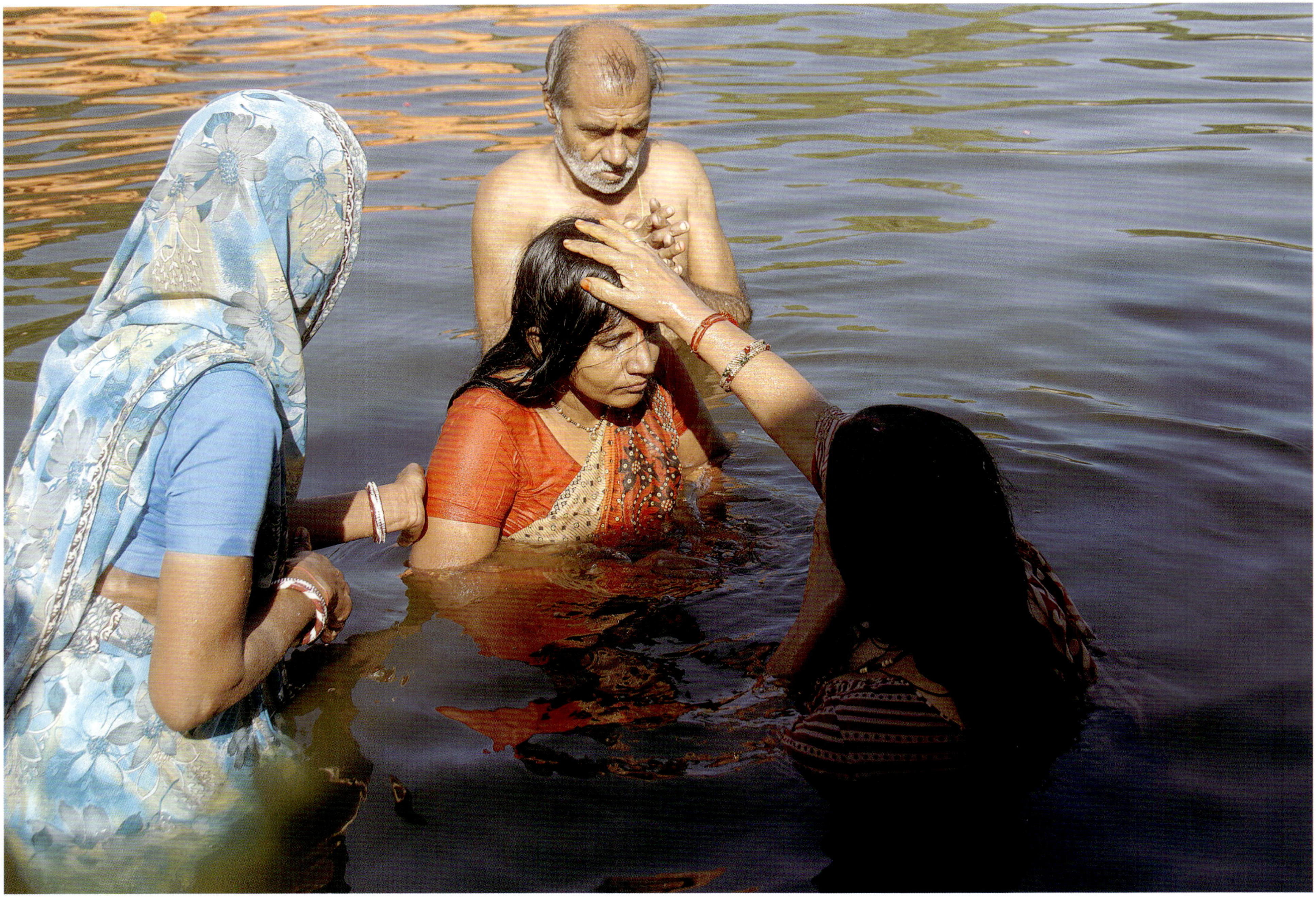

People bathe and perform Hindu rituals in the Shipra River in Ujjain, one of the four cities that hosts Kumbh Mela, a major Hindu religious festival.

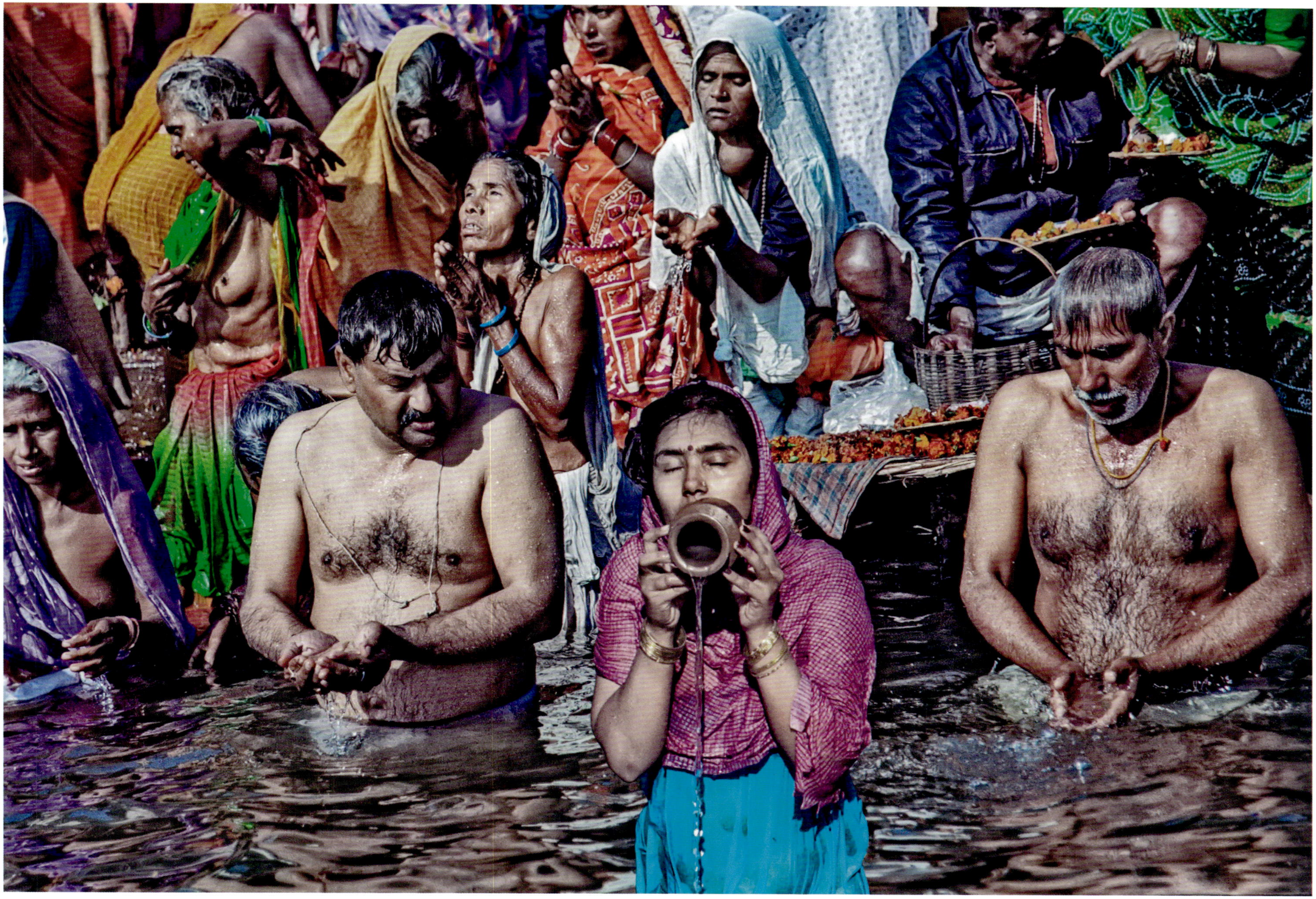

People bathe and pray in the holy Ganges River, which runs through Varanasi. According to Hindu legend, Varanasi is the oldest living (continuously inhabited) city in the world.

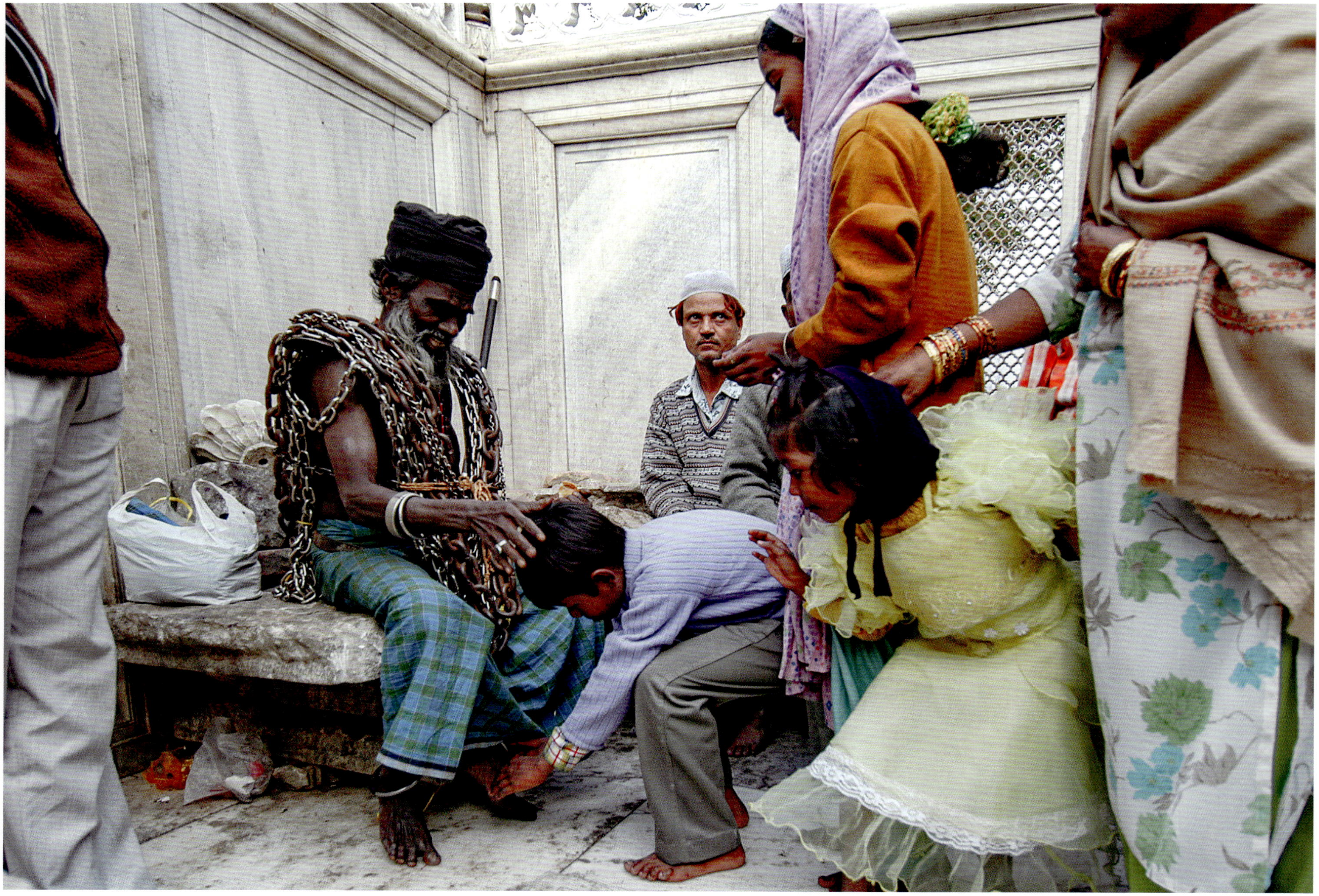

At Hazrat Nizamuddin Aulia Dargah, a Sufi shrine, a family reveres a Malang, a Sufi saint, who is weighed down by chains.

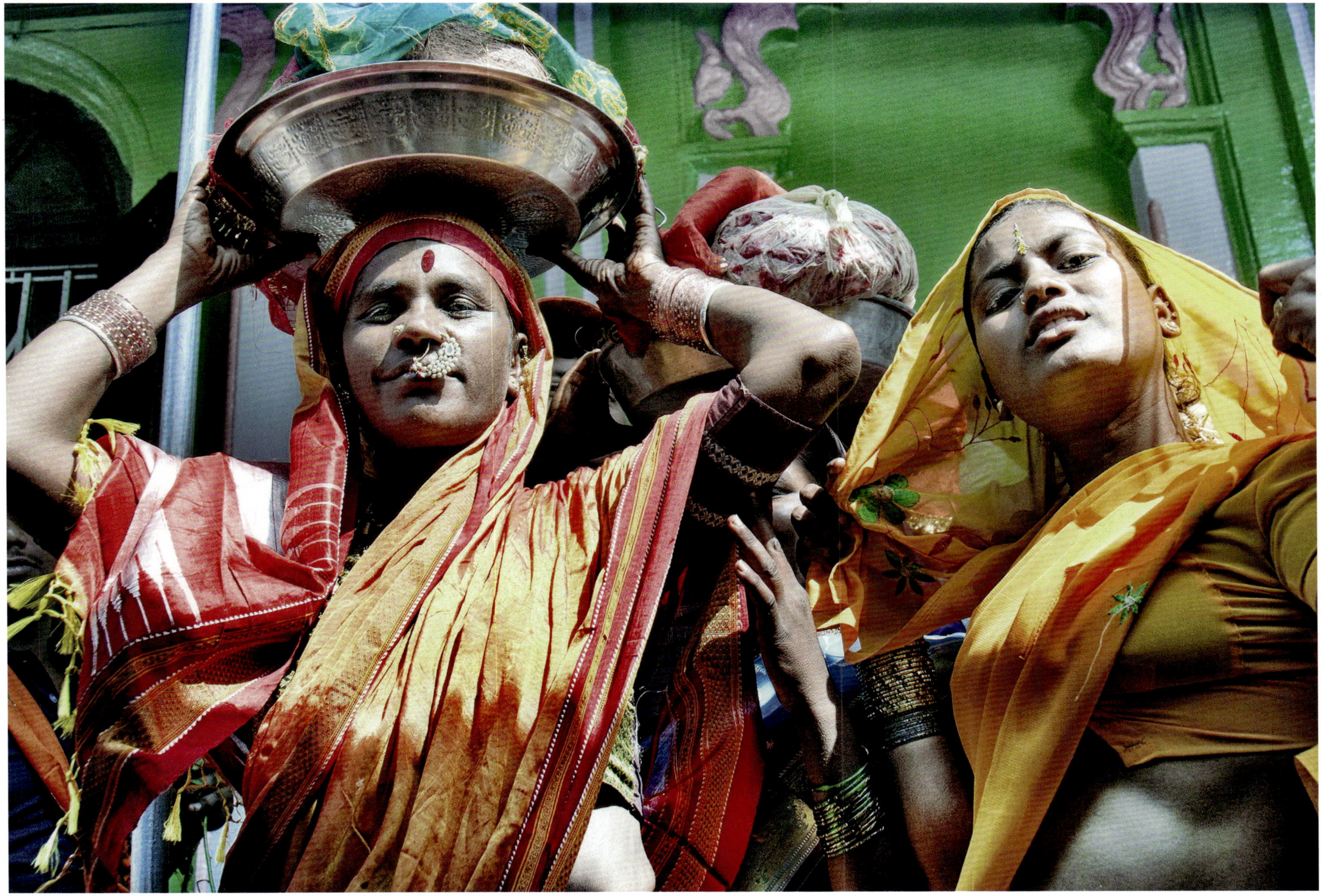

Women carry gifts for the Sufi saint Haji Malang to his dargah, or shrine, at the top of the Malang Gad hill in the town of Kalyan.

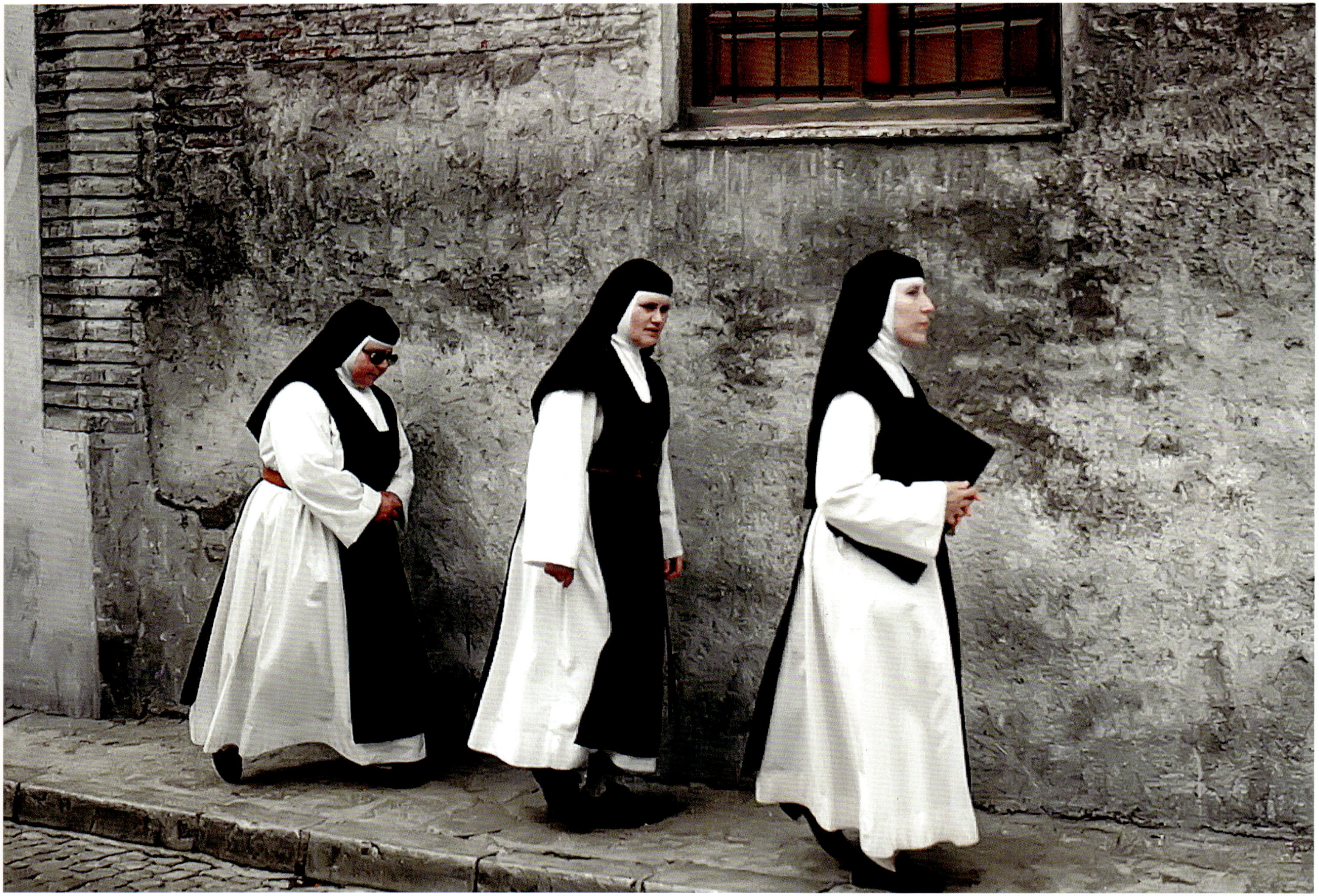

Three Roman Catholic nuns in traditional habits and dress. A Roman Catholic designation inheres full loyalty to the pope, who lives in Rome.

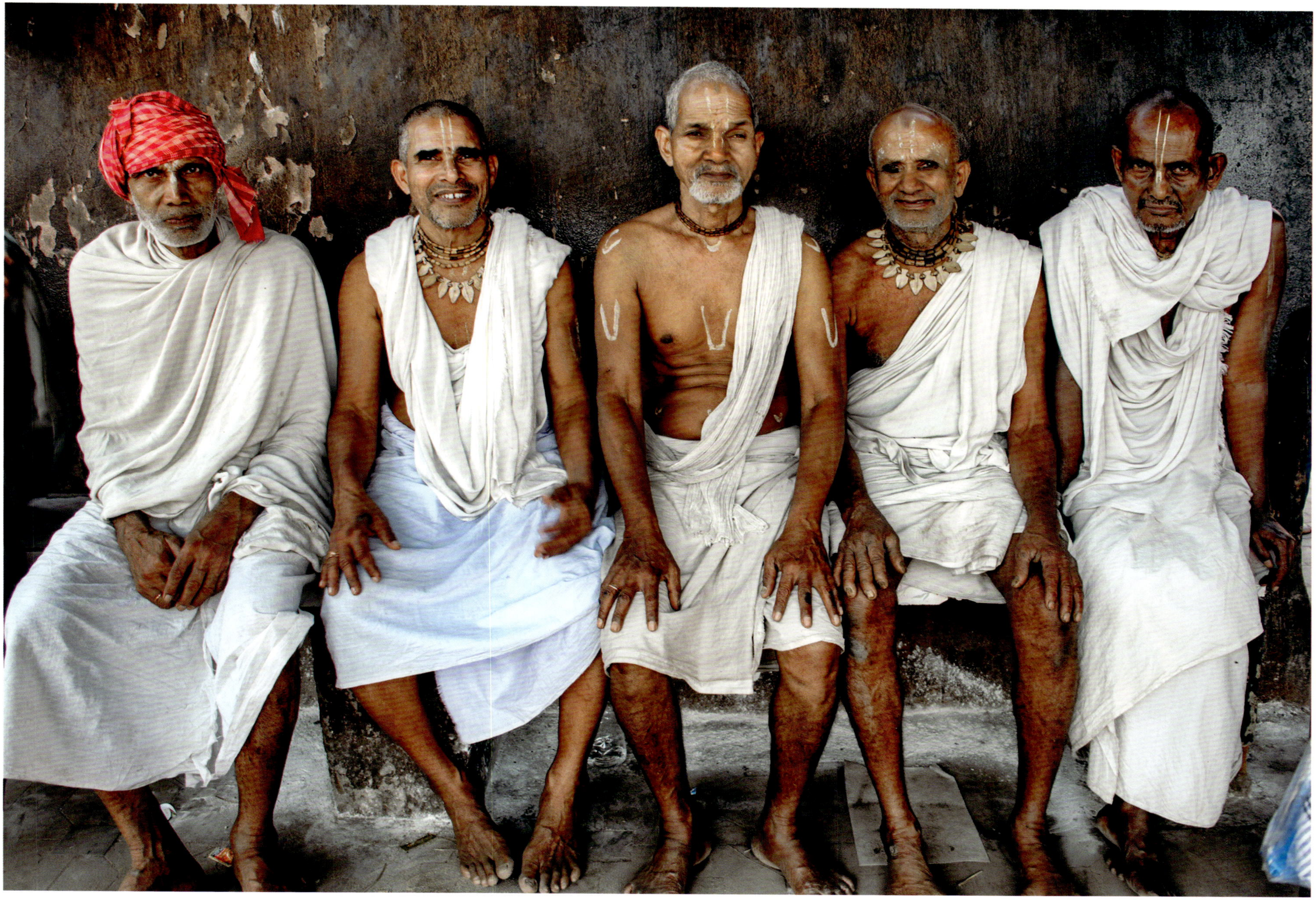

Swargadwar is a cremation ground for Hindus where dead bodies are brought in from different parts of India. These men in white robes are paid by the families of the dead to carry the corpses and play music.

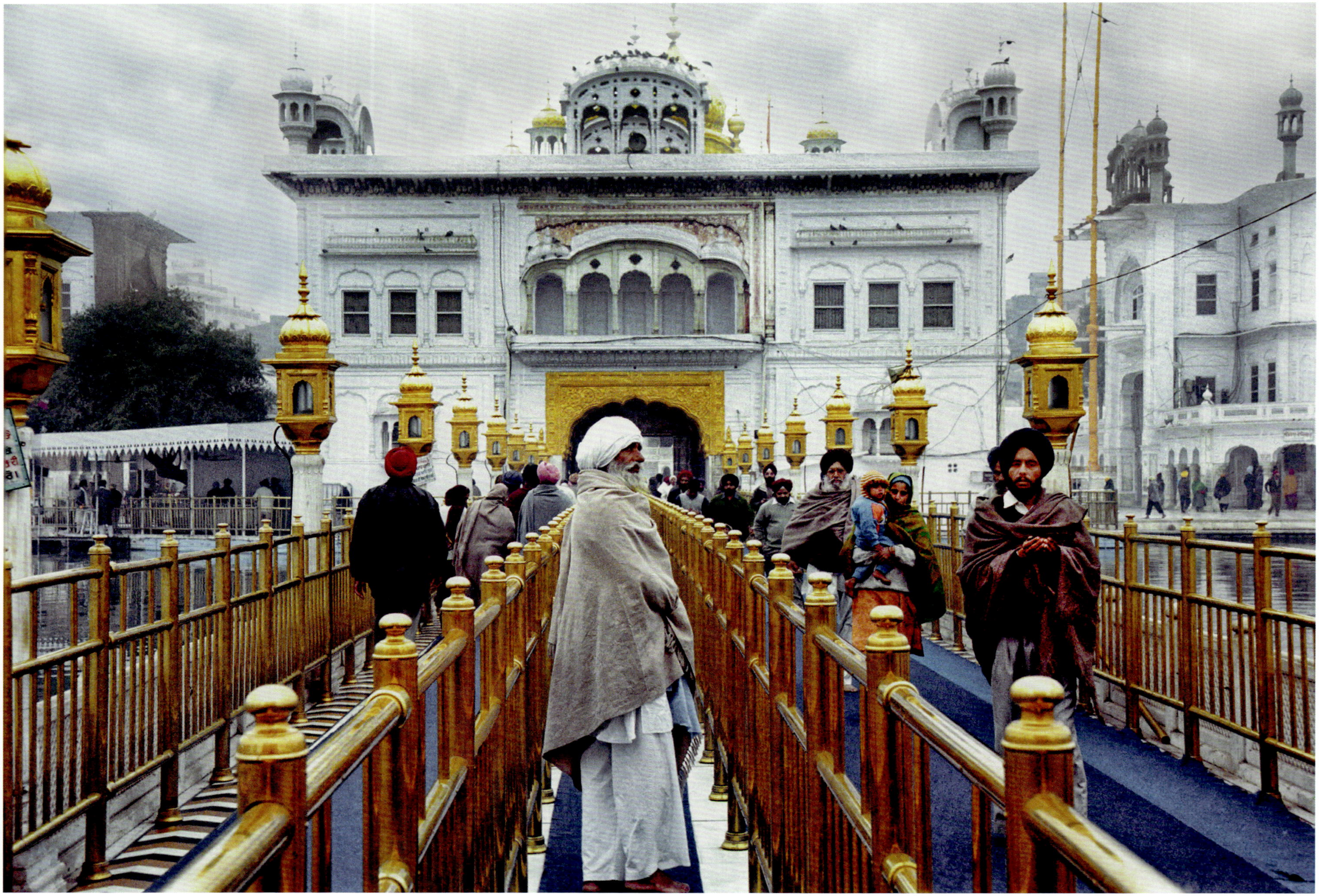

The Golden Temple is the holiest temple and the most important pilgrimage site of Sikhism.

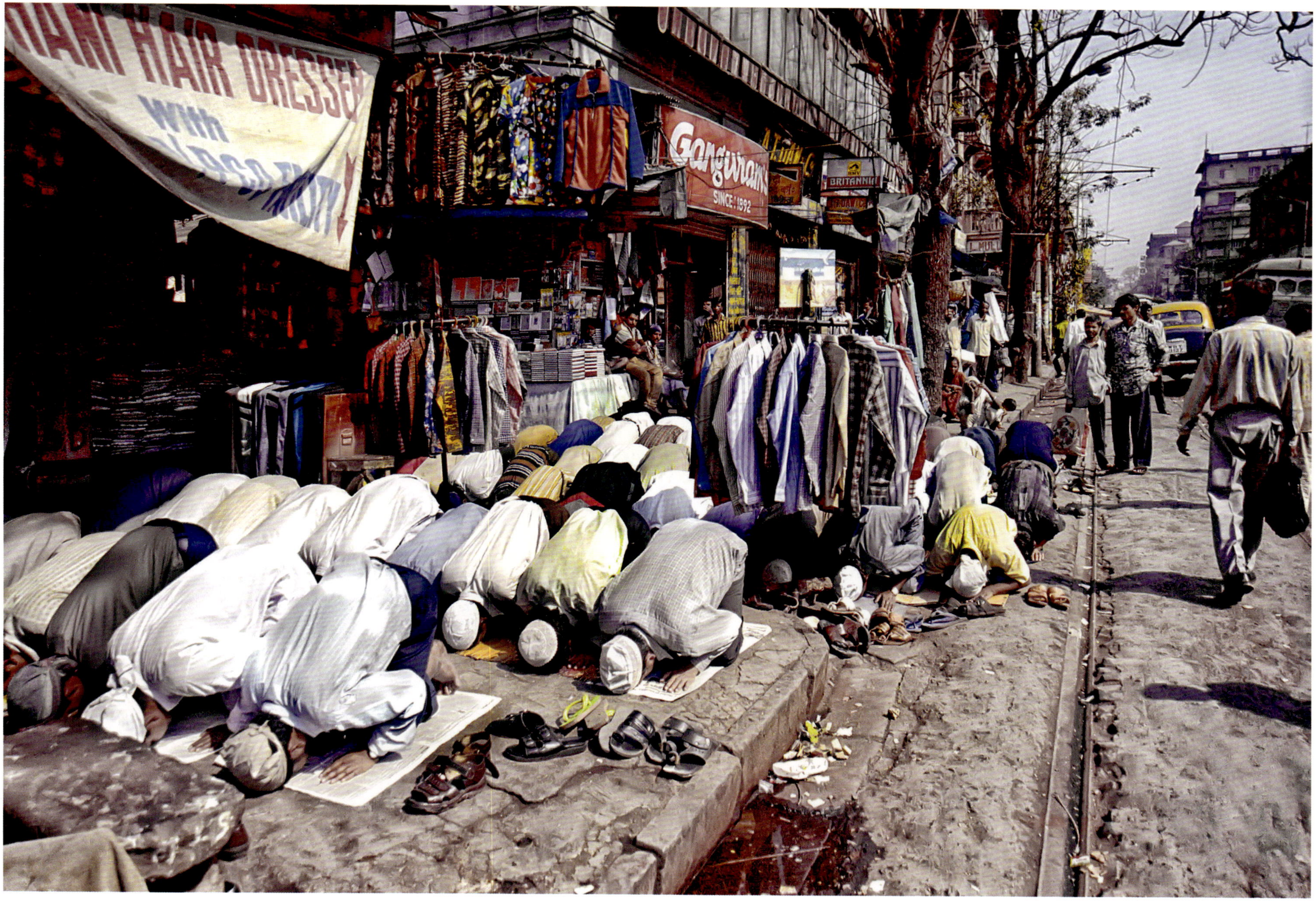

According to Islamic law, Muslims must pray five times a day. In India, where space can be limited, there are dedicated areas that face Mecca where Muslims can pray.

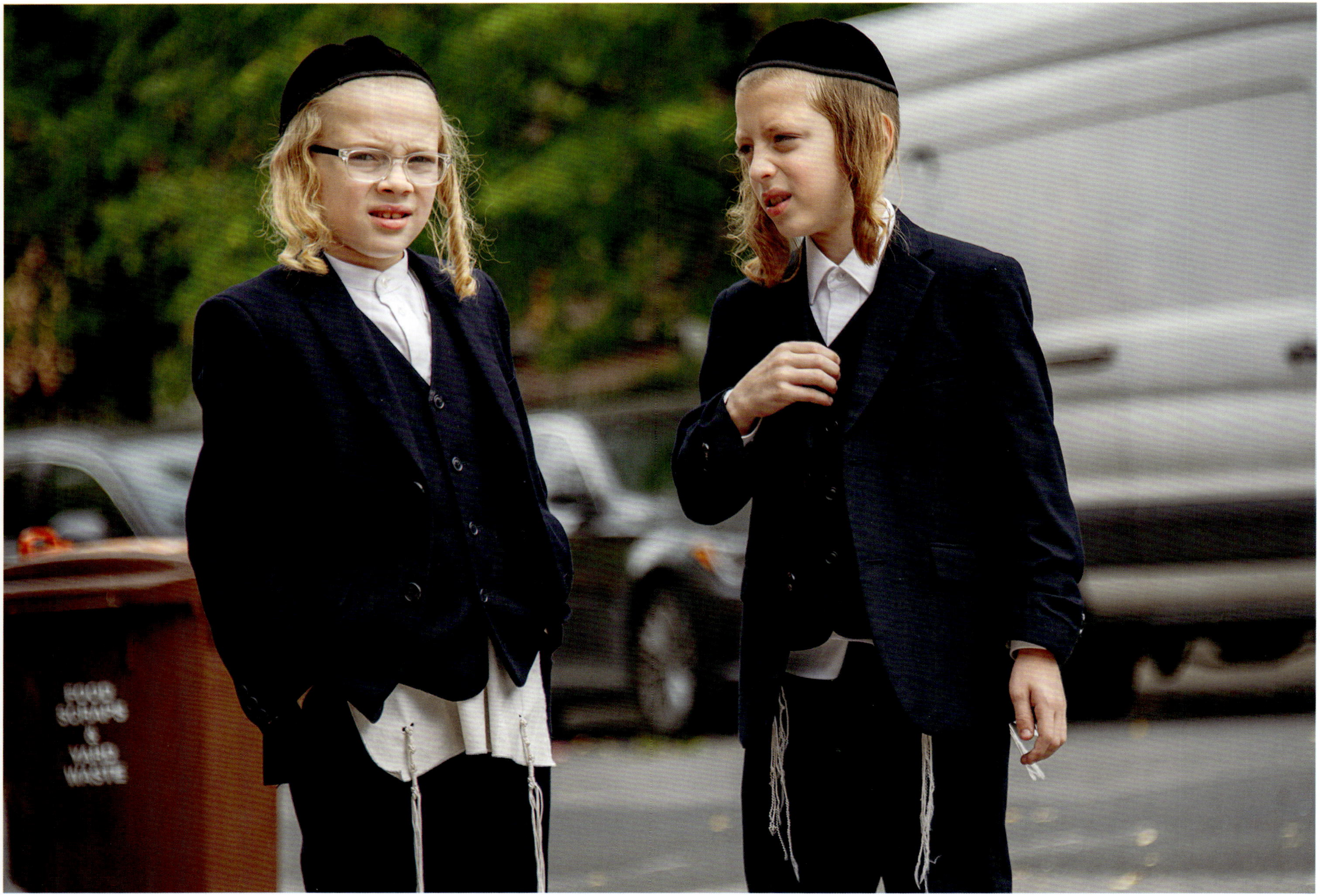

Two Hasidic boys with payot, the curls that hang by their ears, and yarmulkes. Hasidim are adherents of a form of ultra-Orthodox Judaism. These boys and tens of thousands of other Hasidim live in Williamsburg, Brooklyn.

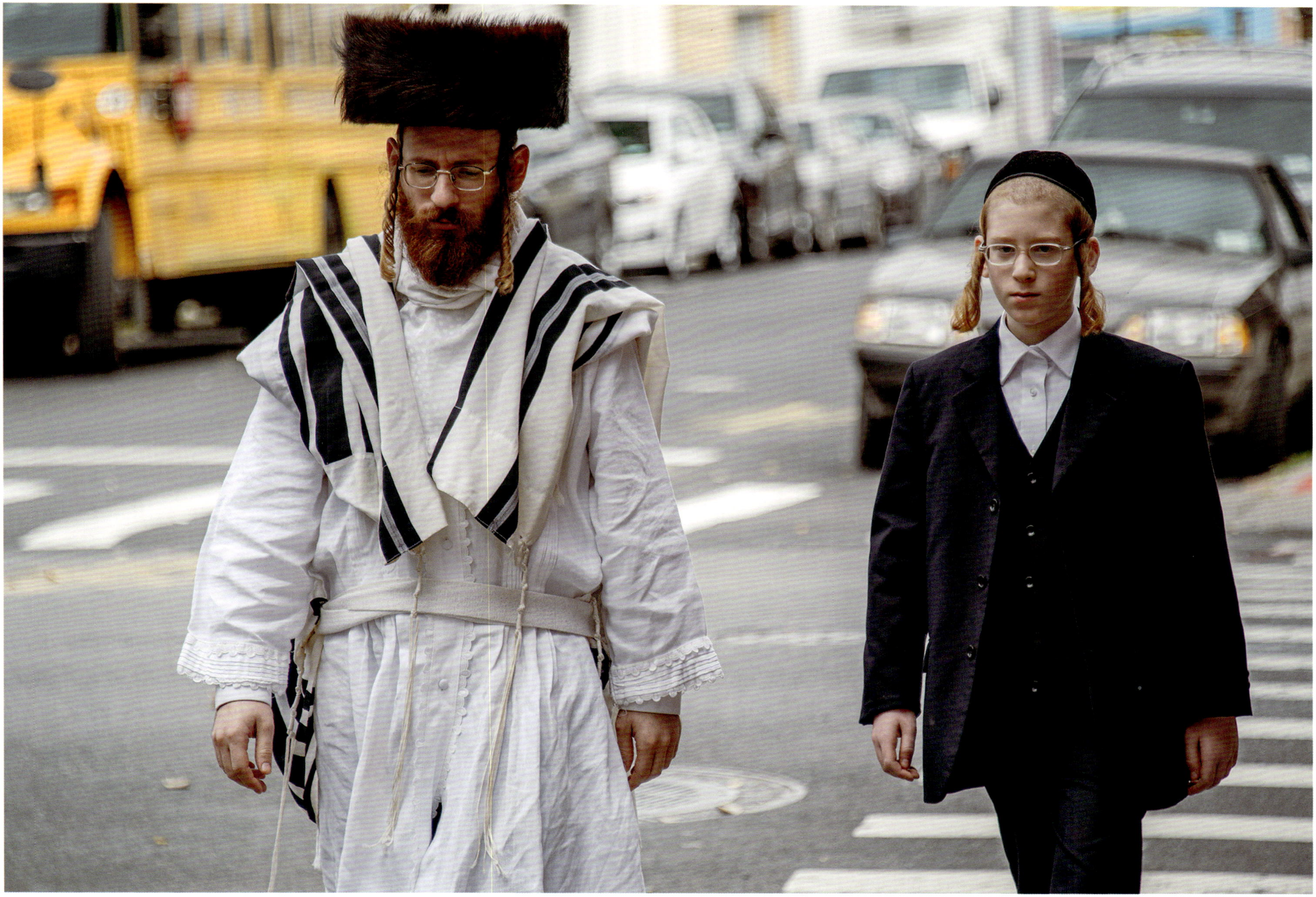

In Williamsburg, Brooklyn, Hasidic Jews head to synagogue on Yom Kippur, the holiest day of the year for Jews. The man on the left wears a shtreimel, a round fur hat worn by Hasidic men on Jewish holidays.

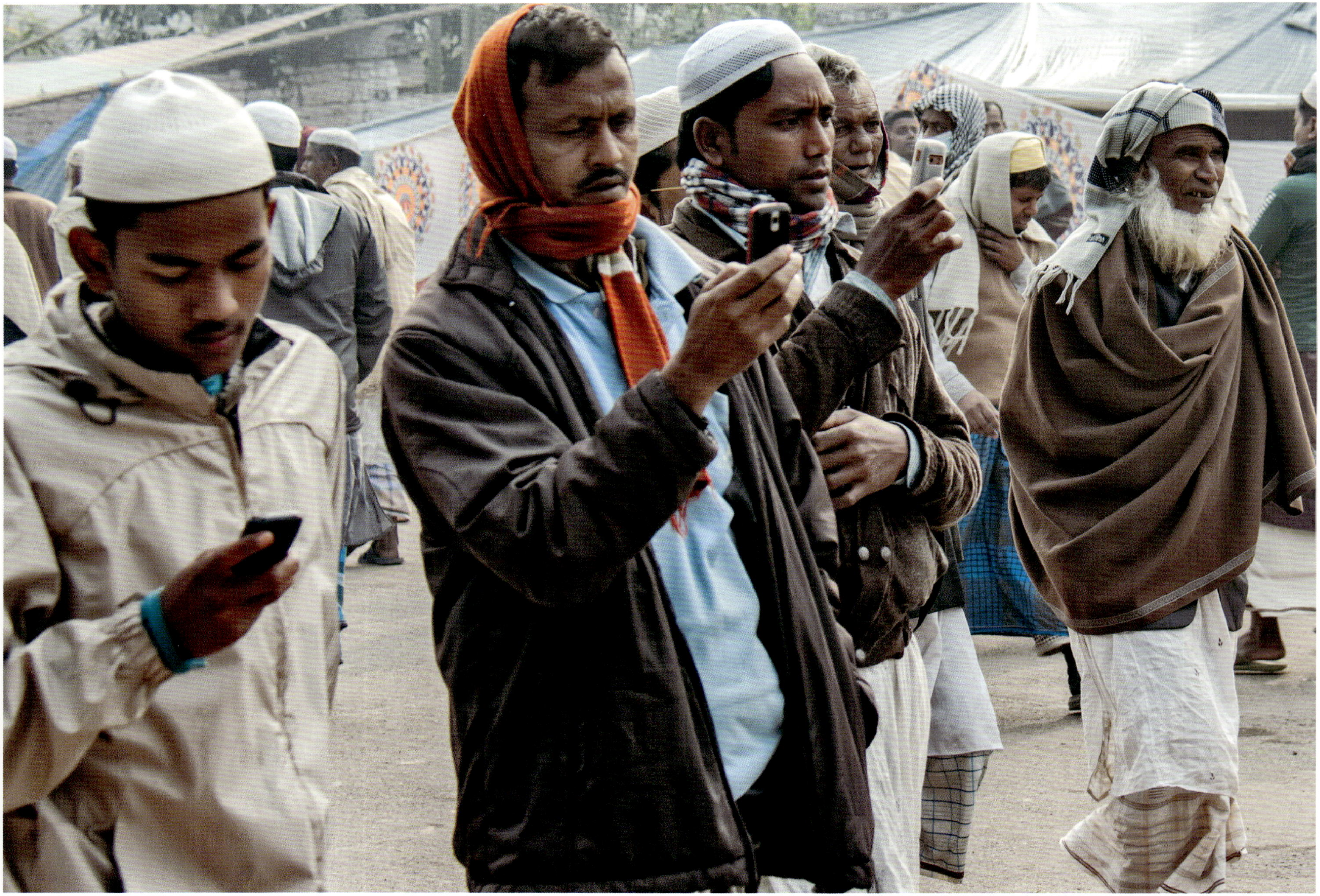

Men head to the Turag River for Bishwa Ijtema, a three-day gathering attended by millions of people each year. The event embraces daily prayers and concludes with a prayer for peace.

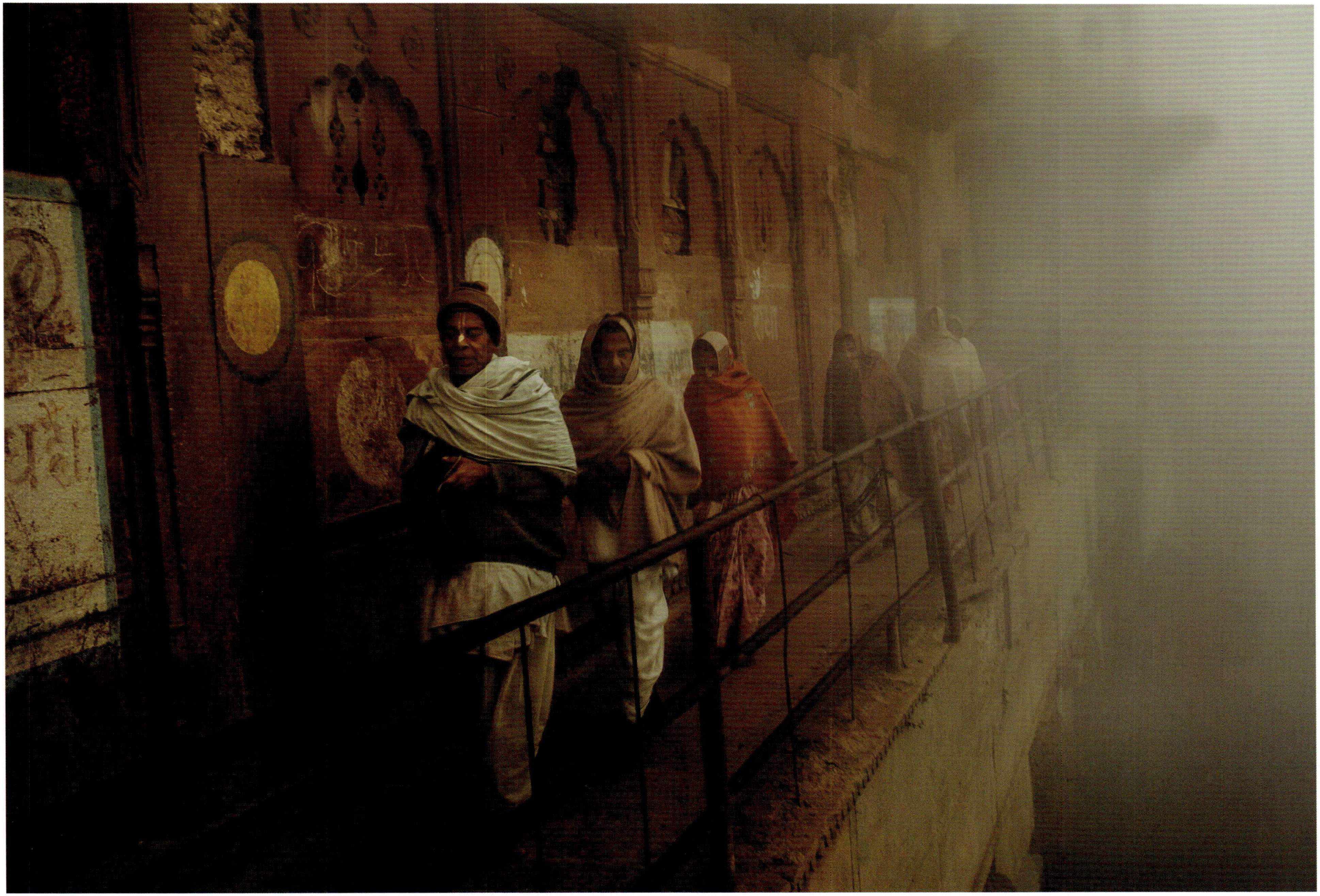

A heavy early morning mist is common in the holy town of Vrindavan, where the deity Krishna is said to have spent his childhood. Many of its temples are dedicated to Krishna and his lover, the deity Radha.

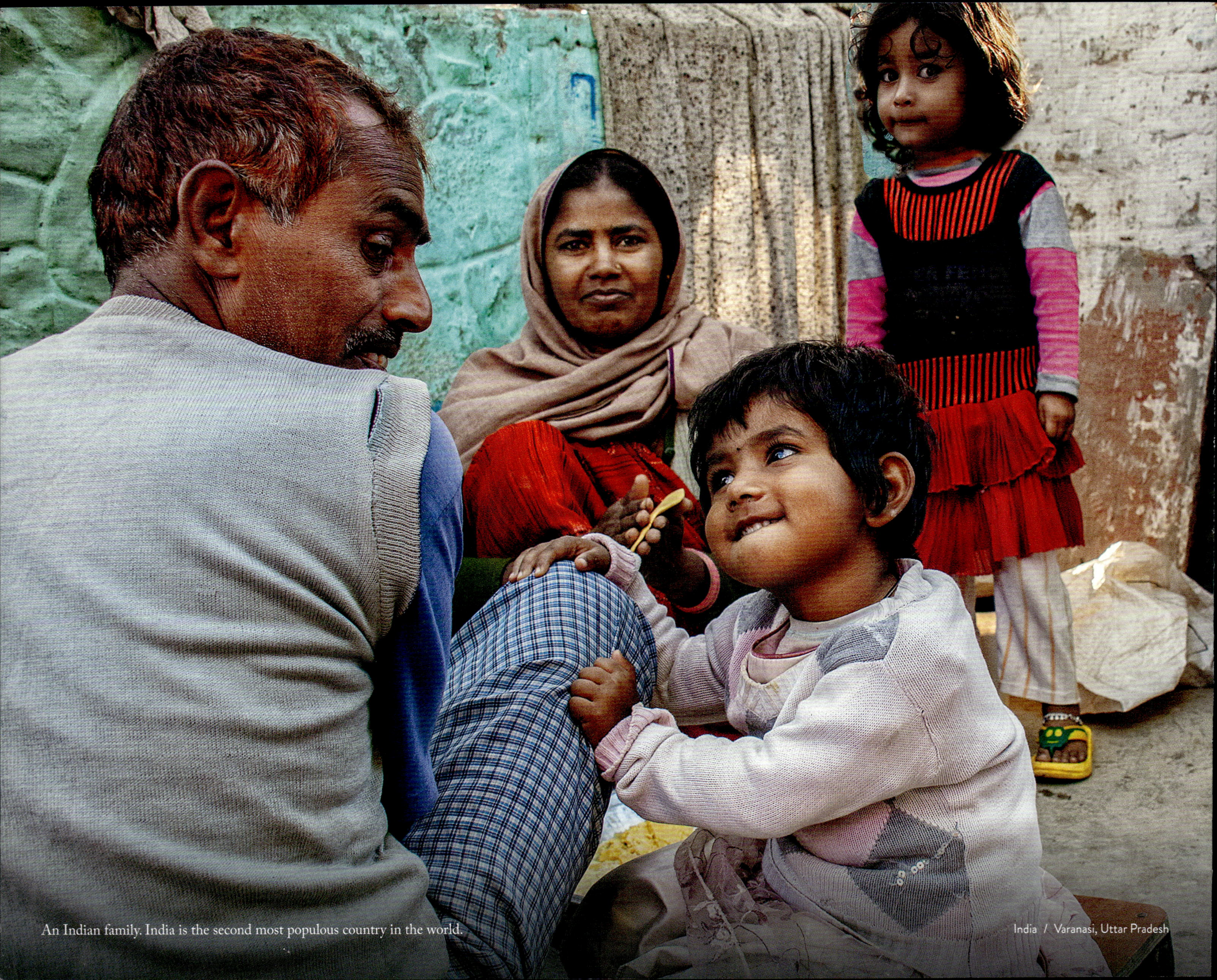

An Indian family. India is the second most populous country in the world.

India / Varanasi, Uttar Pradesh

INHERITANCE

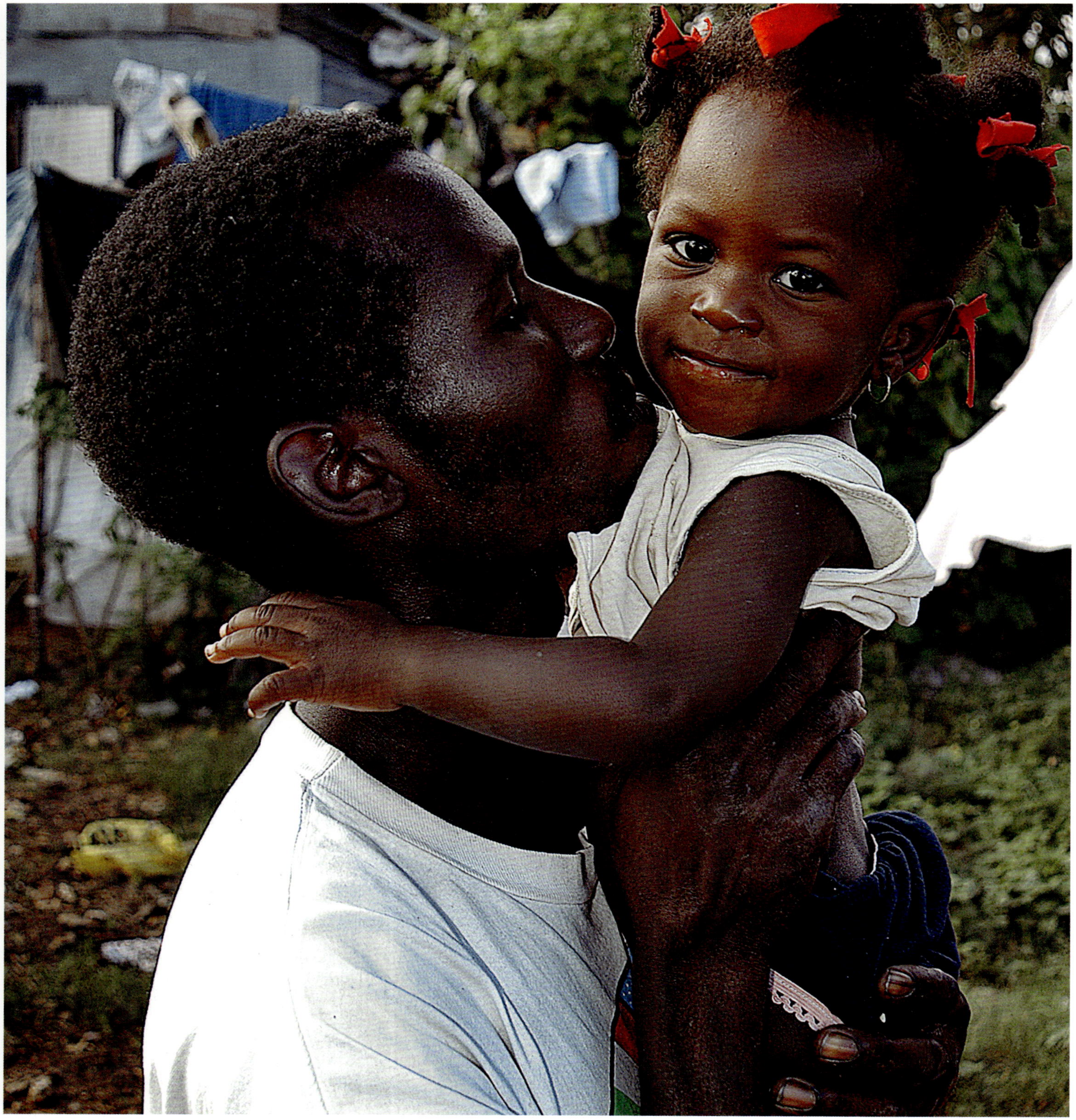

A Haitian man holds his daughter. They live in a slum in the Dominican Republic. Because opportunities for work and wages are higher in the DR, many Haitians cross the border to make a living and provide for their families, but the risk of deportation is high.

Dominican Republic / Sosúa, Puerto Plata

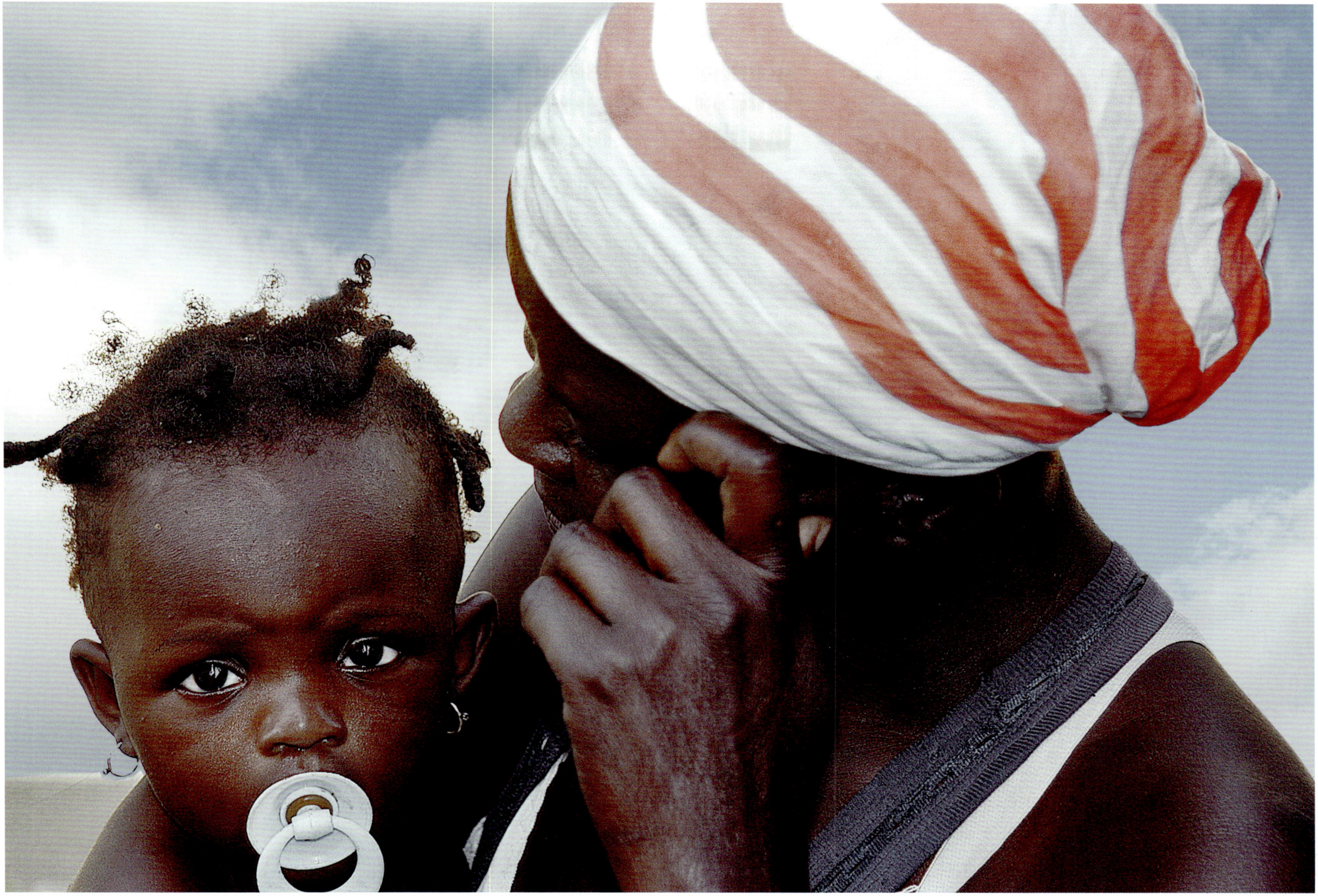

A woman looks tenderly at her infant daughter. In the Dominican Republic, there is great wealth and extreme poverty.

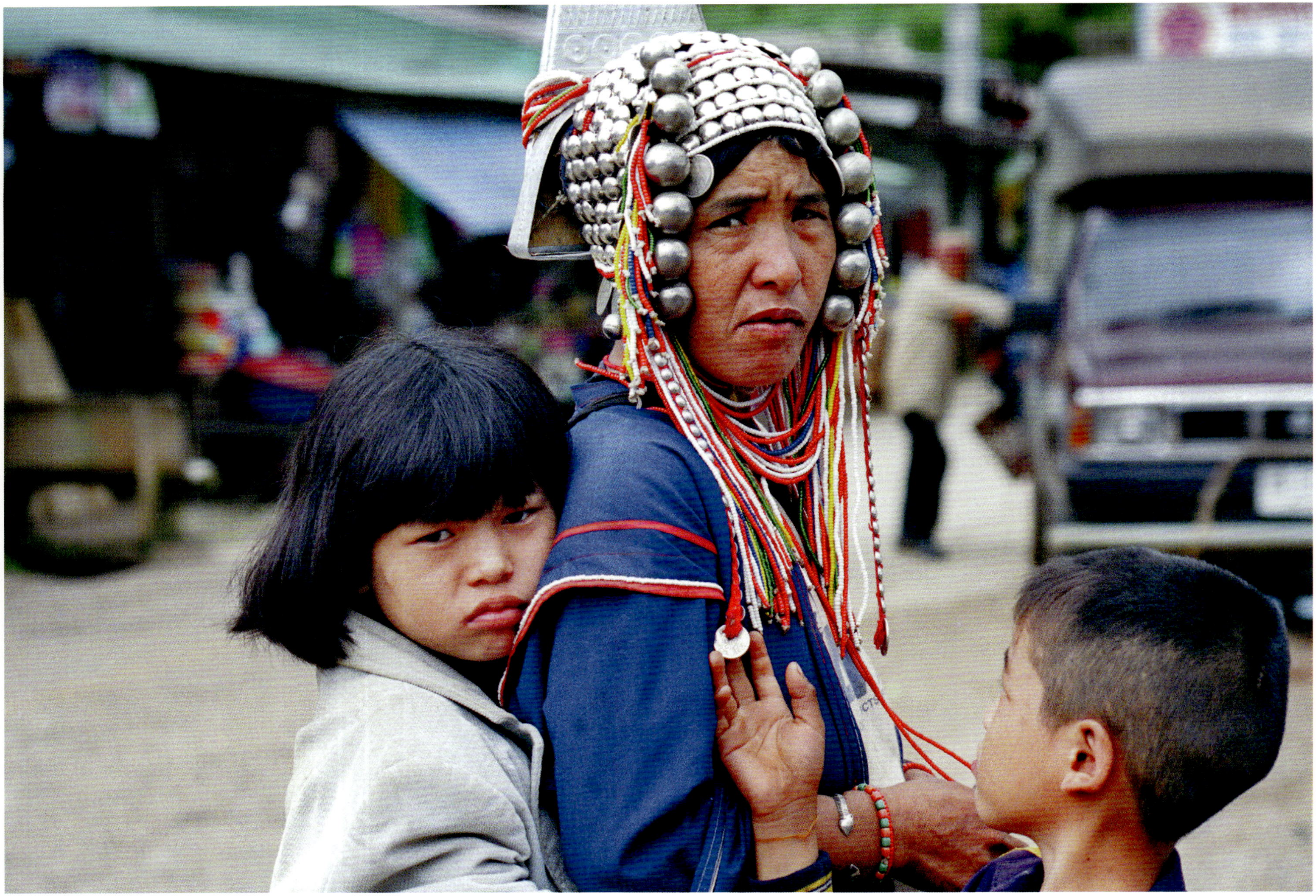

Members of the Akha ethnic group, who live in the mountains of northern Thailand. There are about eighty thousand Akha people in the northern provinces of Chiang Rai and Chiang Mai.

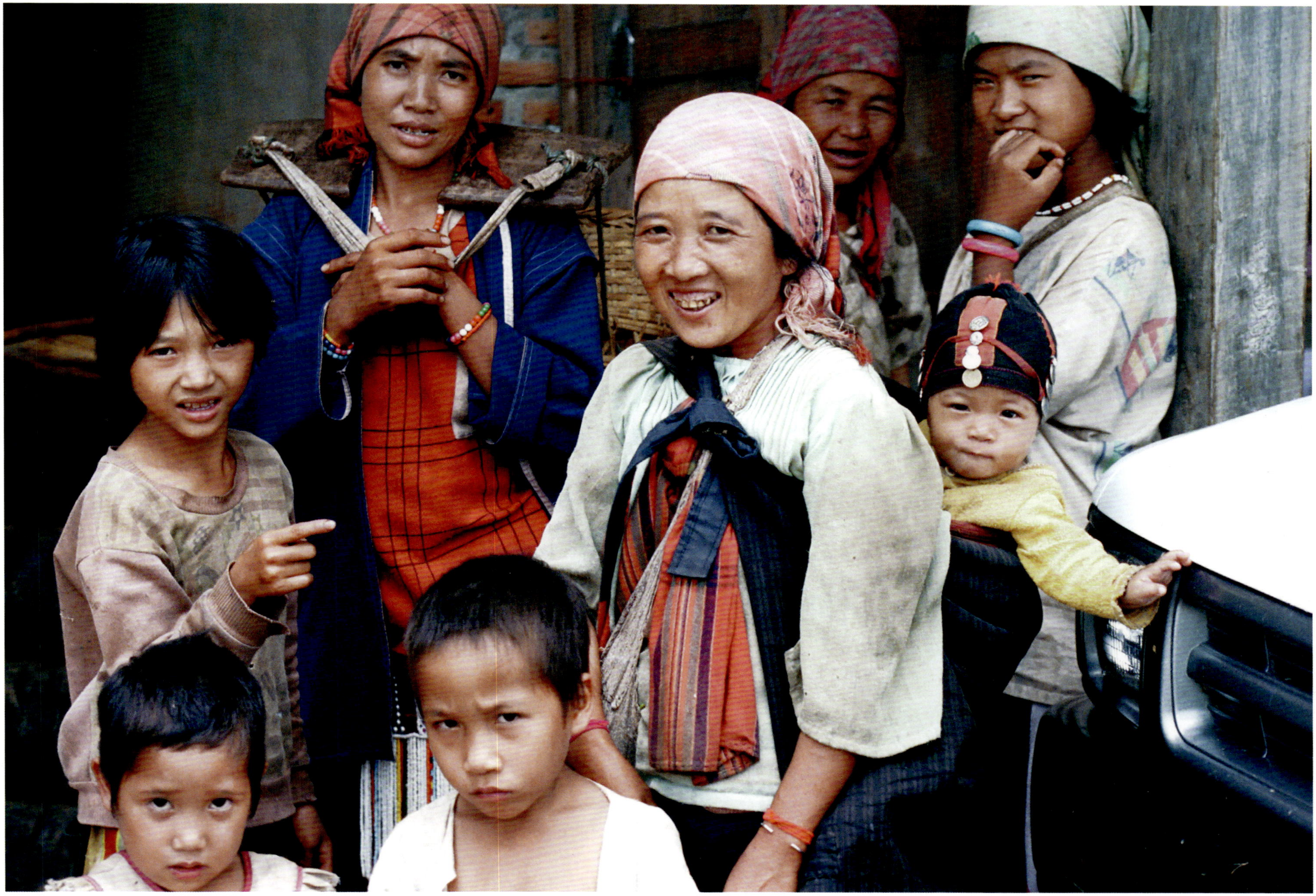

Tribal locals in Chiang Rai, a city in northern Thailand that is rich in temples and history related to Thailand's Lan Na Kingdom.

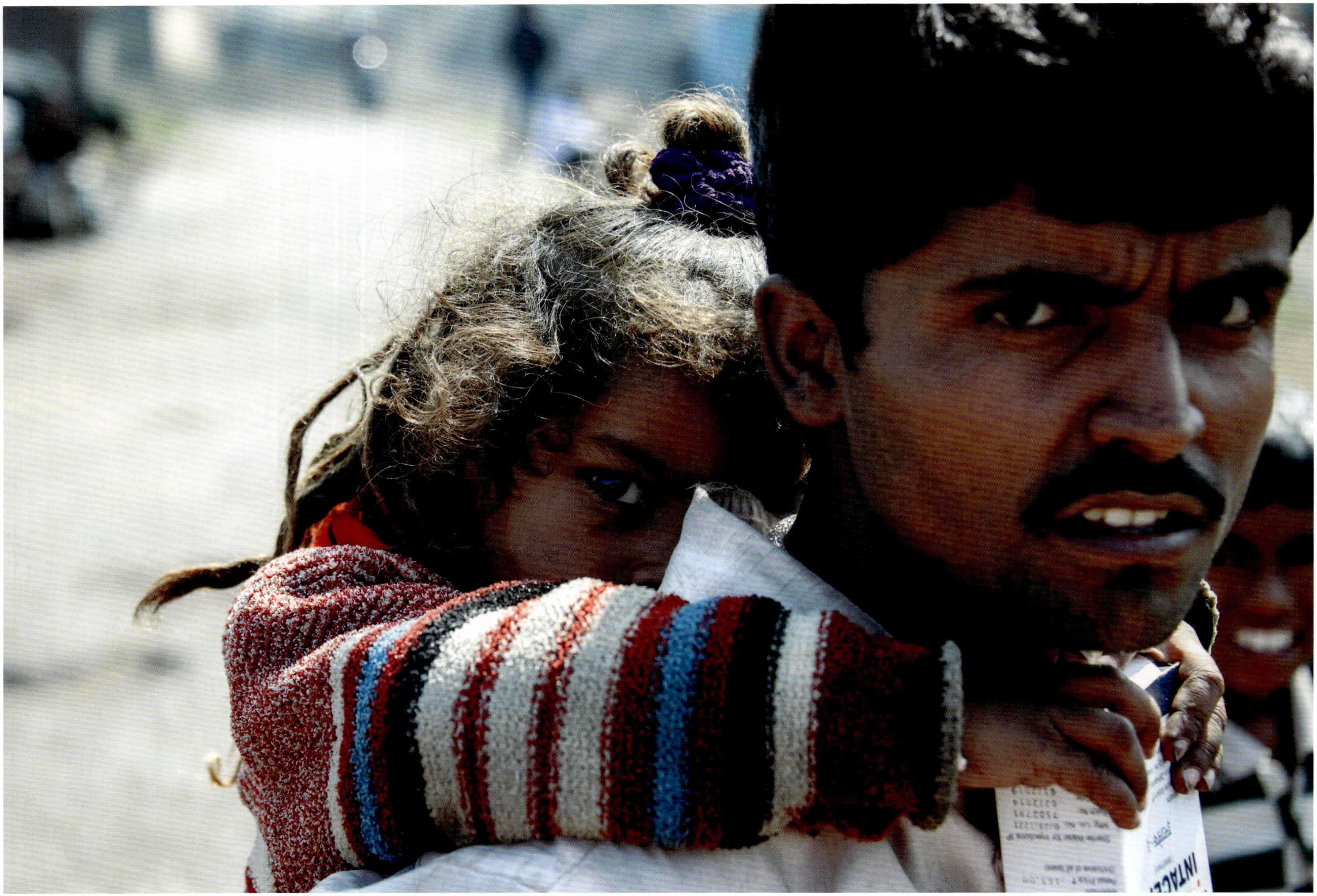

A man and his daughter in Dhanbad. The city is surrounded by more than one hundred coal mines.

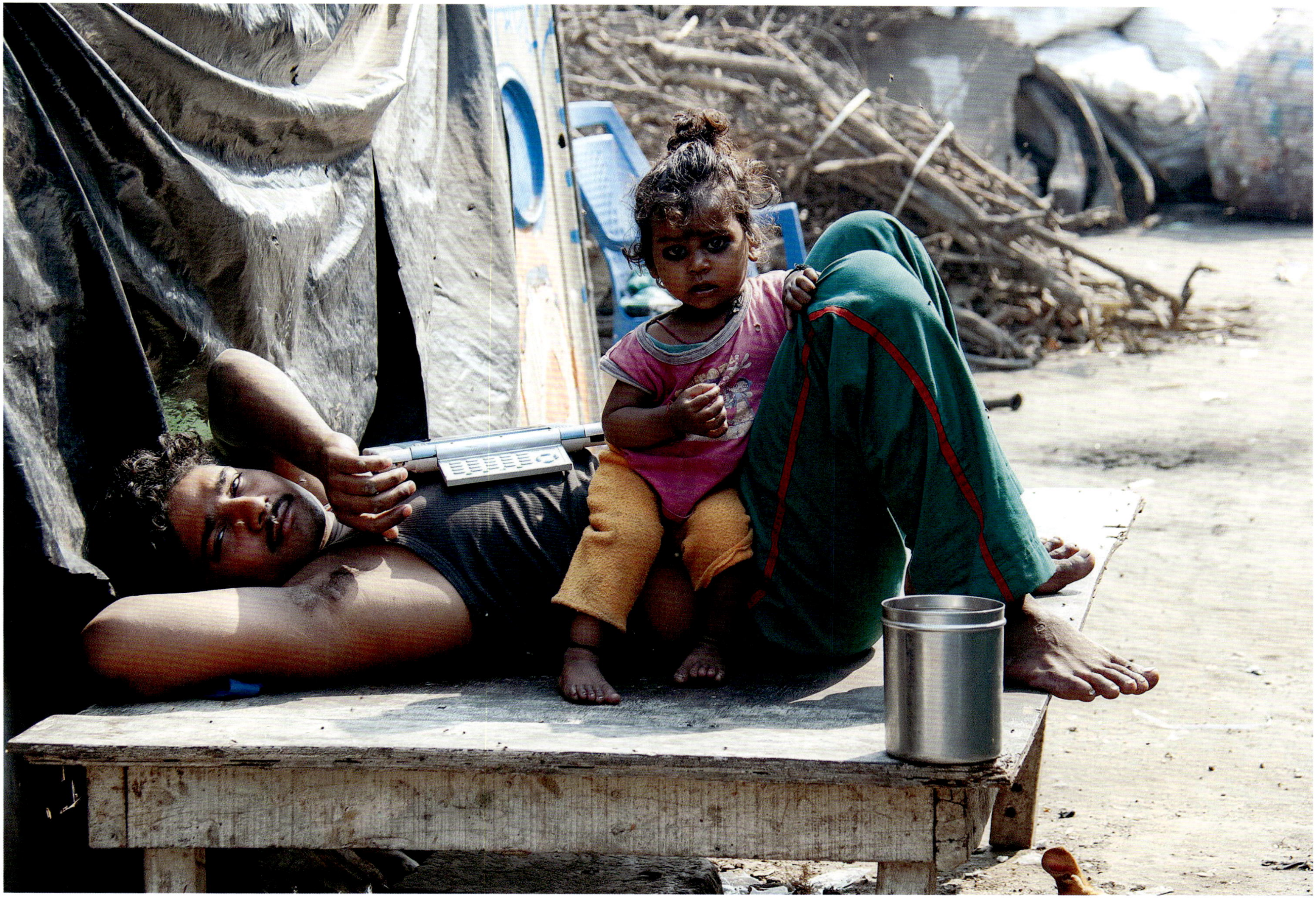

A man and his daughter rest during a hot, sunny day. The very poor people of India live in bustees, makeshift slums, like this one.

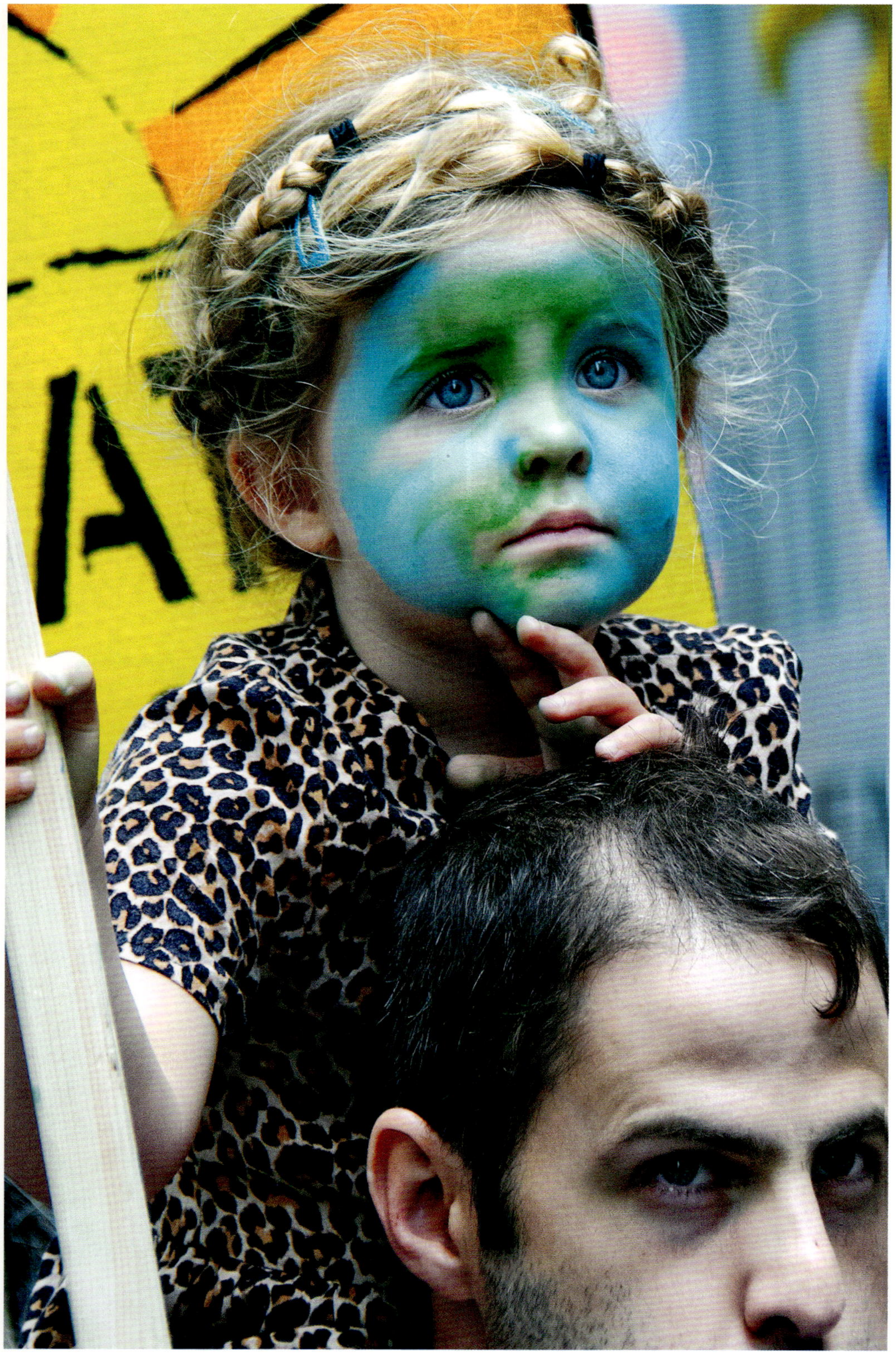

A man and his daughter on Earth Day in Columbus Circle. They stand with others who have marched from Central Park in support of protecting the planet. The girl's face is painted like a map of the world.

United States / New York, New York

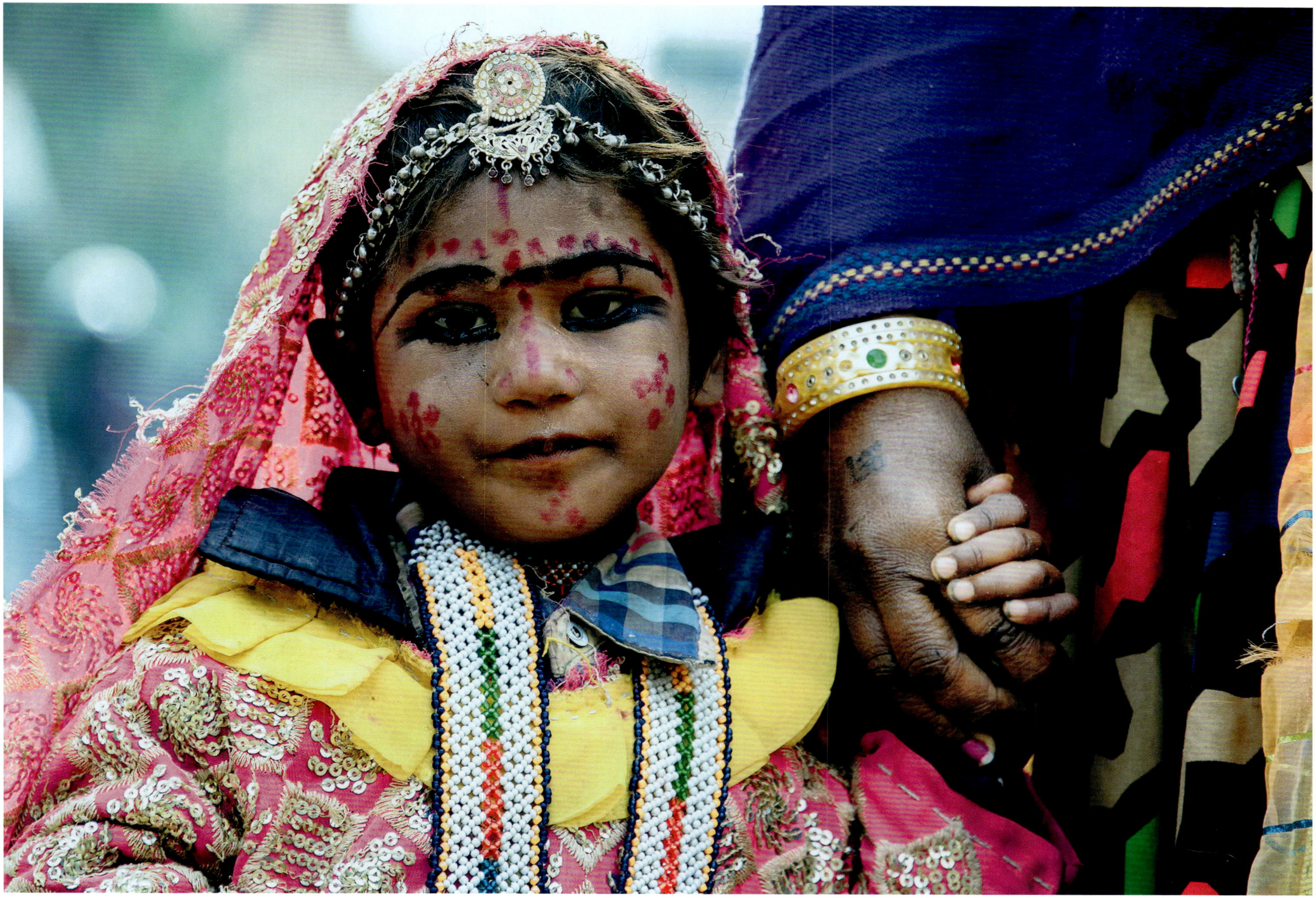

A young girl at the Jaisalmer Desert Festival in the Thar Desert.

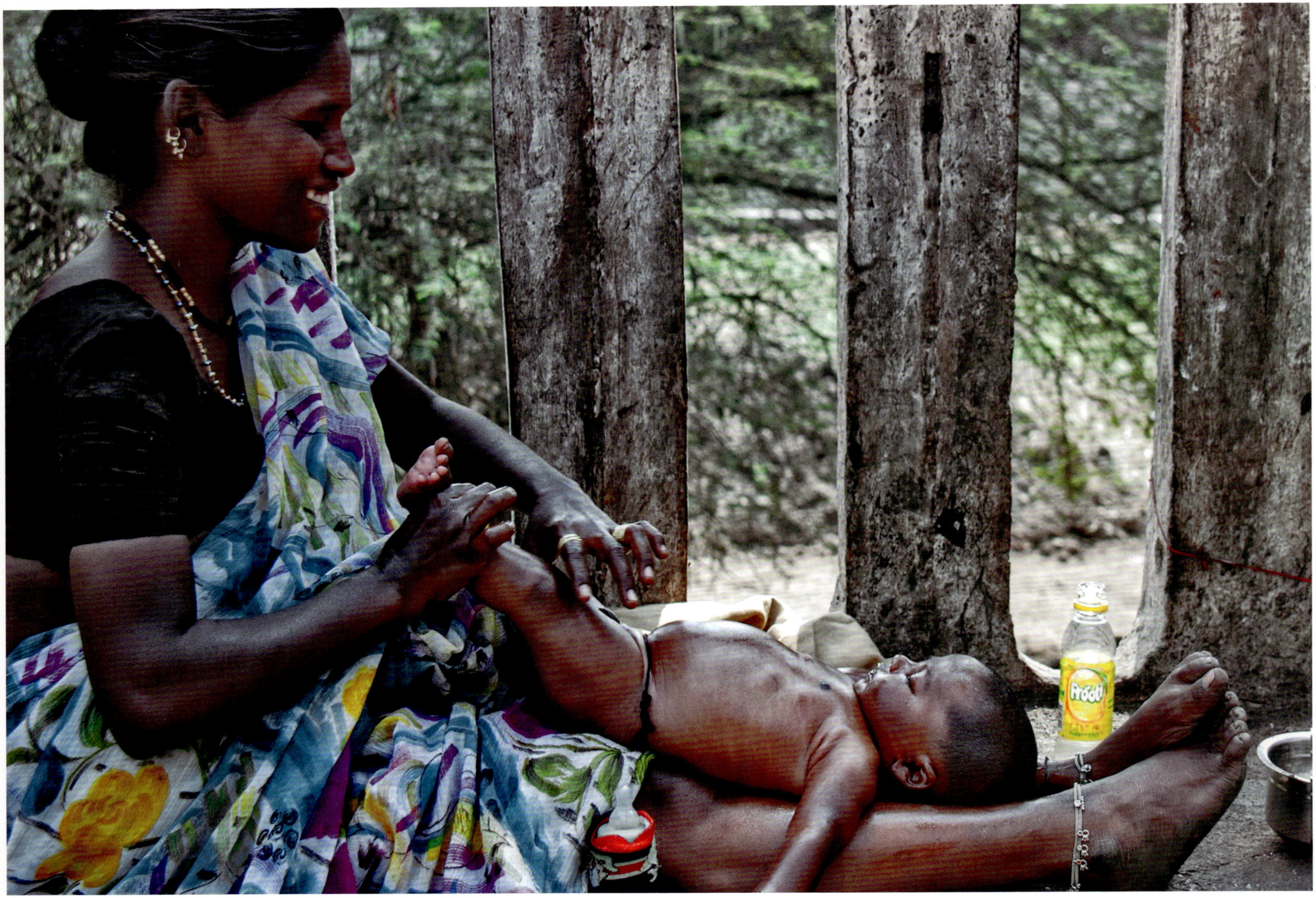

A mother entertains her child.

India / Pune, Maharashtra

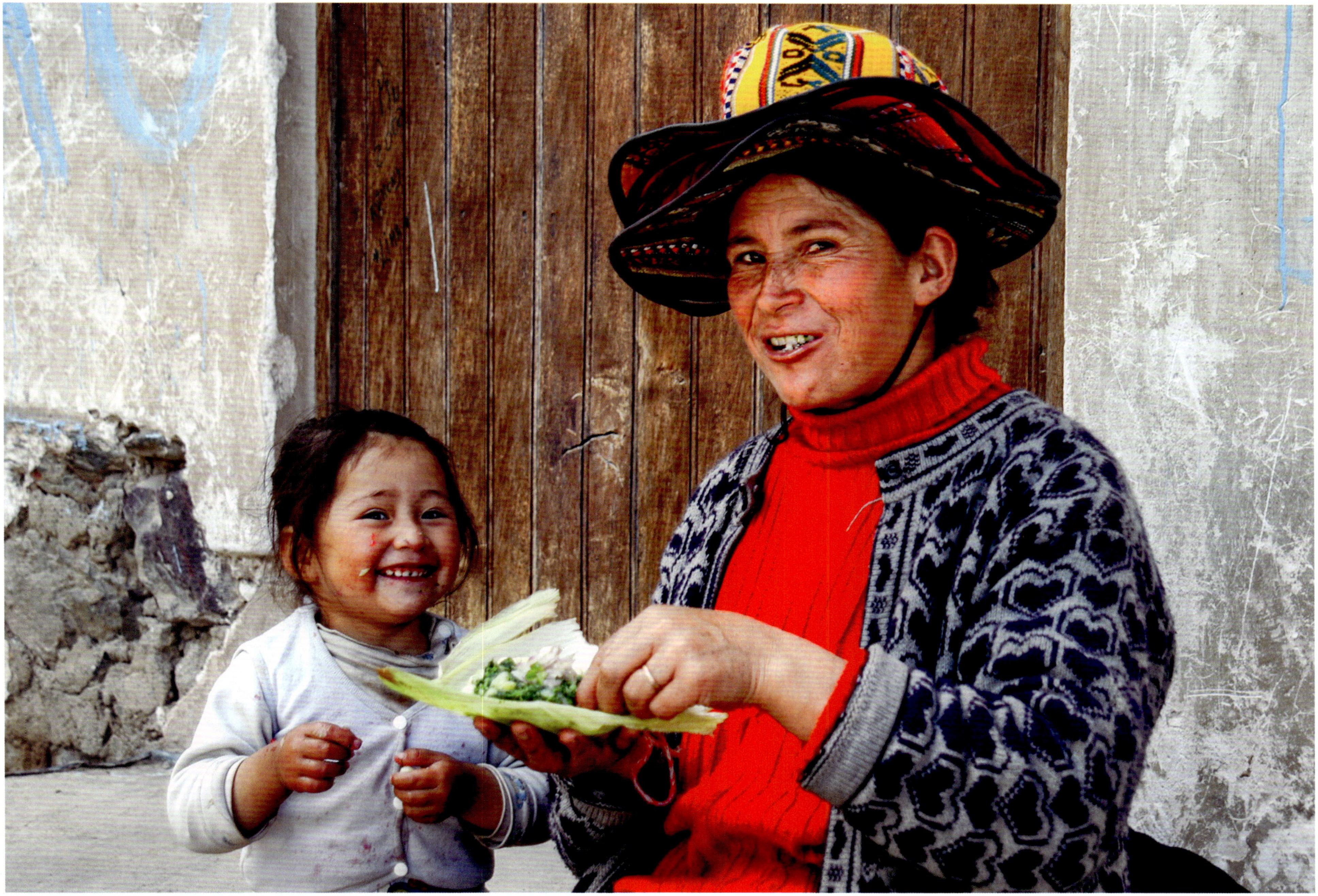

A woman and child enjoy cuy, or guinea pig.

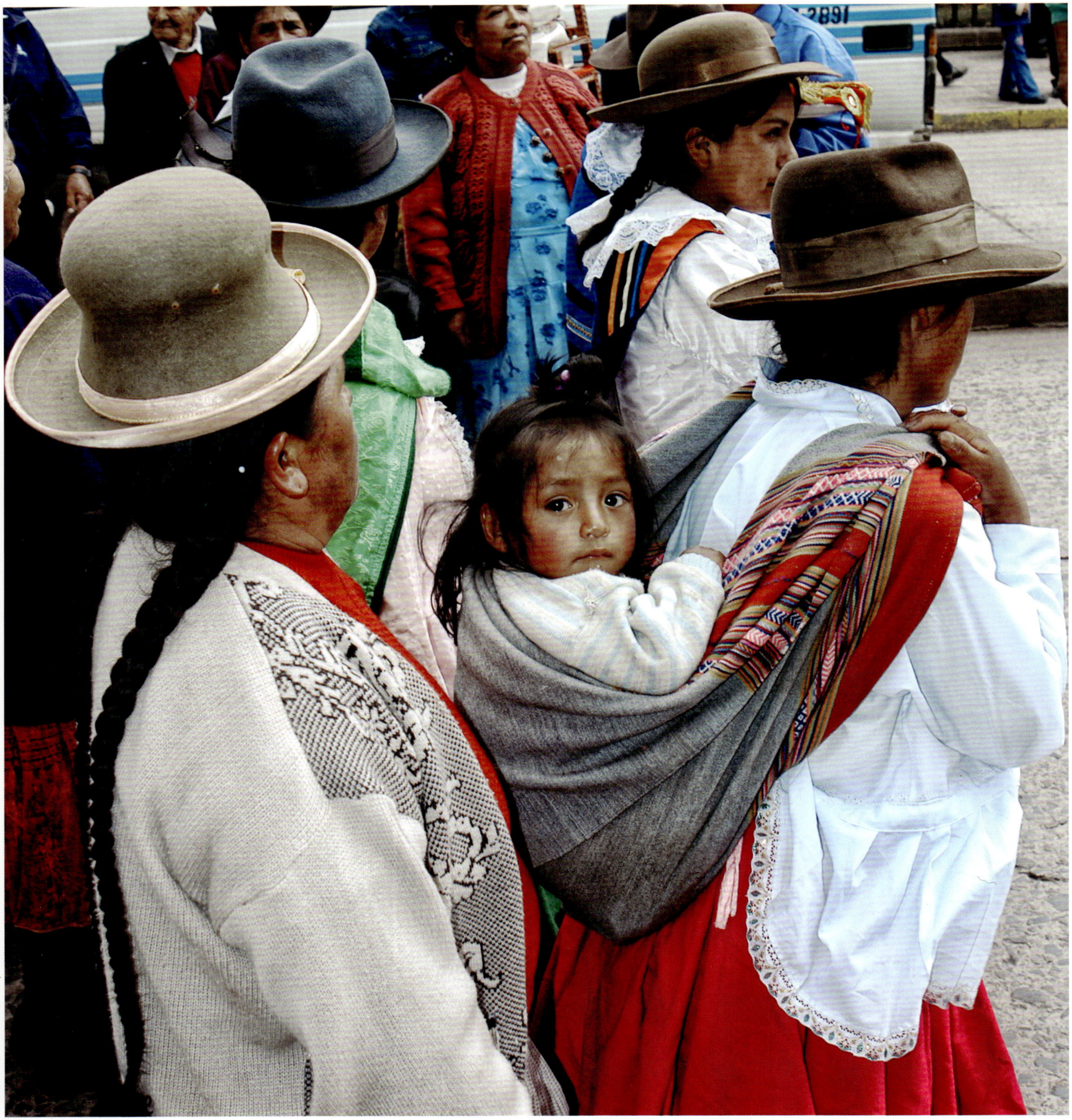

In the Peruvian Andes, a young girl rests in a manta, a traditional carrying cloth, tied to her mother's back. Women often carry children on their backs when walking, cooking, eating, or working.

Peru / Cuzco

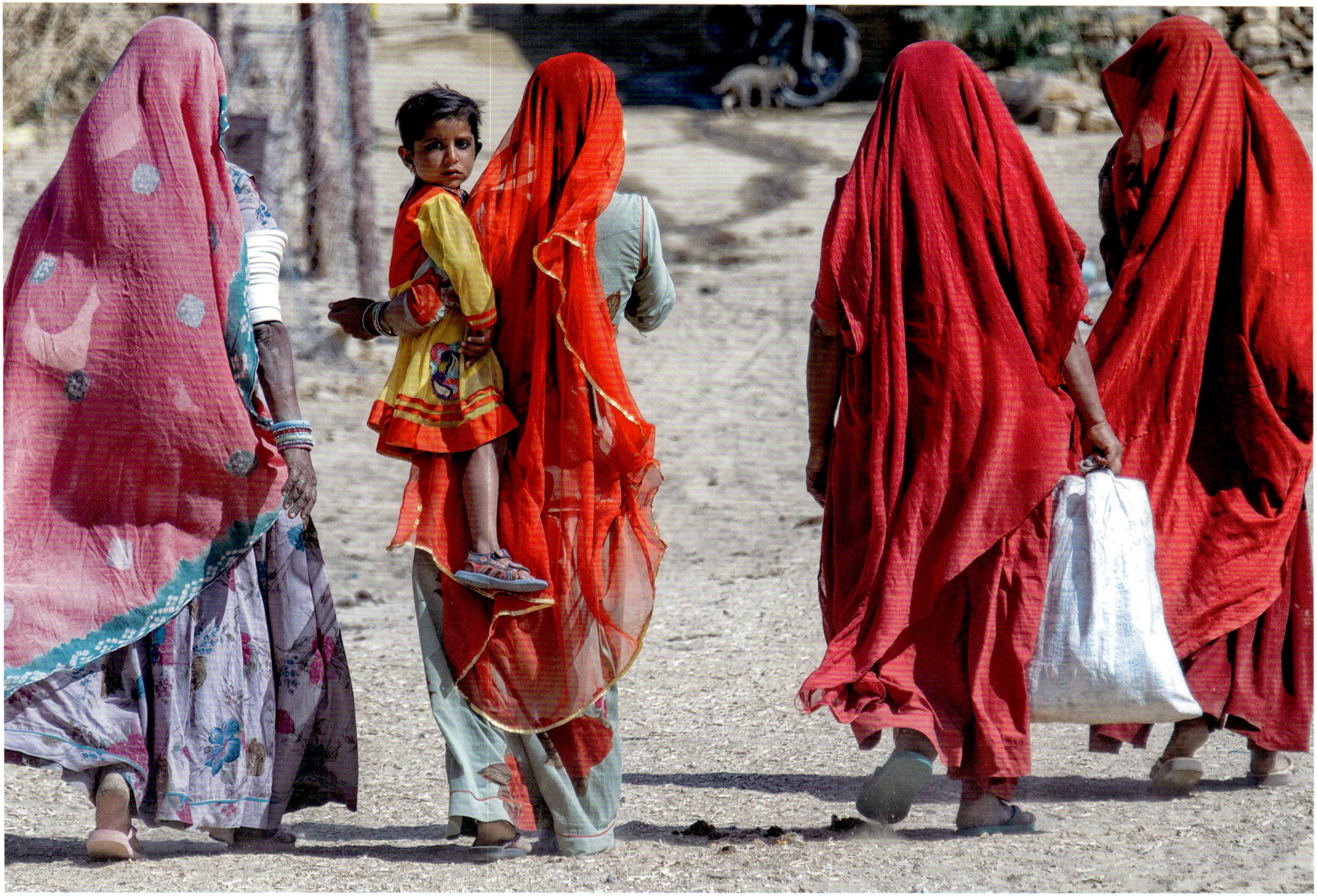

Women walk in a town in the Thar Desert by the Pakistani border.

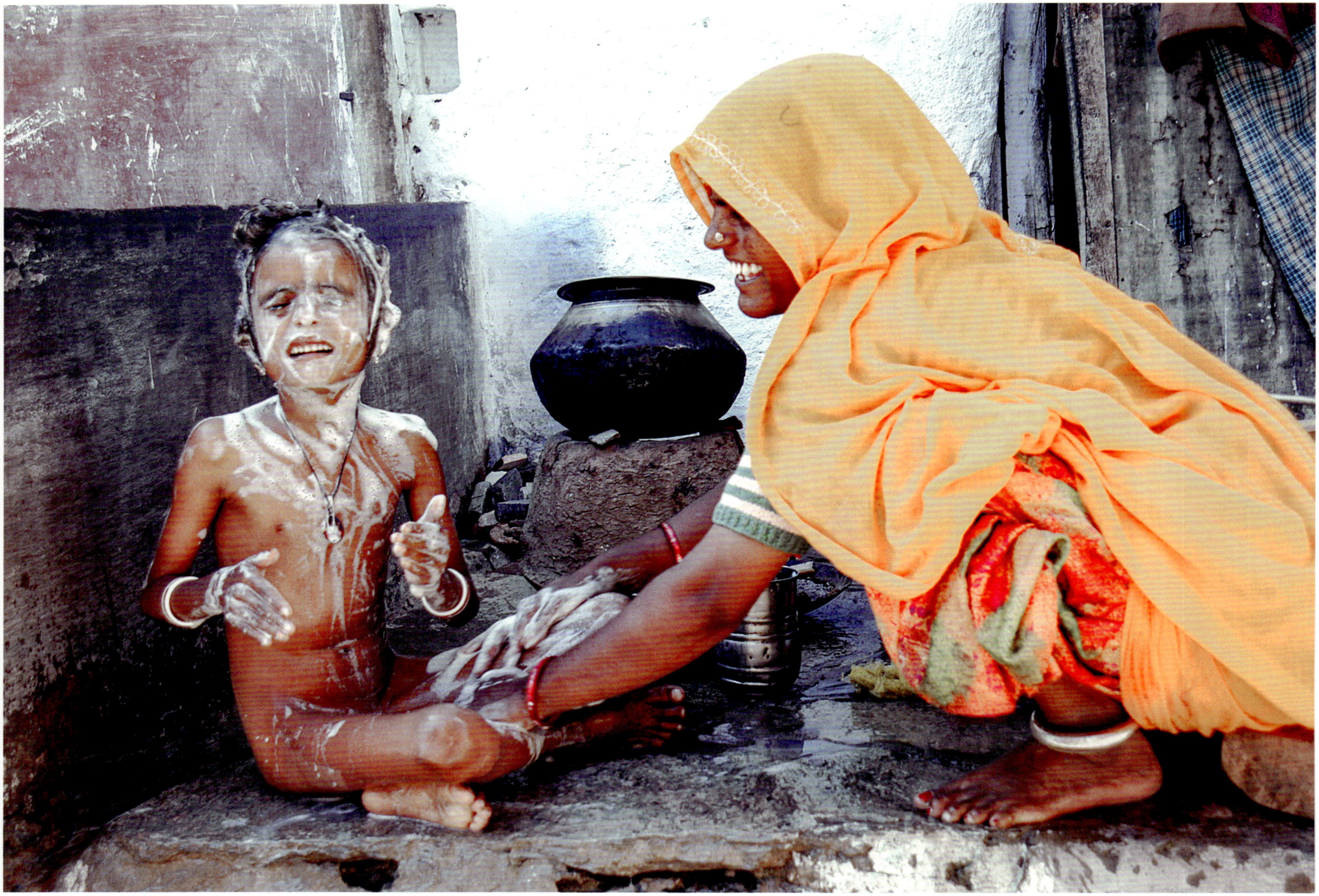

A mother bathes her child. The mother is covered up even though it is 100 degrees Fahrenheit outside.

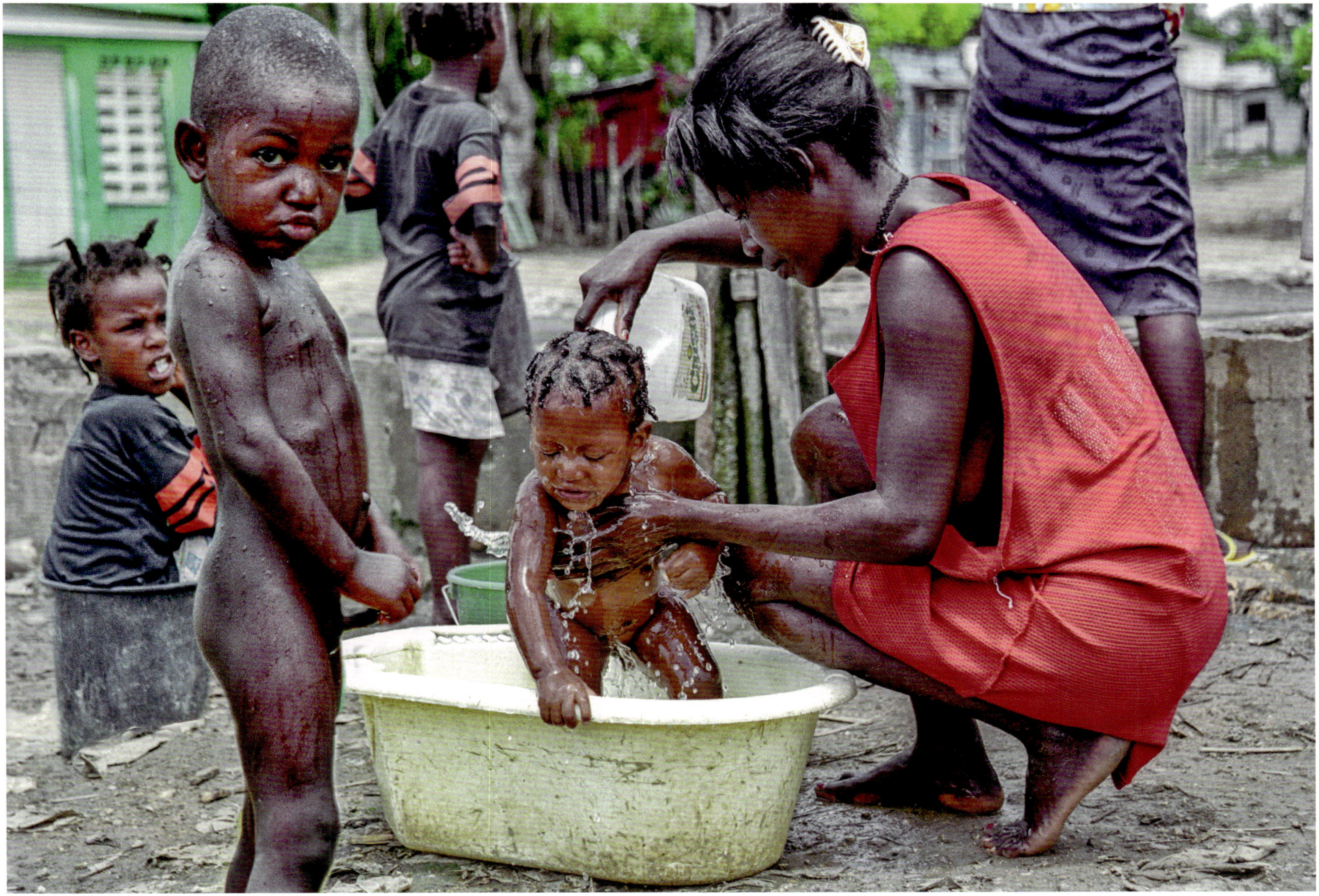

A mother washes her children in a makeshift shower in batey el Jamon.

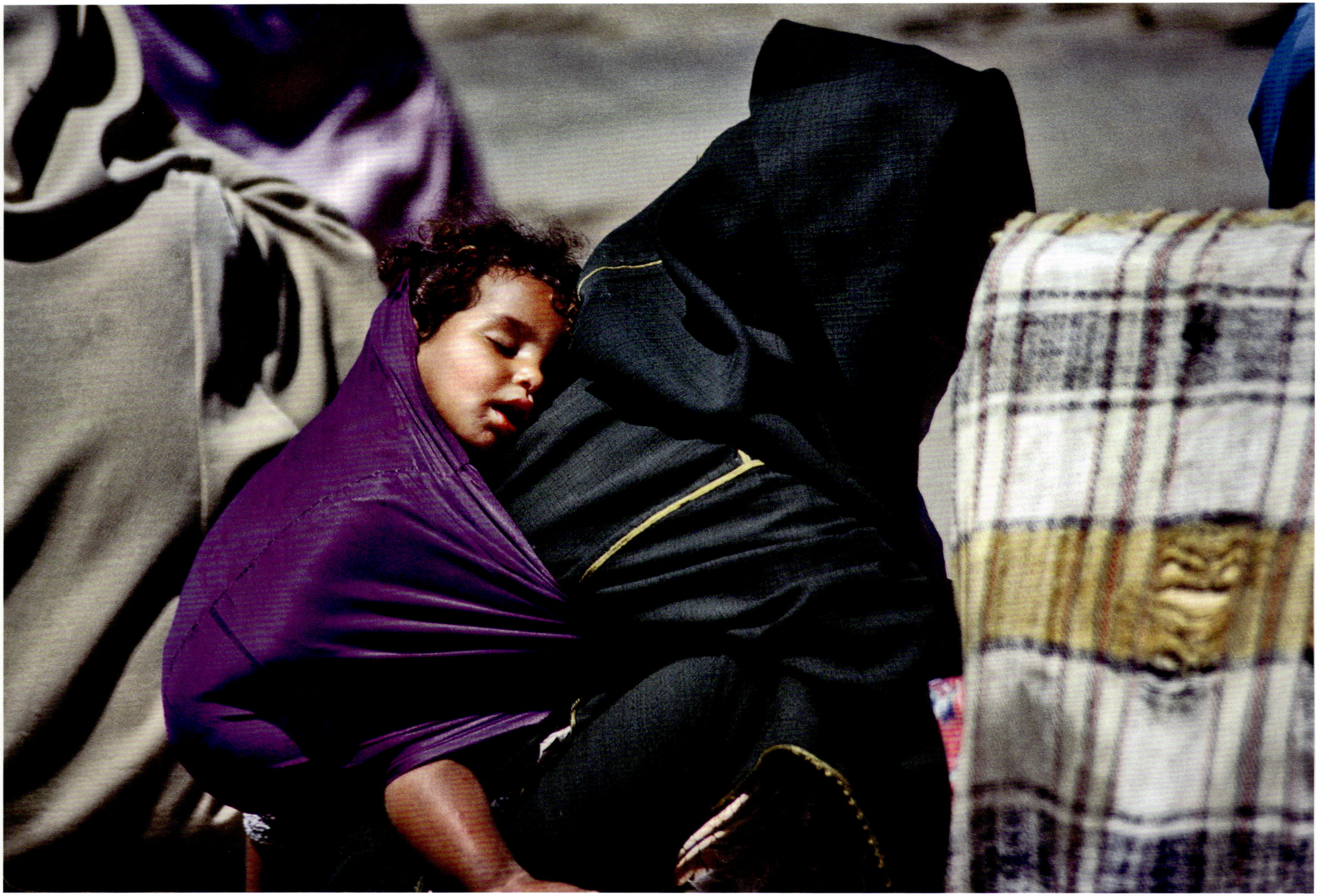

A mother carries her sleeping child while shopping at a market in the town of Ürgüp.

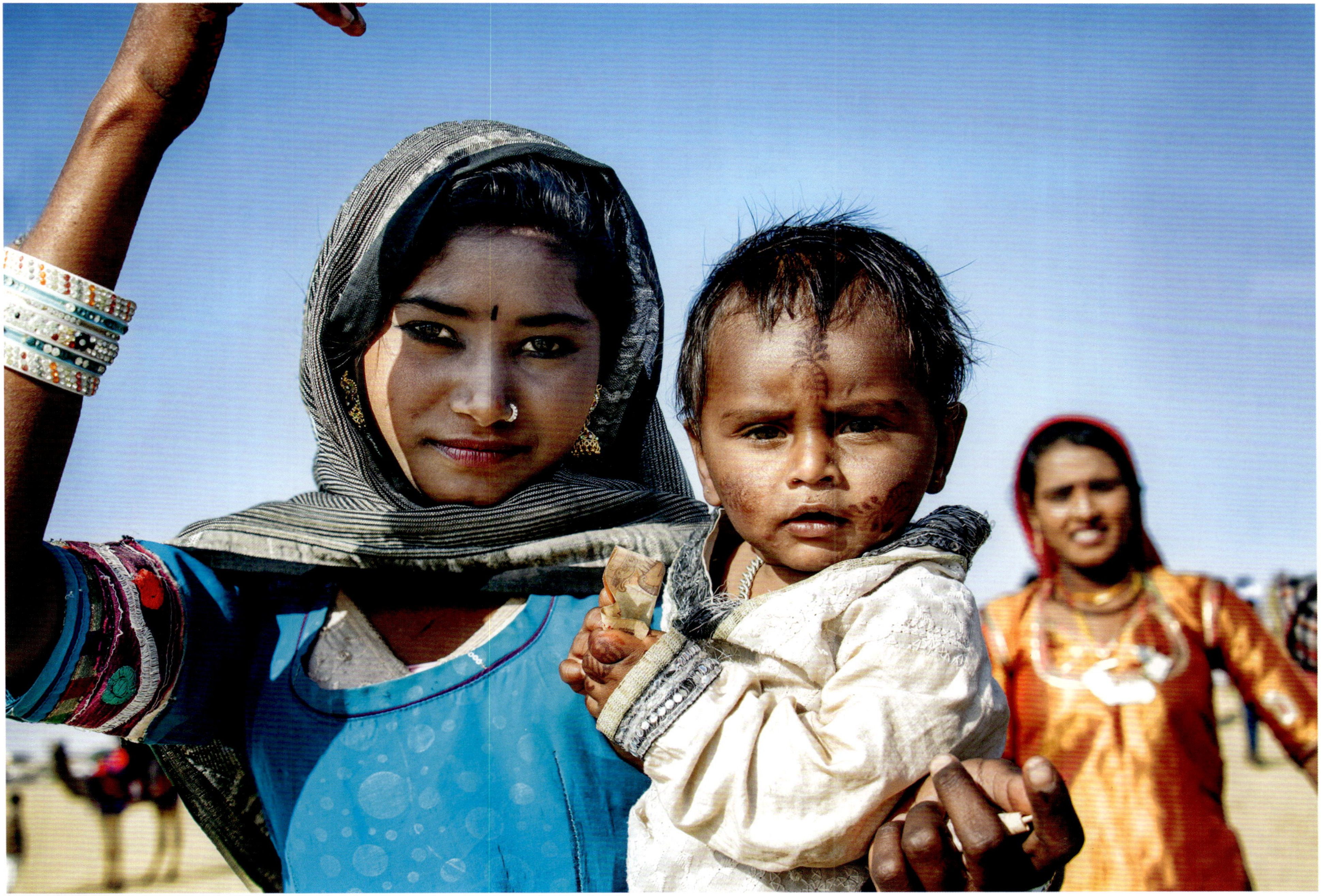

Roma, known by the pejorative term gypsy, perform for baksheesh, or tips, on the touristed dunes in western Rajasthan near the Pakistani border.

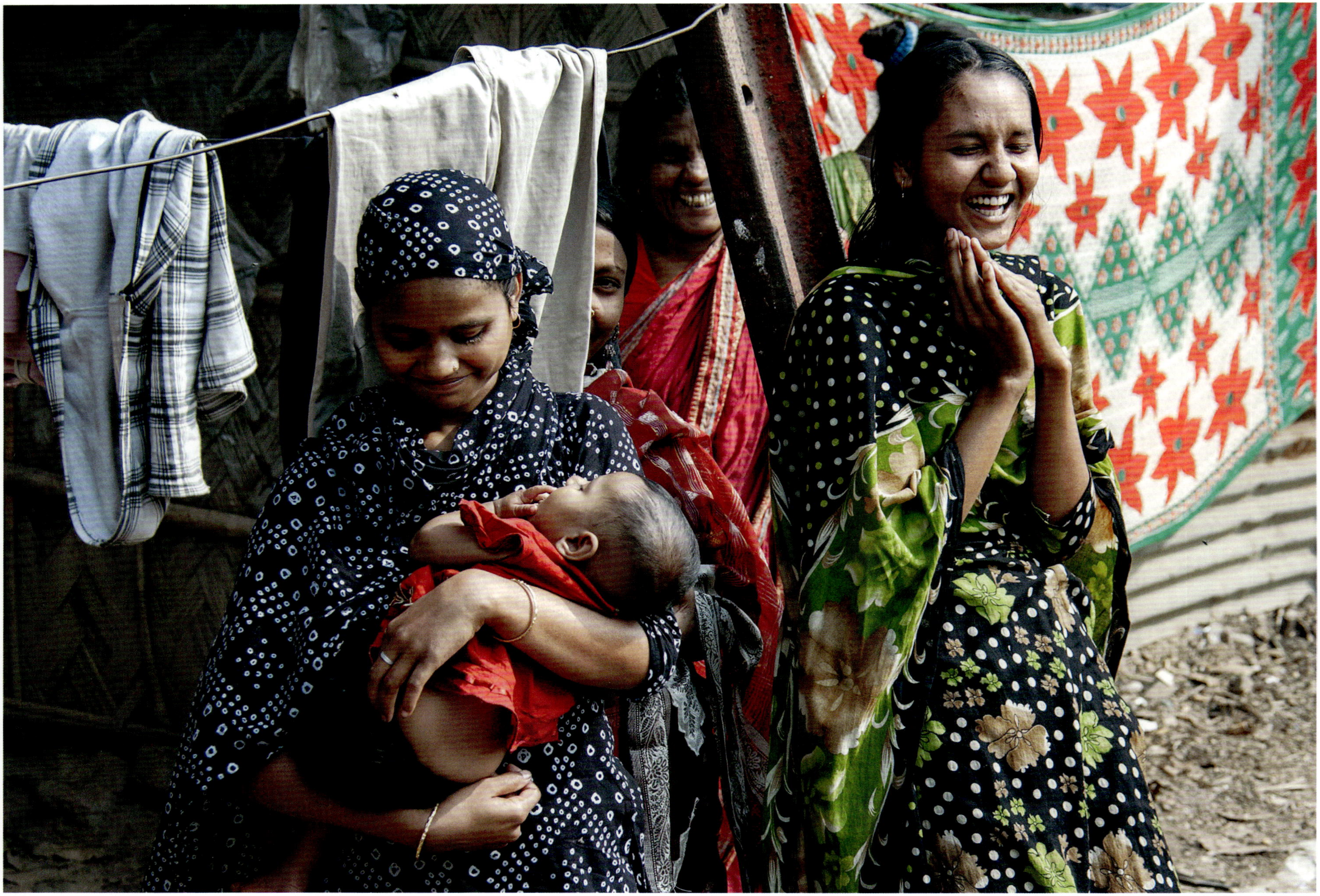

In a Dhaka slum, women smile and one looks sheepishly.

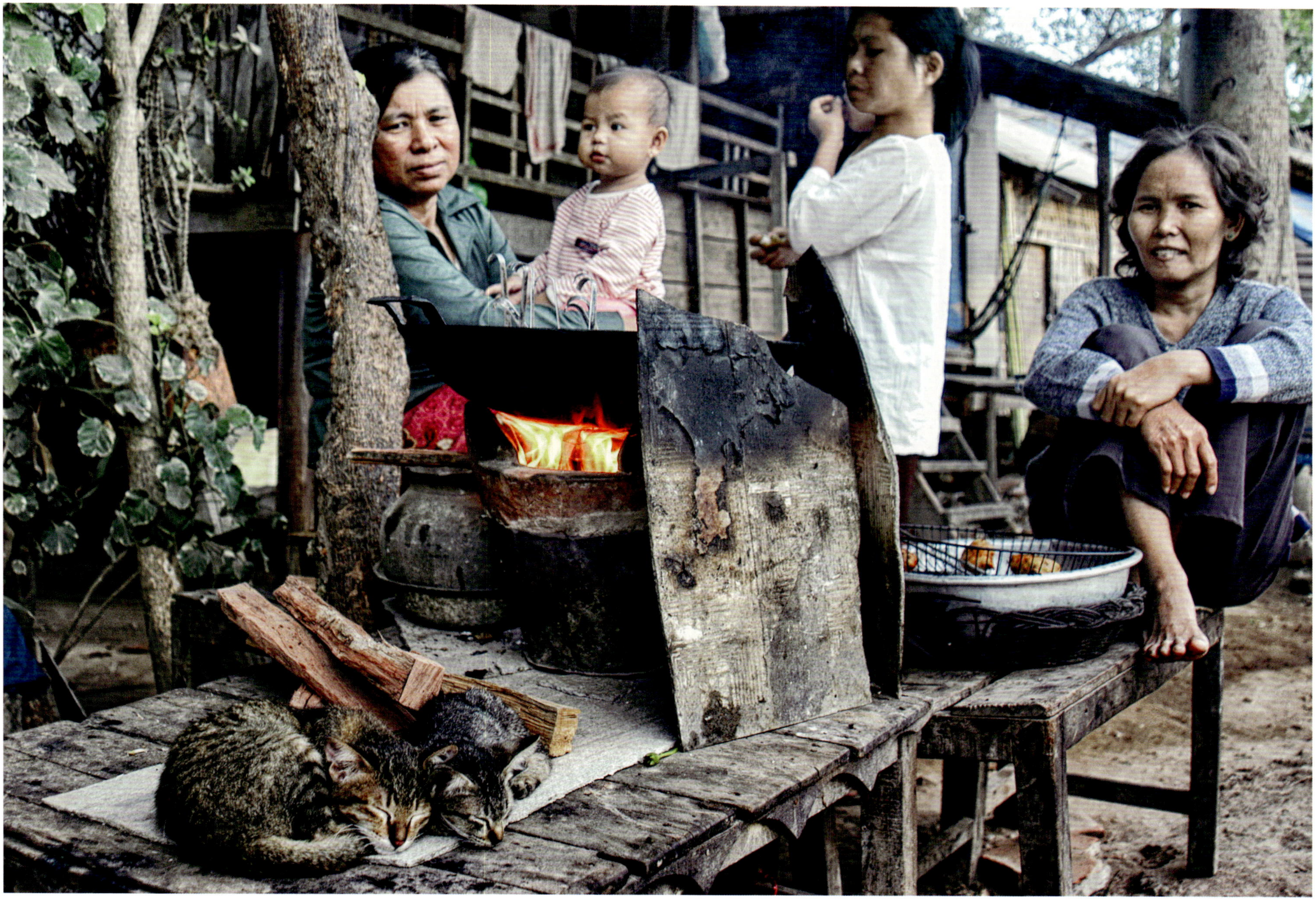

In the capital of Cambodia, locals sell food and cats catch catnaps.

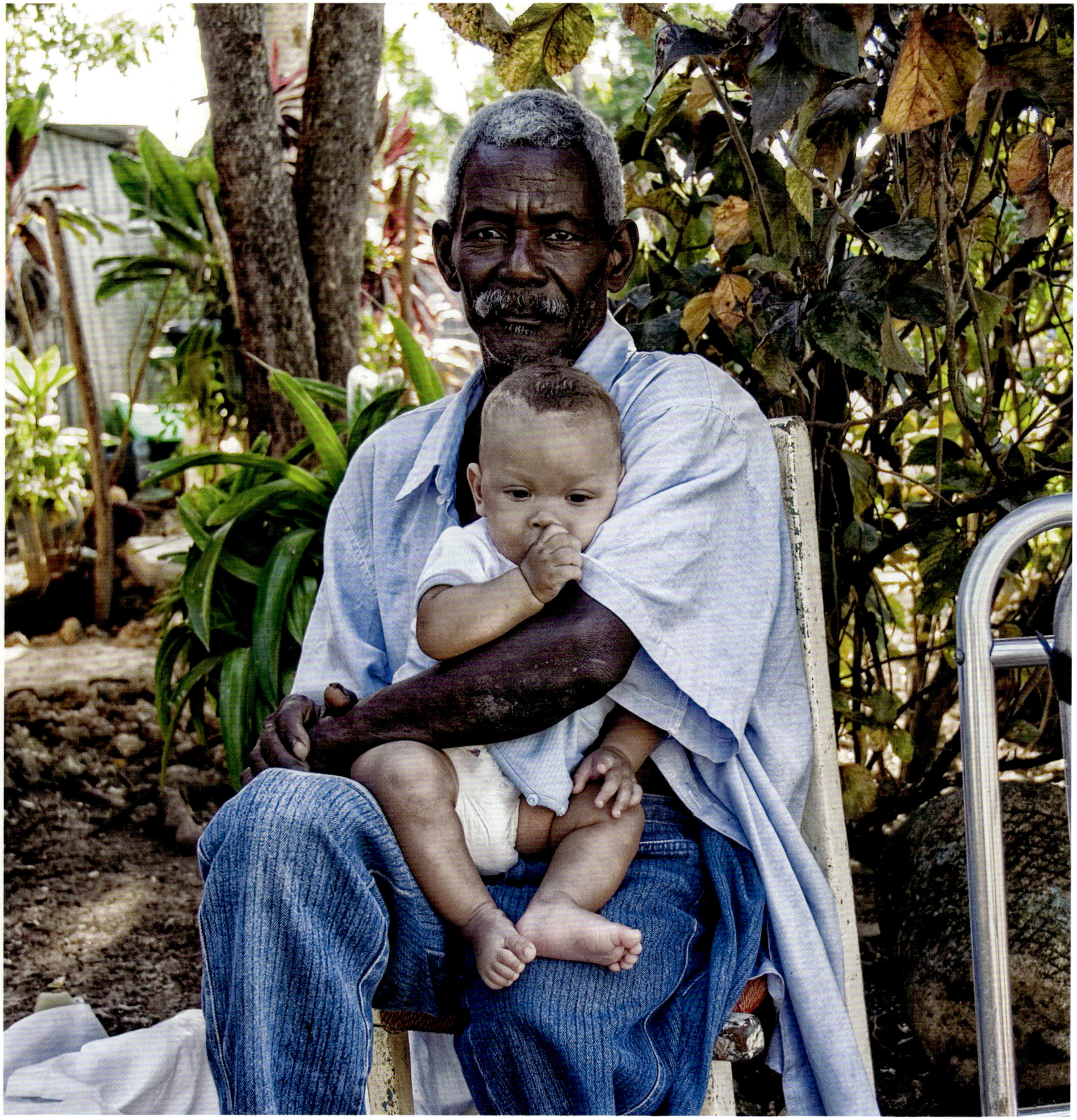

On batey Angelina, a cane cutter from Haiti holds his grandson. The man has lost a leg to diabetes and can no longer work.

Dominican Republic /
San Pedro de Macorís,
San Pedro de Macorís Province

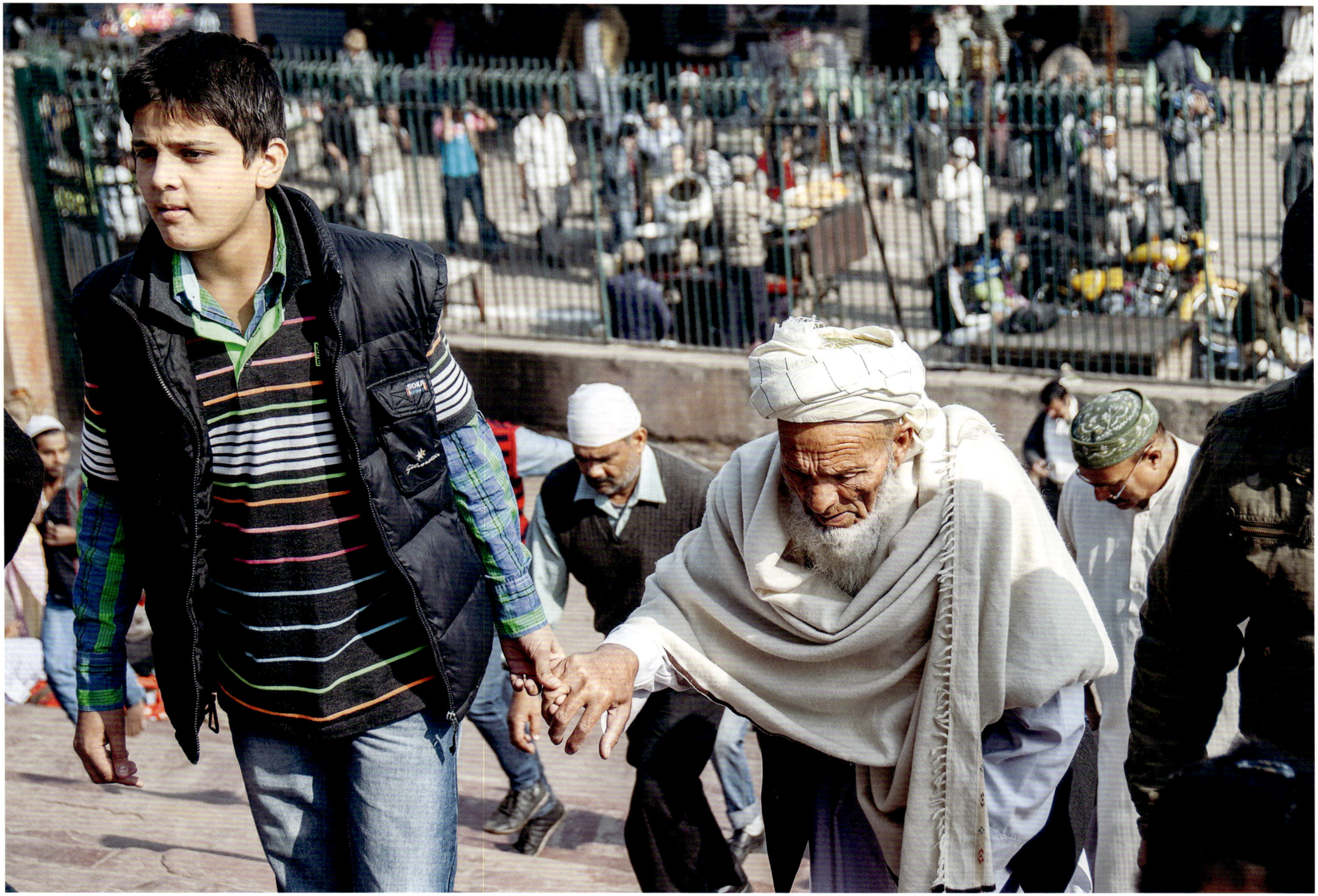

A young man helps an older man up the steps to Jama Masjid, the largest mosque in India, for Friday prayer.

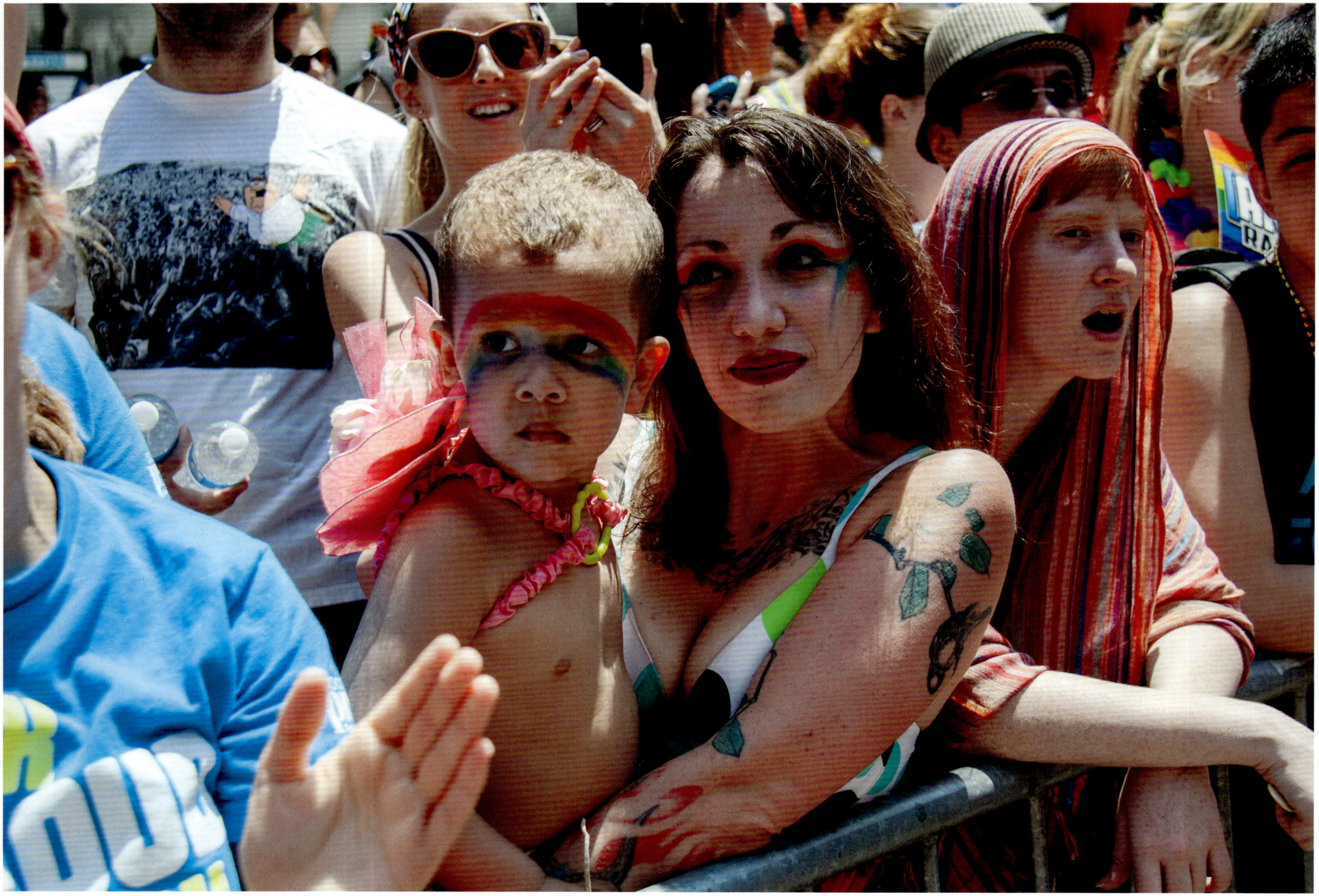

A woman and her son on the sidelines of the New York City Pride March. One of the largest annual pride marches in the world, the NYC Pride March traverses south on Fifth Avenue through Greenwich Village and passes the Stonewall National Monument, which memorializes the June 1969 riots that launched the modern movement for LGBTQ+ rights.

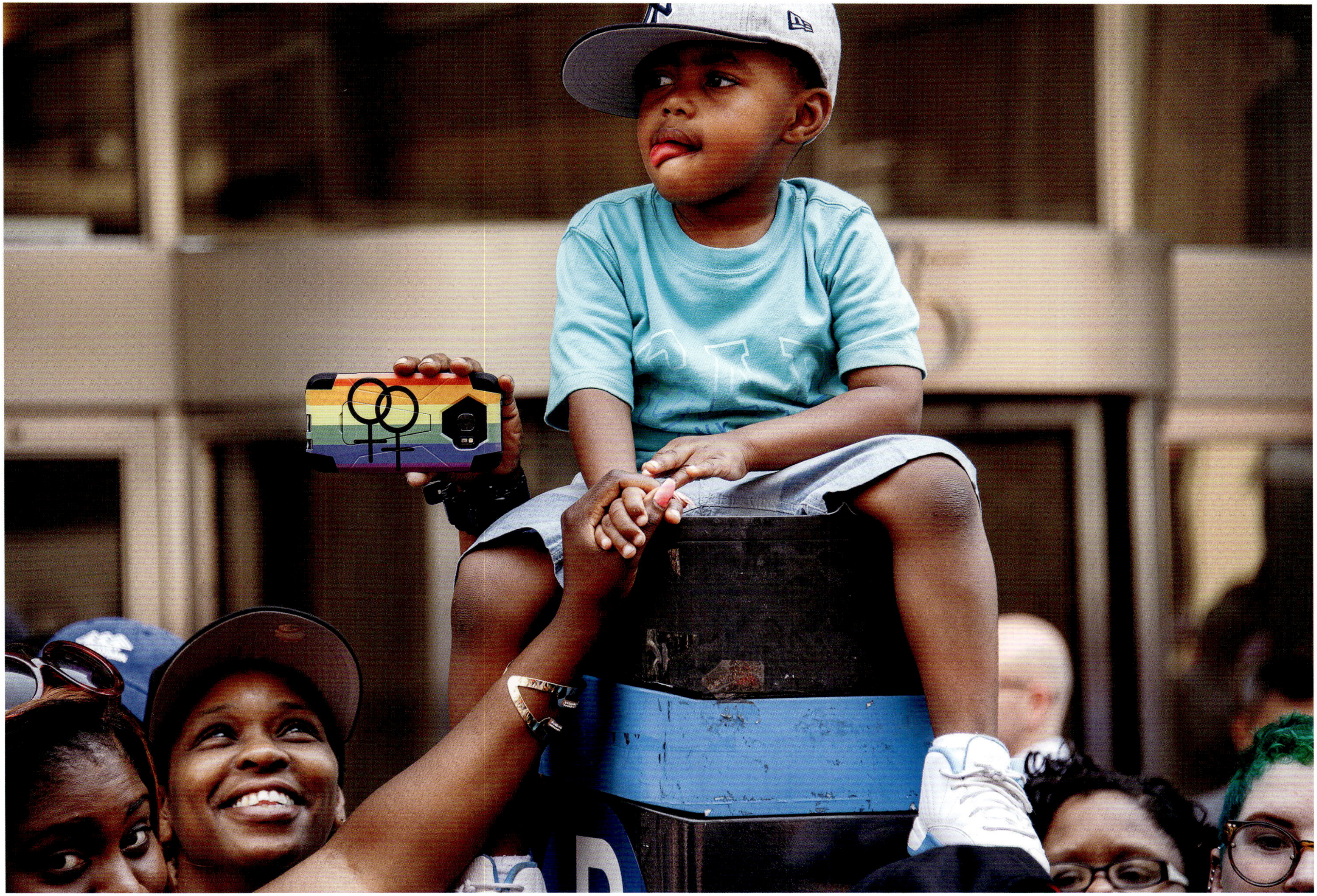

A child watches the celebrants of the Pride March.

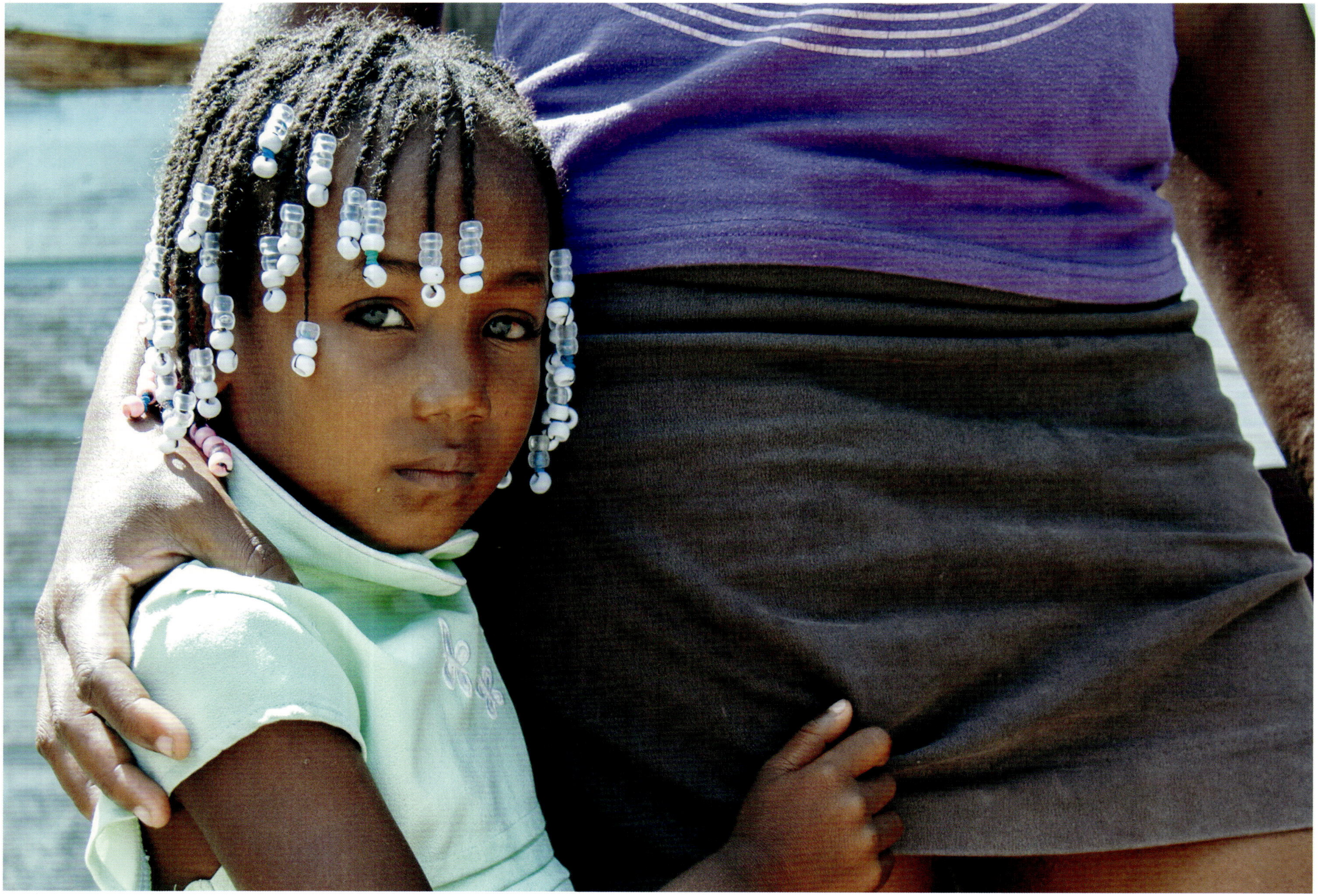

A girl clutches her mother's skirt. Beauty exists in the slums around San Pedro de Macorís.

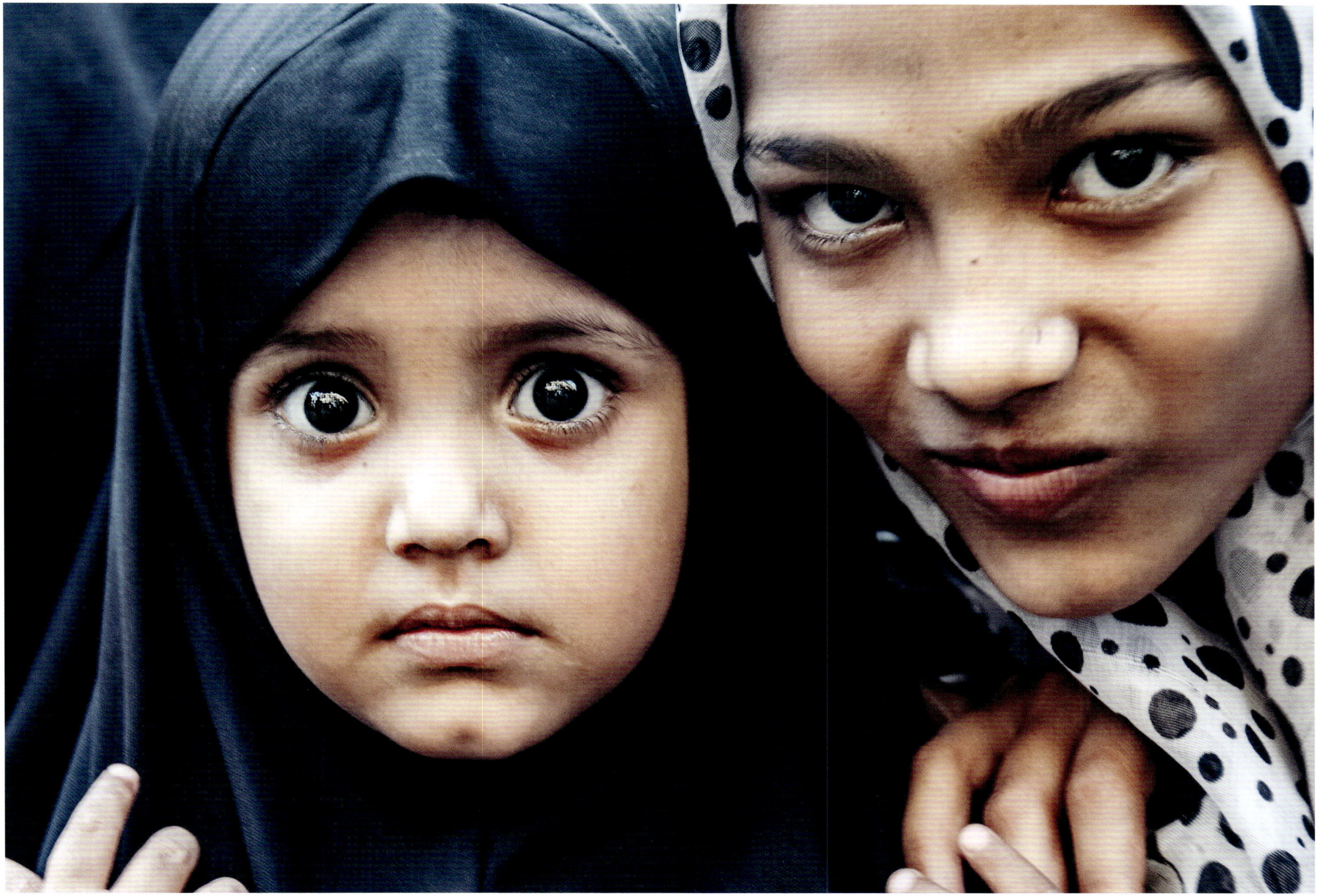

A Shiite Muslim mother and daughter mourn during Muharram, the first month of the Islamic calendar. Storytelling, weeping, self-flagellation, and reenactments of the Battle of Karbala form the crux of the observances.

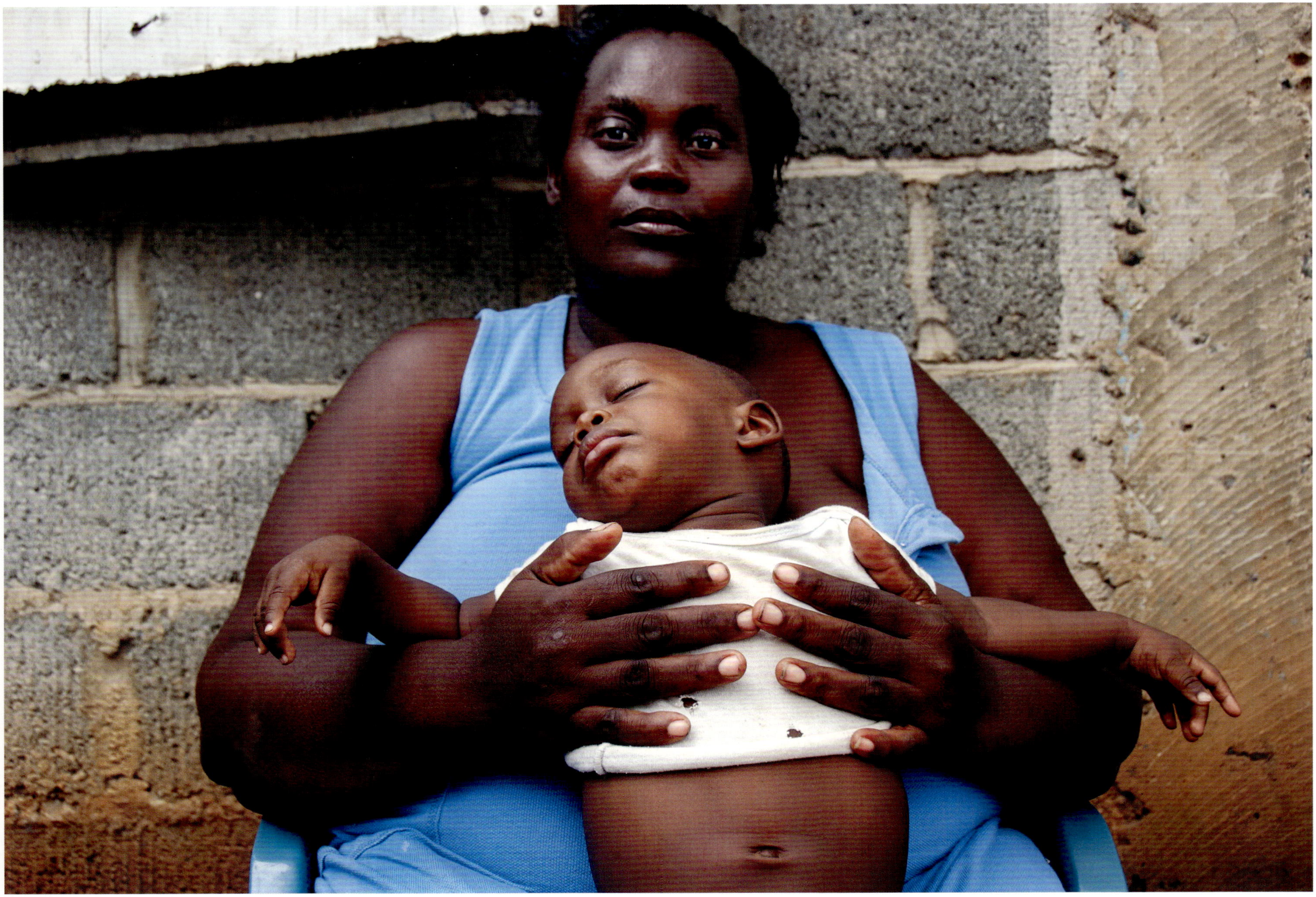

A woman holds her sleeping son.

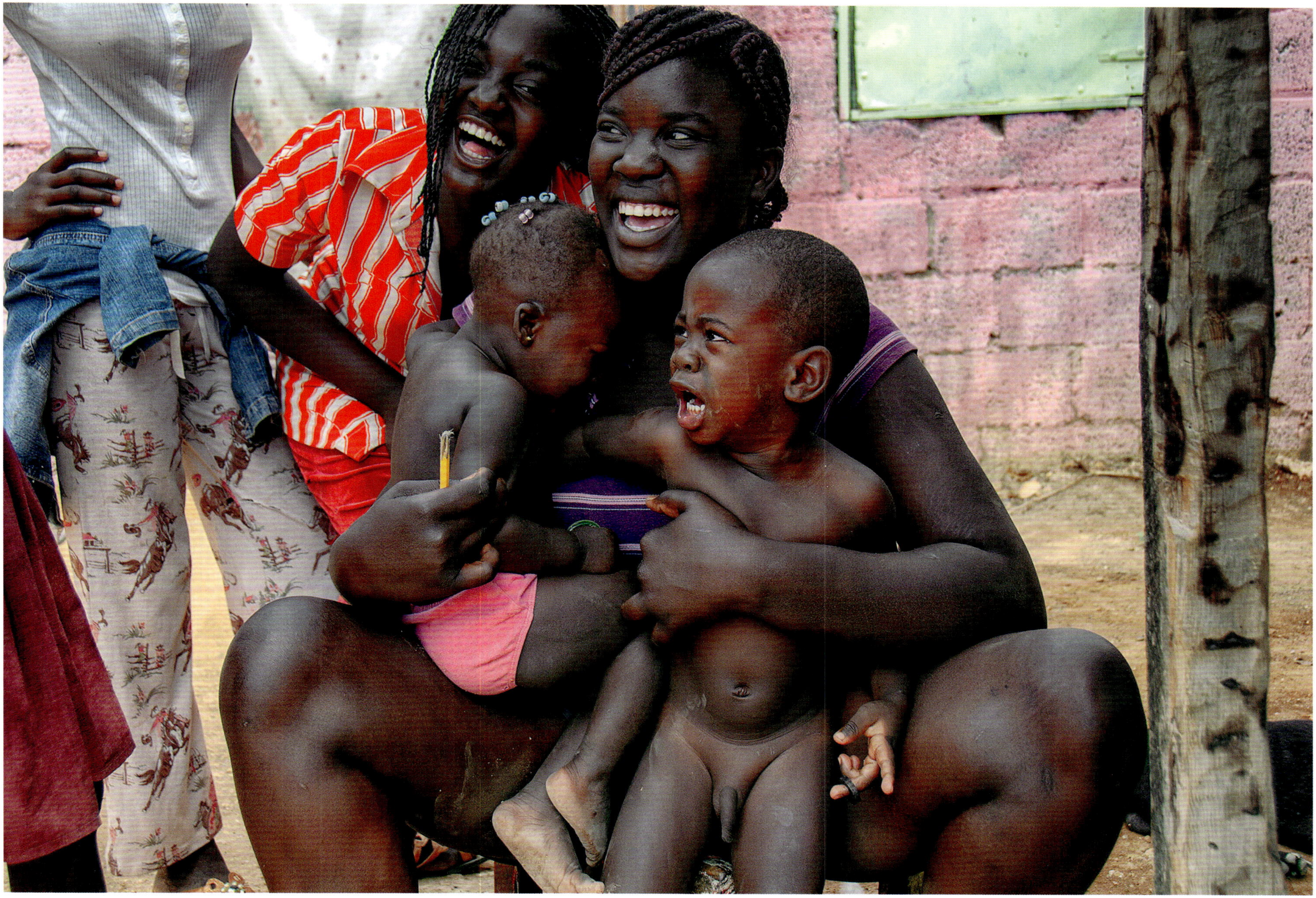

A mother's joy in spite of poverty.

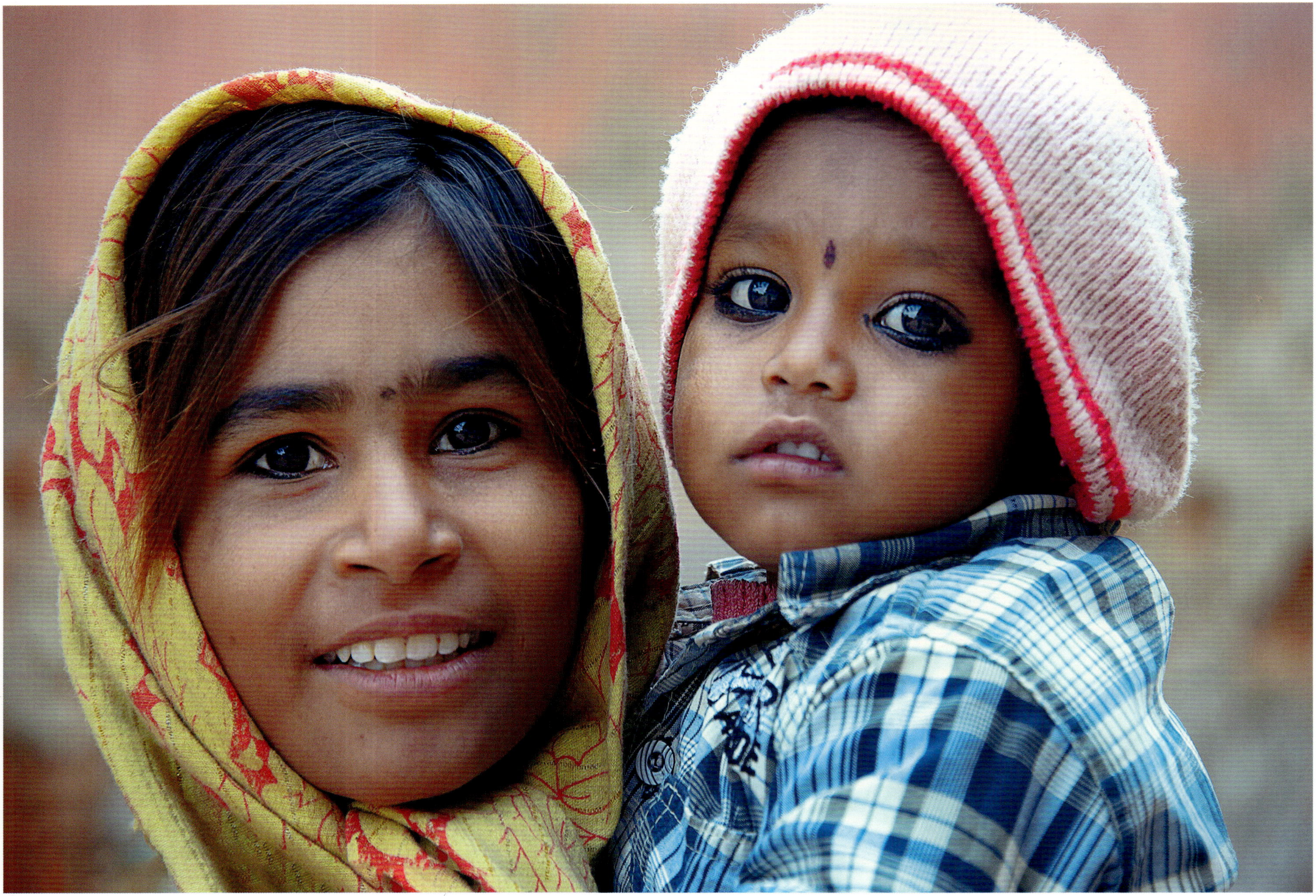

A woman and child. Each has a bindi and wears kajal, or kohl, eyeliner. Kohl has been used for centuries by women, and often children and men as well. It's thought that it can protect children's eyes, improve them, or even ward off curses from the evil eye, but it can also lead to lead poisoning.

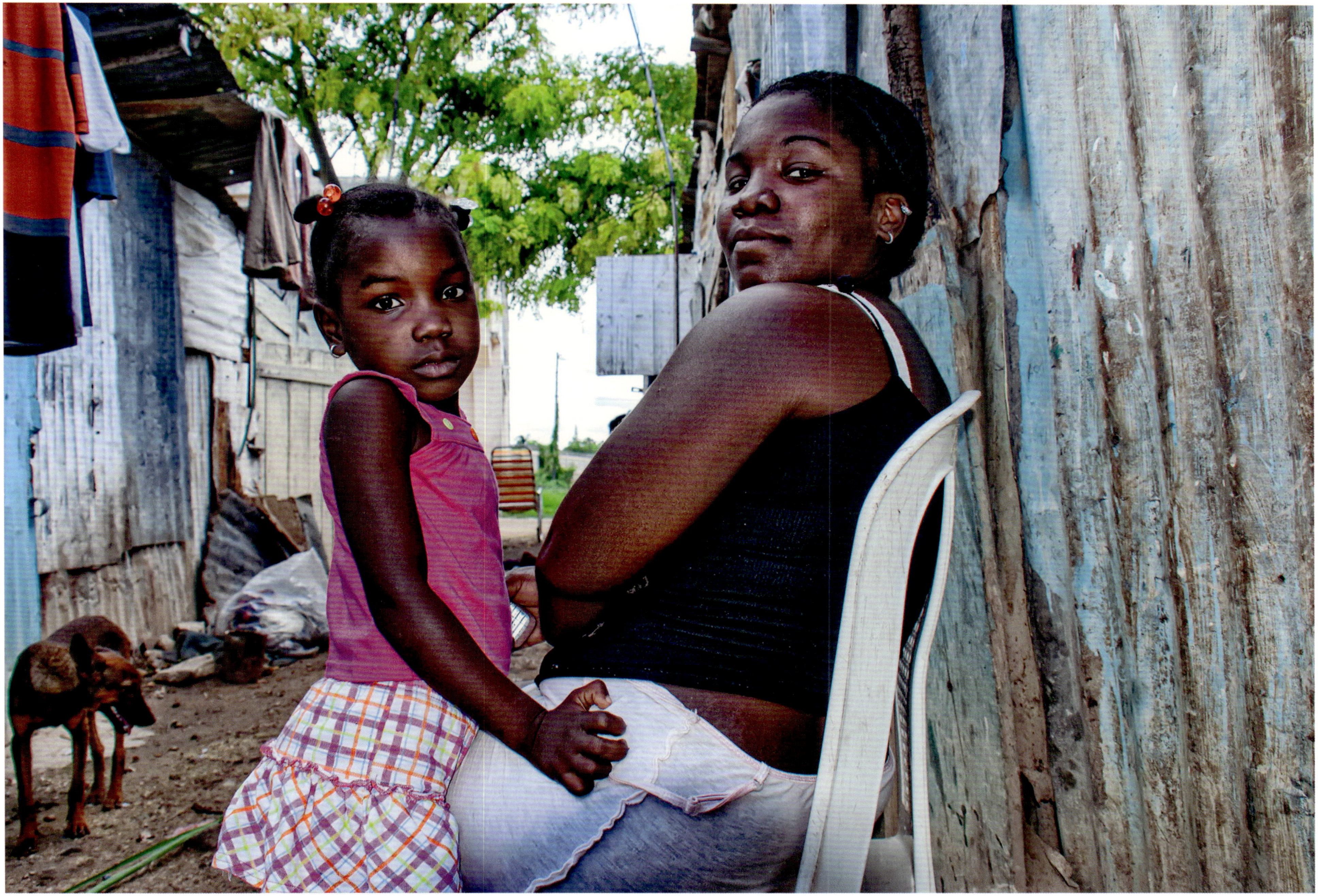

A mother and daughter pose for a portrait.

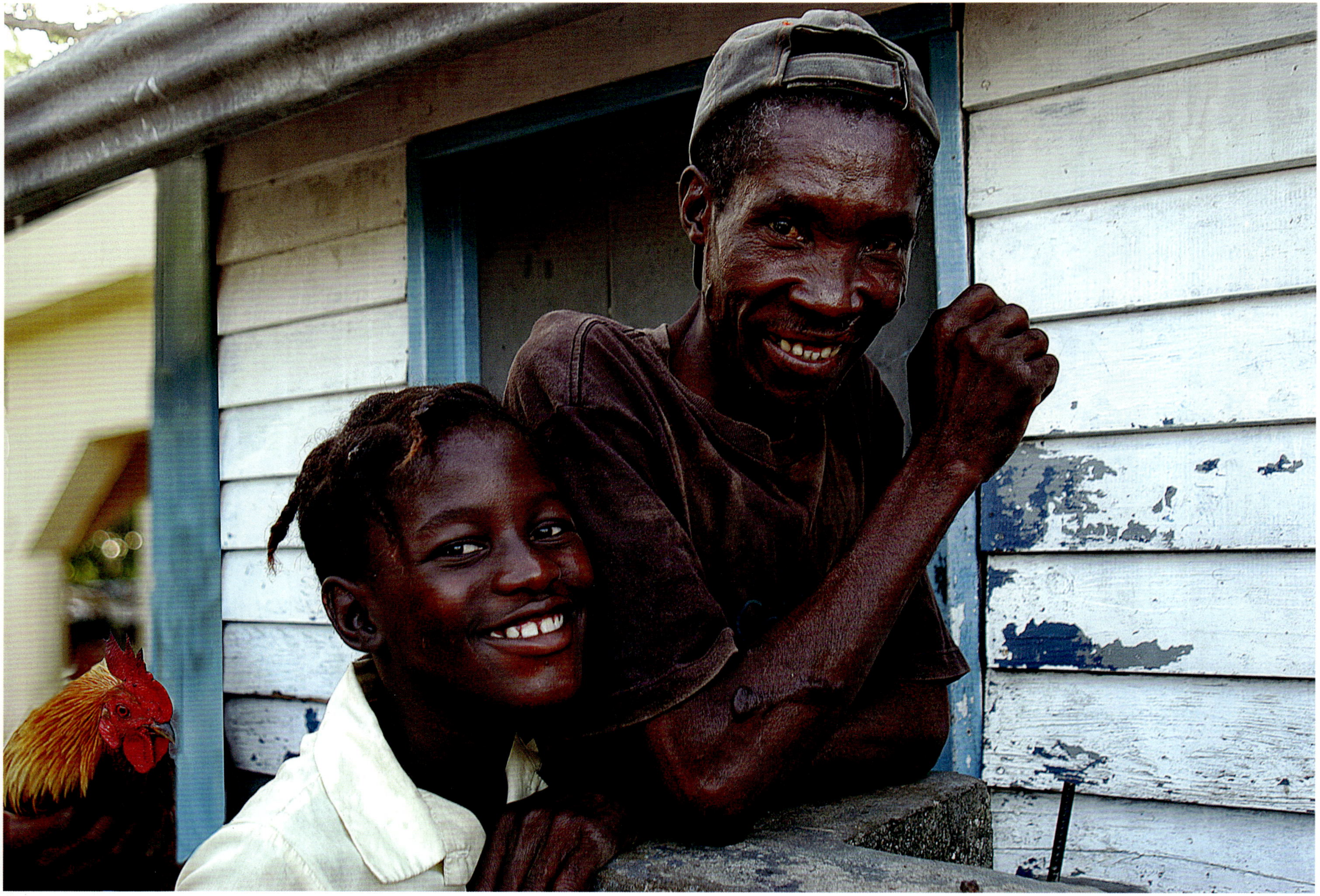

Despite arduous lives and intense heat, these Haitian immigrants wear smiles.

A father and son rest for a minute.
They're in the central market of
San Pedro de Macorís, where
they've come to shop for food.

Dominican Republic / San Pedro de Macorís, San Pedro de Macorís Province

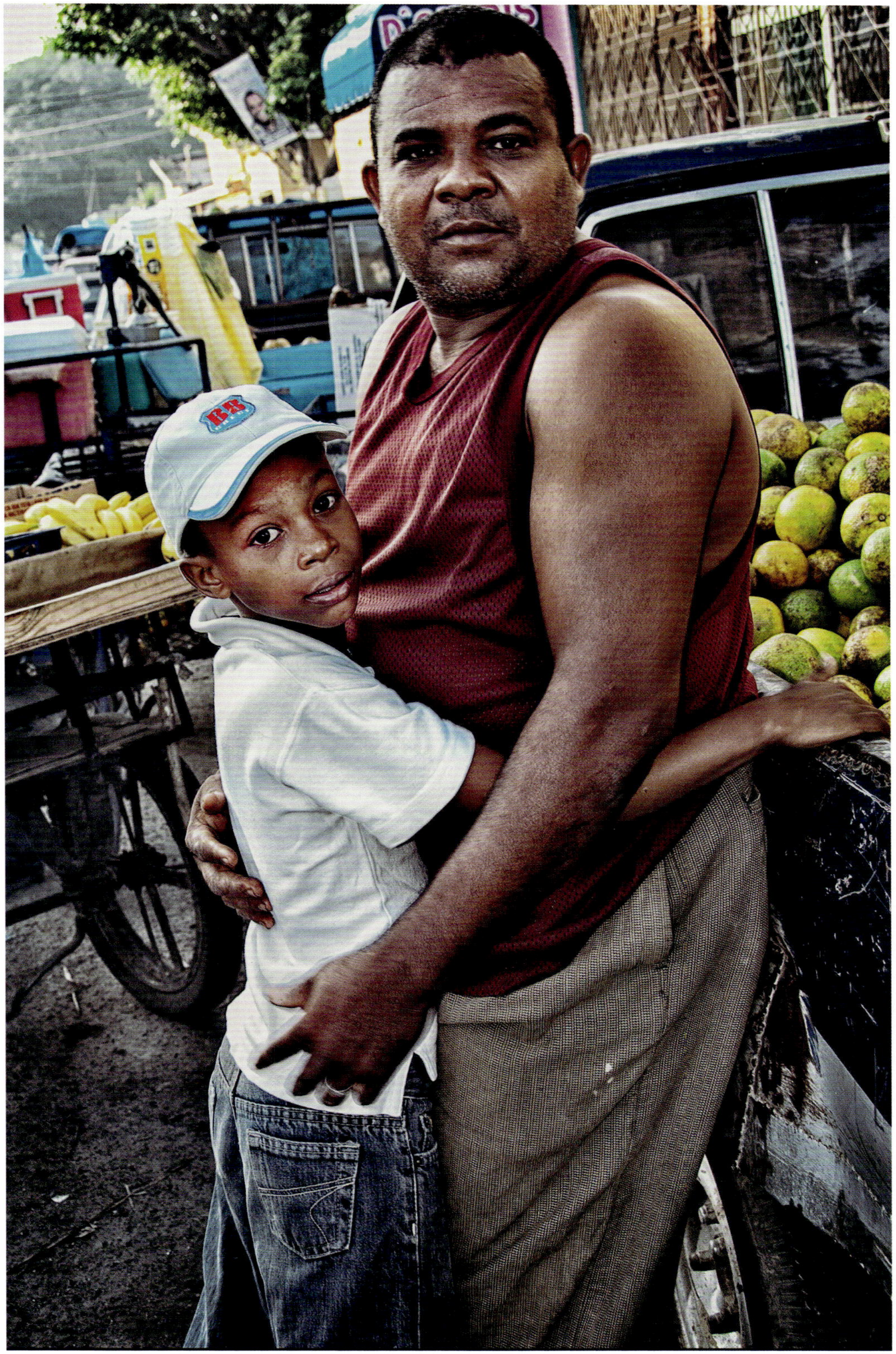

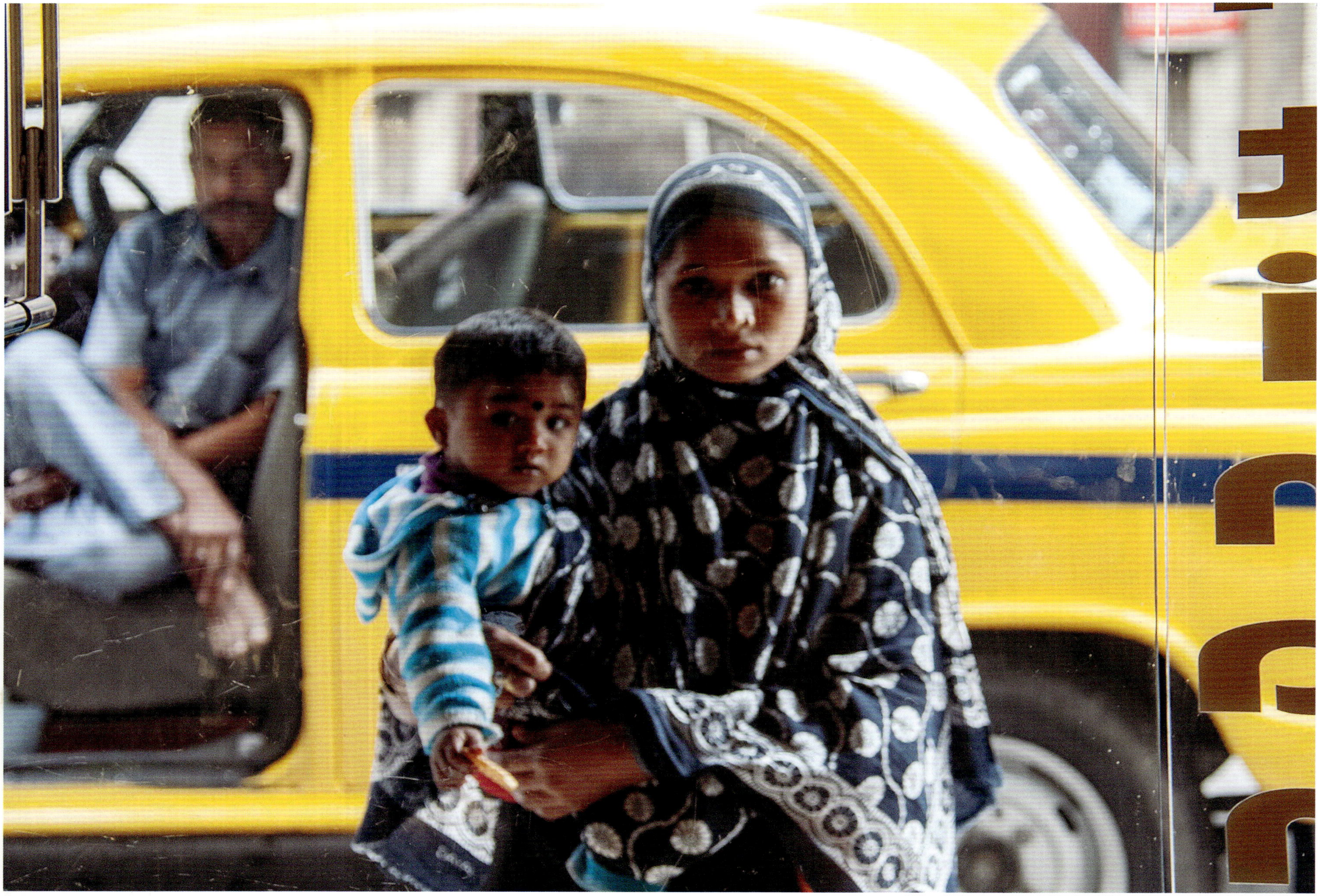

A mother and her son look through the glass window of a hotel. She is a beggar, hoping that the guests in the hotel will give her money.

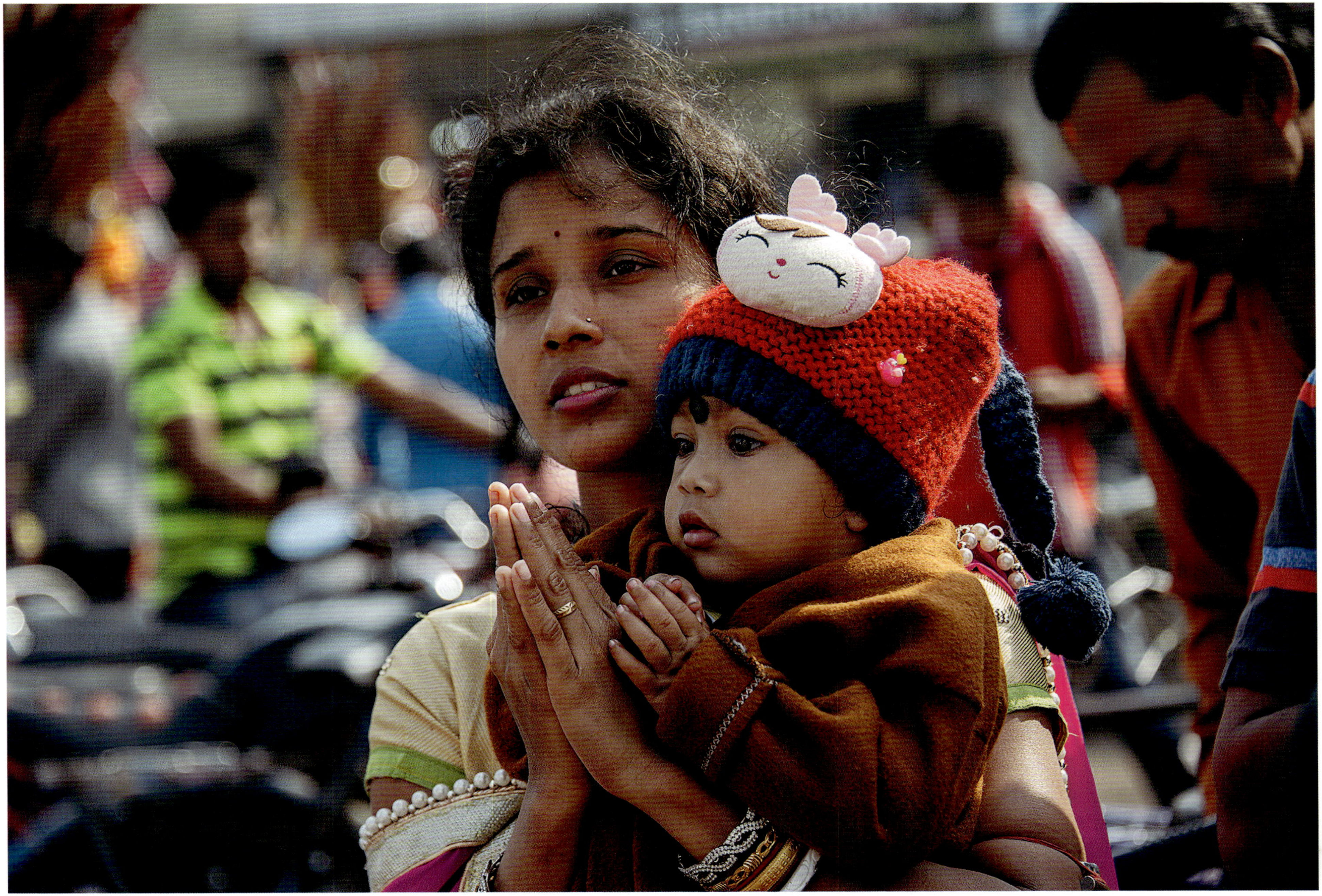

A mother and child worship at the Shree Jagannatha Temple, a Hindu temple dedicated to Mahaprabhu Shree Jagannatha, a form of the deity Vishnu.

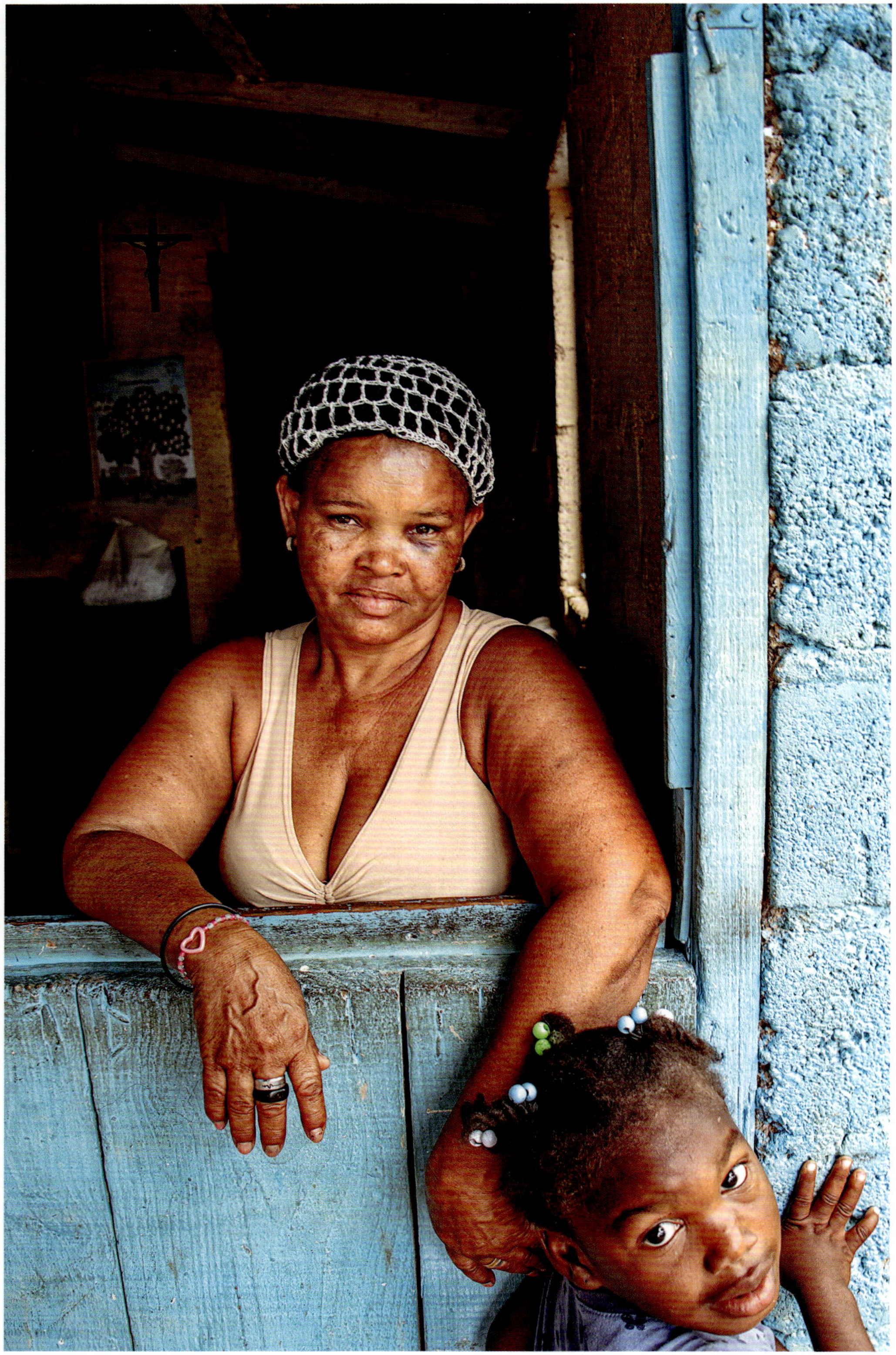

A woman and child in San Pedro de Macorís. The sky-blue paint is common in their barrio—a bright contrast to the poverty they struggle with.

Dominican Republic / San Pedro de Macorís, San Pedro de Macorís Province

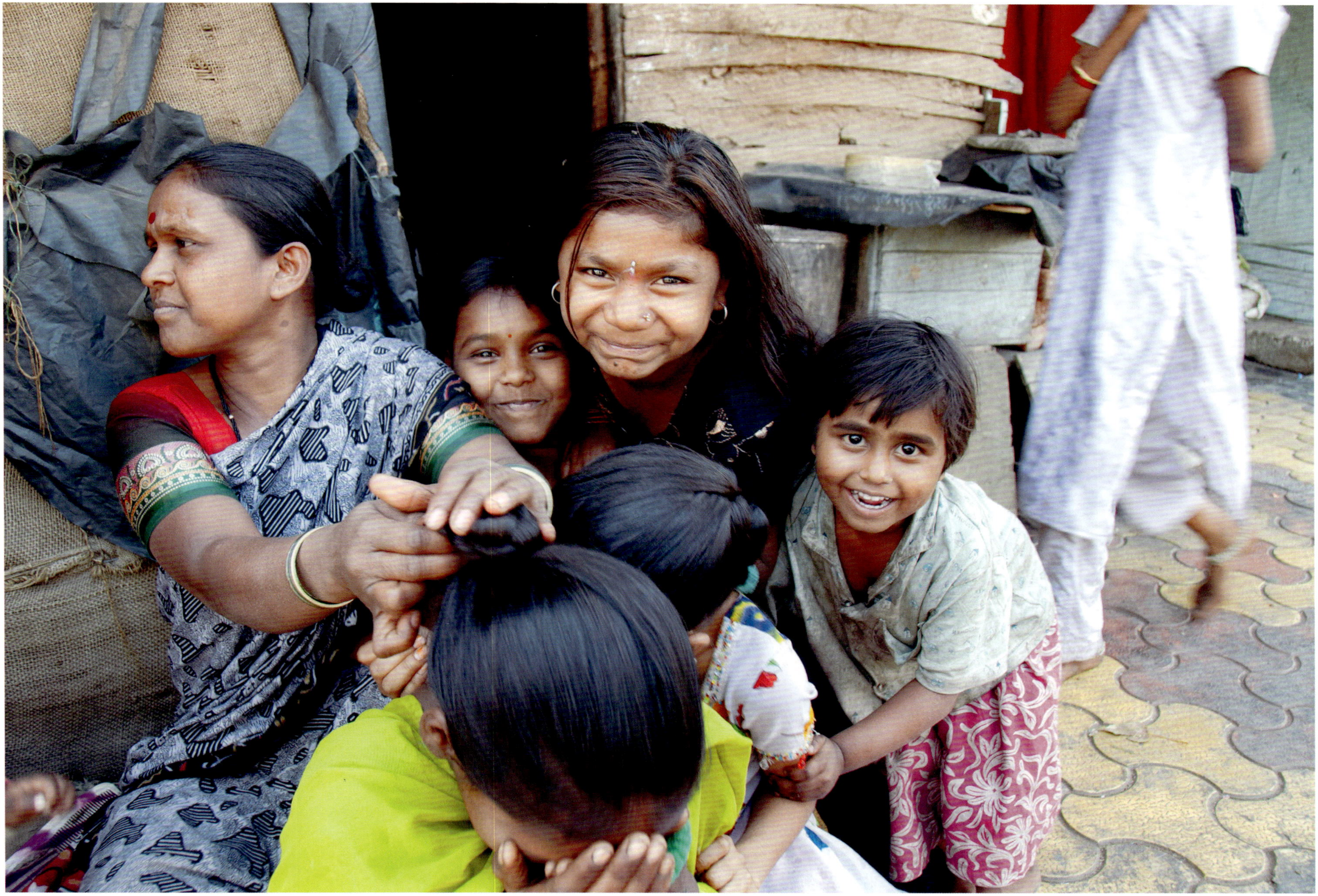

A family in Nashik, one of the four cities that are riverbank pilgrimage sites during the Hindu religious festival Kumbh Mela. During Kumbh Mela, scores of Hindu devotees come to worship on the banks of the Godavari River.

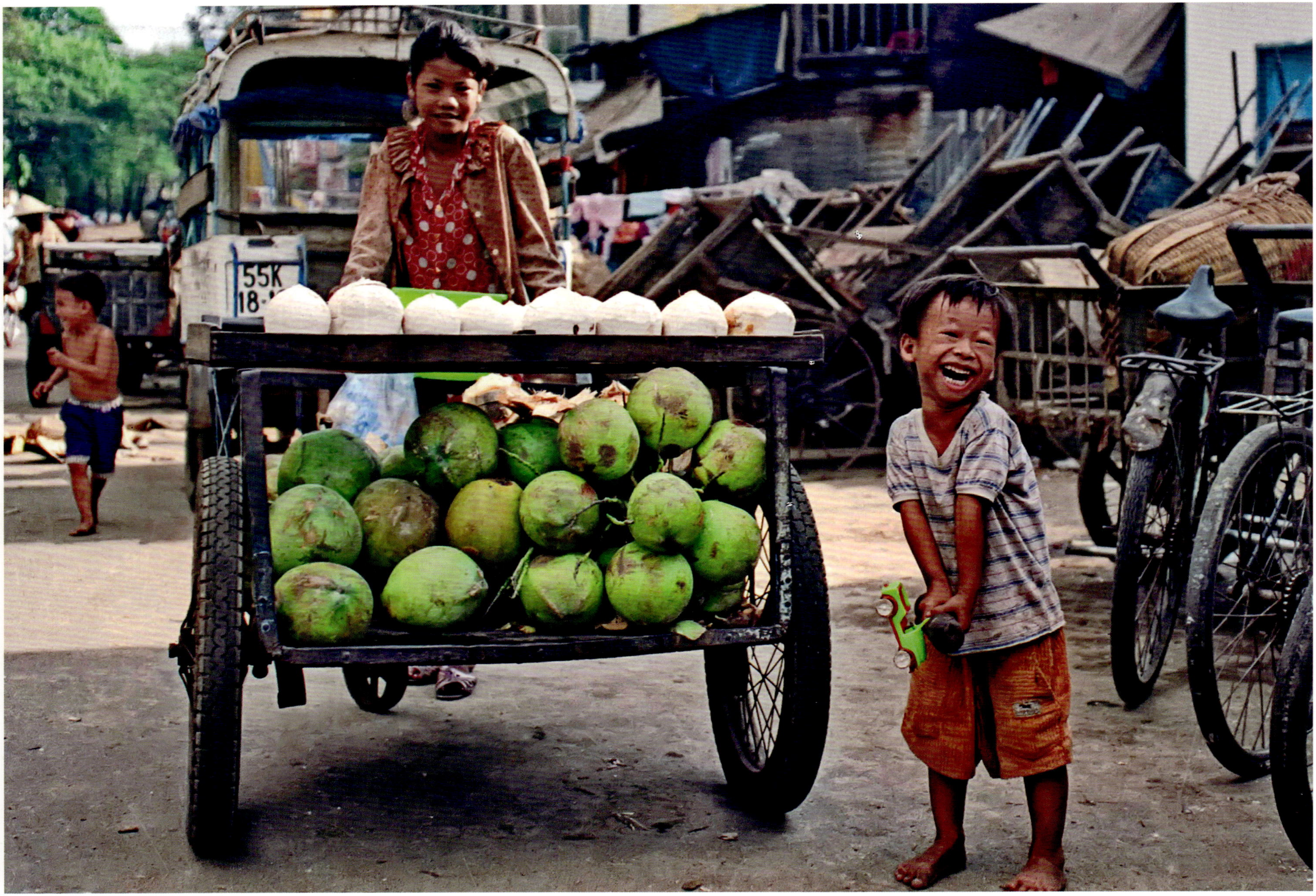

A woman sells coconuts at Ho Chi Minh City's bustling Bến Thành Market, a famous attraction.

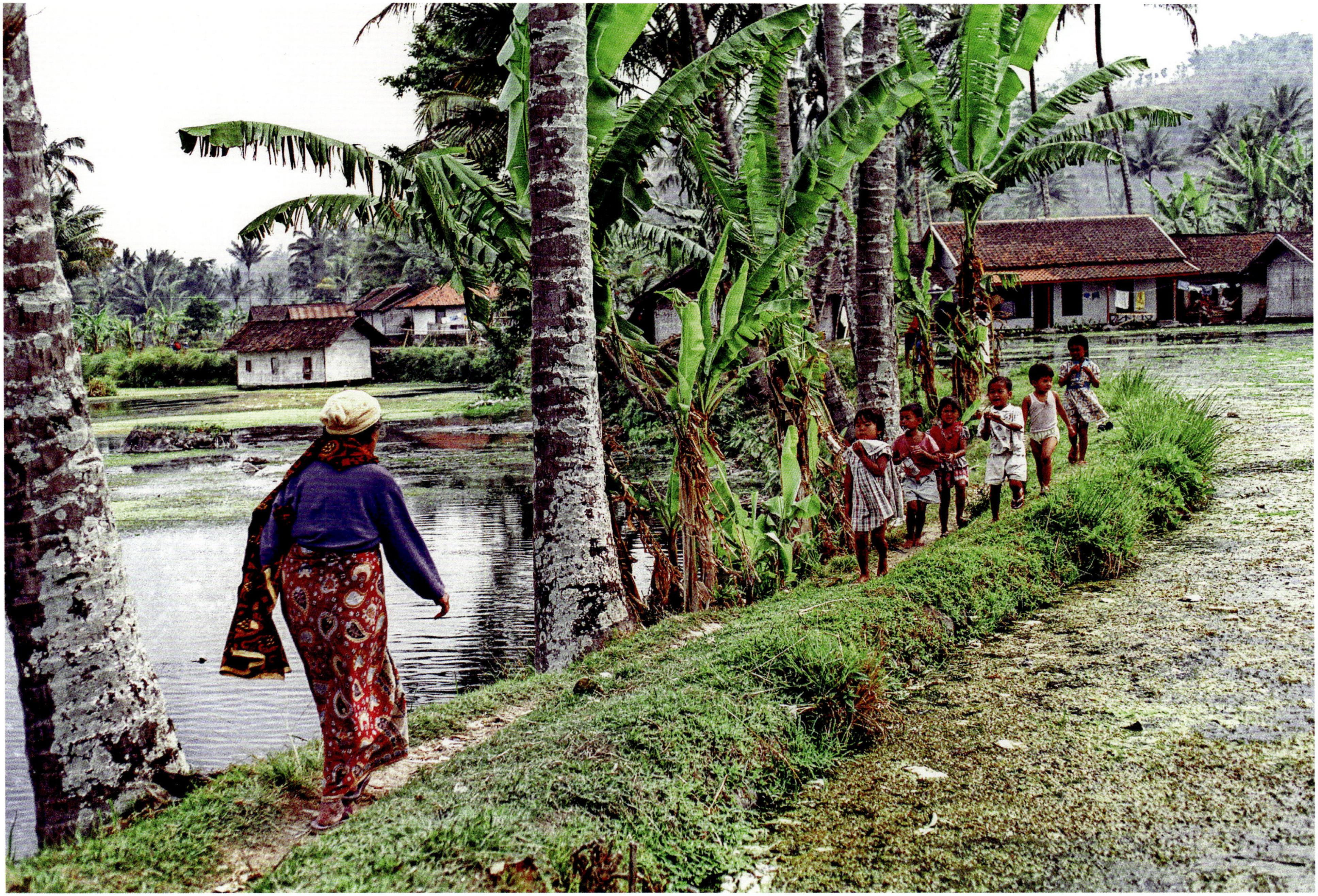

A grandmother arrives home to her family. They live by Garut's famous hot springs.

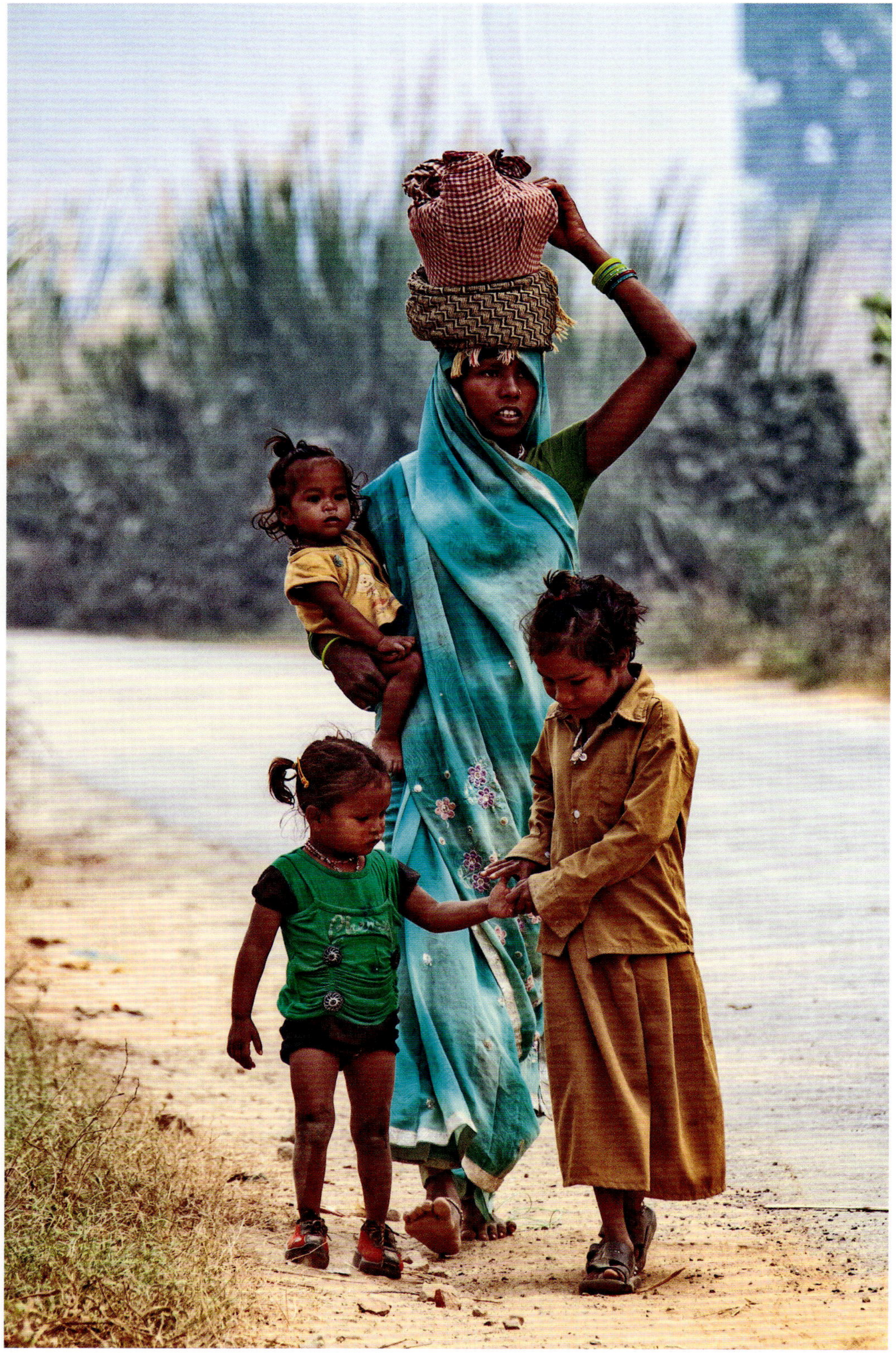

A woman and three children
in Bodh Gaya.

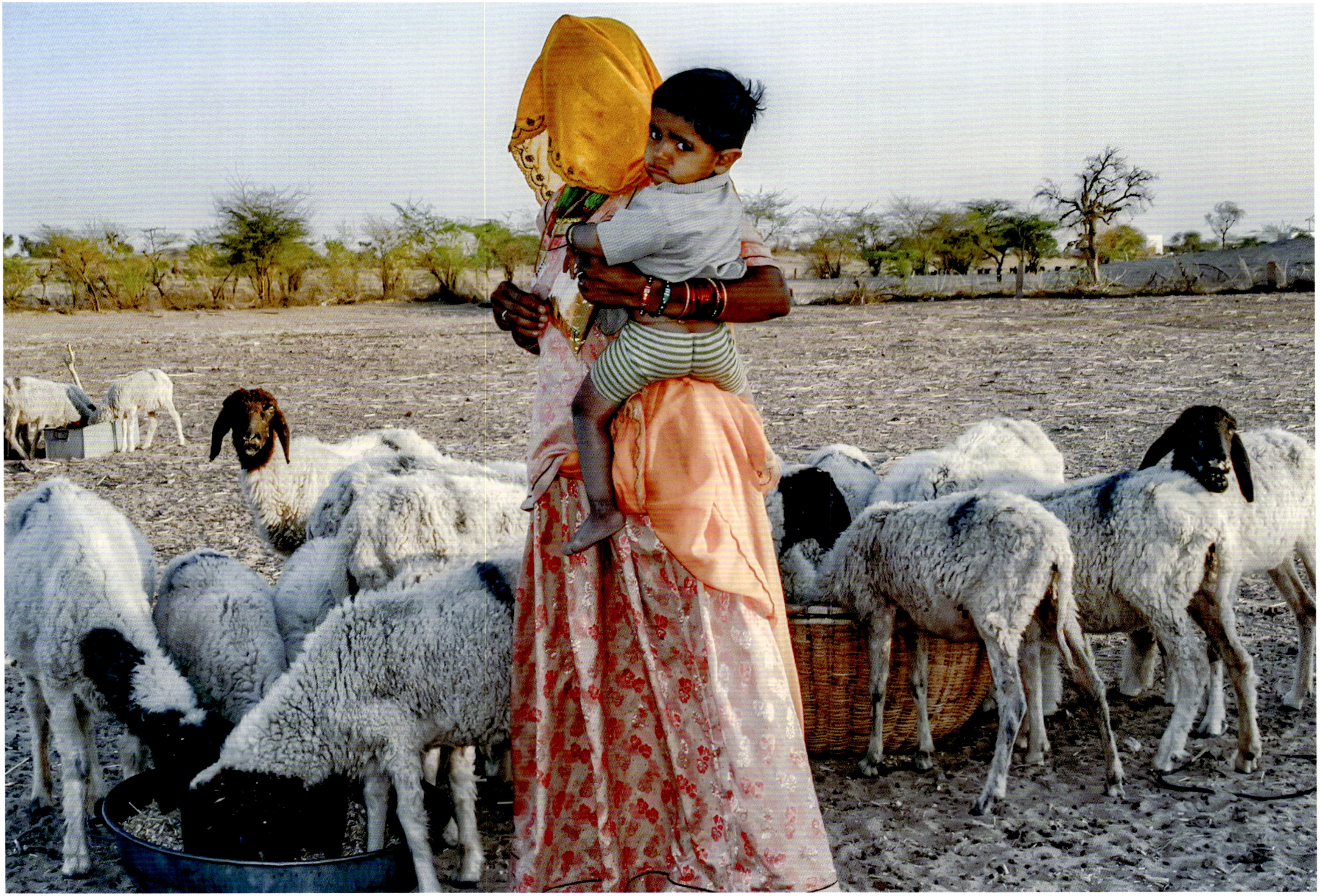

A mother and son and their sheep in the Thar Desert. Many people who live in the desert are herders.

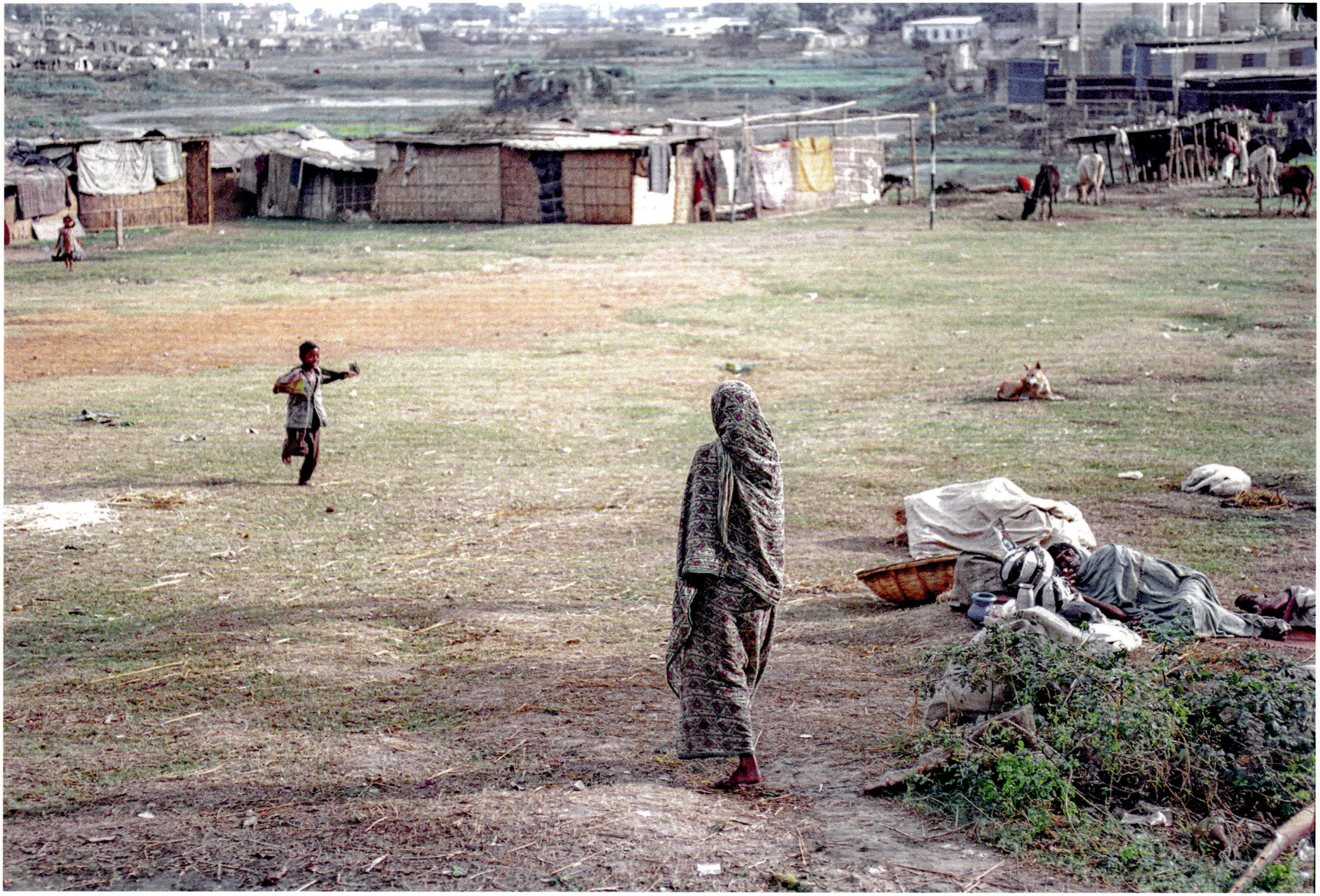

A boy runs across a rural shantytown. There are more than twenty-one million people in the urban area surrounding Dhaka, making it one of the most densely populated urban areas in the world. Shantytowns and slums are scattered throughout.

A woman and her child in front of what was once a huge, busy sugar refinery and sugar mill. Sugarcane is grown in the Dominican Republic and exported all over the world. Domino Sugar gets its name from the island nation.

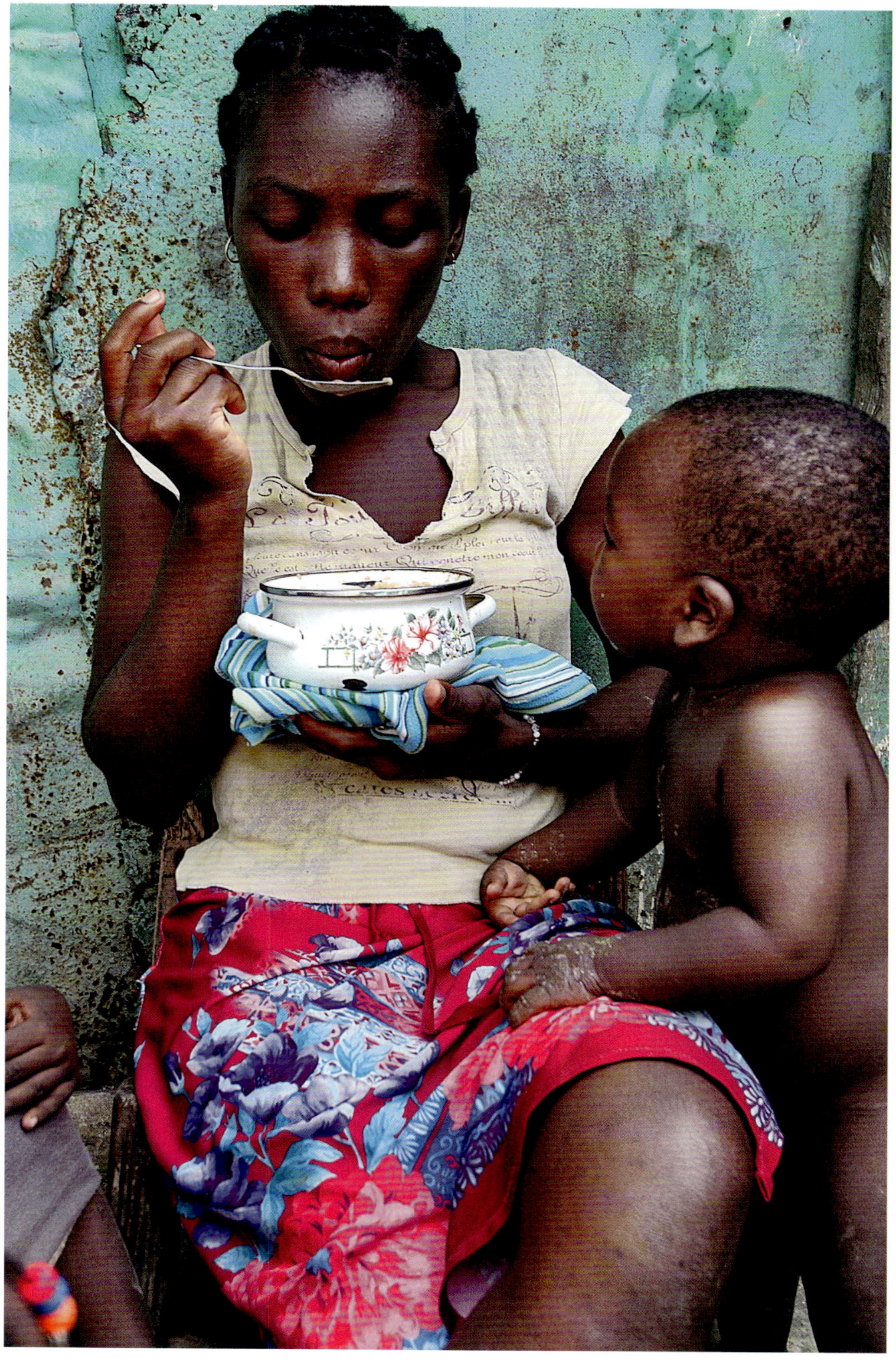

Dominican Republic /
Porvenir, San Pedro de Macorís Province

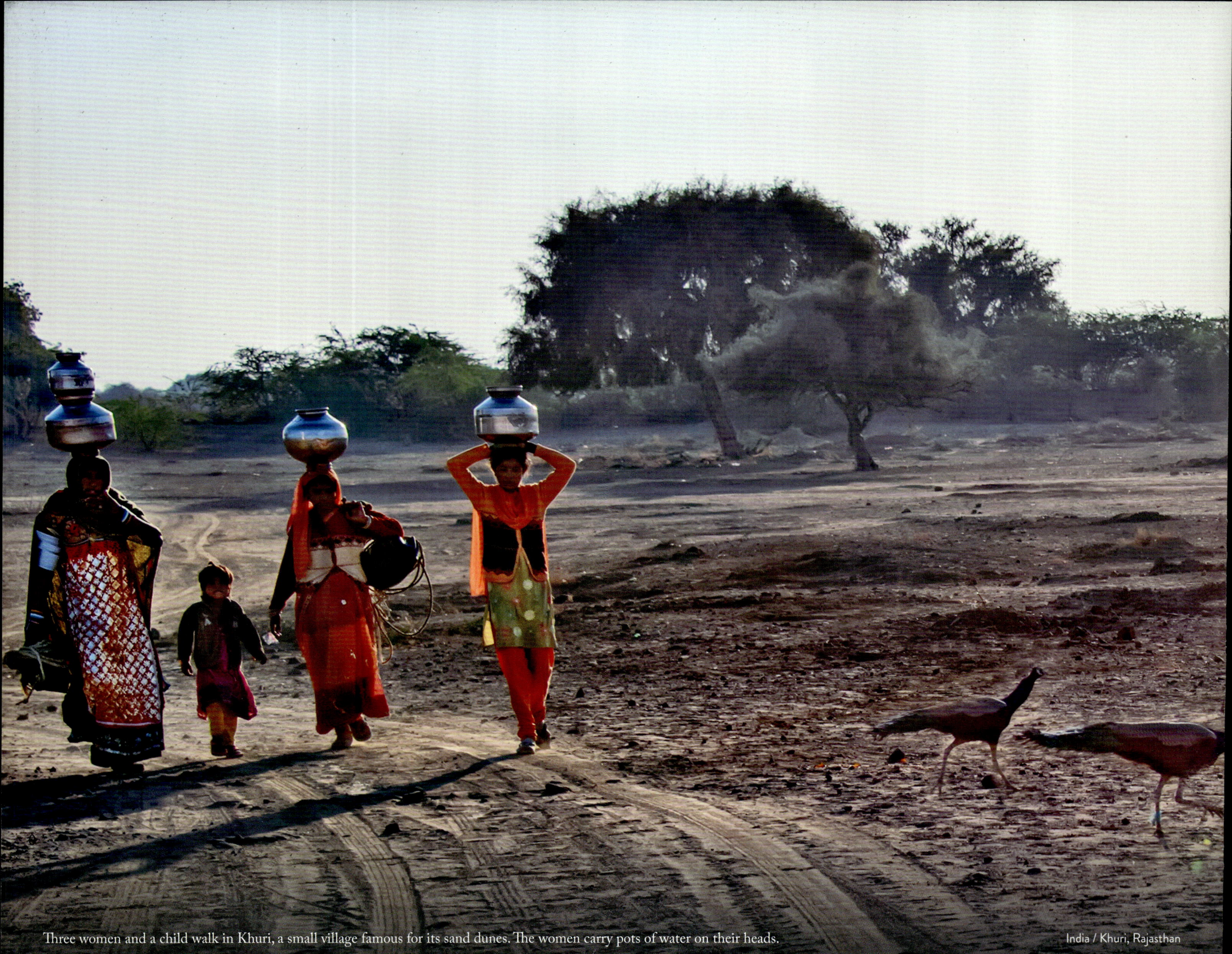

Three women and a child walk in Khuri, a small village famous for its sand dunes. The women carry pots of water on their heads.

India / Khuri, Rajasthan

JOURNEY

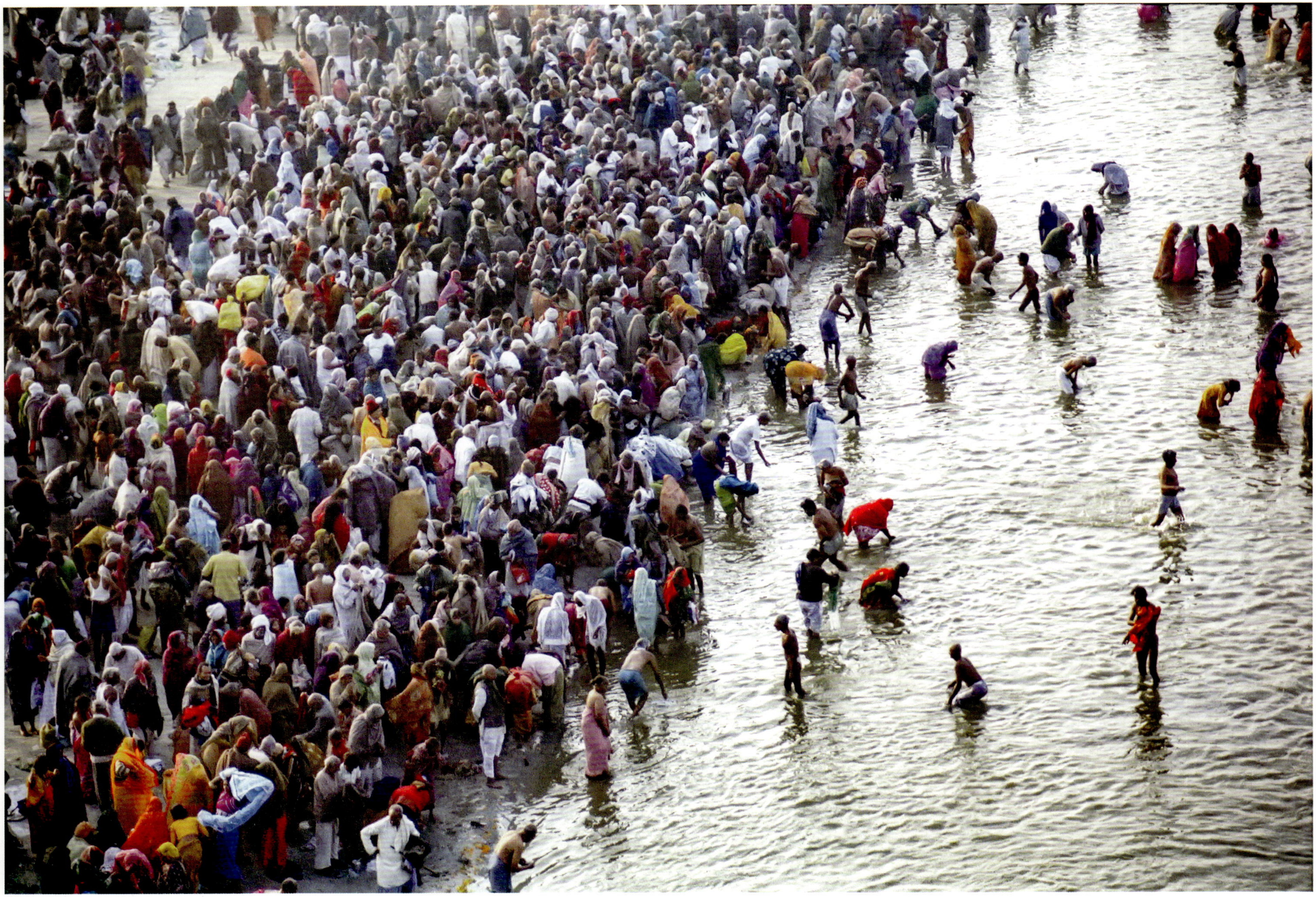

A bird's-eye view of the attendees of Prayag Kumbh Mela, the part of Kumbh Mela (a major Hindu pilgrimage) held at Prayag Triveni Sangam: the meeting points of the Ganga, Yamuna, and mythical Sarasvati rivers.

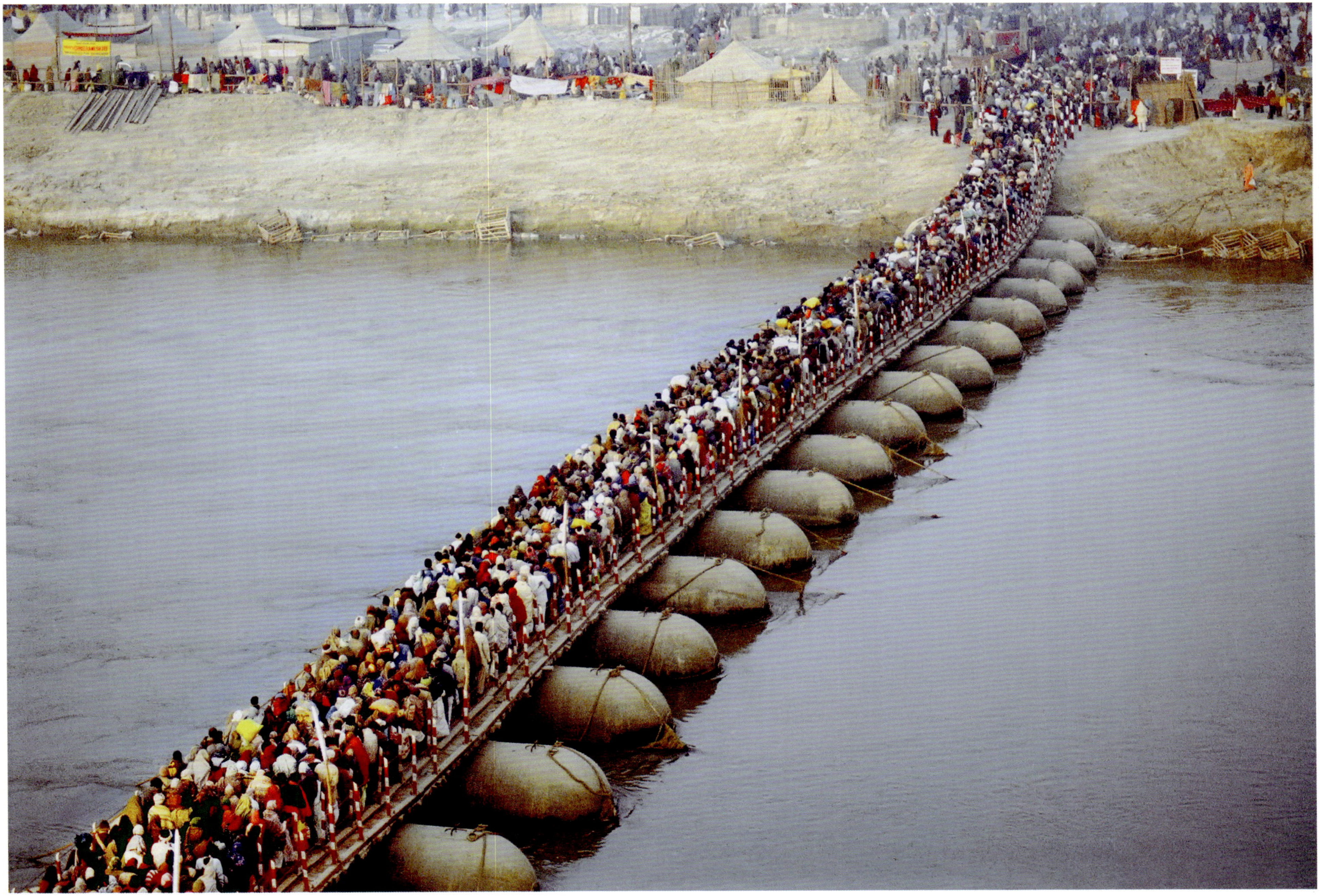

Pontoons support a bridge traversed during Ardh Kumbh Mela (half Kumbh Mela).
In 2019, Ardh Kumbh Mela brought 120 to 150 million attendees to Allahabad, one of the four riverbank pilgrimage sites.

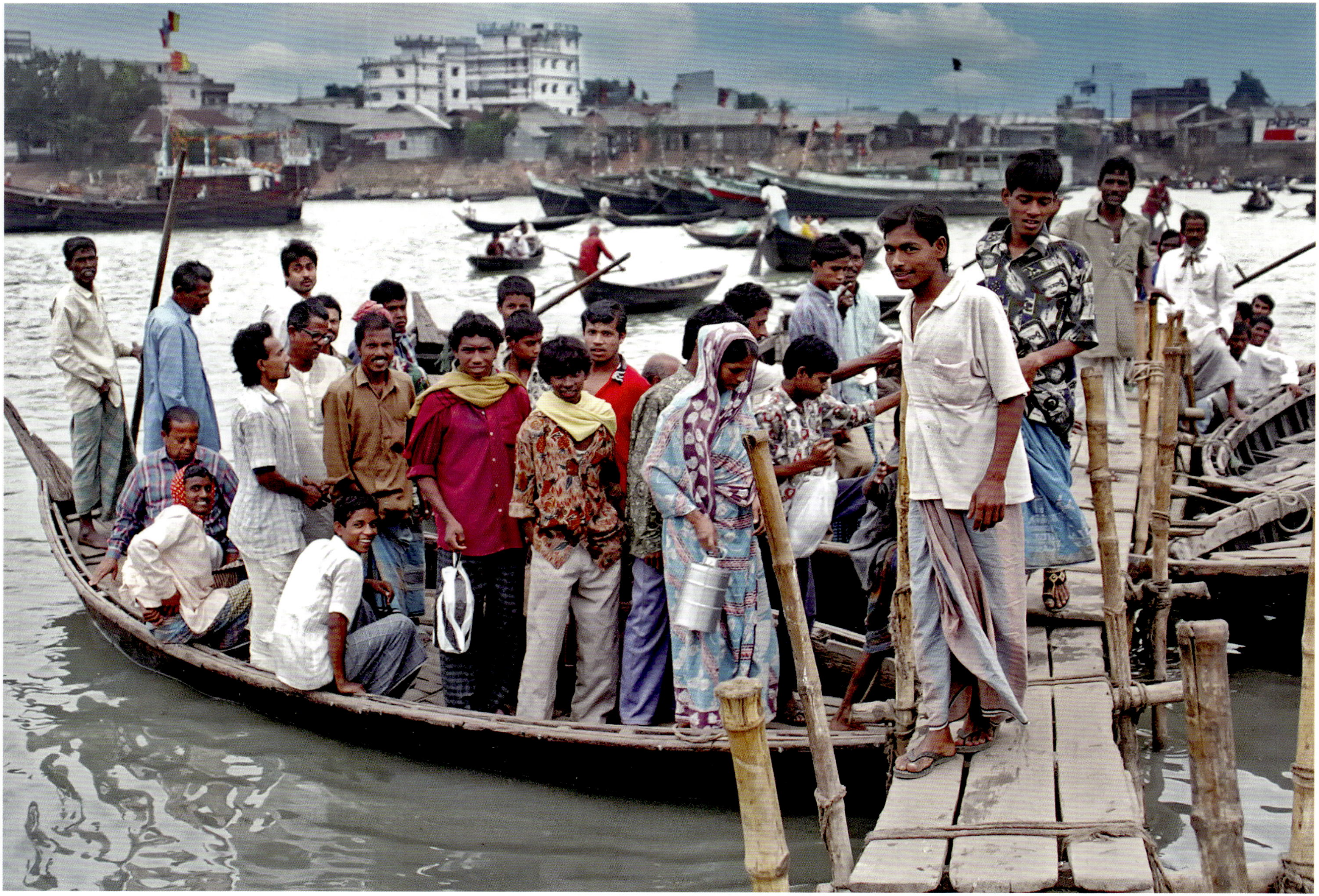

Few bridges cross the Buriganga River, so the twenty-five thousand people who commute daily between the commercial area on one side and the residential area on the other side often rely on a sampan—a type of small wooden boat—to cross.

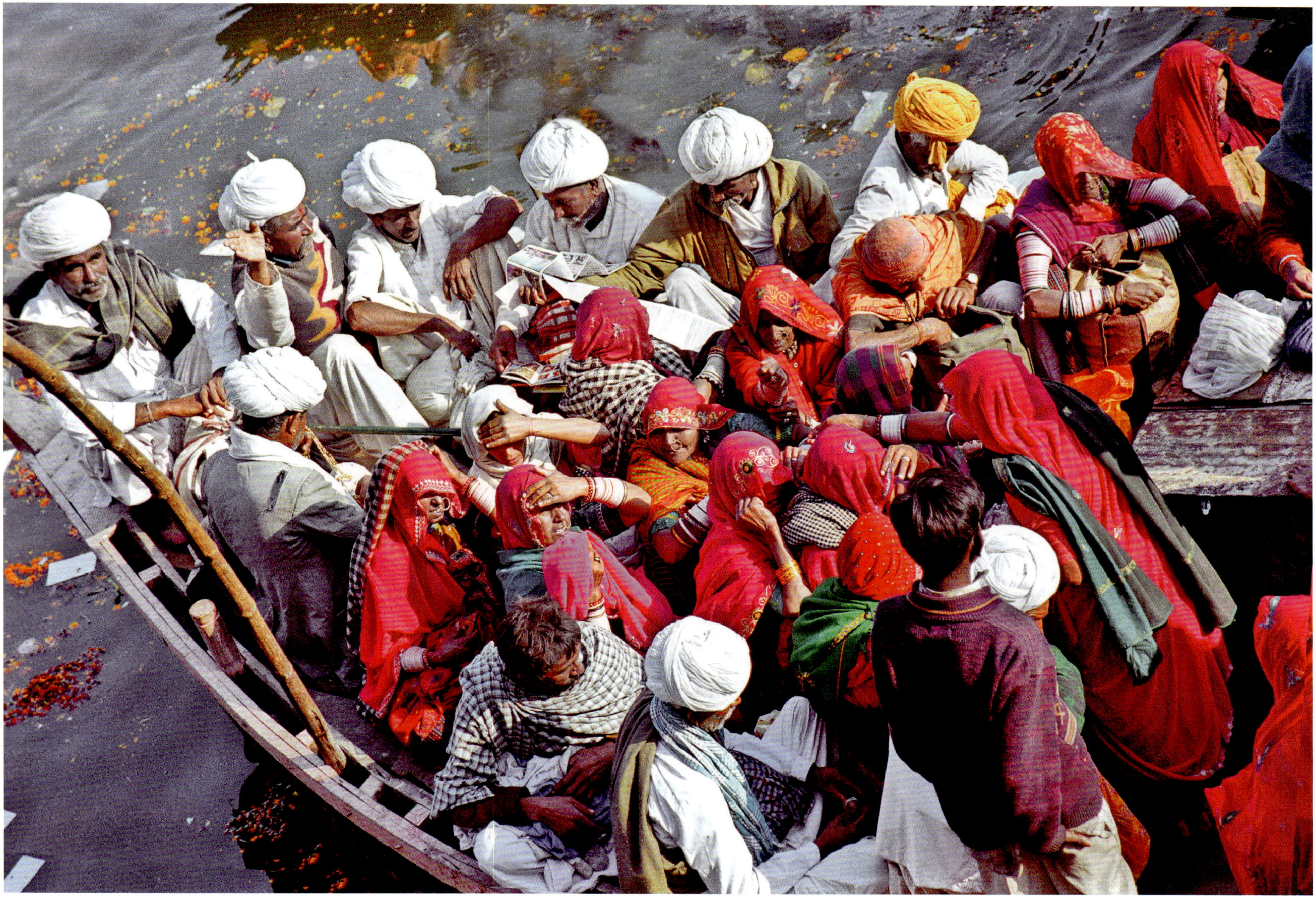

Millions of pilgrims visit Varanasi annually, and taking a boat ride on the holy Ganges River is a very spiritual event for a Hindu.

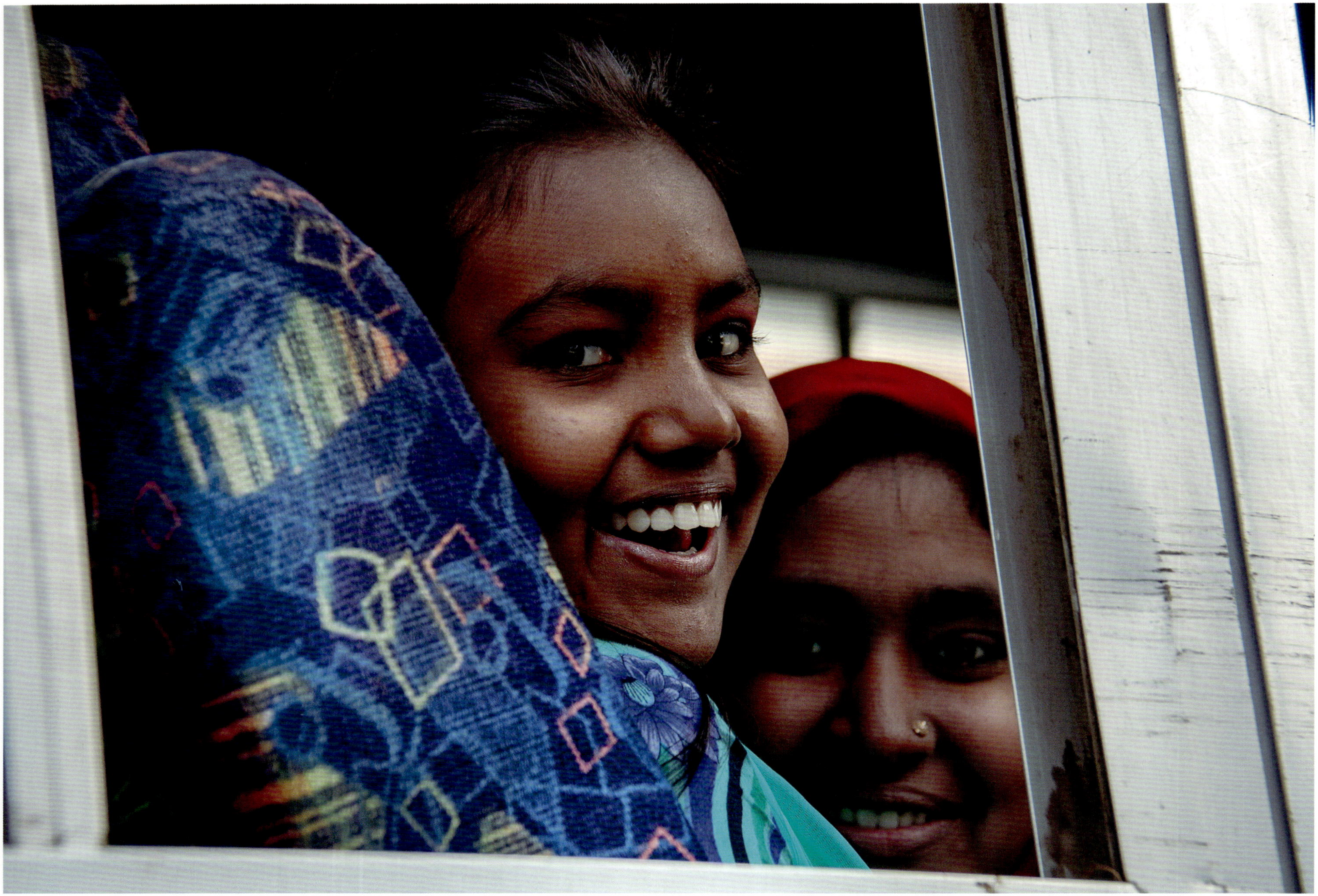

Women traveling by bus in Dhaka. The woman on the right has a nose piercing, which is common in Southeast Asia. They have been worn since classical times.

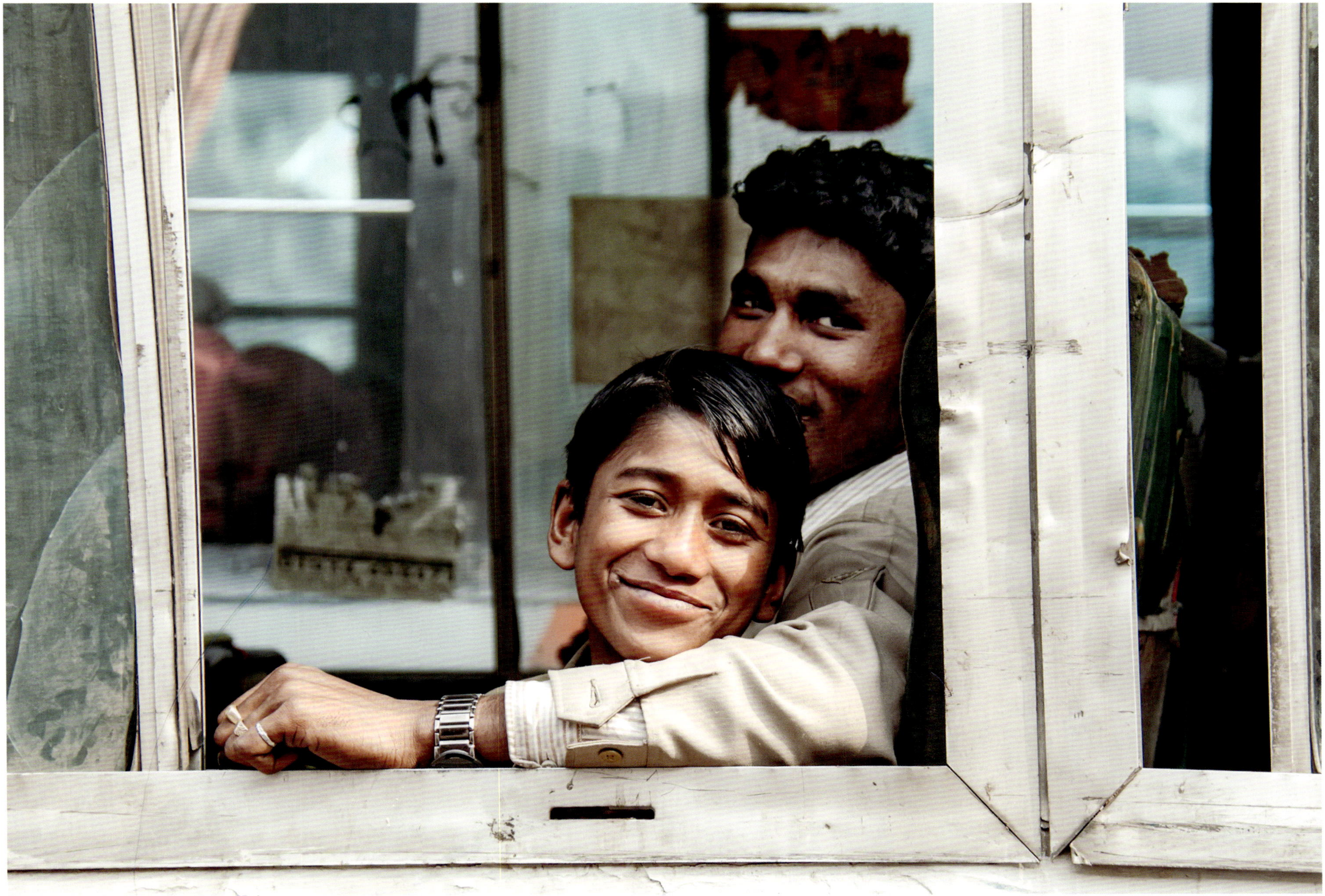

Passengers on a bus in Dhaka smile at the camera.

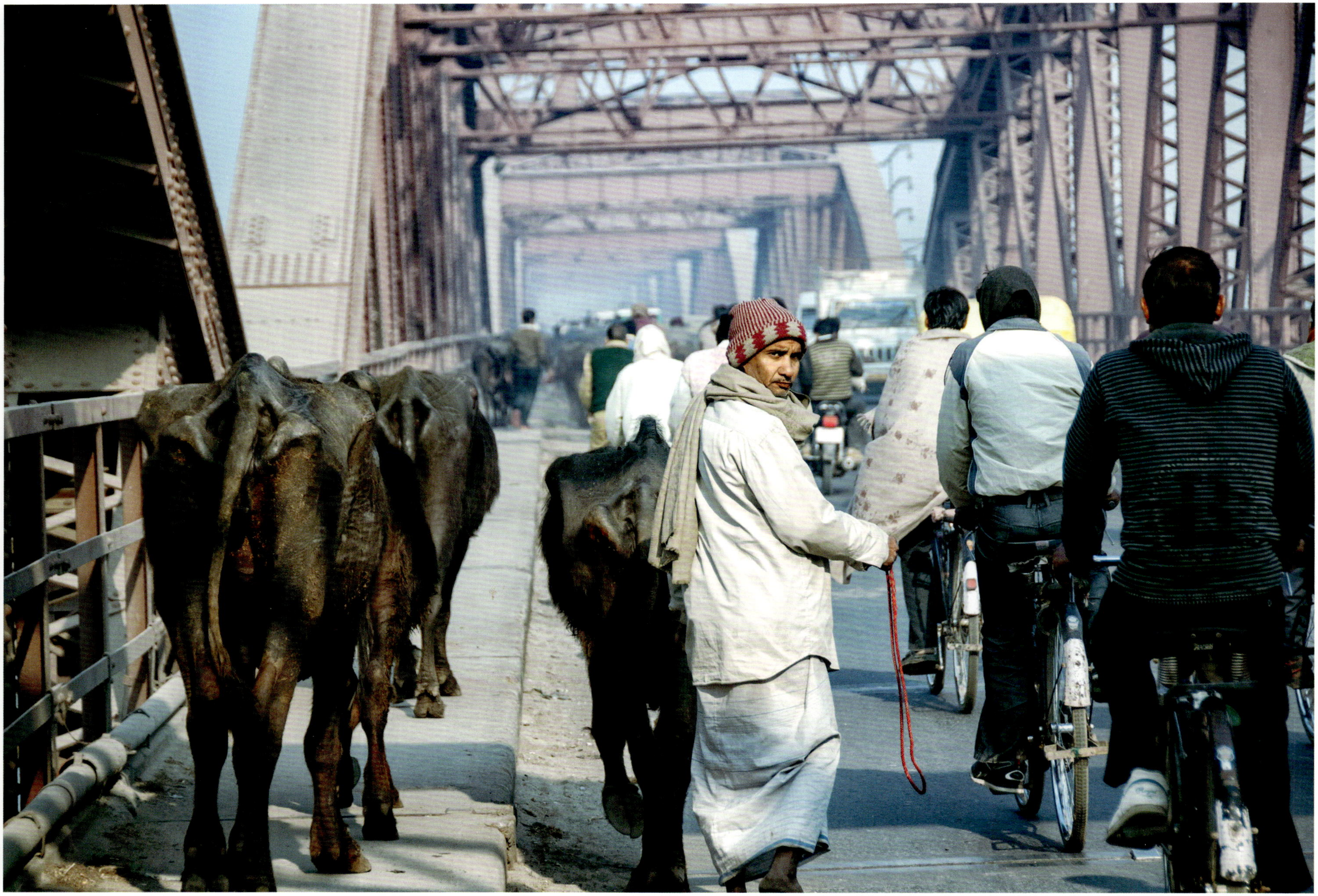

People cross the Ganges by way of the Malviya Bridge, which is often called the Raj Ghat Bridge because of its proximity to Raj Ghat.

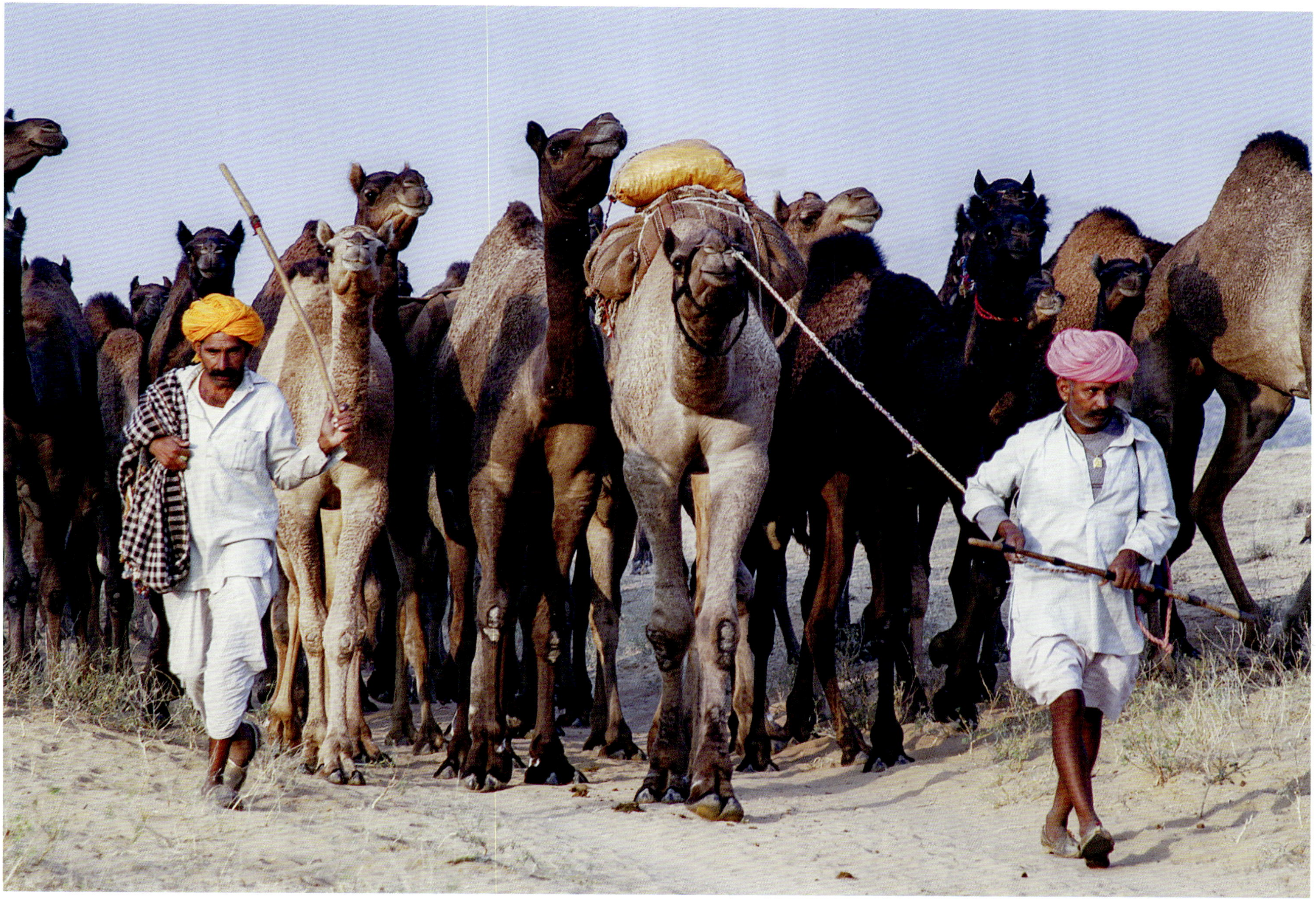

Men trek to Pushkar, a quaint town bordering the Thar Desert, to sell camels at a camel fair. The fair hosts wealthy Rajasthanis and some thirty thousand camels each year.

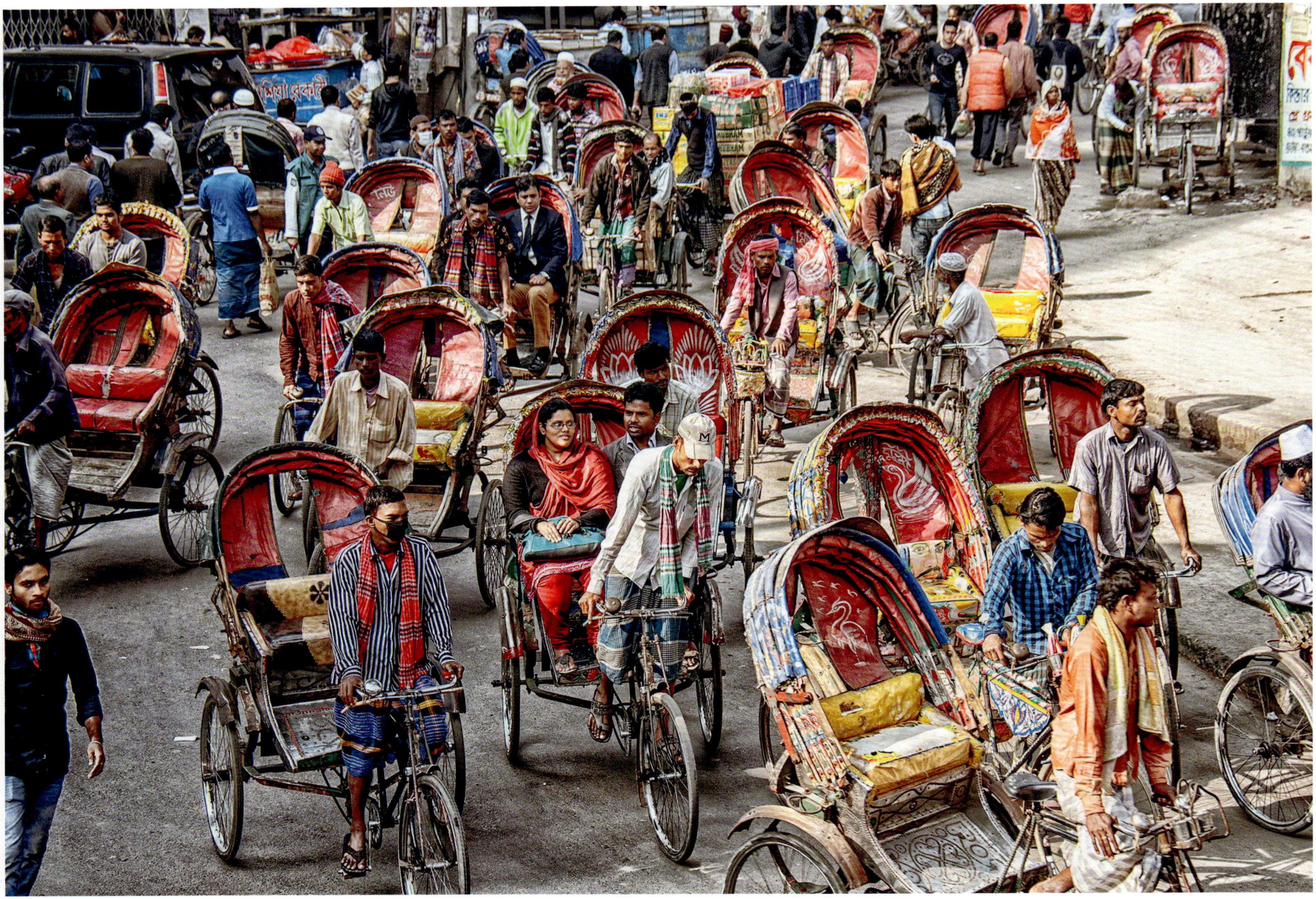

With nearly one million rickshaws in densely populated Dhaka, traffic can cause hours-long jams. Some officials have called for a rickshaw ban, which would put millions of drivers out of work.

People sit on the roof of a train as they travel to the Bishwa Ijtema gathering.

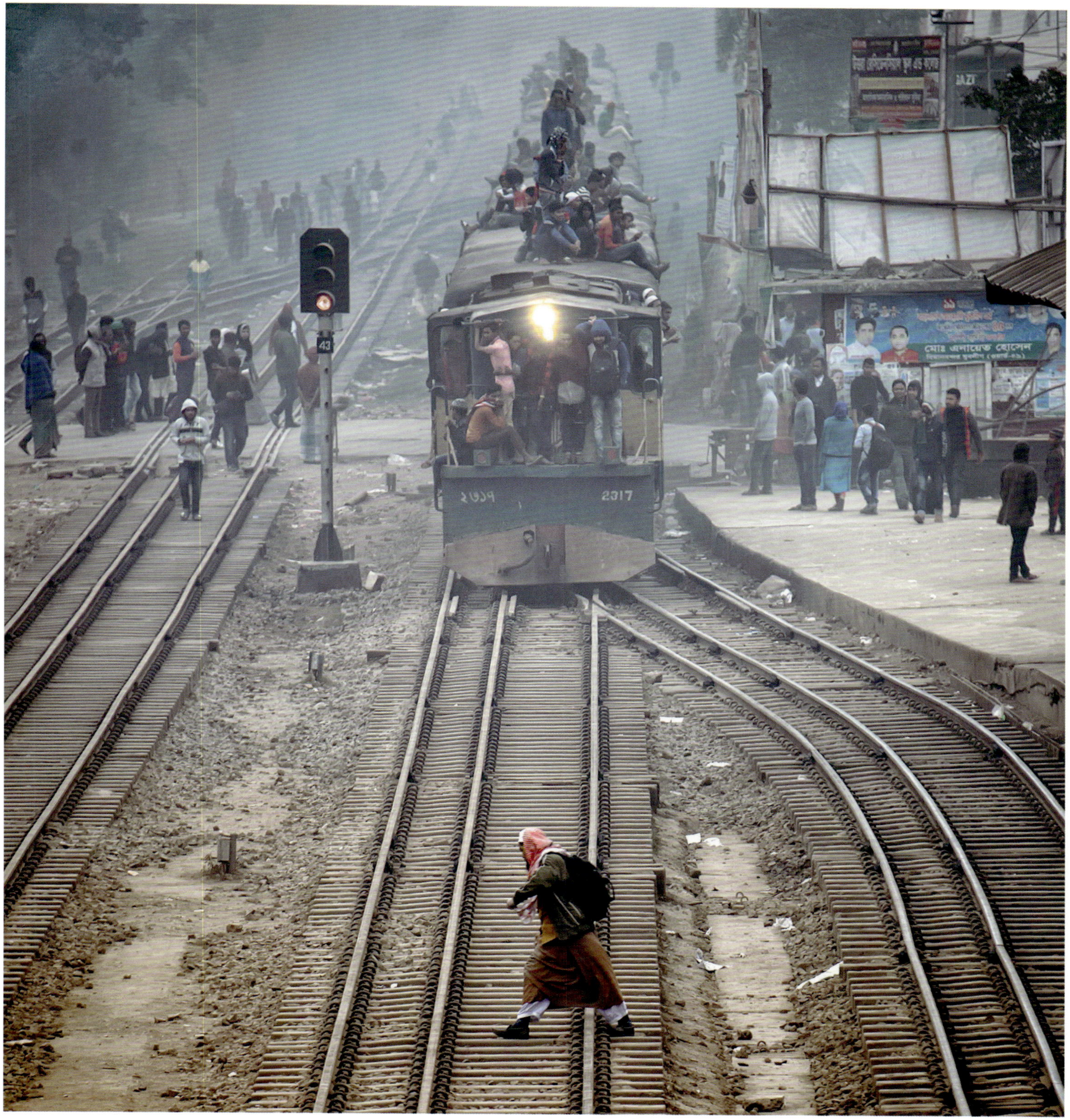

Bangladesh / Dhaka, Dhaka District

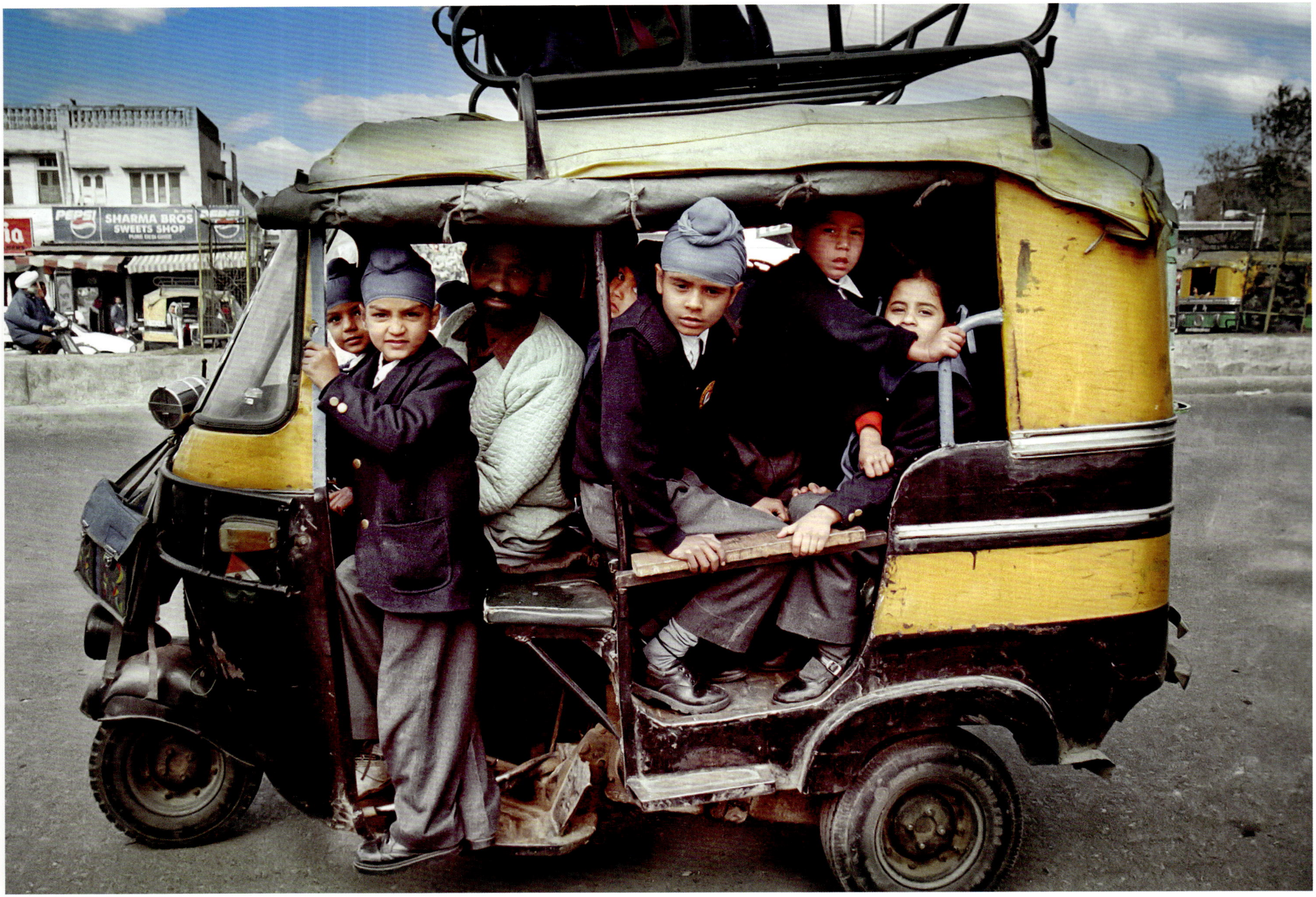

Schoolchildren and a driver fill a tuk-tuk.

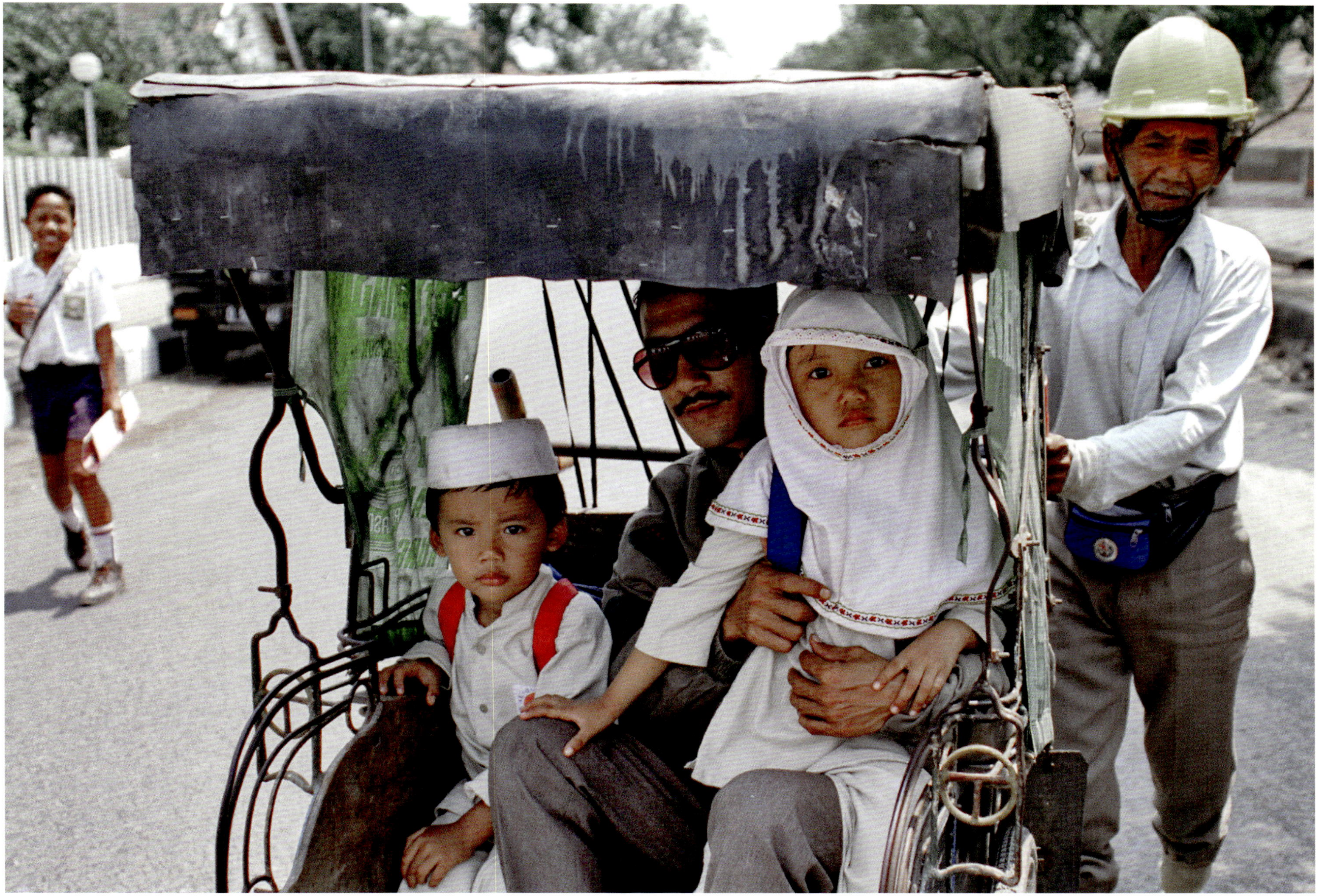

A father and his children in a pedicab in George Town, the capital of Penang. George Town was once a key trading hub. Today it is a UNESCO World Heritage site that is home to both historic and modern buildings. Pedicabs transport both locals and tourists.

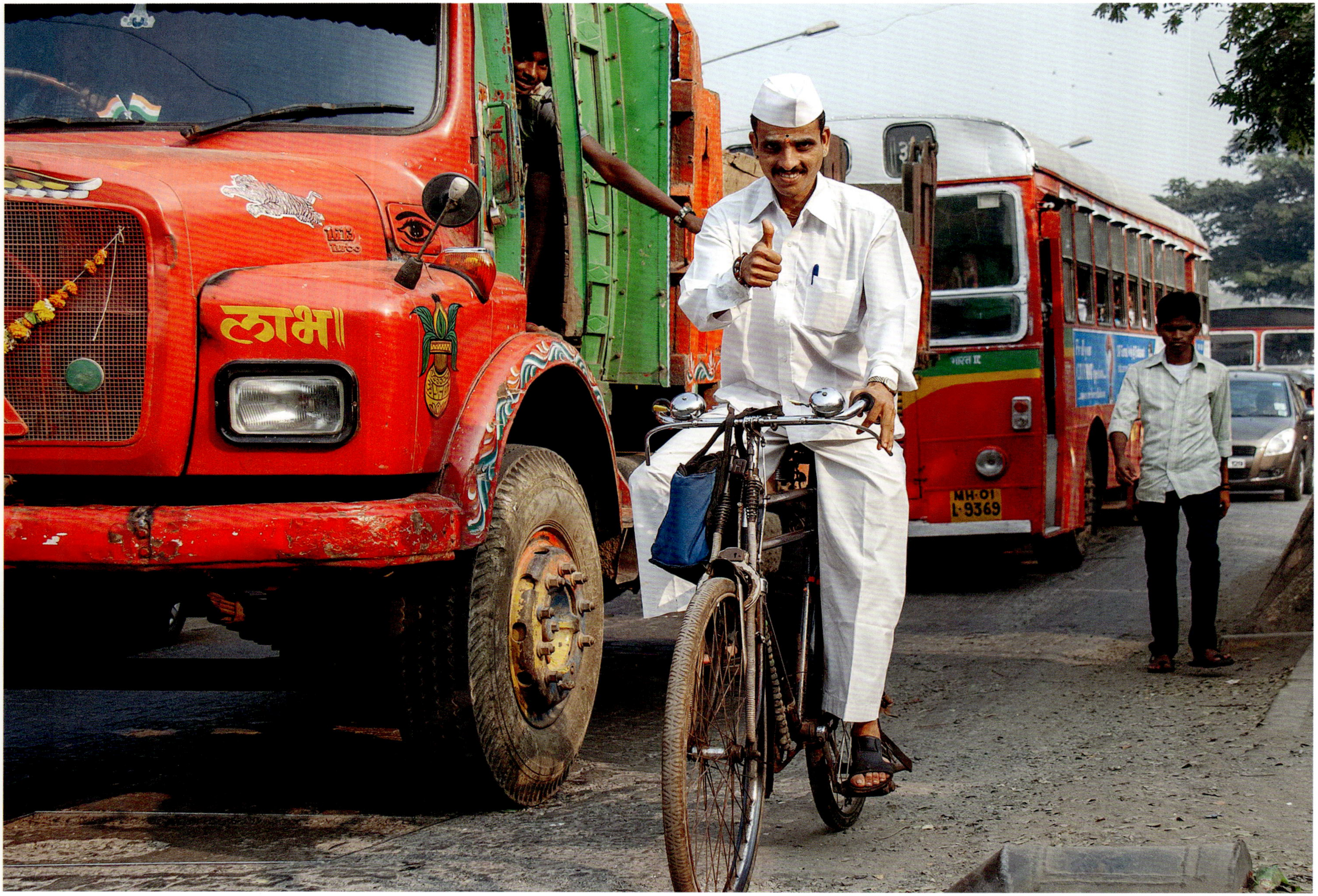

For many residents of Mumbai, such as this man, bikes are a common way of getting around the city.

A family heads toward the Old Yamuna Bridge. In the back of the wagon are four more children with their mother. The wood will probably be used for cooking or heating.

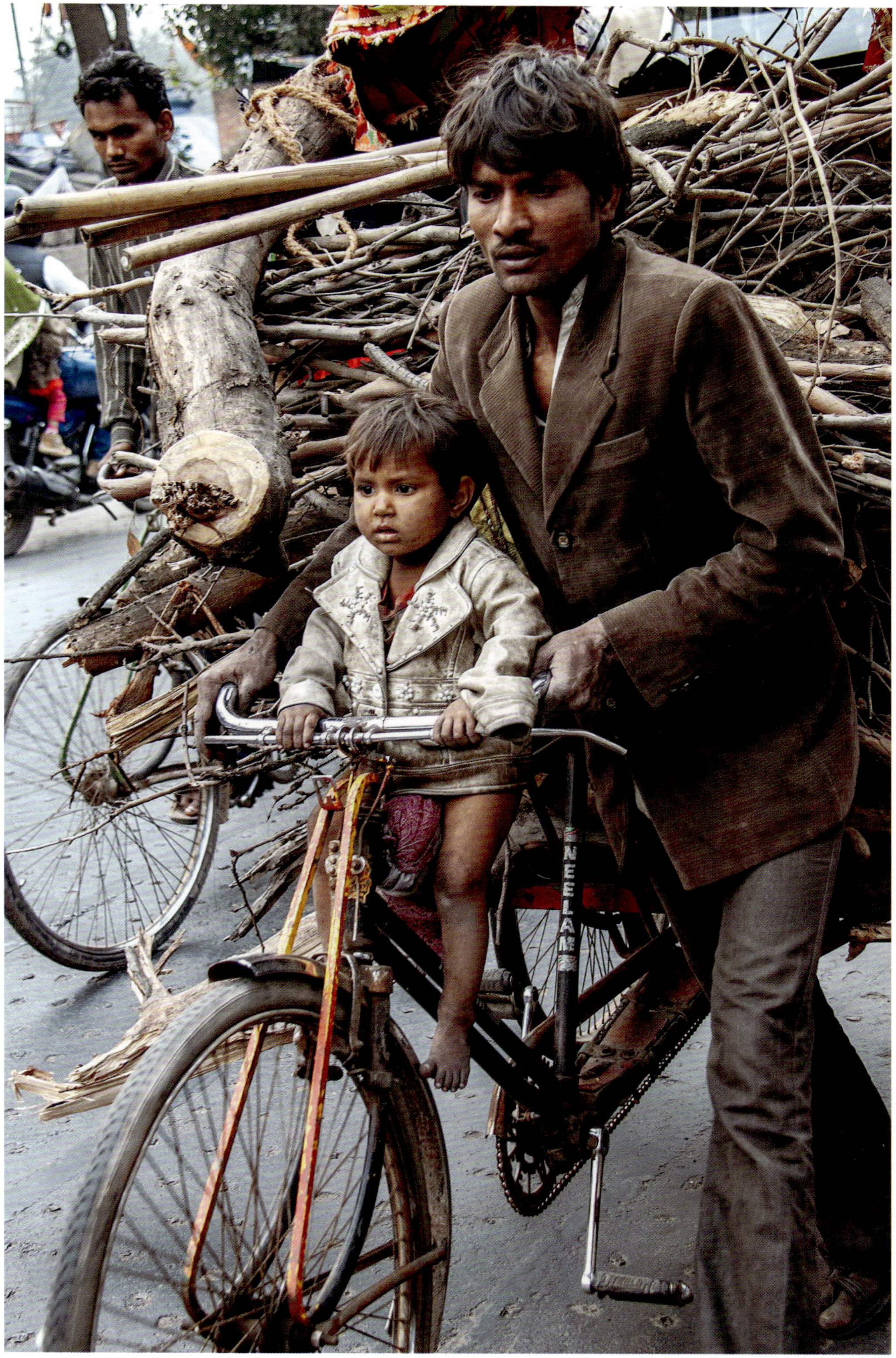

India / New Delhi, Delhi

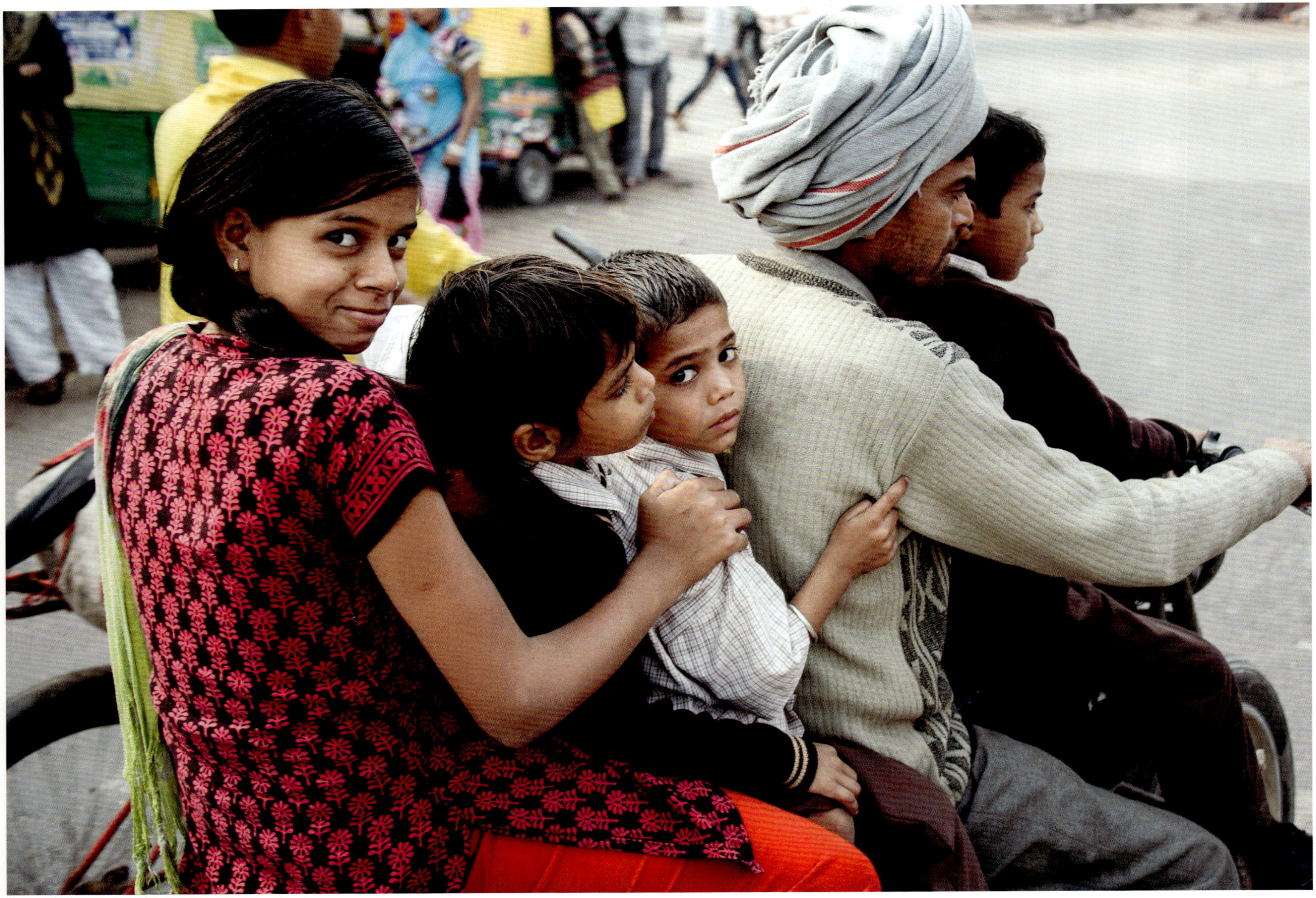

A family squeezes onto a vehicle.

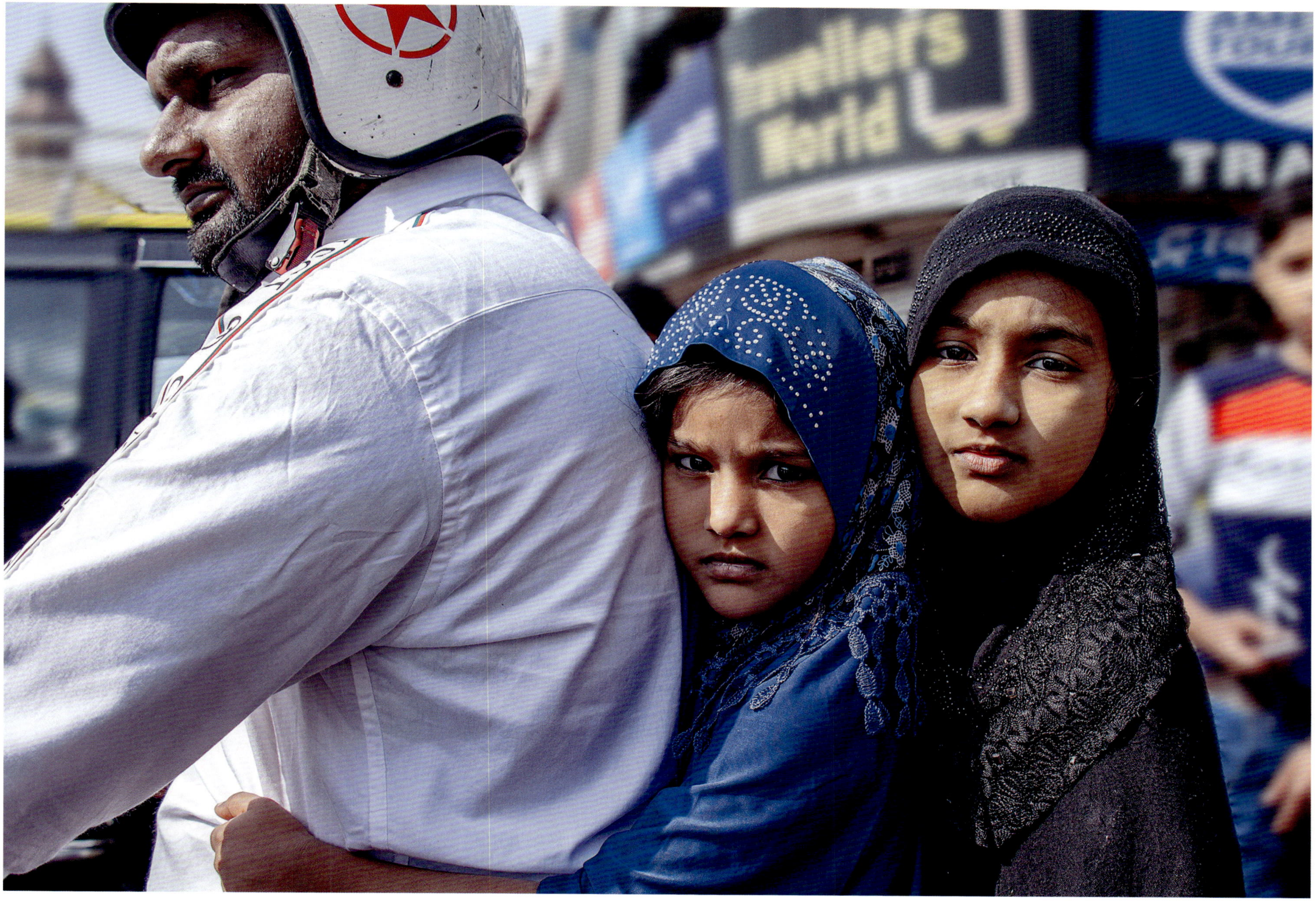

Passengers in transit. Some bikes can carry up to five people.

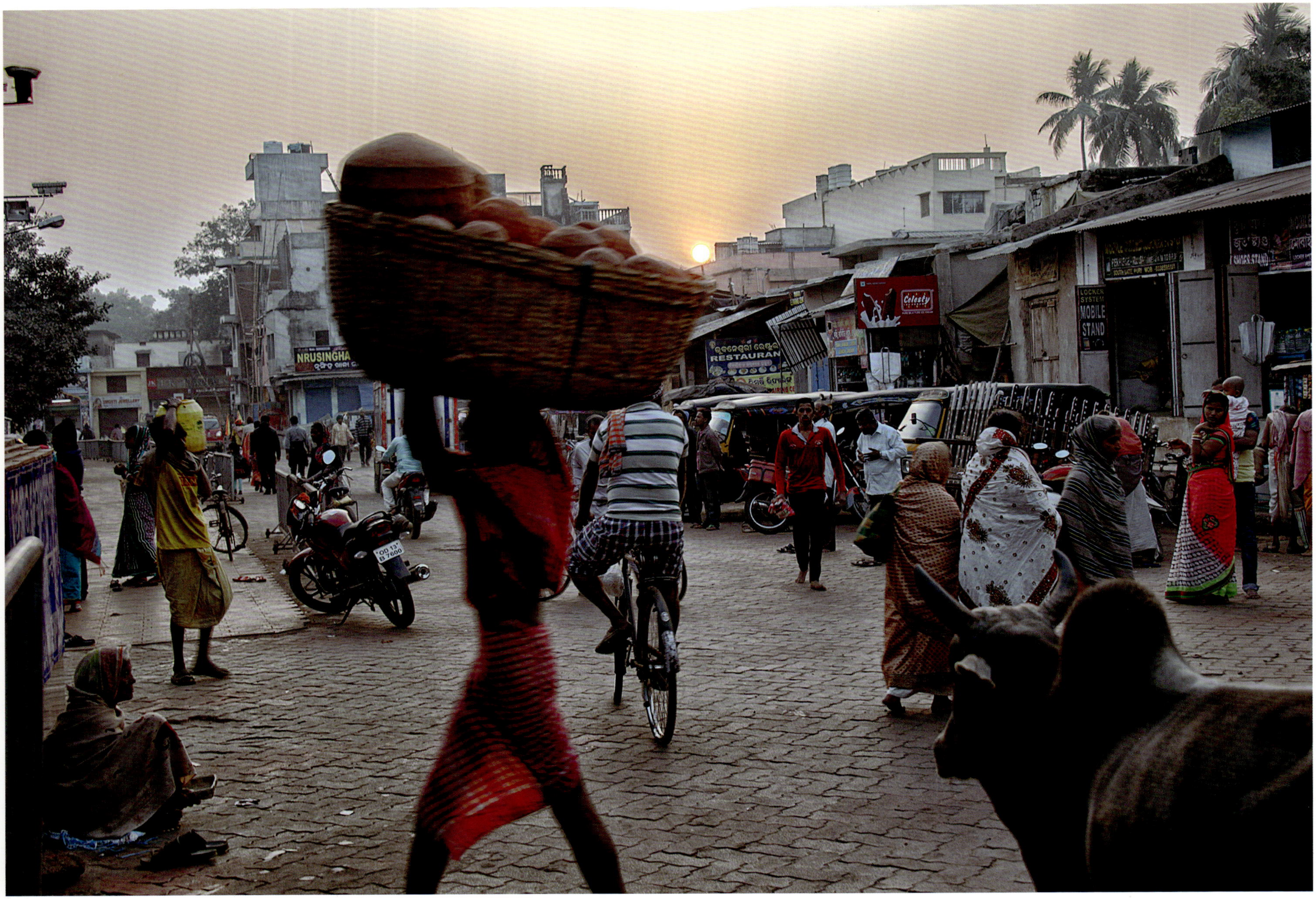

Sunrise brings action to the streets of Puri, home to the Shree Jagannatha Temple.

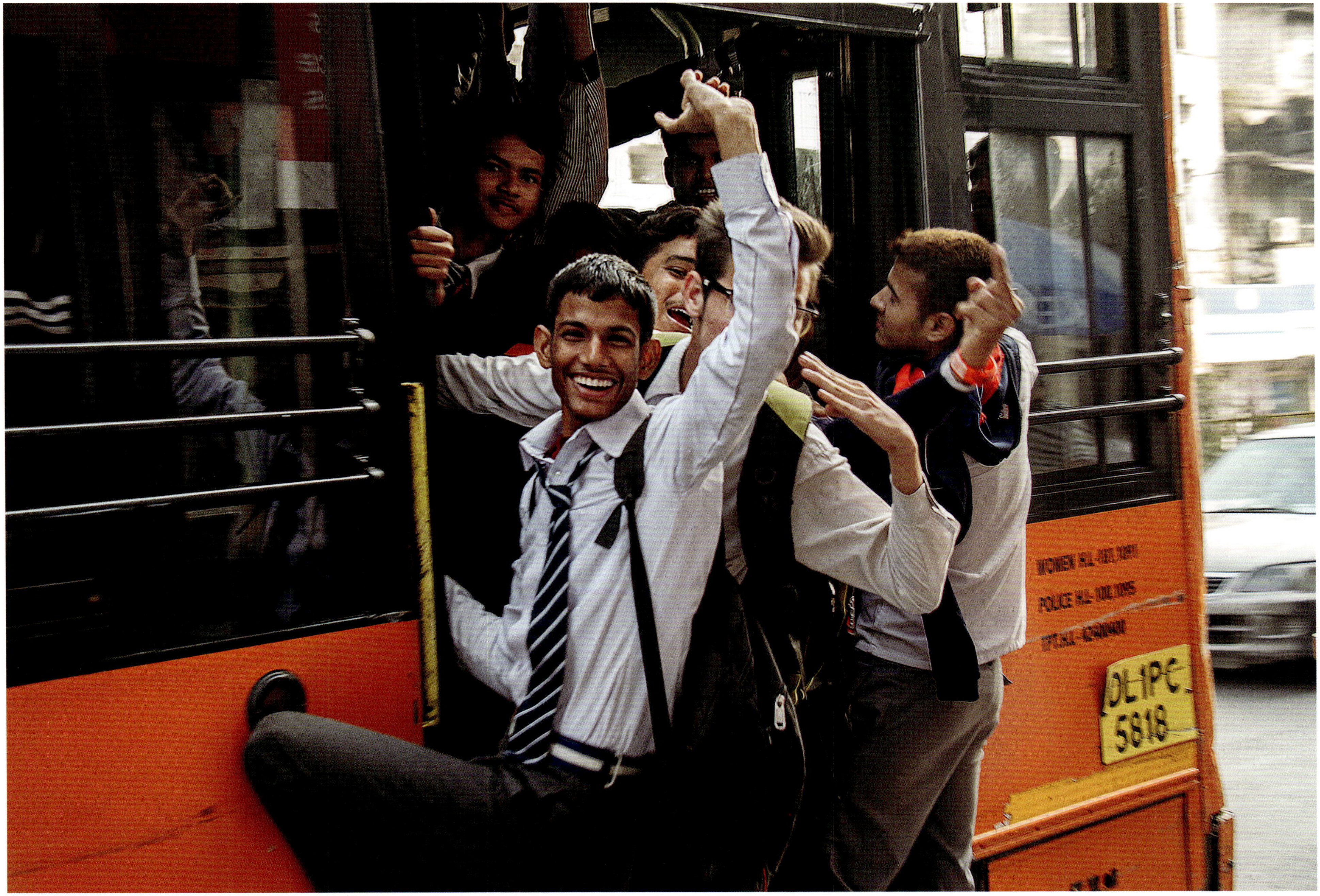

Teenagers cram into a bus in New Delhi.

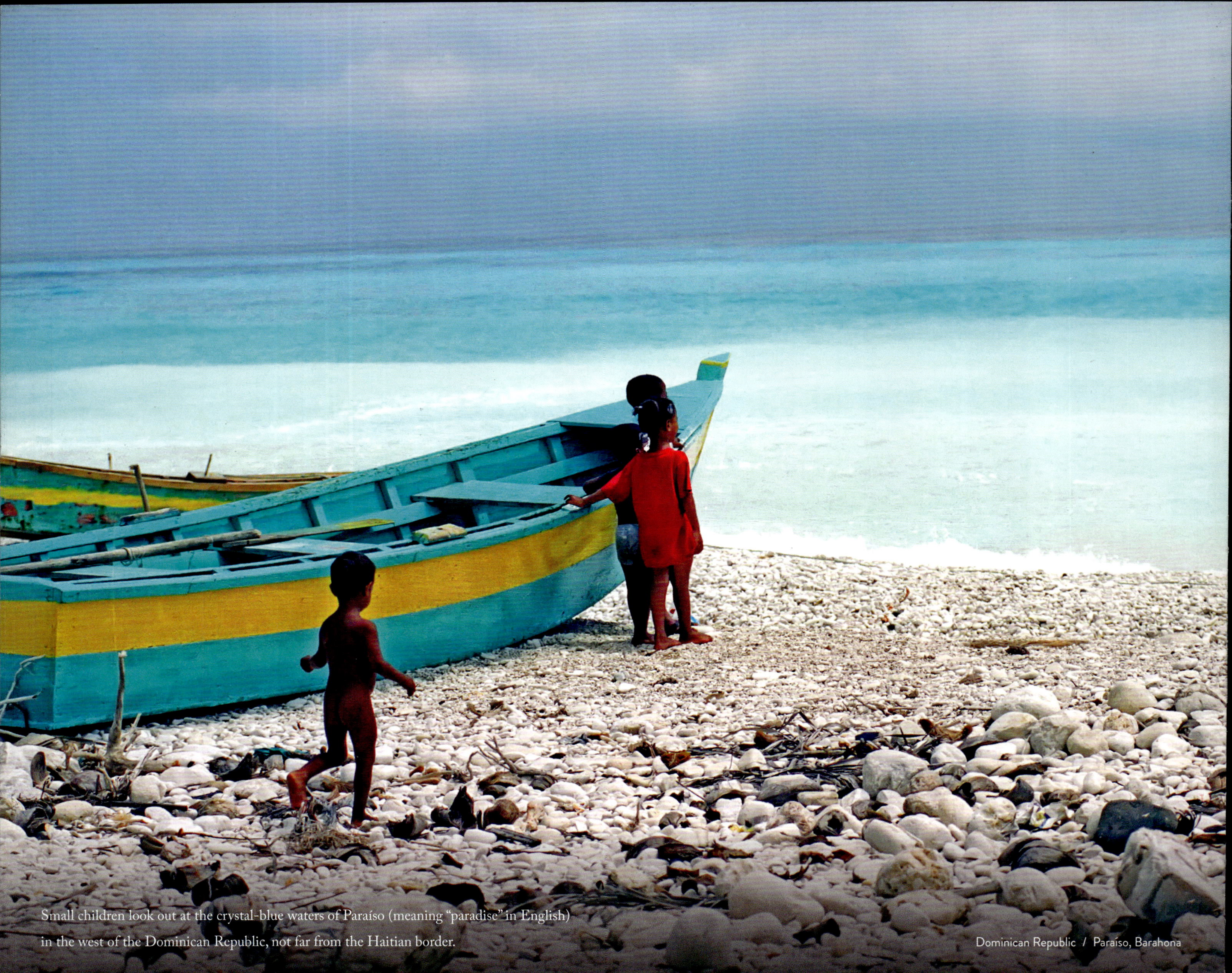

Small children look out at the crystal-blue waters of Paraíso (meaning "paradise" in English) in the west of the Dominican Republic, not far from the Haitian border.

Dominican Republic / Paraíso, Barahona

PASTIME

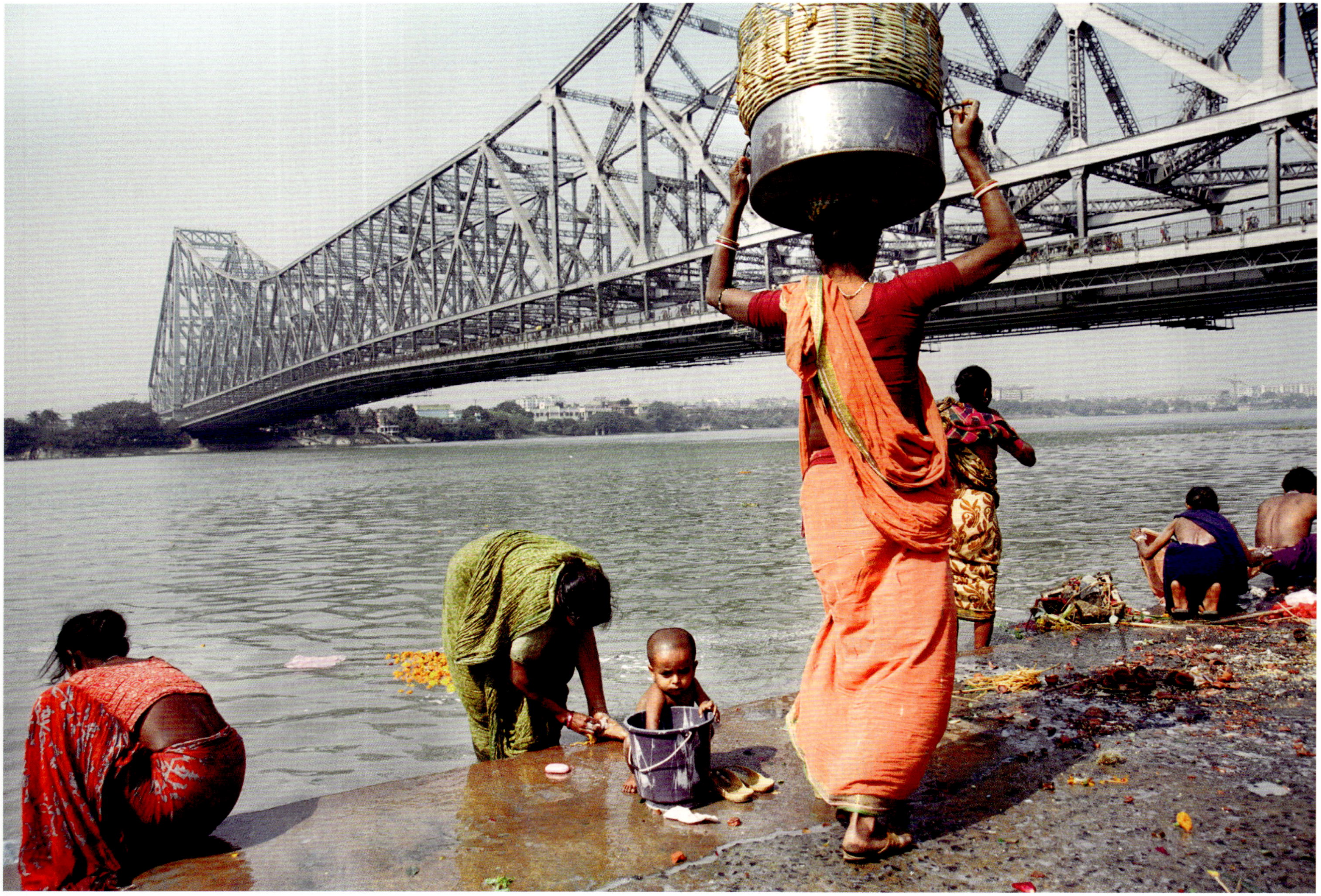

Women wash clothes in the Hooghly River. The Howrah Bridge soars above.

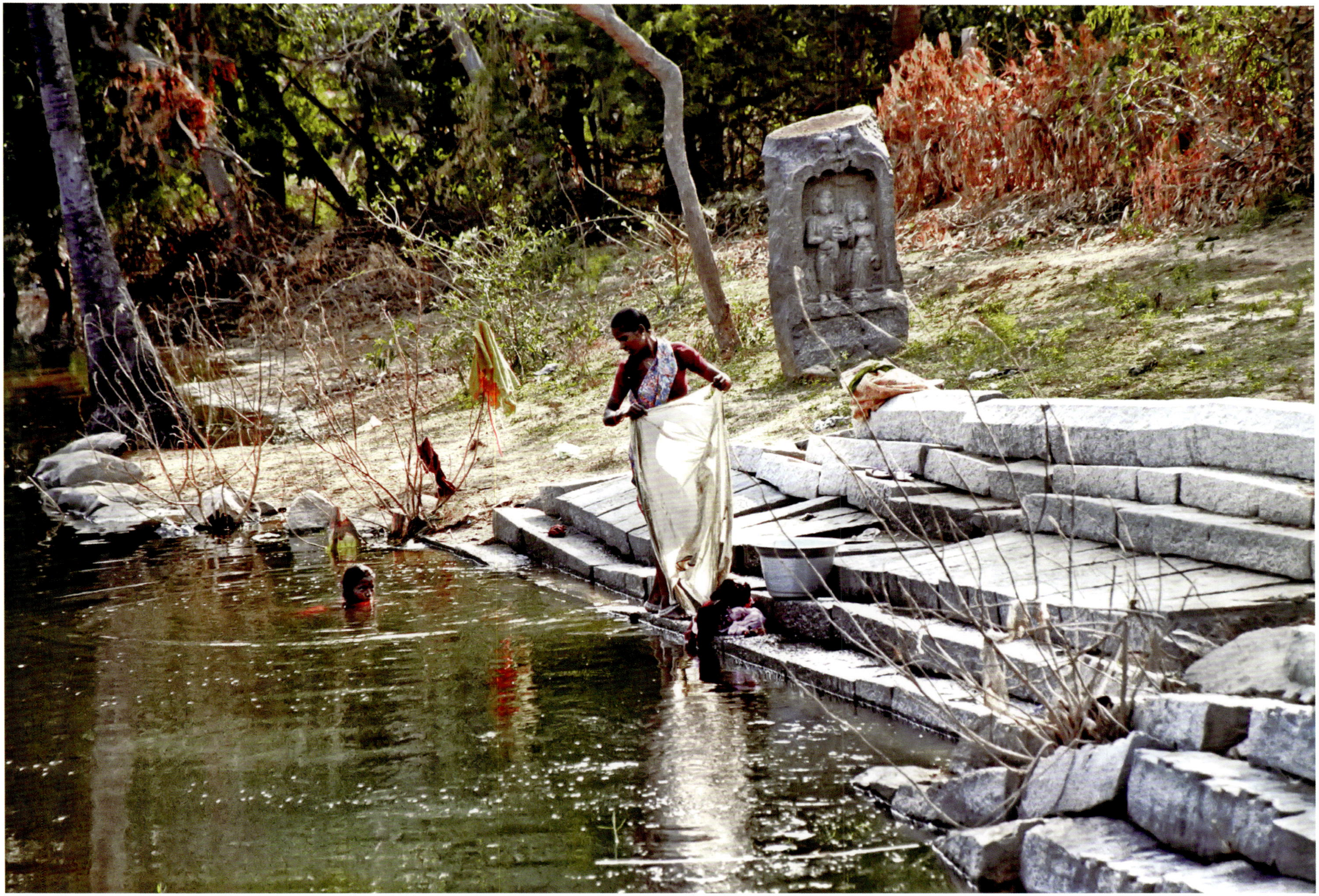

In the town of Mamallapuram, a woman washes clothes while her daughter cools off.

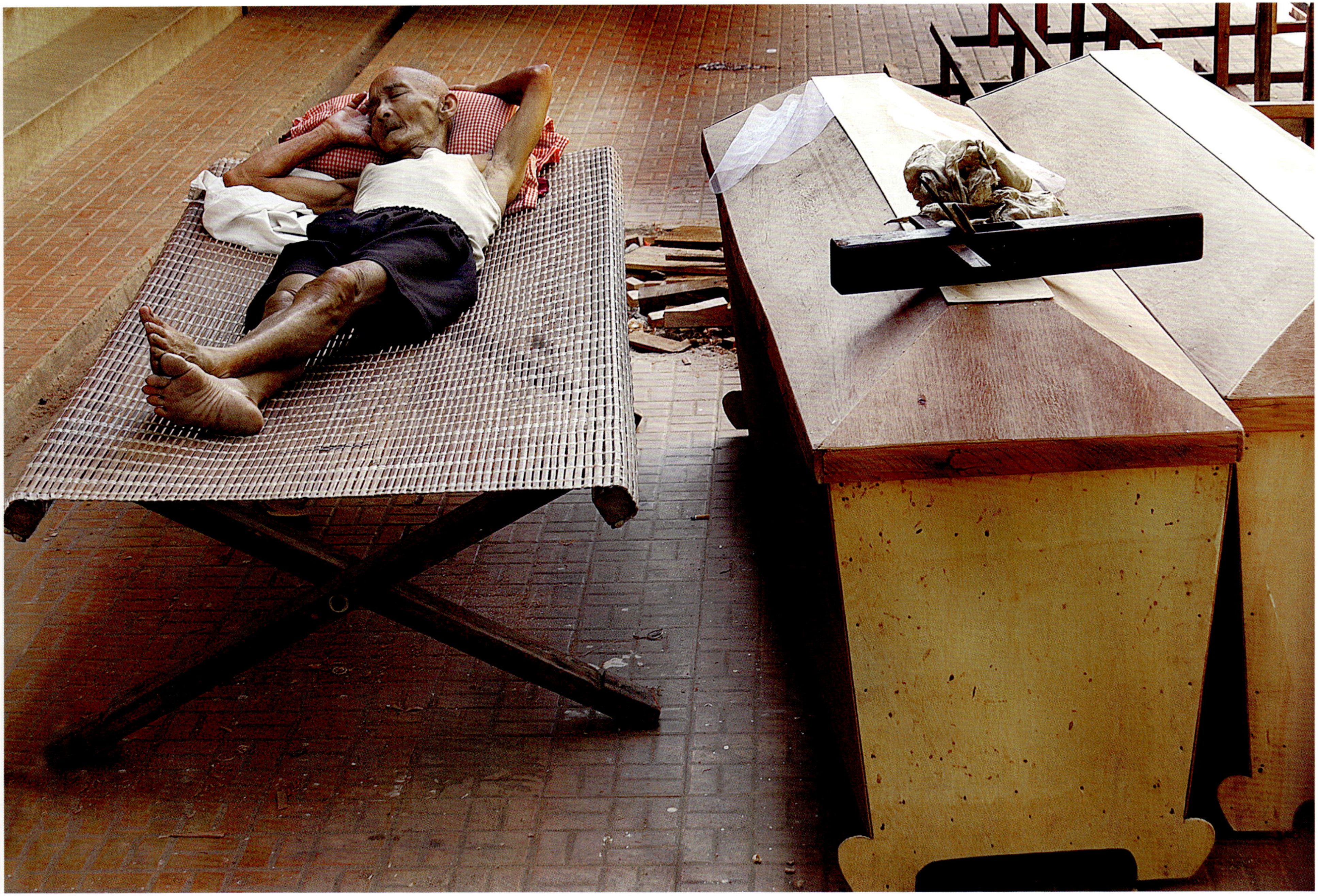

A man with carpenter tools sleeps next to a coffin. The saying goes that if someone builds their own coffin, they have to lie in it: they've gotten themselves into a bad situation. This man was merely napping in the daytime heat of Phnom Penh.

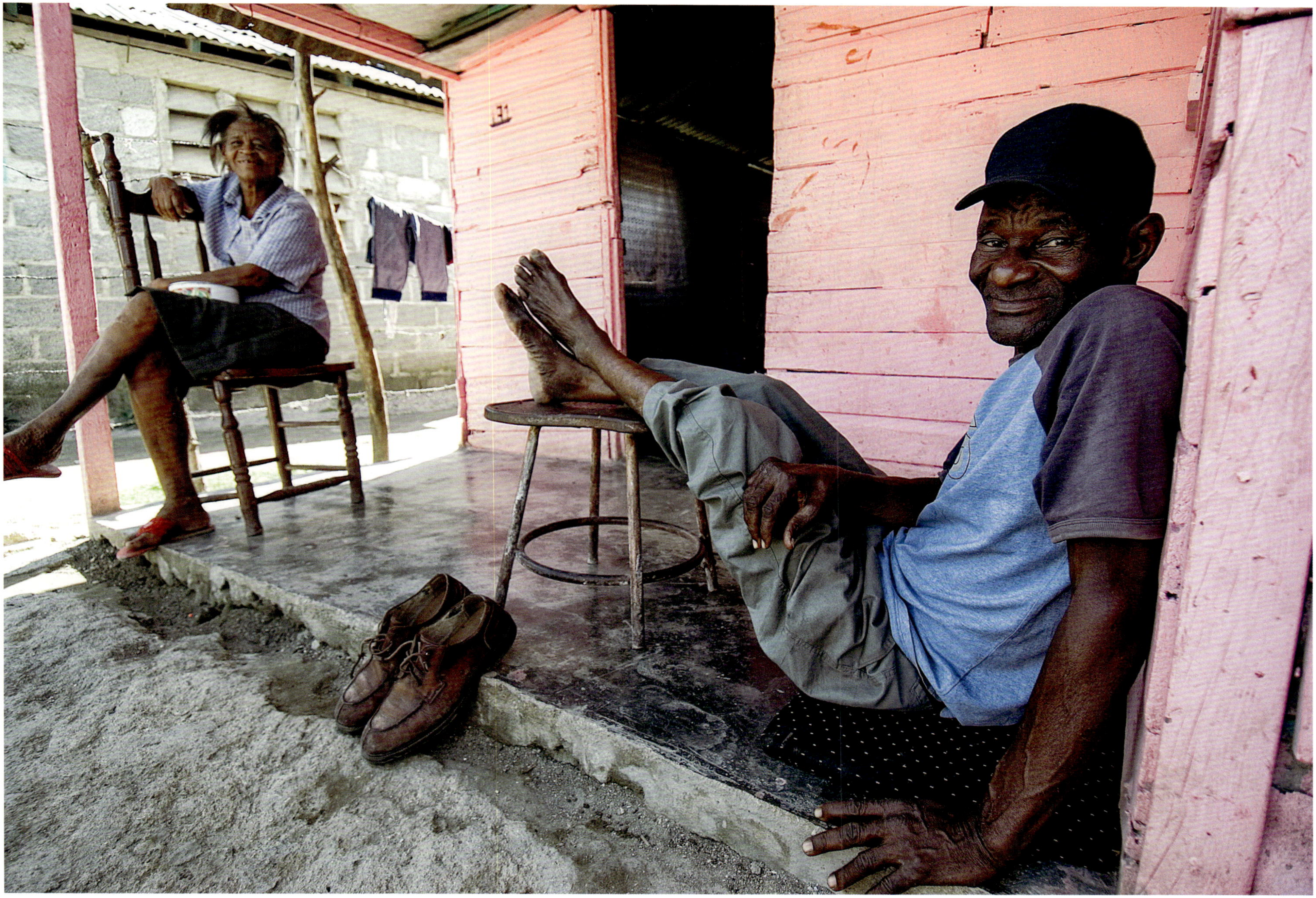

A happy couple relax in front of their home.

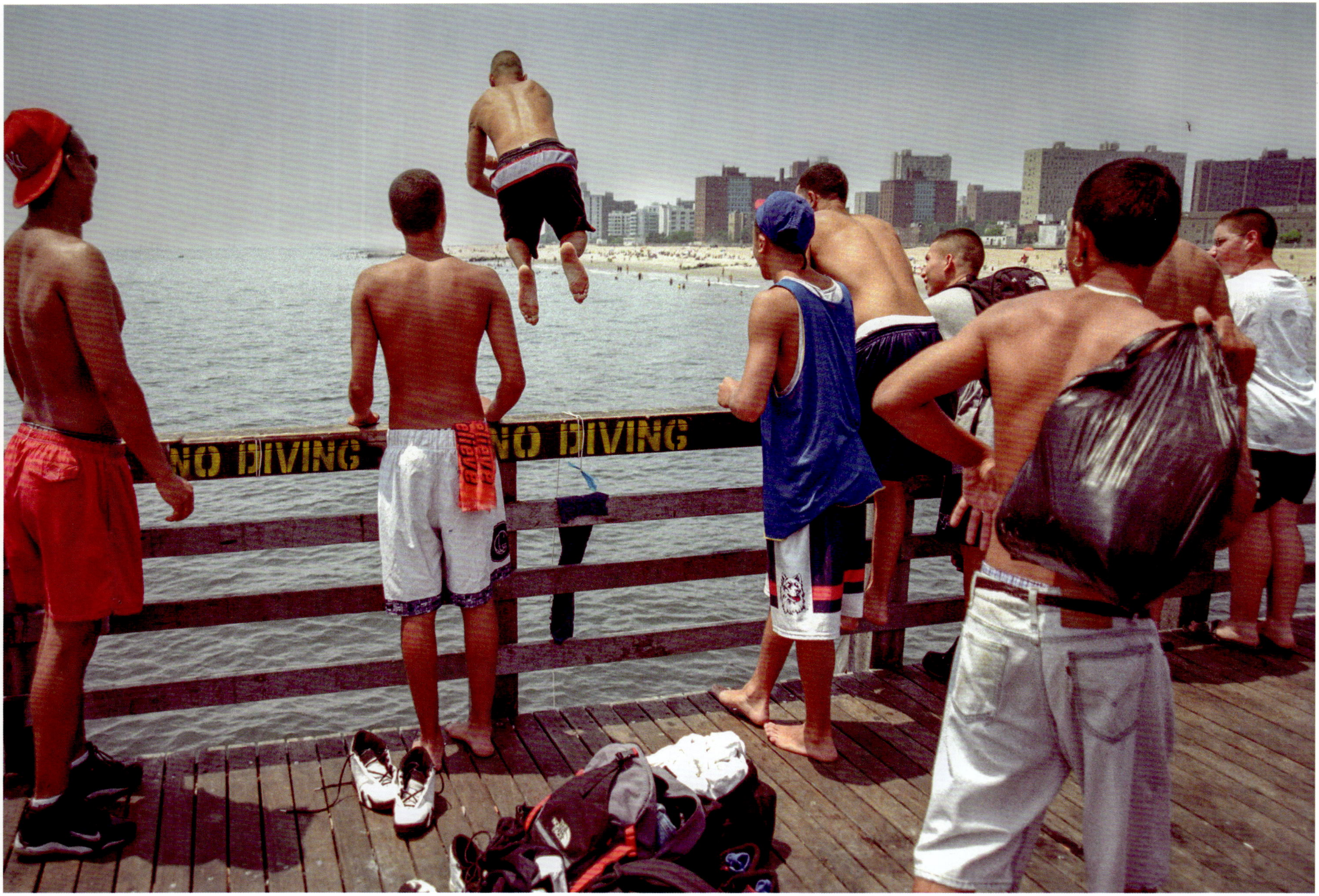

Boys on a hot day in Brooklyn's Coney Island.

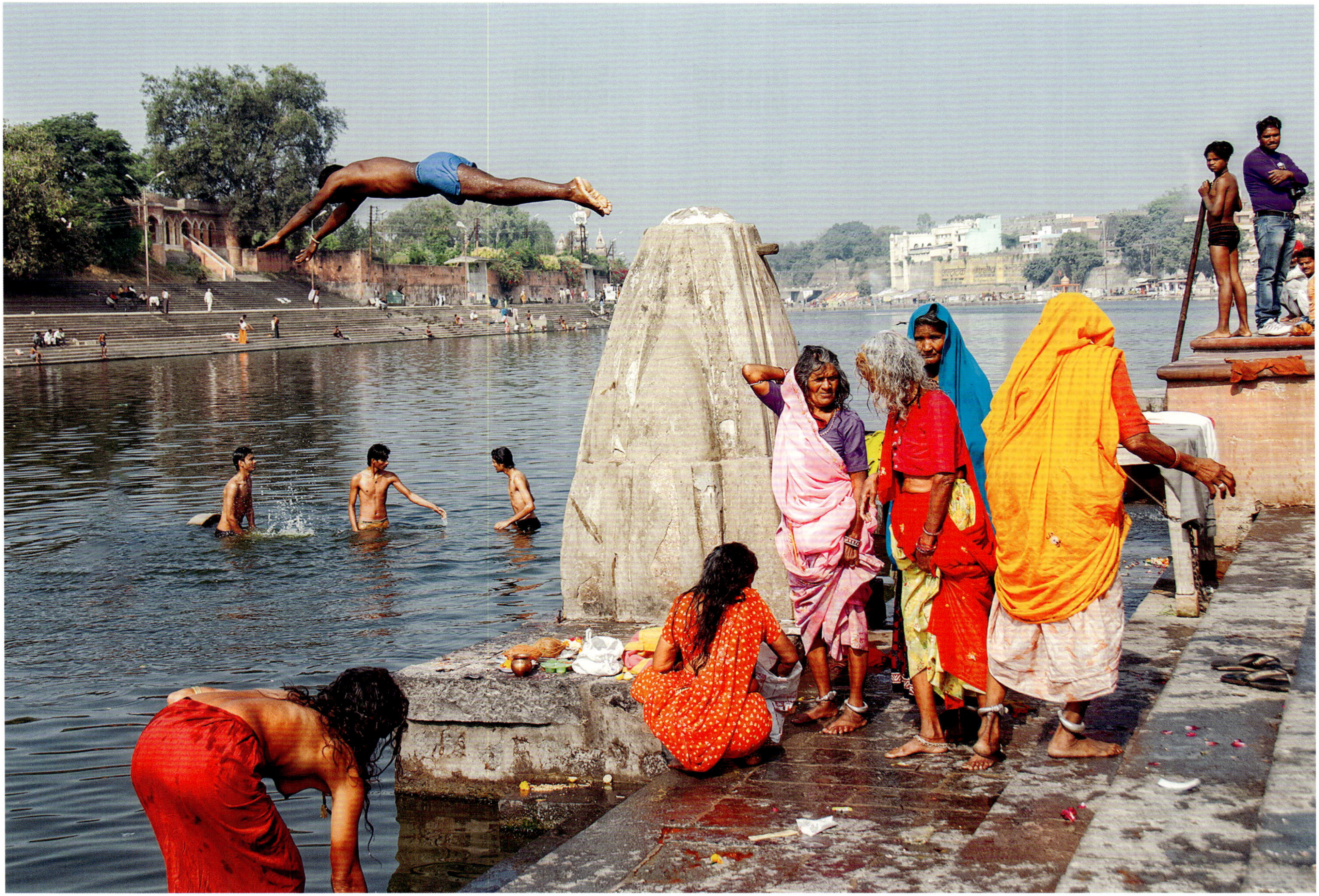

People enjoying time in the Shipra River. It is an essential place for Hindu rituals and pilgrimages but increasingly polluted and drying up.

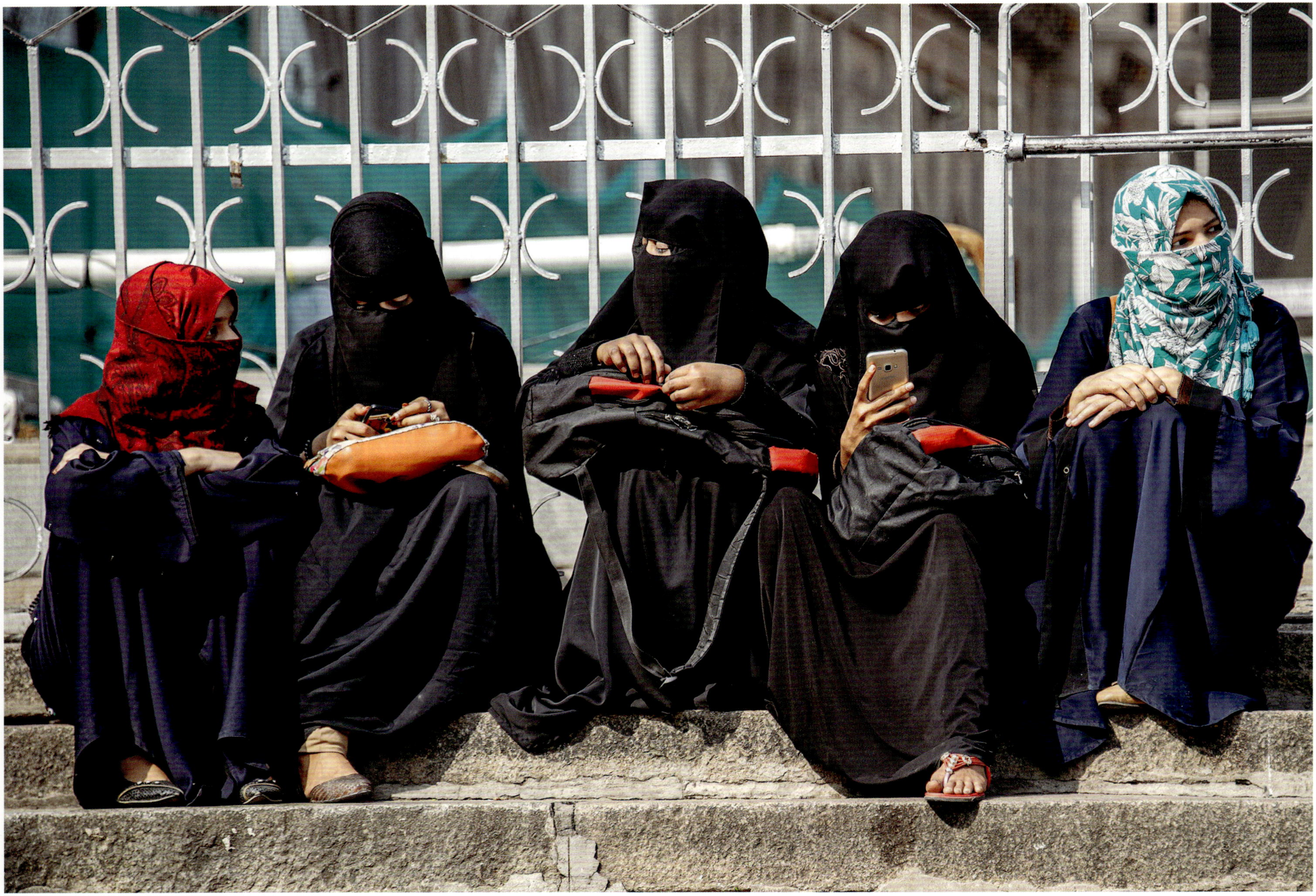

Women sit in front of the masjid, or mosque, as they wait for jum'ah.

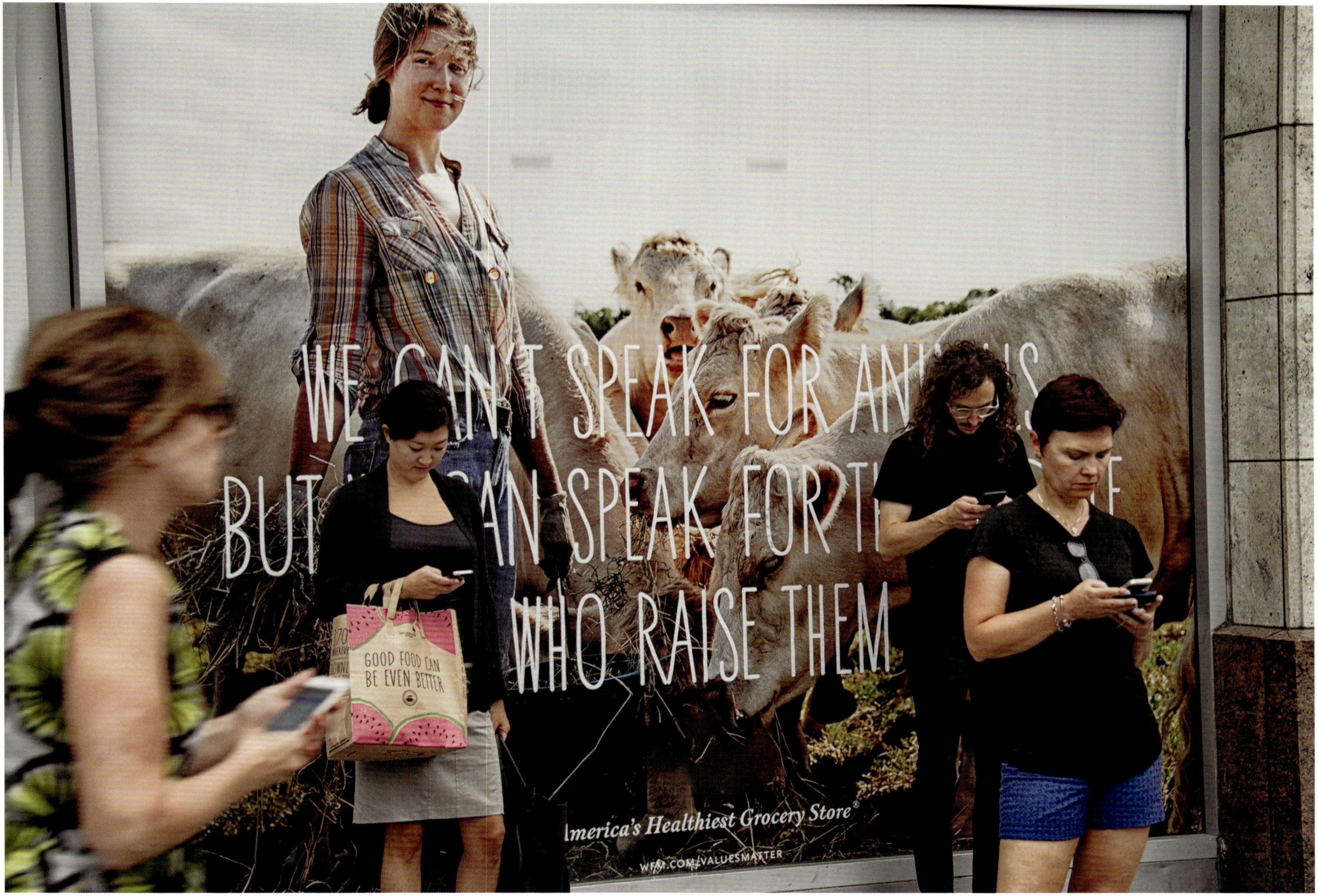

People look at their cell phones near Union Square.

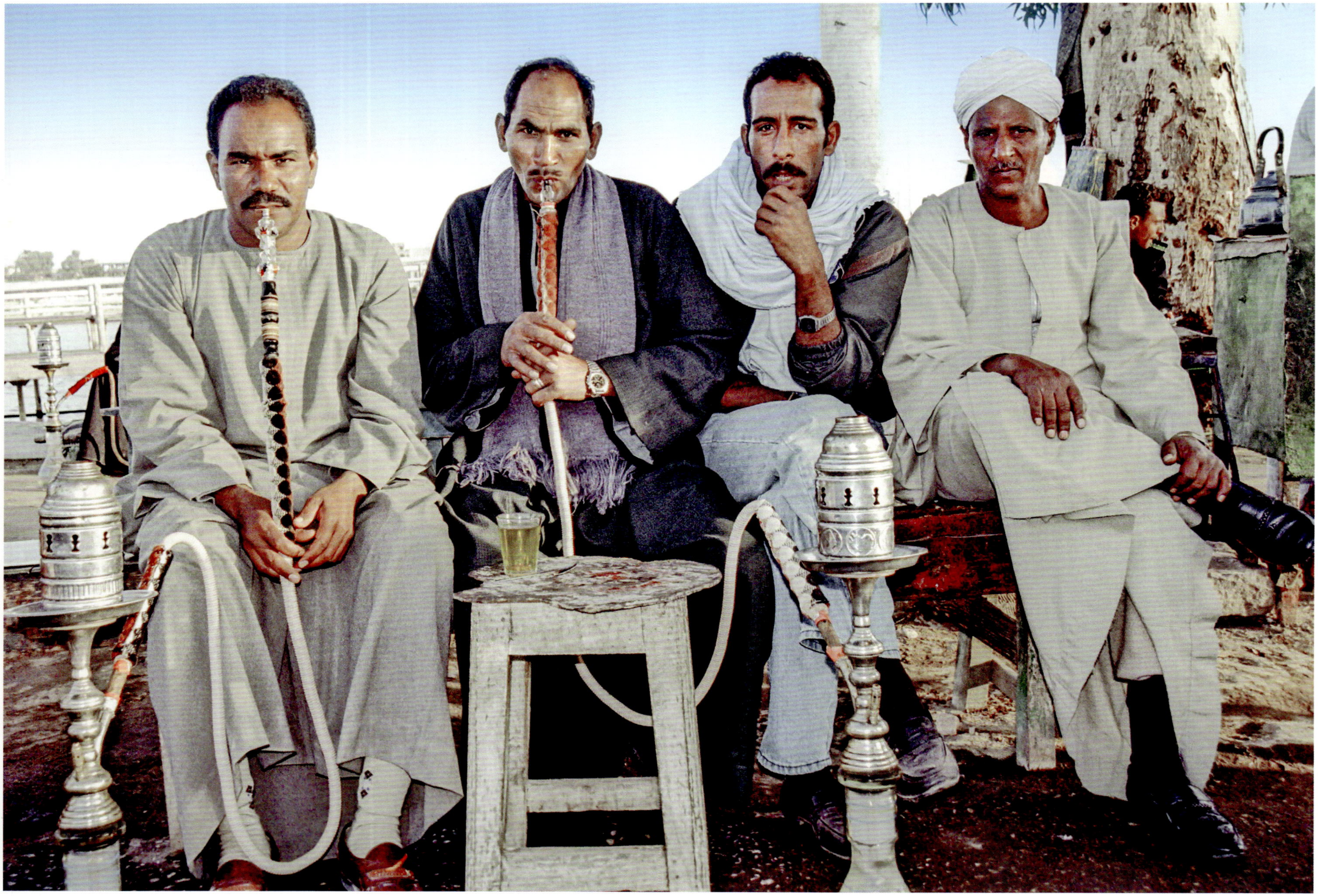

Four men, two hookahs.

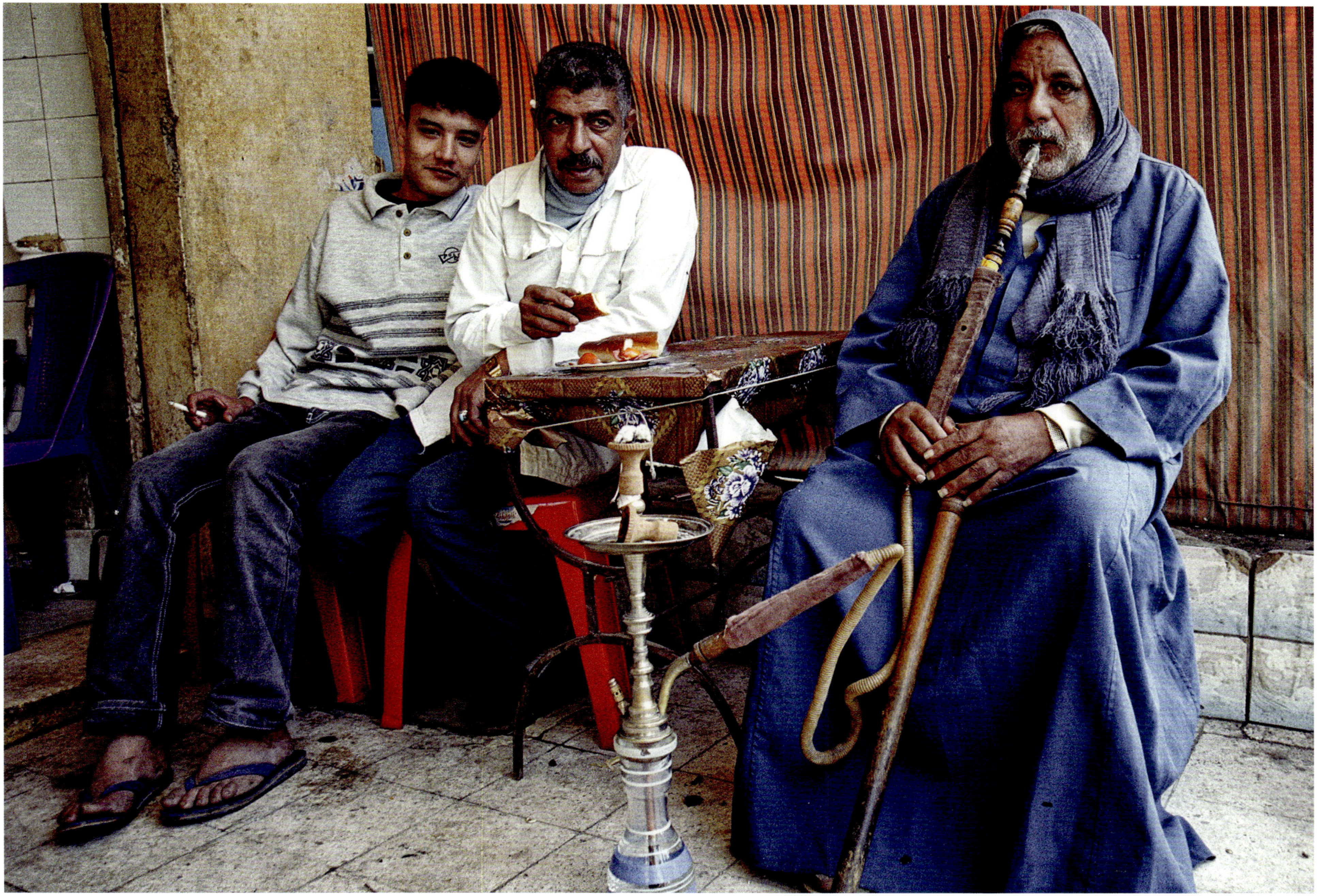

Three men relax while one smokes a cigarette, another eats lunch, and the third uses a hookah.

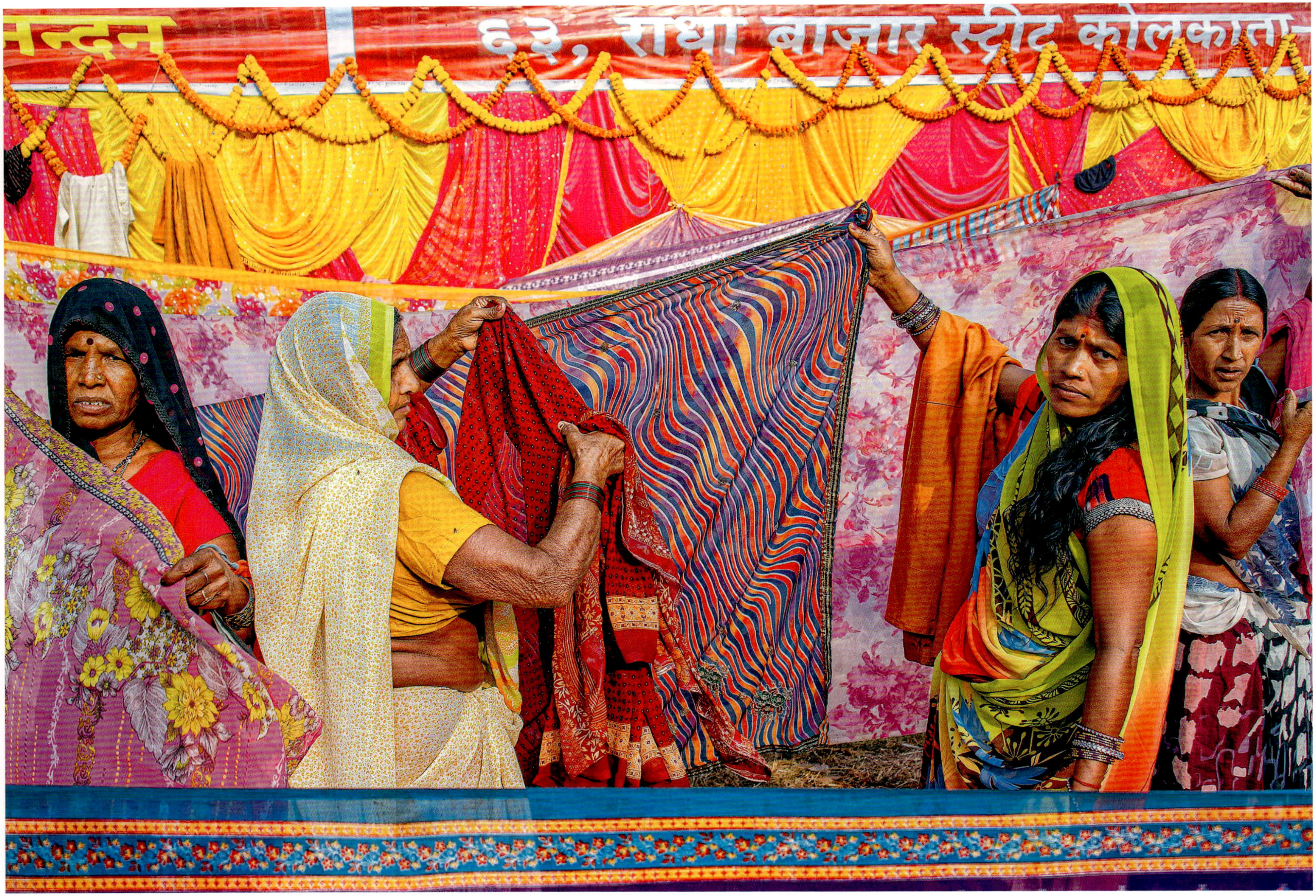

Women hang colorful silks at the Gangasagar transit camp in Kolkata. It is a rest stop from which tens of thousands of people travel to Sagar Island for Gangasagar Mela, an annual pilgrimage where hundreds of thousands of Hindus gather to take a holy dip in the Ganges.

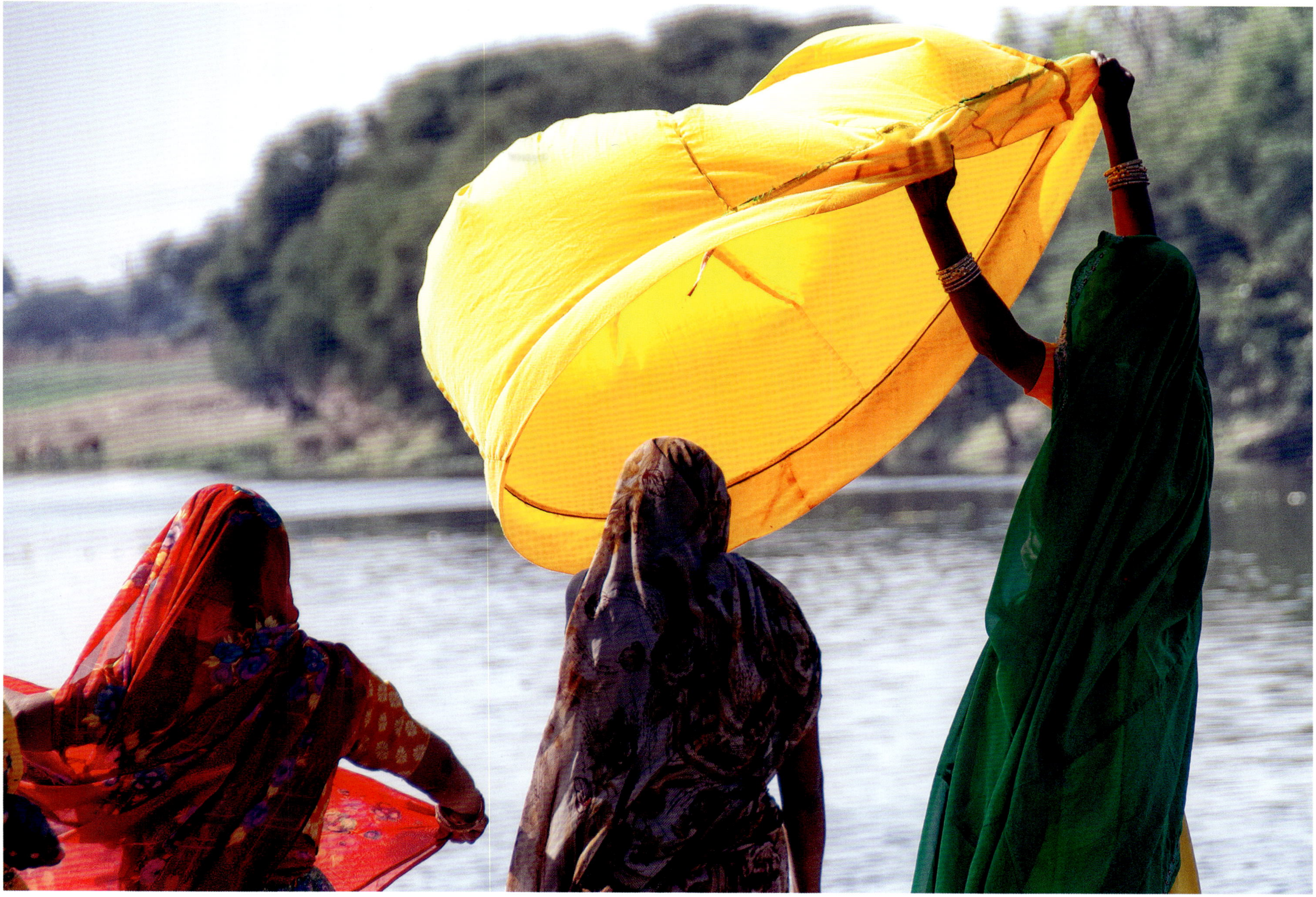

Women air-dry their garments after washing them in the sacred Shipra River.

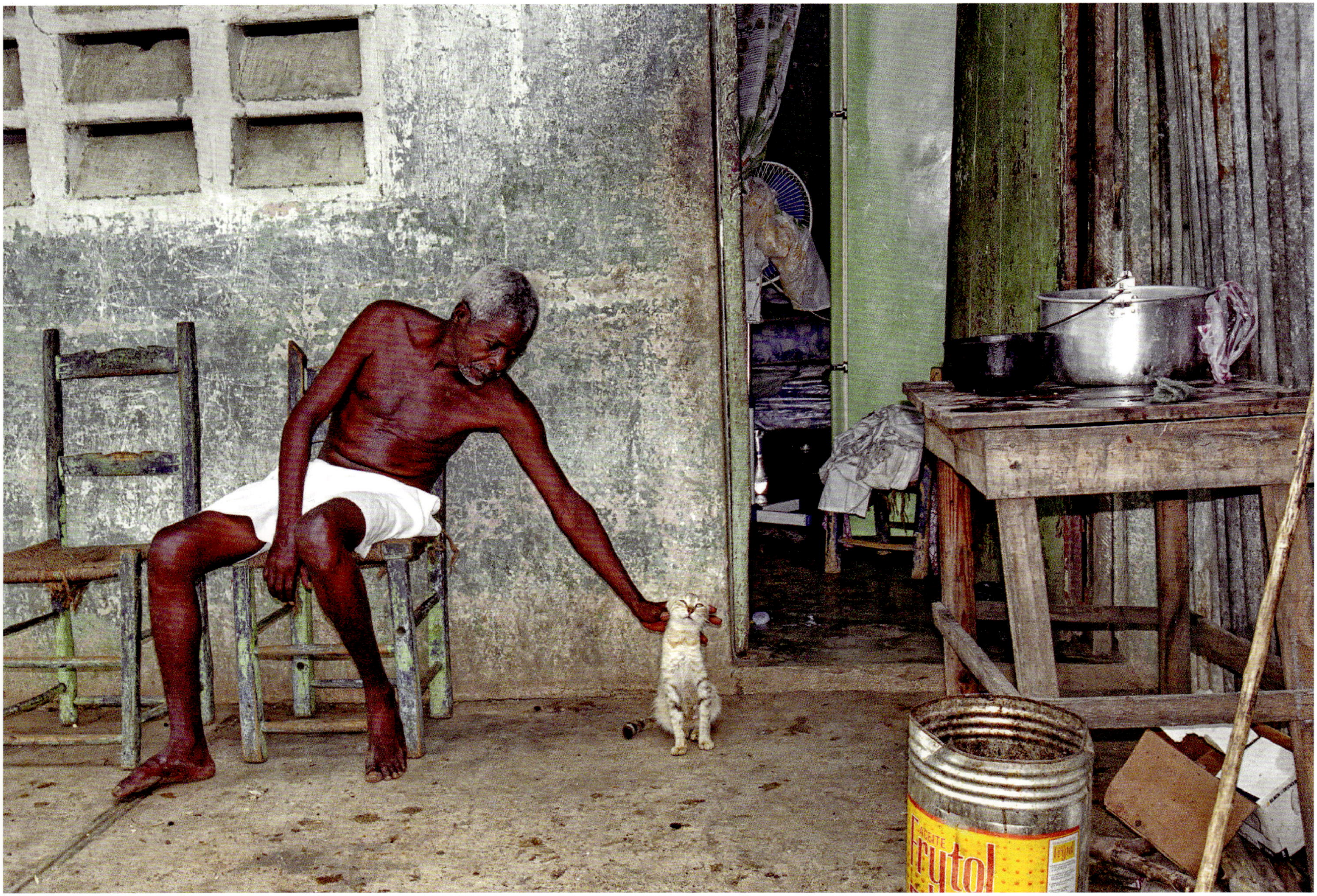

In batey Aleman, a Haitian man pets his friend.

In Manhattan's East Village, a woman and her best friend shop for hats.

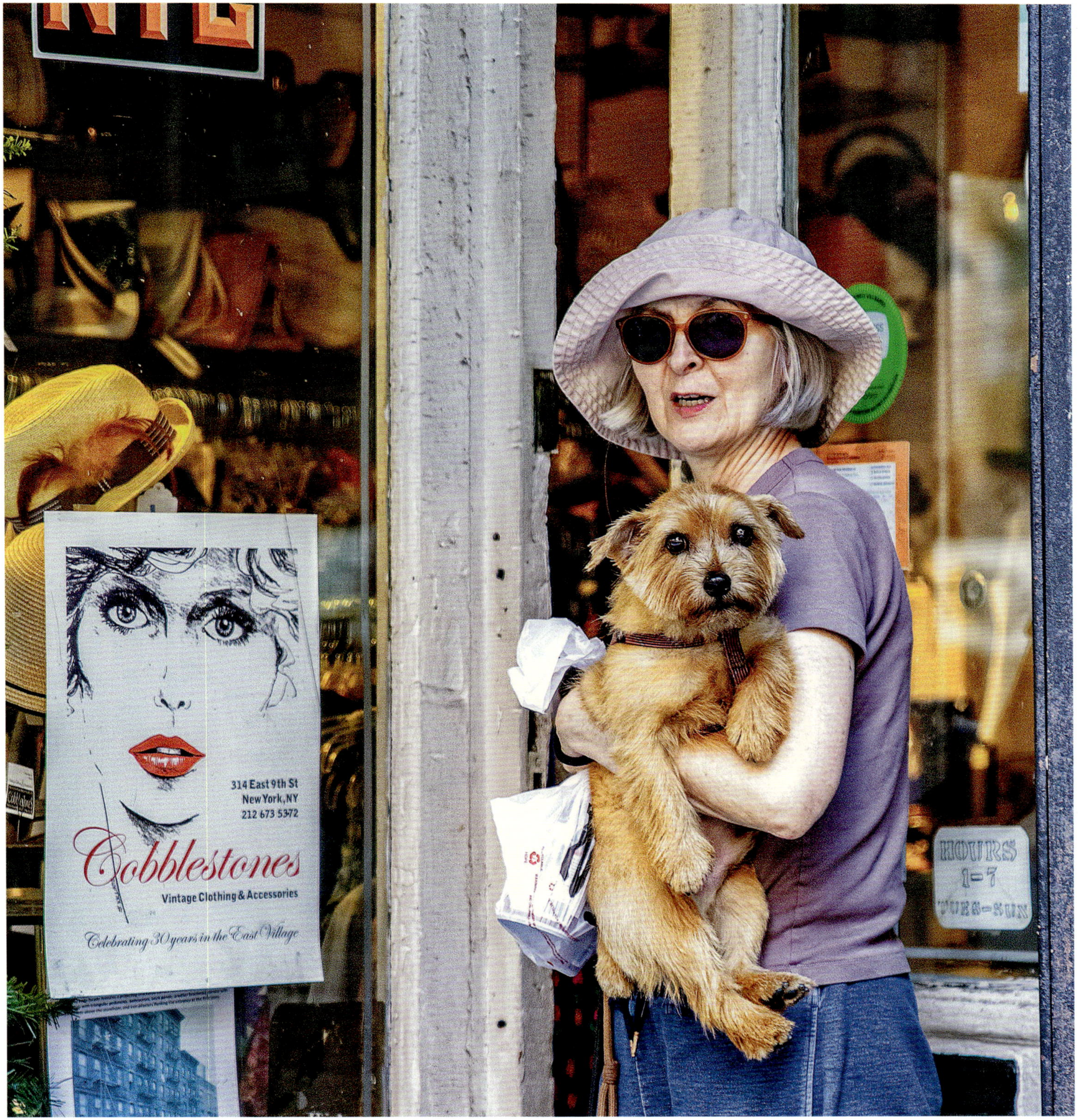

United States / New York, New York

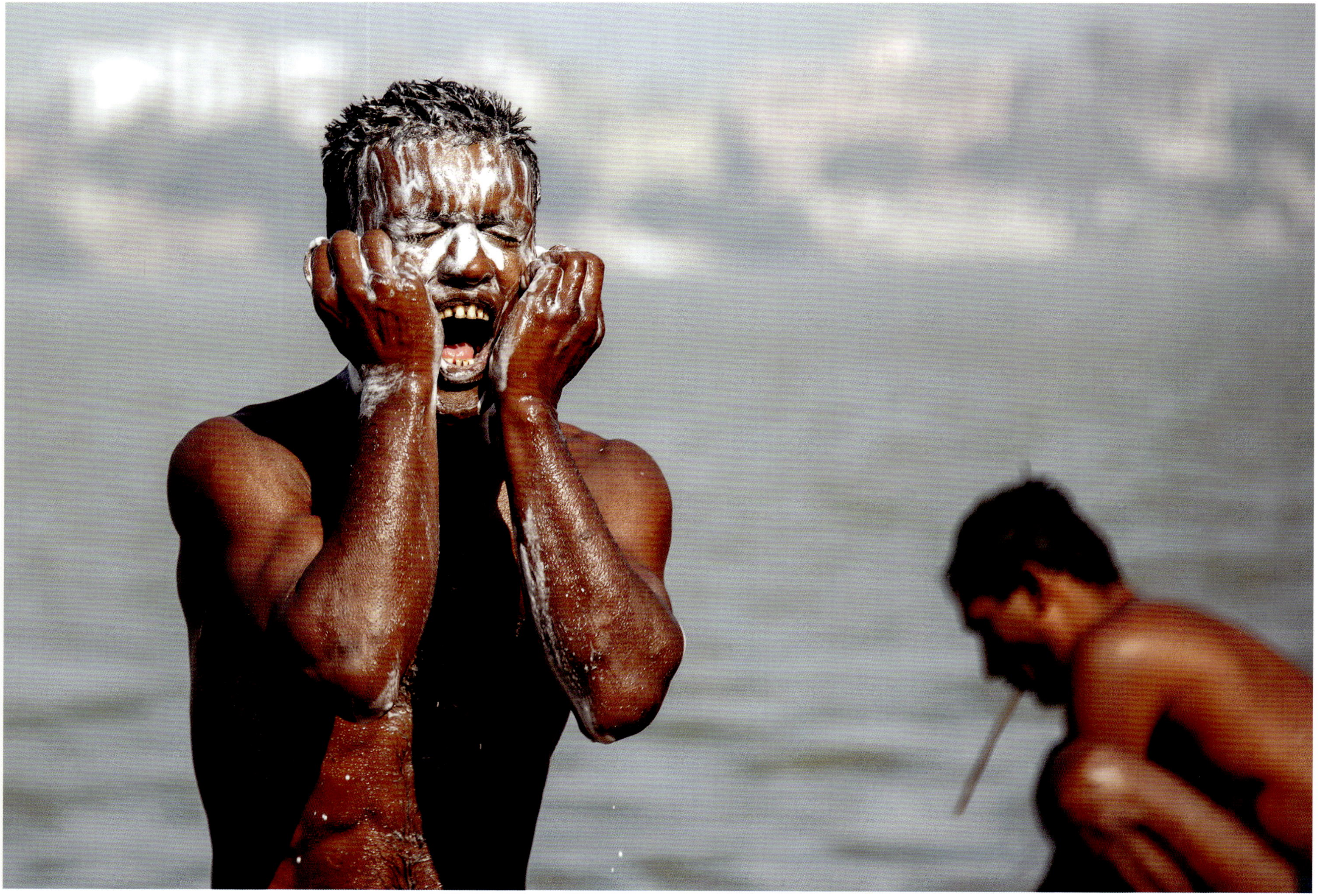

A man soaps up before dipping into the Hooghly River, which flows through Kolkata.

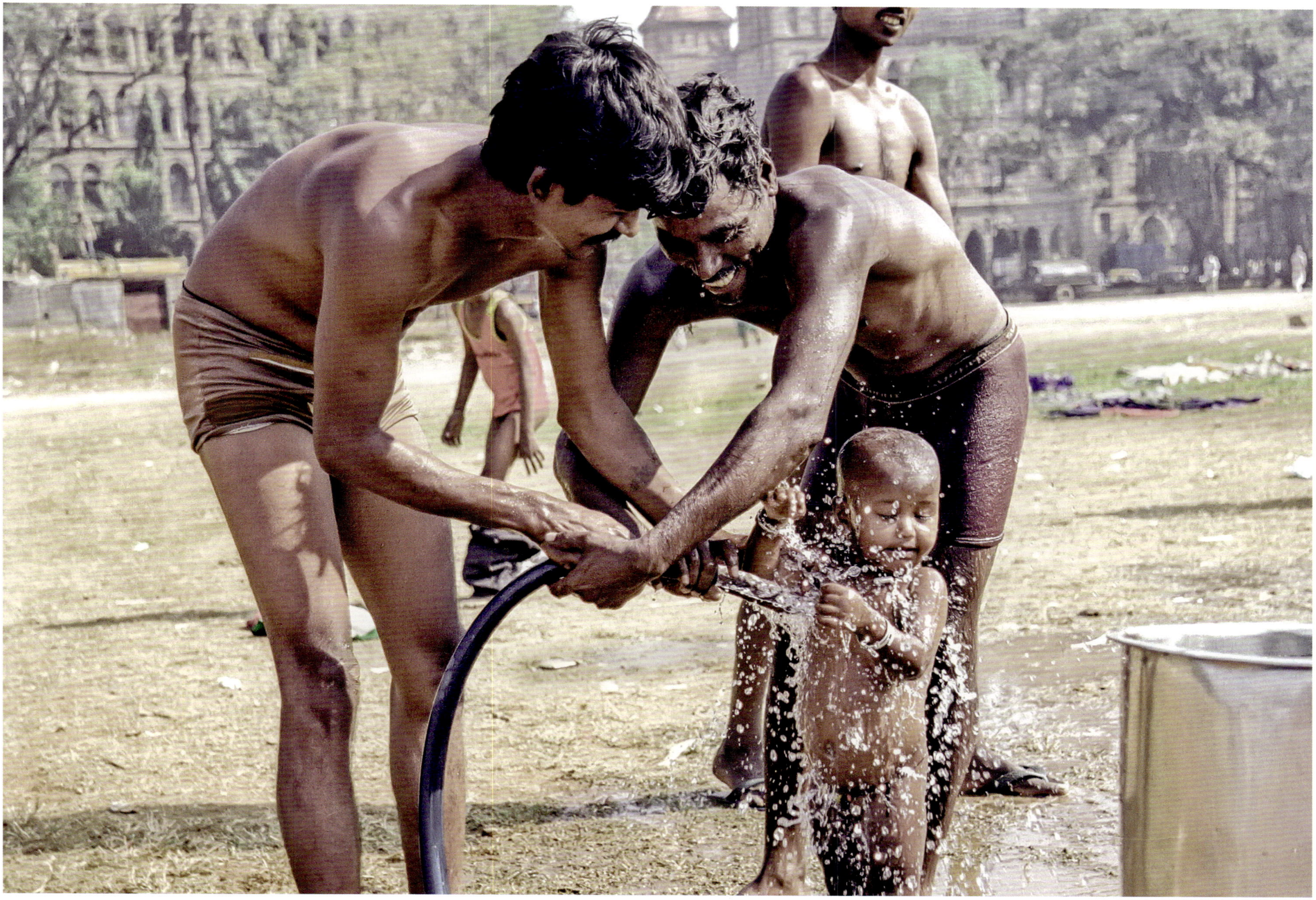

Men in a park near Victoria Terminus (today named Chhatrapati Shivaji Terminus), Mumbai's historic train station, help a child cool down in 100-degree heat.

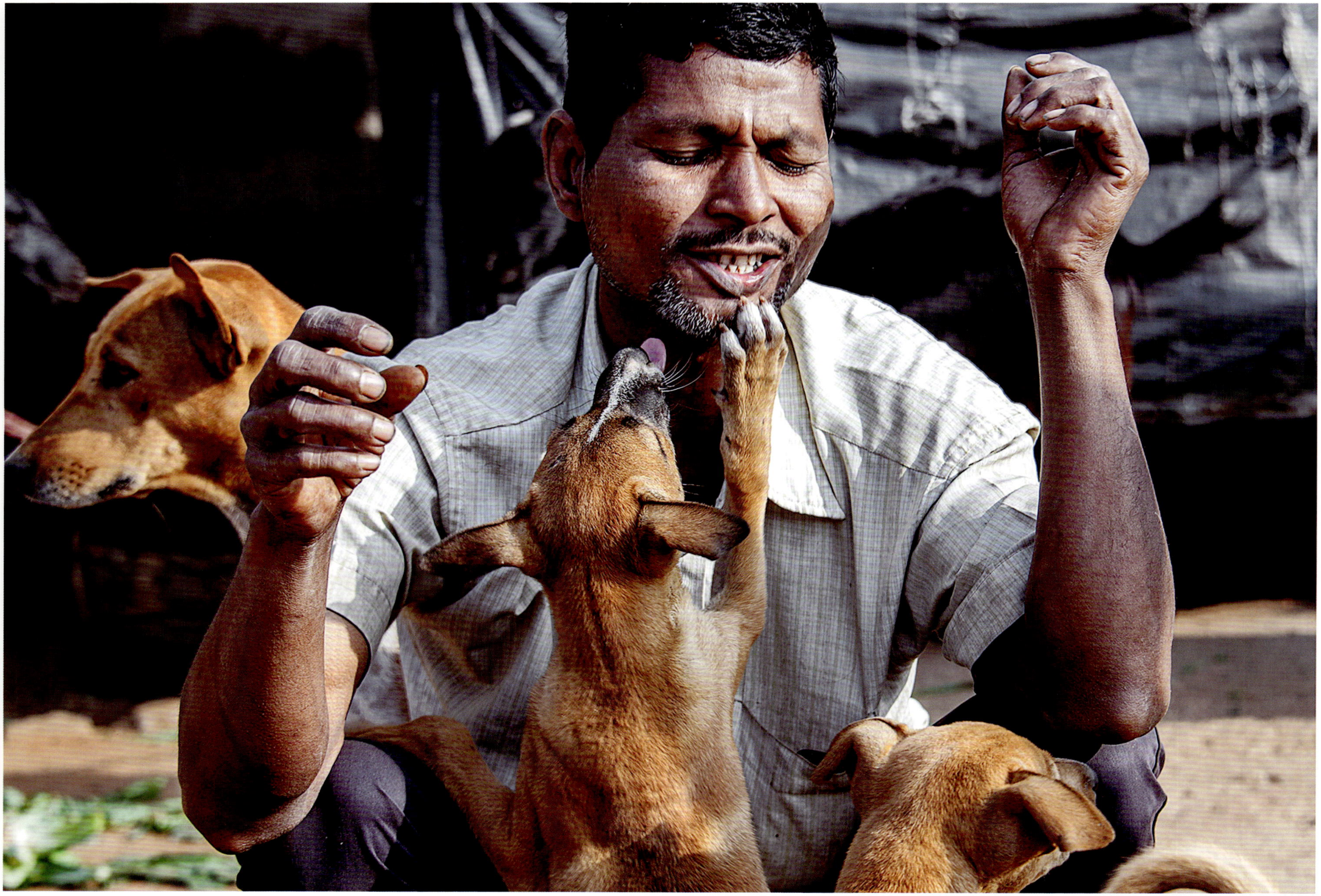

A man plays with puppies in Bhubaneshwar, the capital of Odisha known as the Temple City for being home to hundreds of temples.

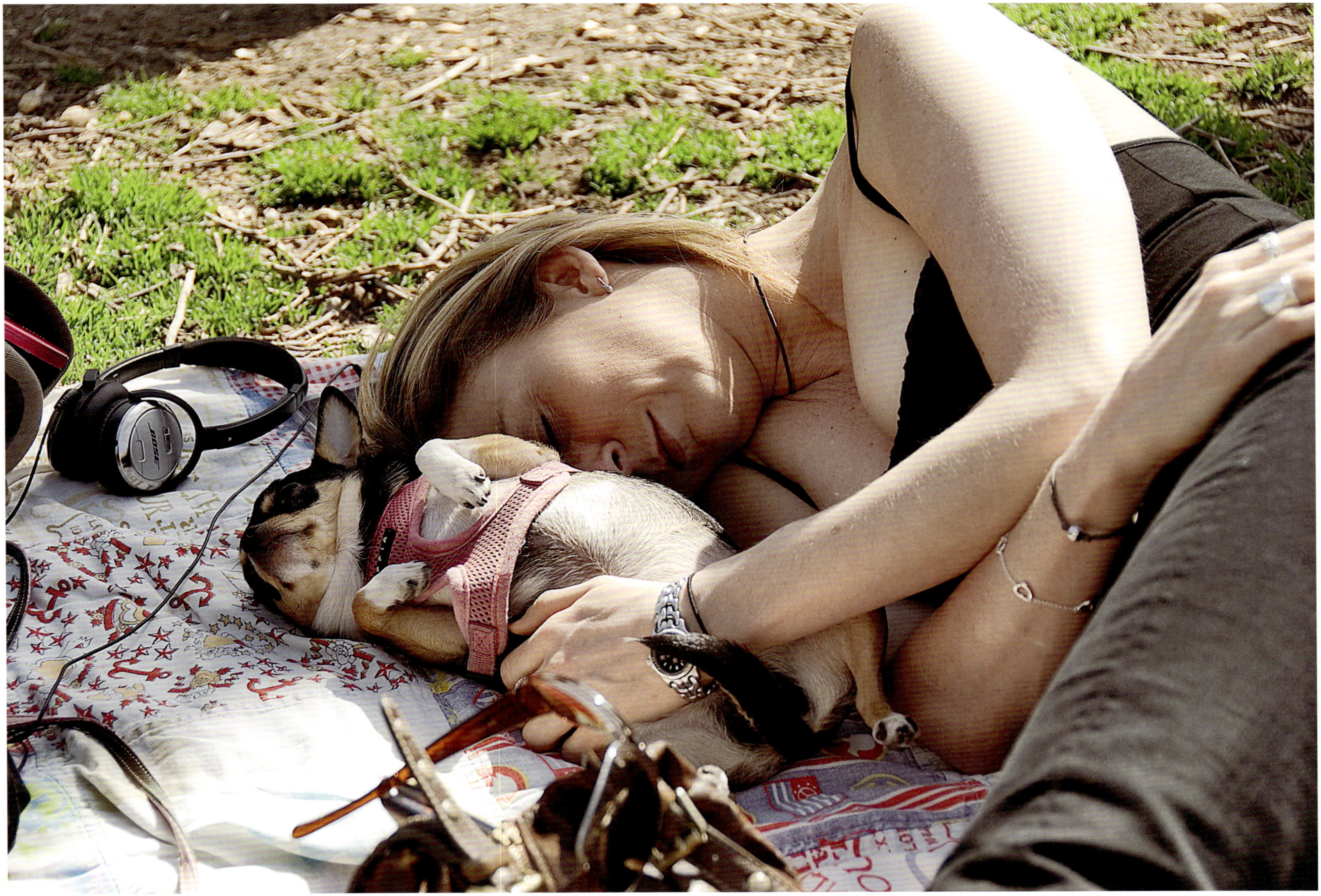

A woman and her puppy nap on a hot summer day in Washington Square Park.

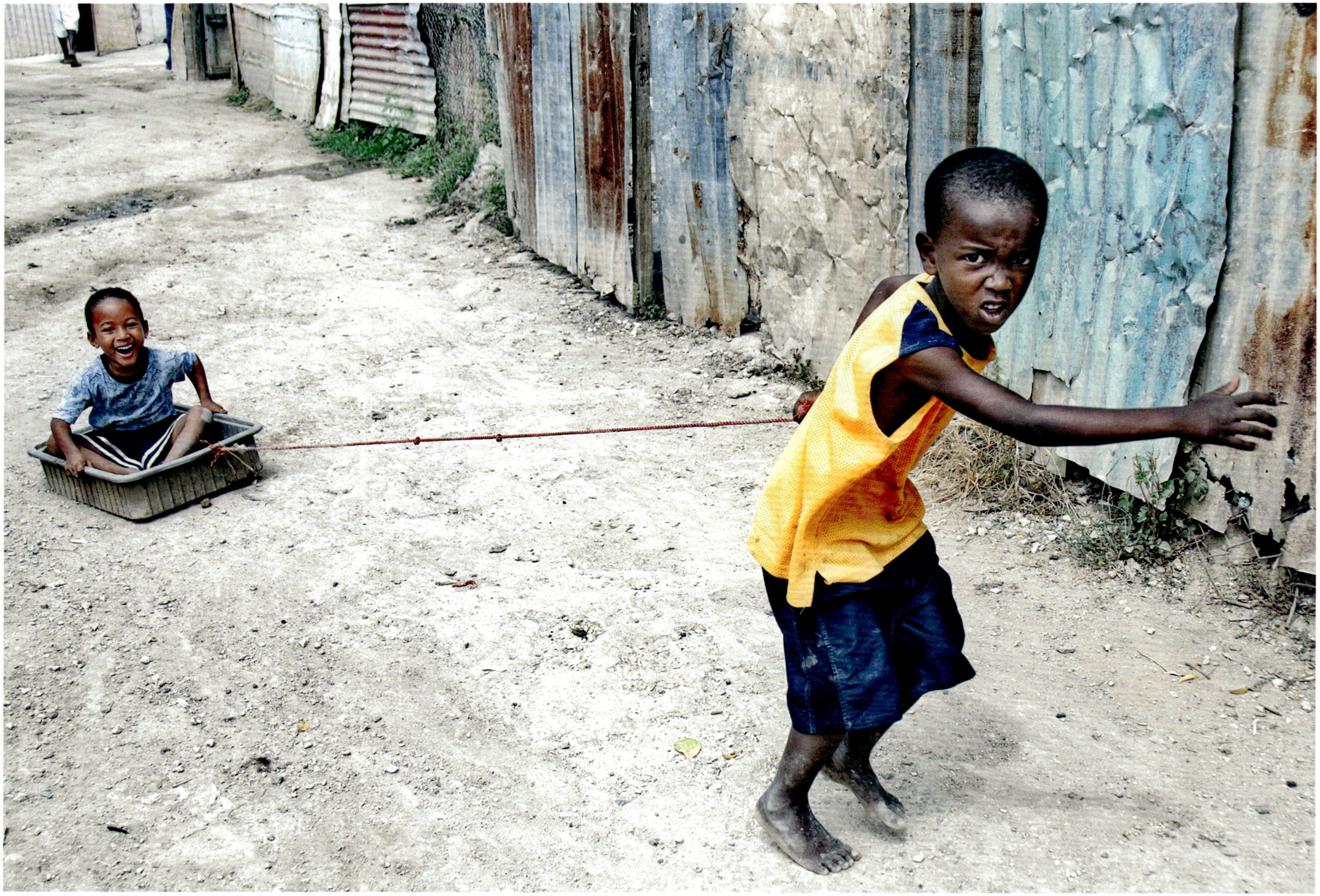

Children play with a makeshift toy.

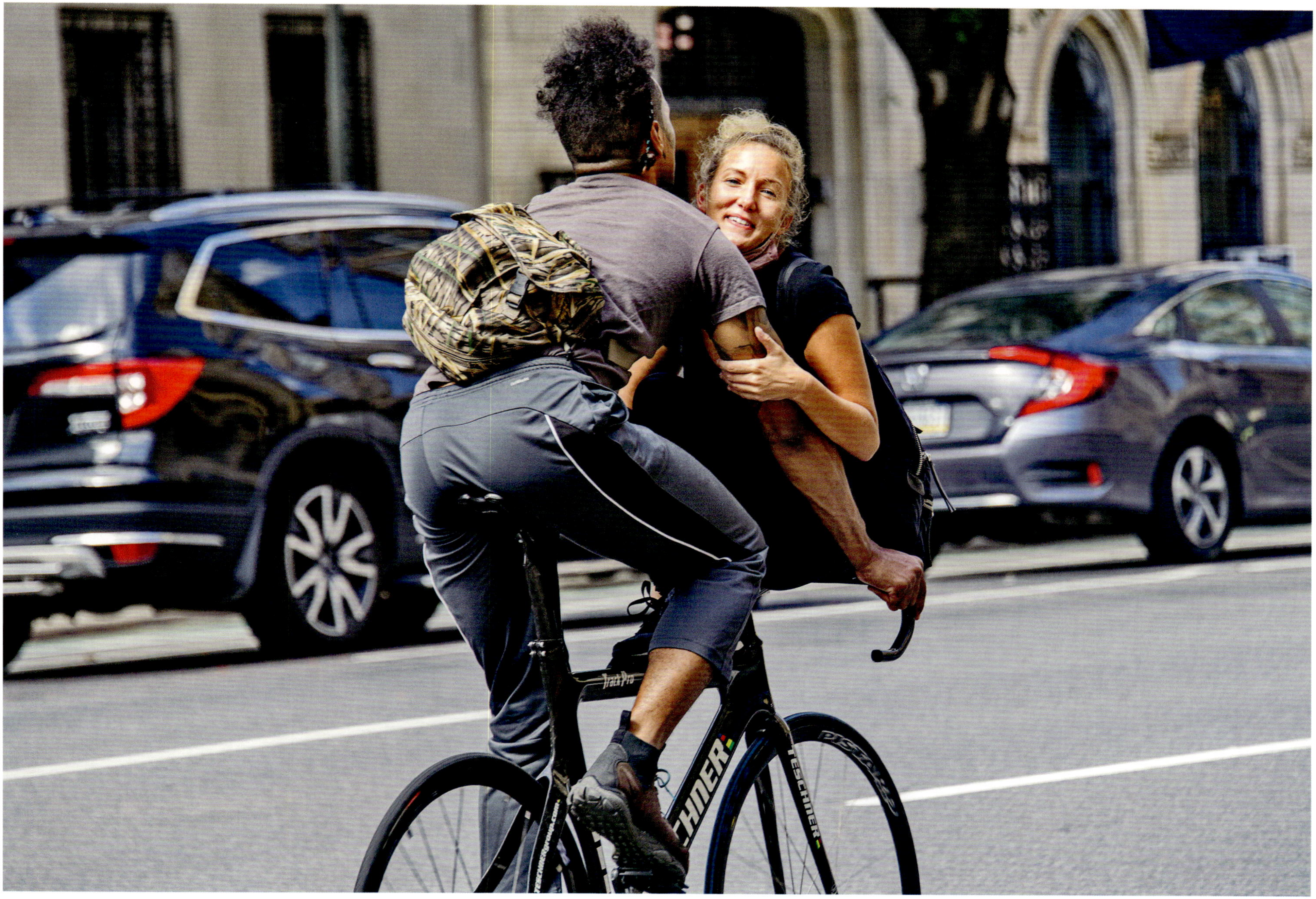

A couple let down their masks during a shared bike ride on a sunny day in Manhattan's East Village.

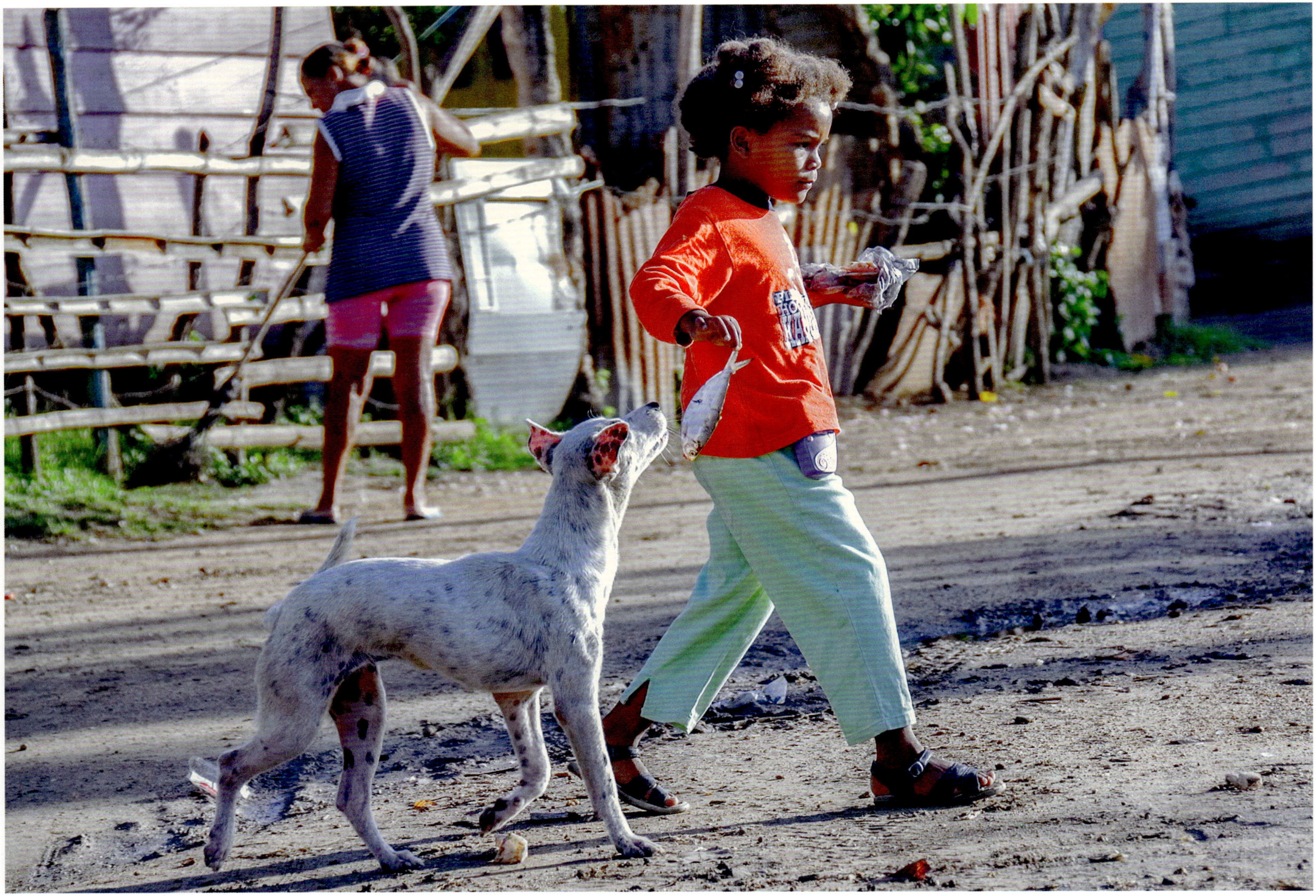

A child in the slums of San Pedro de Macorís carries a fish to be fried and mixed with rice and legumes, potatoes, yuca, or plantains.

A child and her puppy.

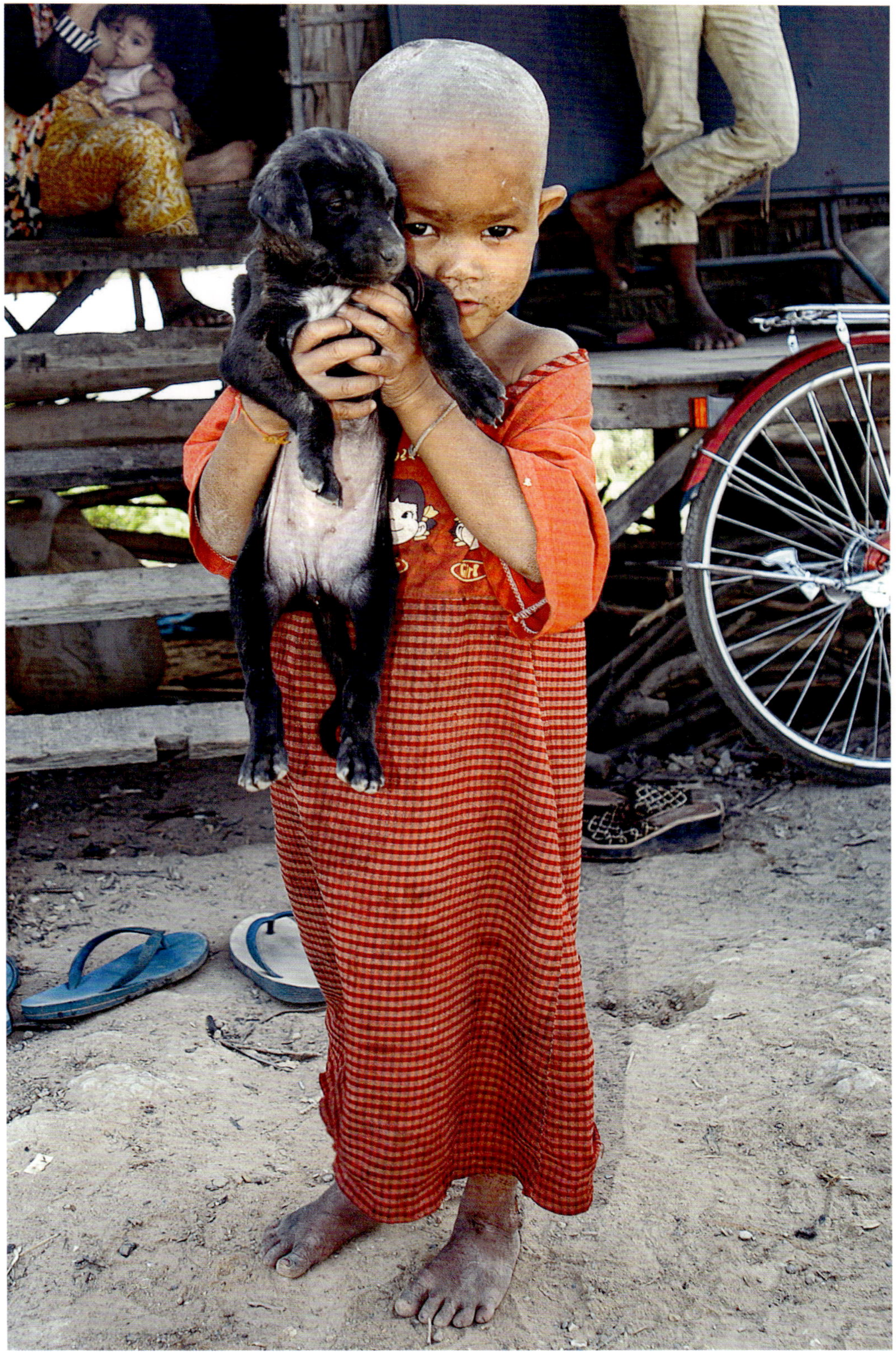

Cambodia / Krong Battambang, Battambang Province

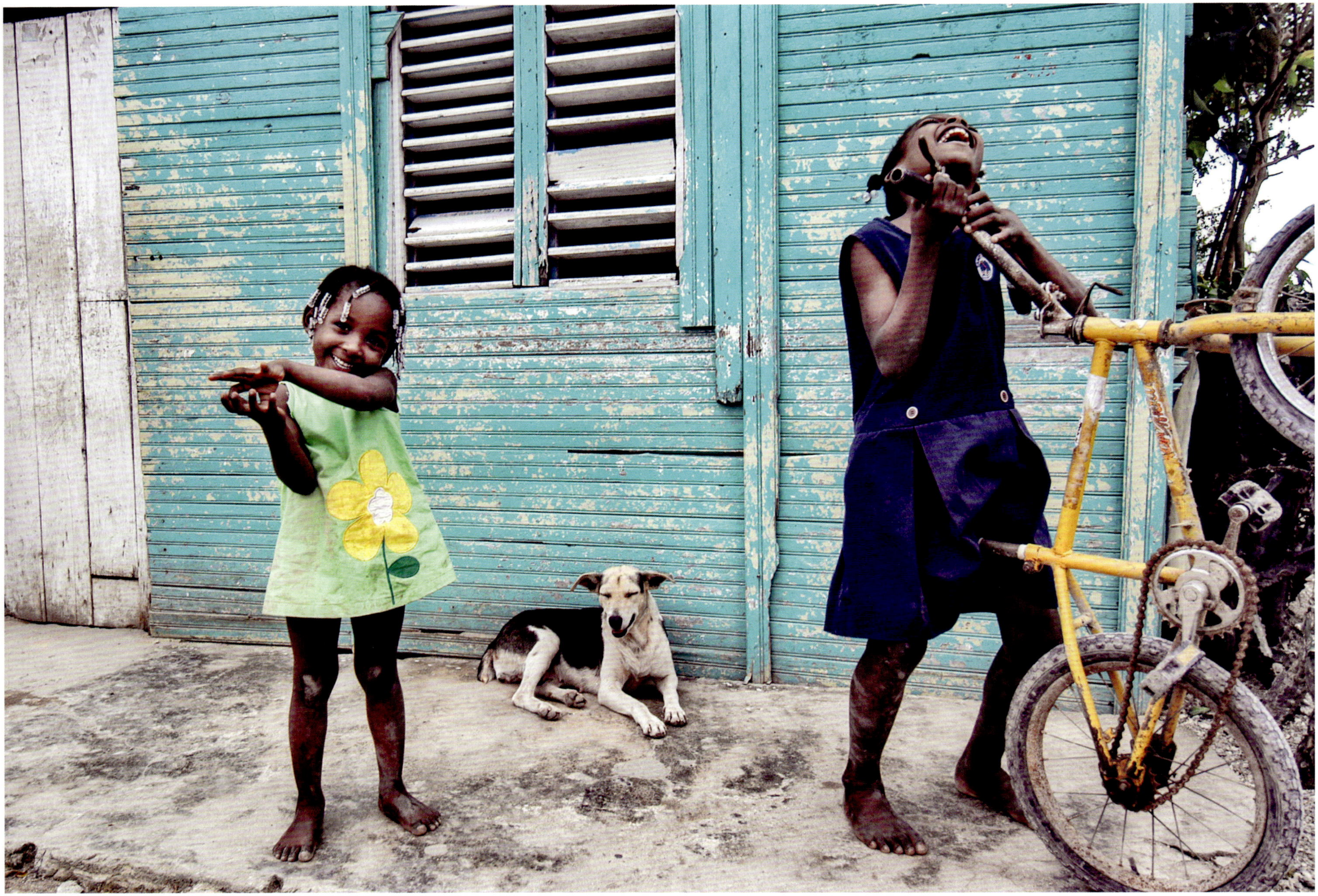

Two girls and a dog—all laughing.

Children and their furry friend in
a village in Krong Battambang,
Cambodia's leading rice-producing city.

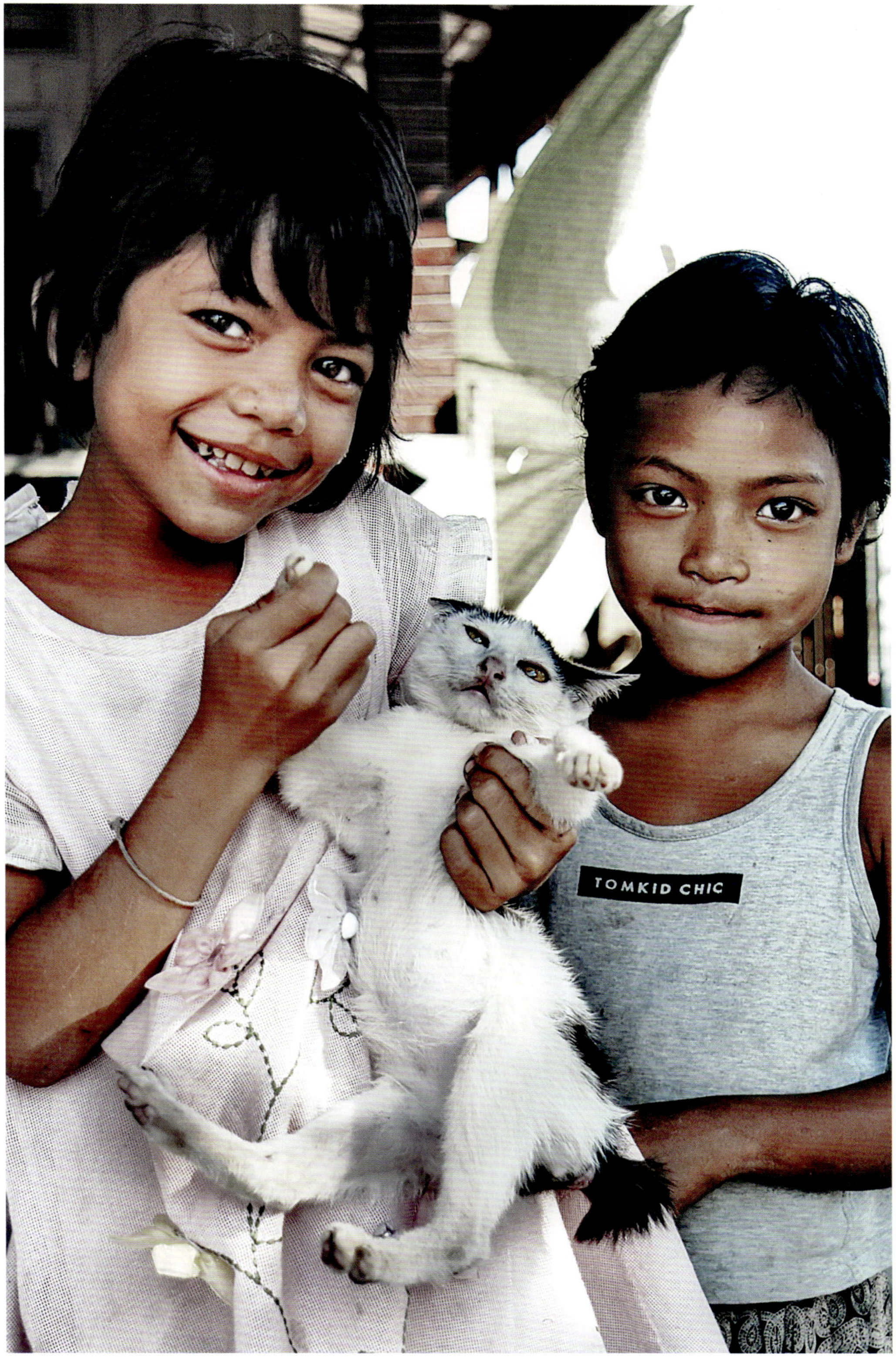

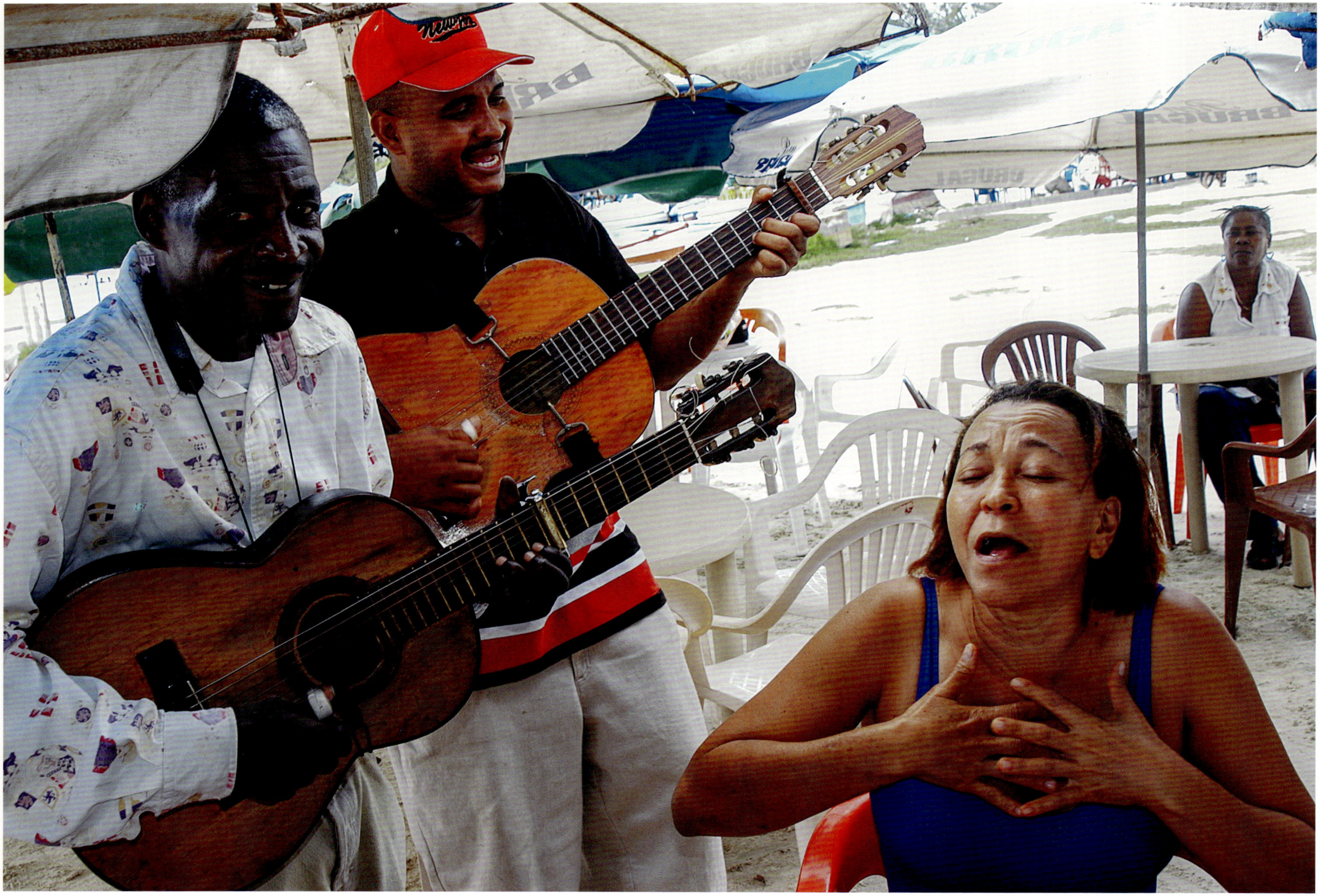

A woman sings and two men play guitar on Boca Chica Beach (Playa Boca Chica). Music is a national treasure in the Dominican Republic.

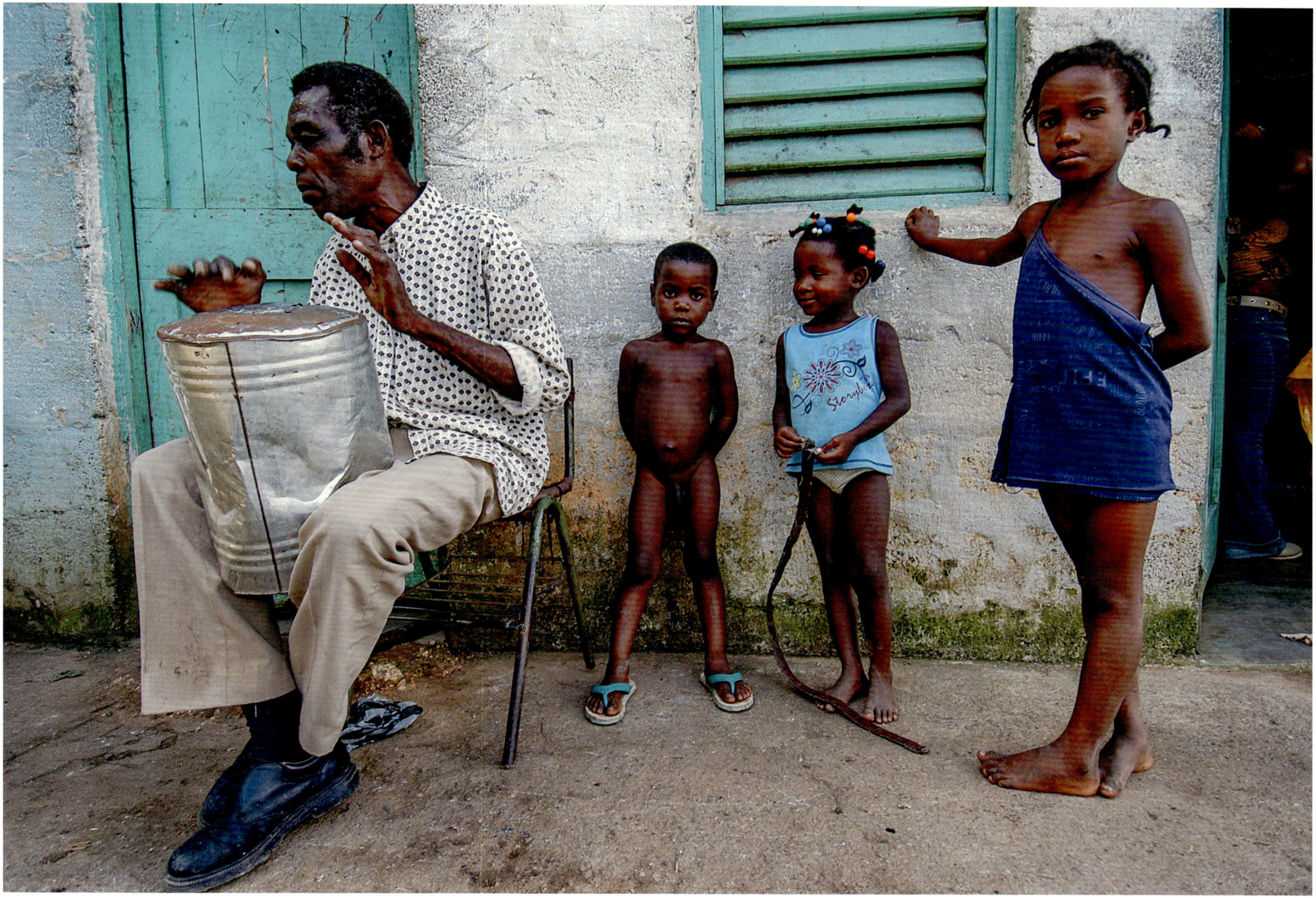

A man uses a makeshift drum to entertain three children.

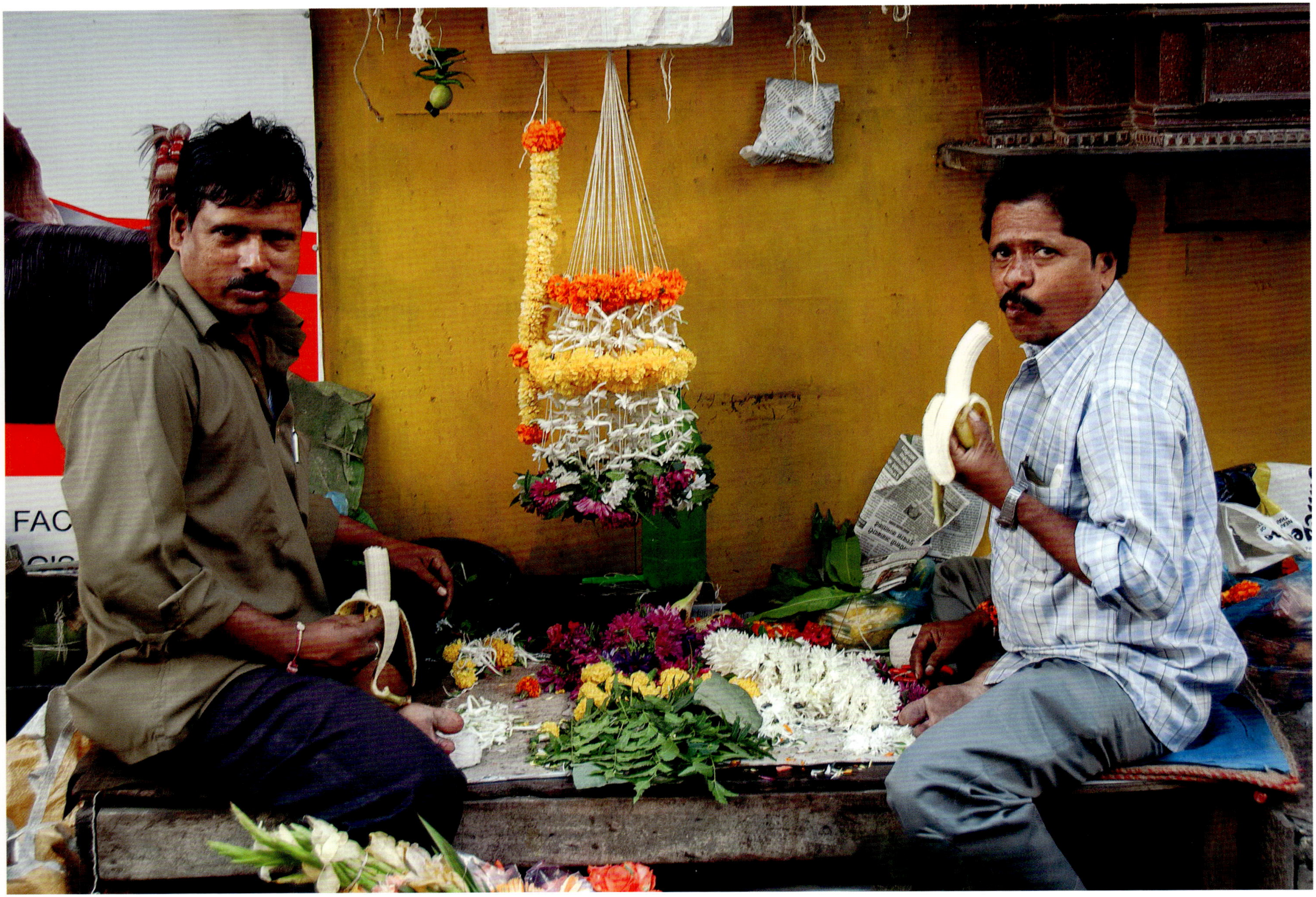

Street florists enjoy a snack on a break from work.

India / Mumbai, Maharashtra

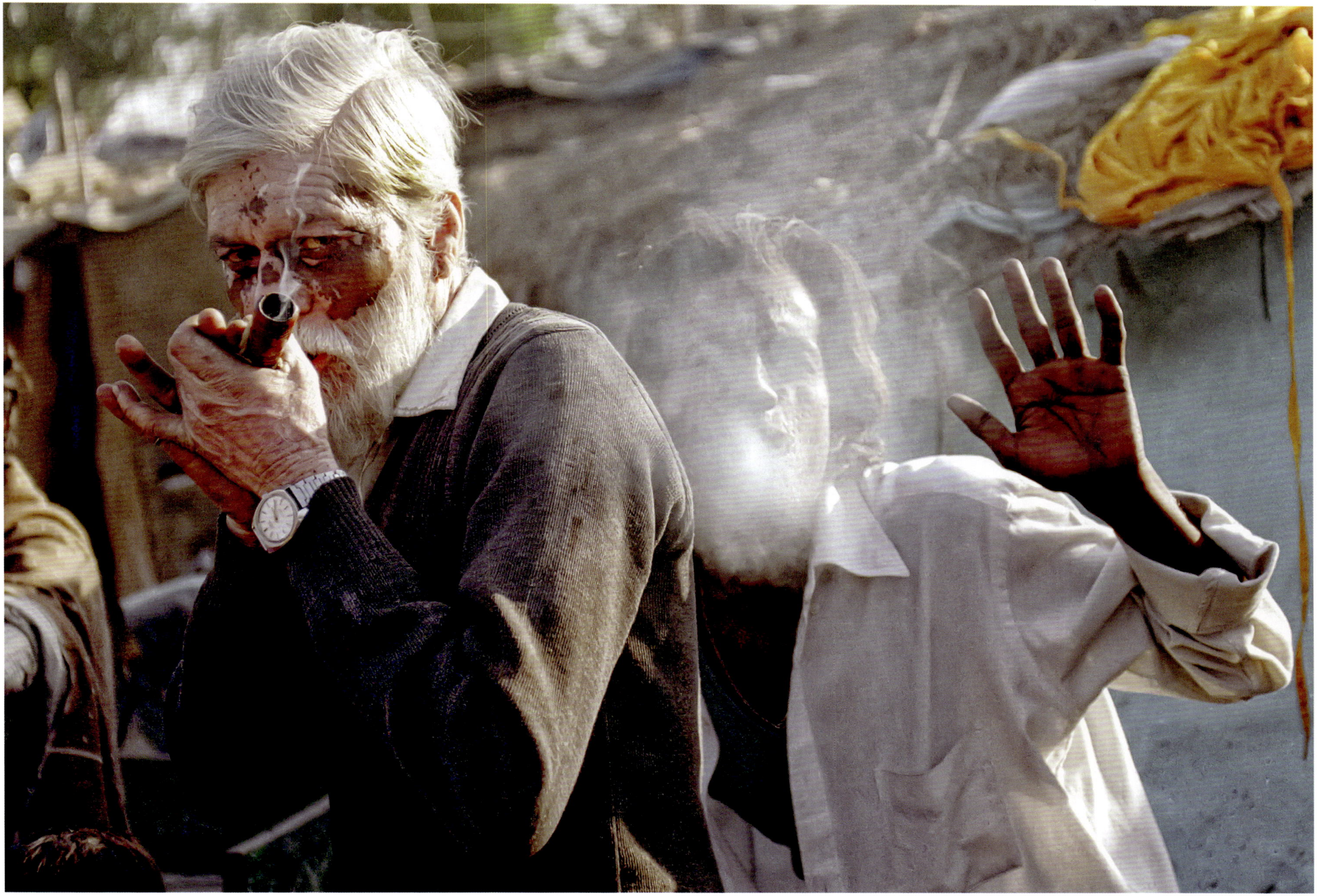

A man with vitiligo smokes from a pipe. Life isn't easy for slum residents like these men, but there are organizations that help. Asha Community Health and Development Society, for example, helps slum residents of Delhi access health care, education, and financial services. Asha means "hope" in Hindi.

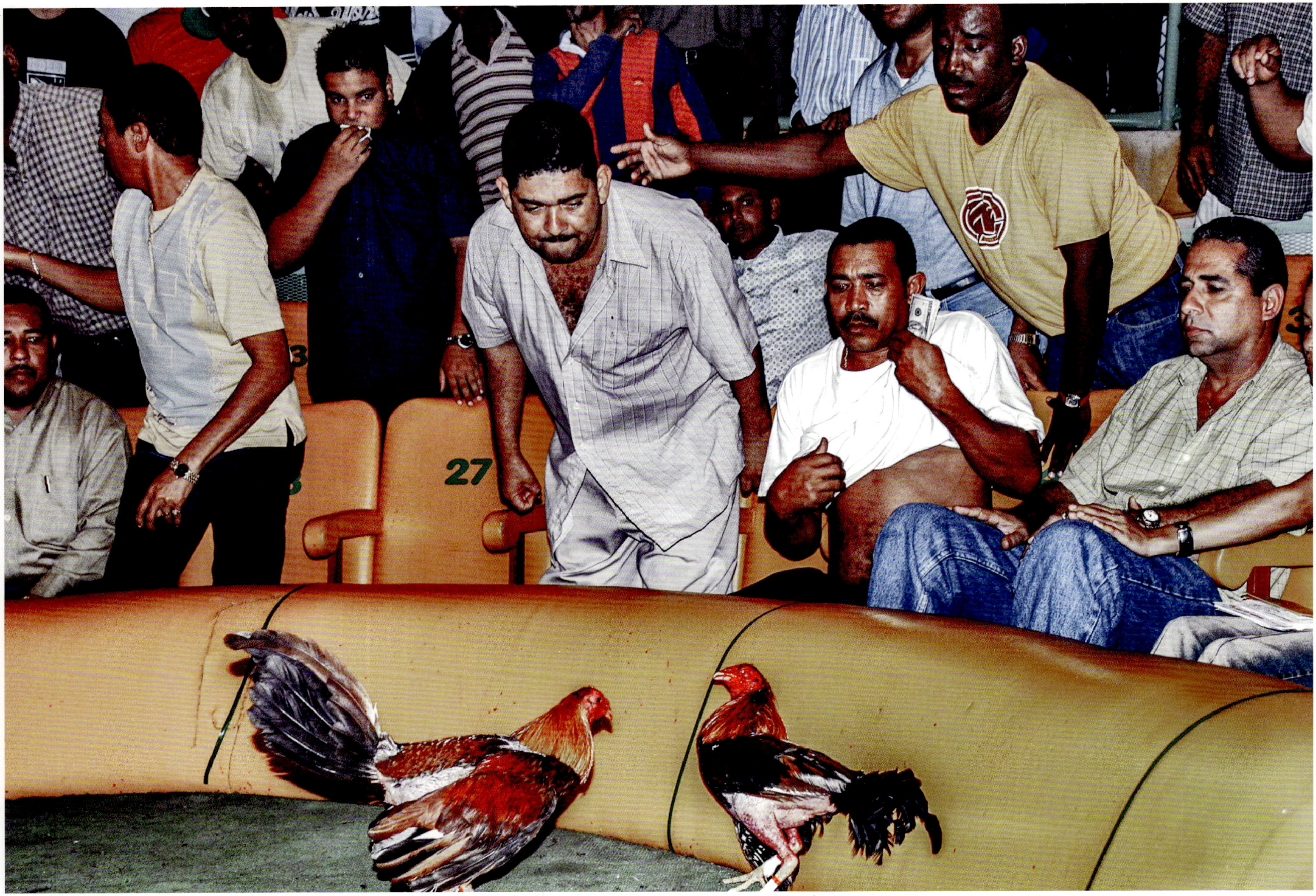

Men in a *gallera*, a cockfight arena, have staged a battle. Dominicans bet on cockfights, which are legal, and some are broadcast on television.

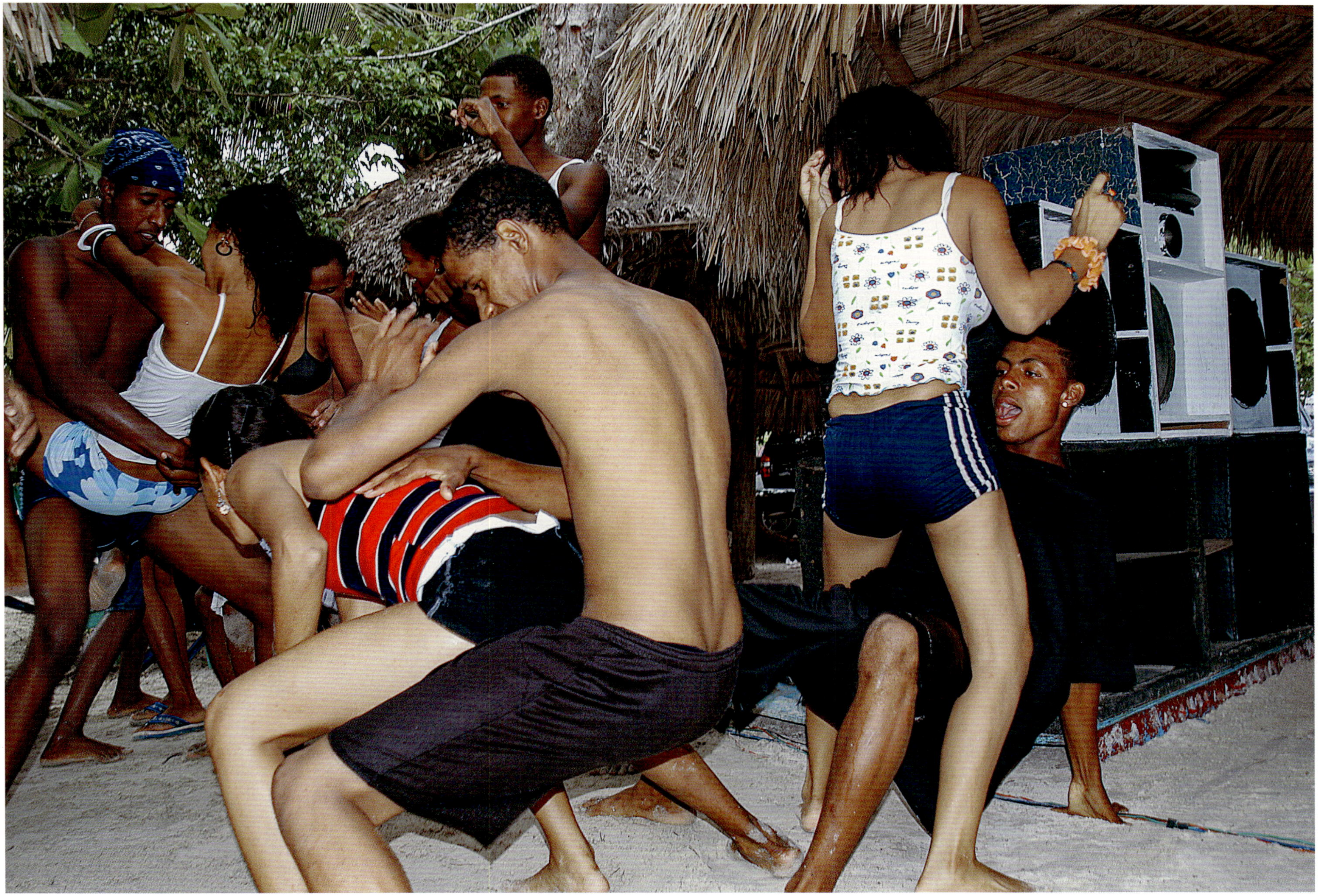

On Boca Chica Beach, lust defines how these teenagers dance. Dominicans have a joie de vivre that is often expressed in their dancing. Dances like the merengue originated in the Dominican Republic.

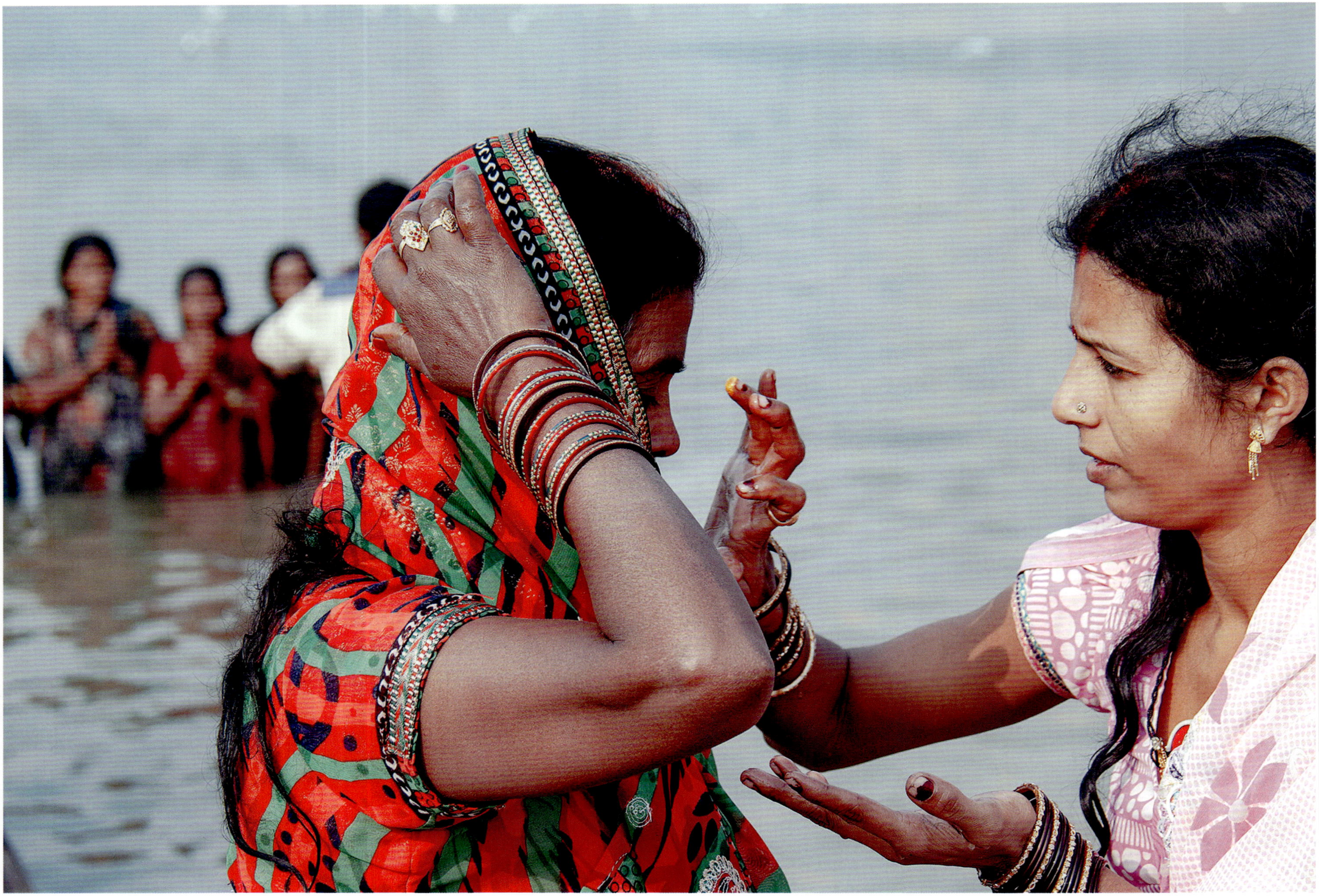

A woman marks another woman with a bindi. Bindis are symbolic of the third eye and much more.

A woman with henna used on her arms for bodily decoration. Henna is often used for celebrations.

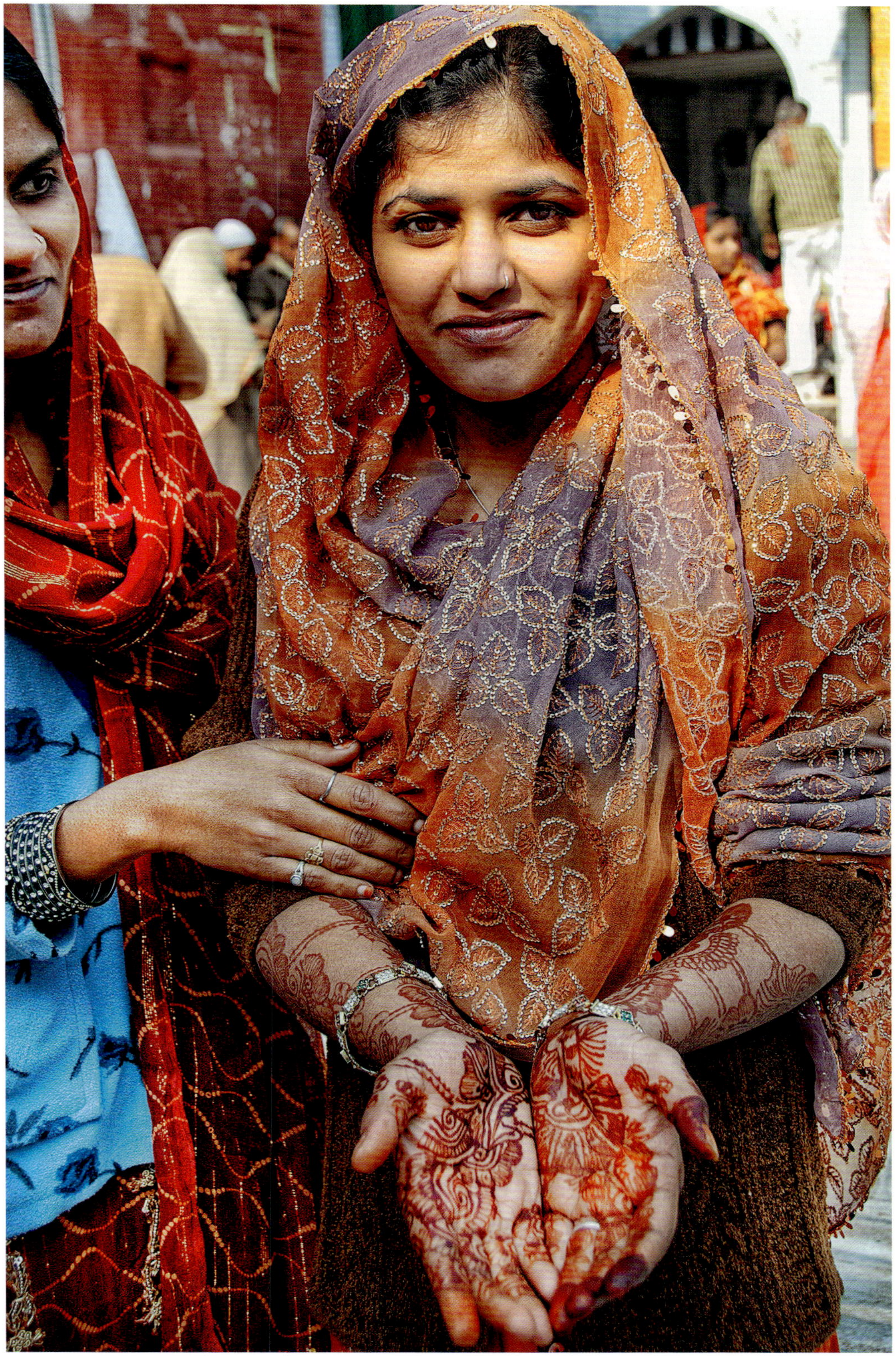

India / Ajmer, Rajasthan

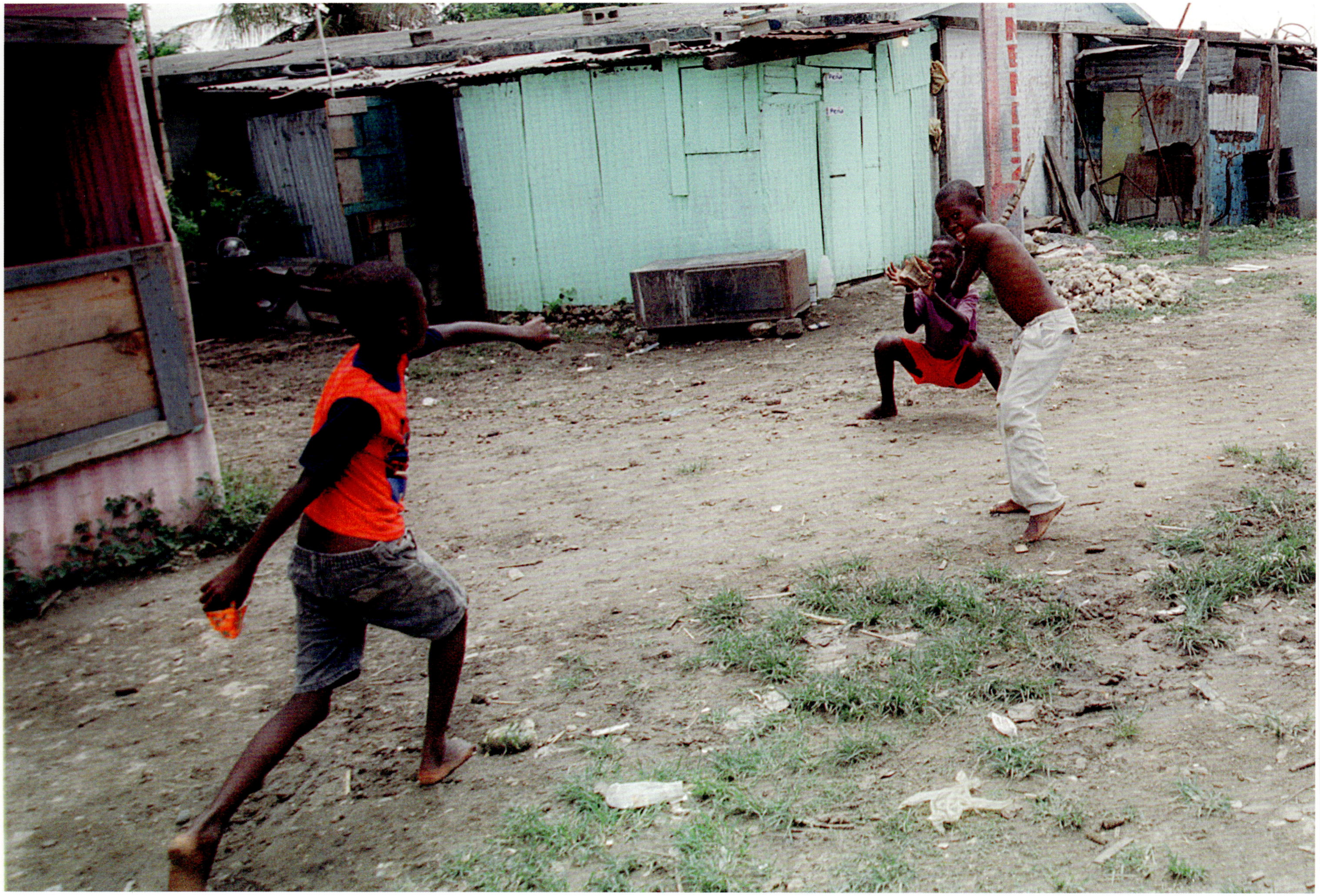

Boys play baseball. There were more than one hundred Dominican players in Major League Baseball on opening day in 2019, the first time players from a nation outside of the United States reached triple digits. Many of these men are born into poverty in Dominican slums. Acquiring an MLB deal is the fantasy of many Dominican children.

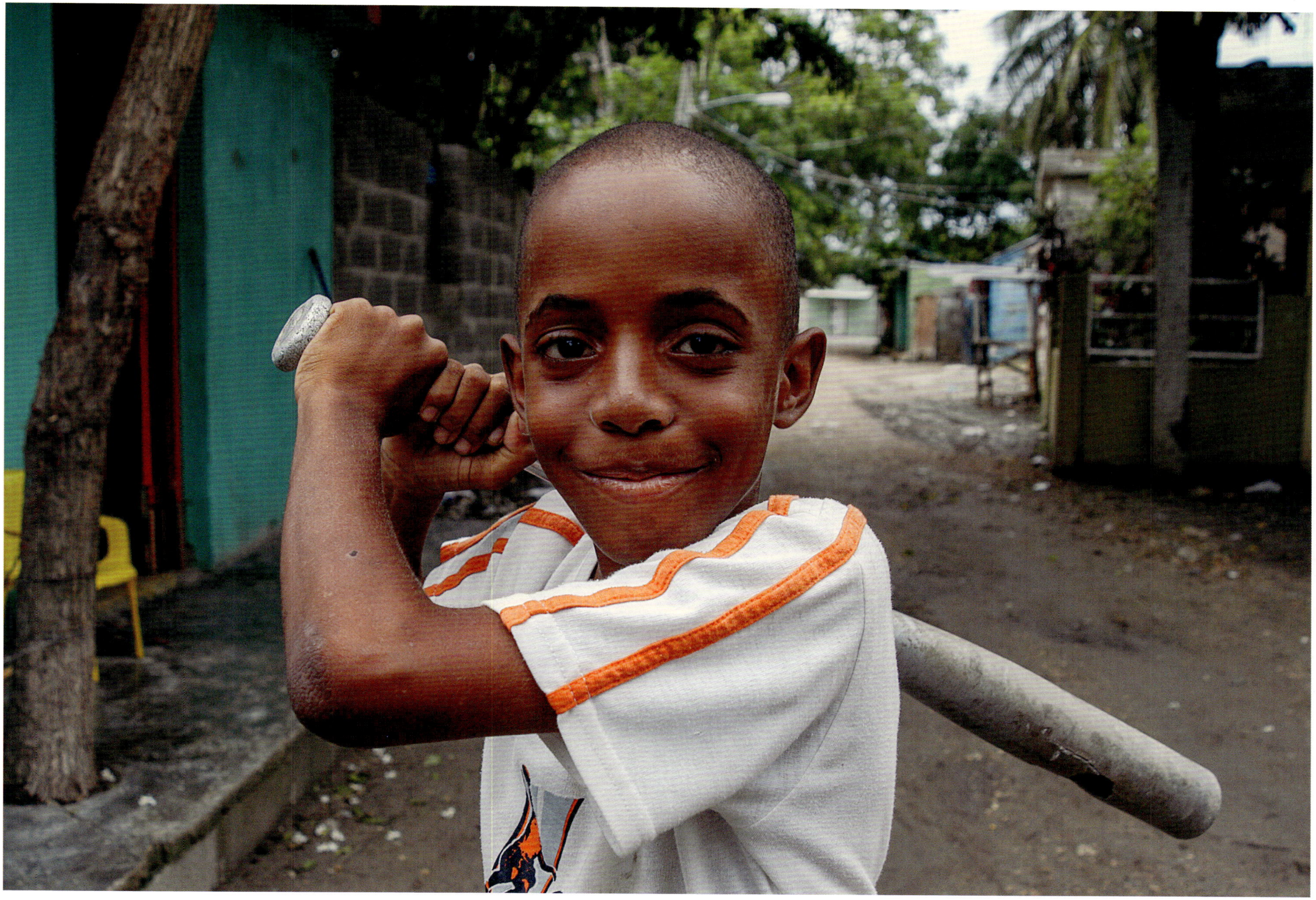

A boy and his bat.

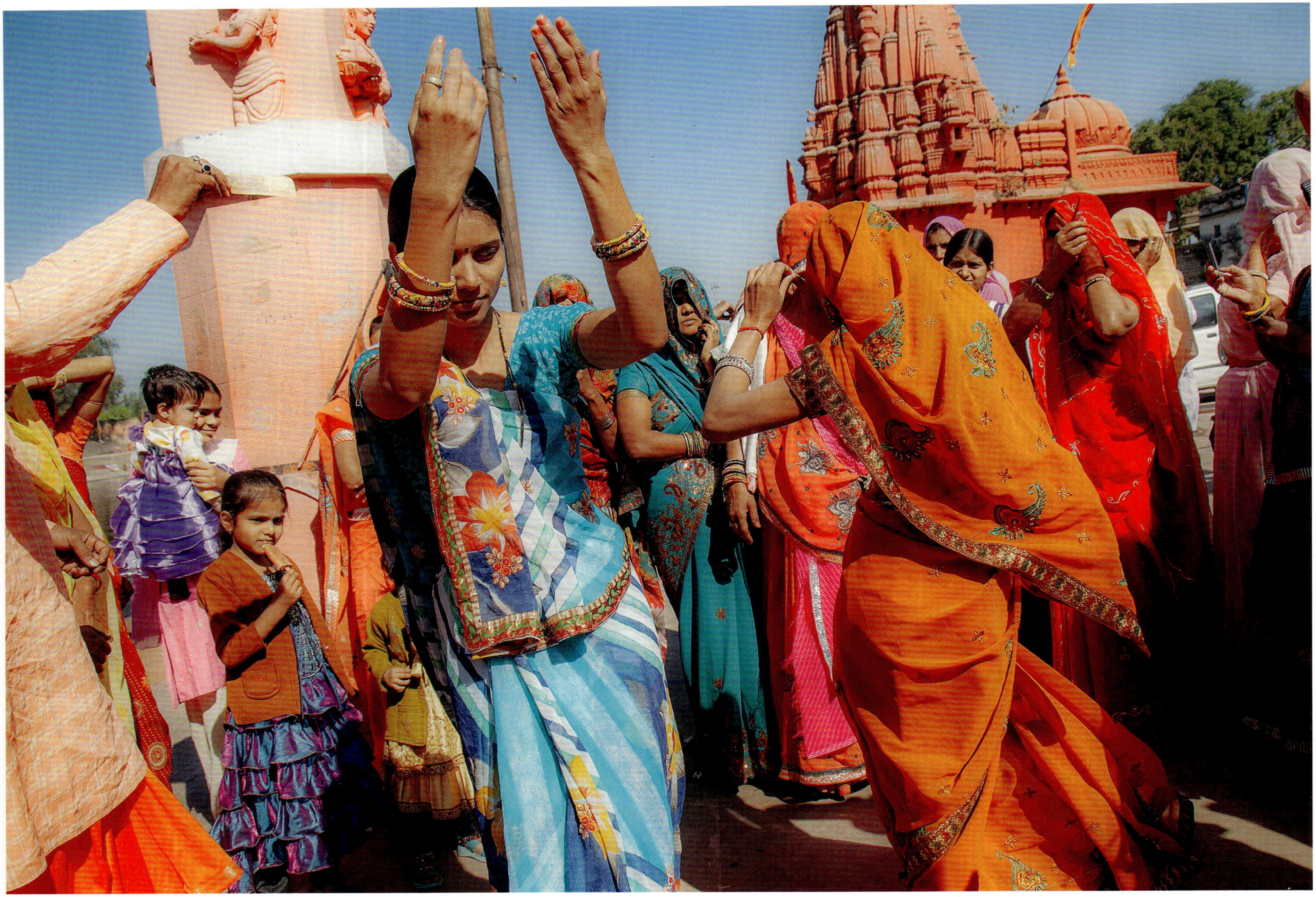

A woman at a wedding in Ujjain, one of the four cities that hold a Kumbh Mela.

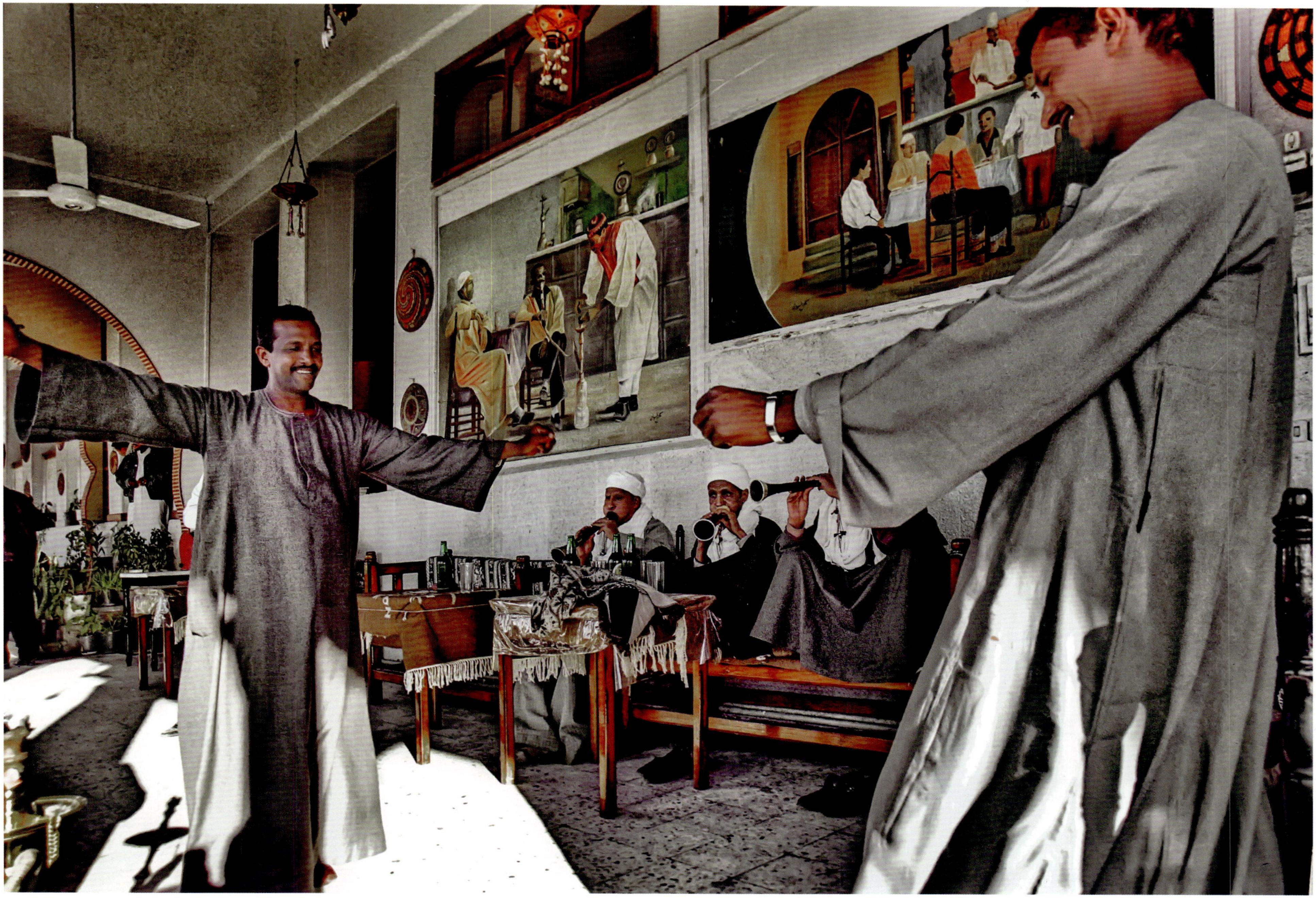

At dinnertime in a café, men dance with one another as musicians play and beer flows.

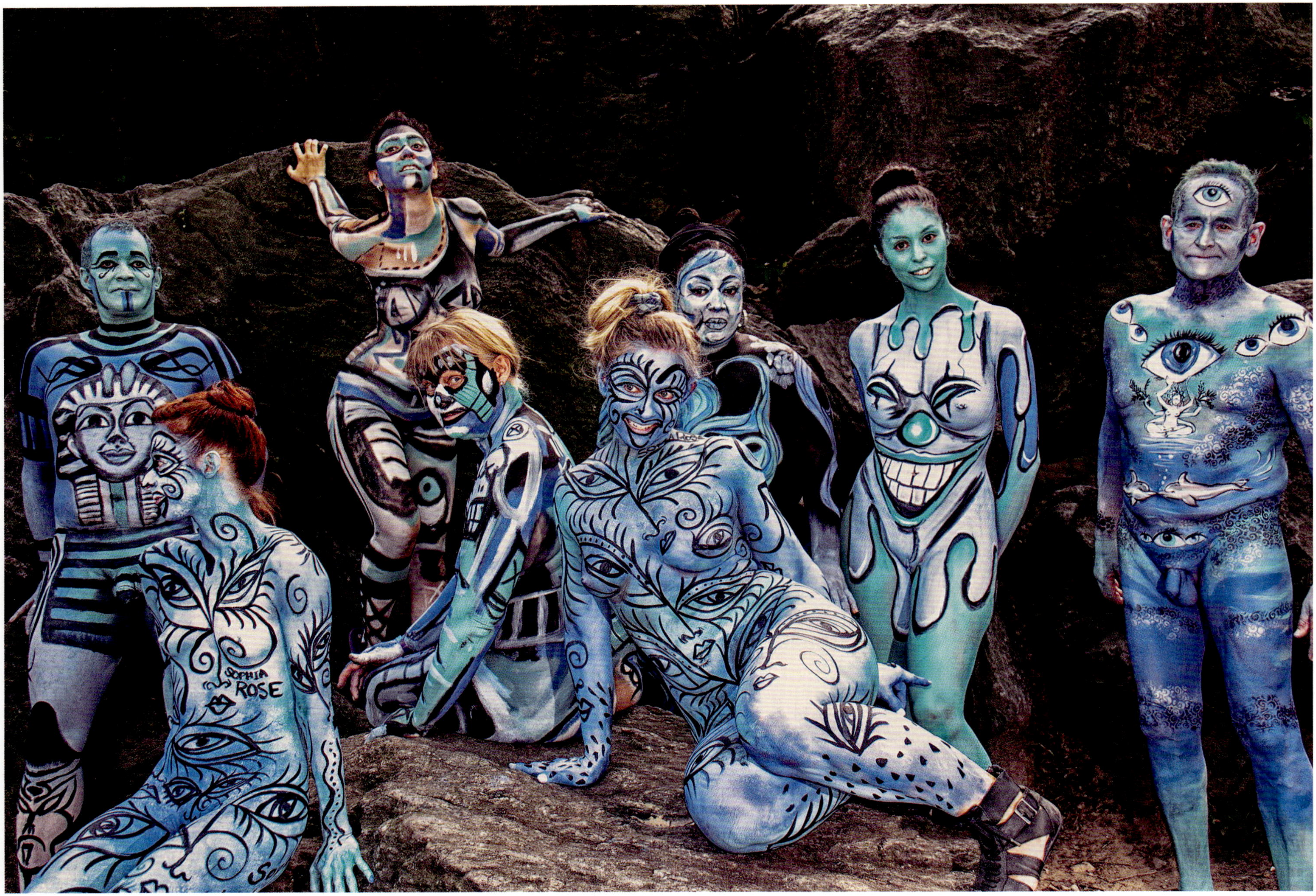

Every year on Body Painting Day, people celebrate the beauty of the human body. Painted in the nude, they march around Manhattan and show off their decorative designs. Here they are in Central Park.

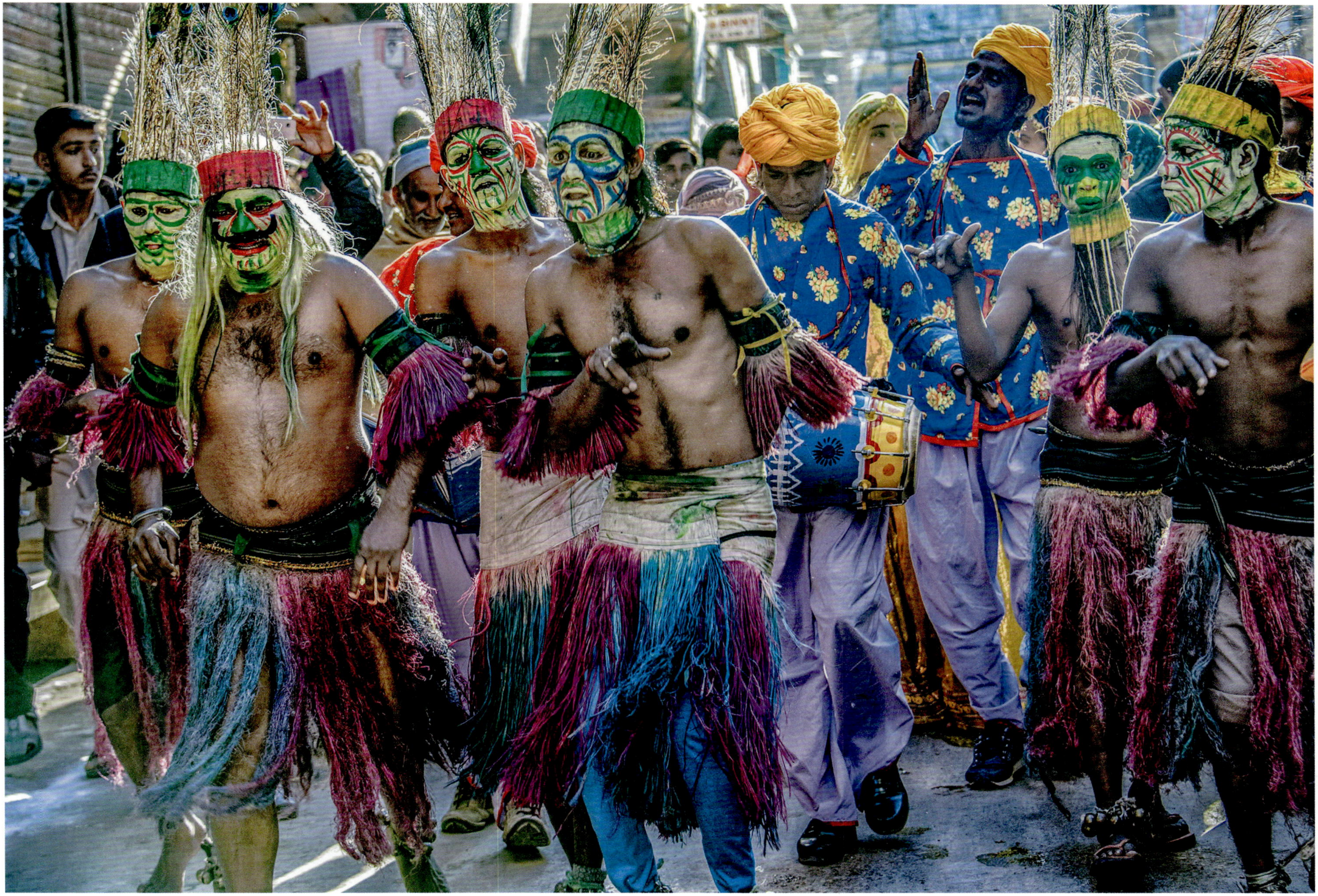

Performers at the Jaisalmer Desert Festival. The festival takes place every February and is intended to show off the traditional culture of Rajasthan in western India.

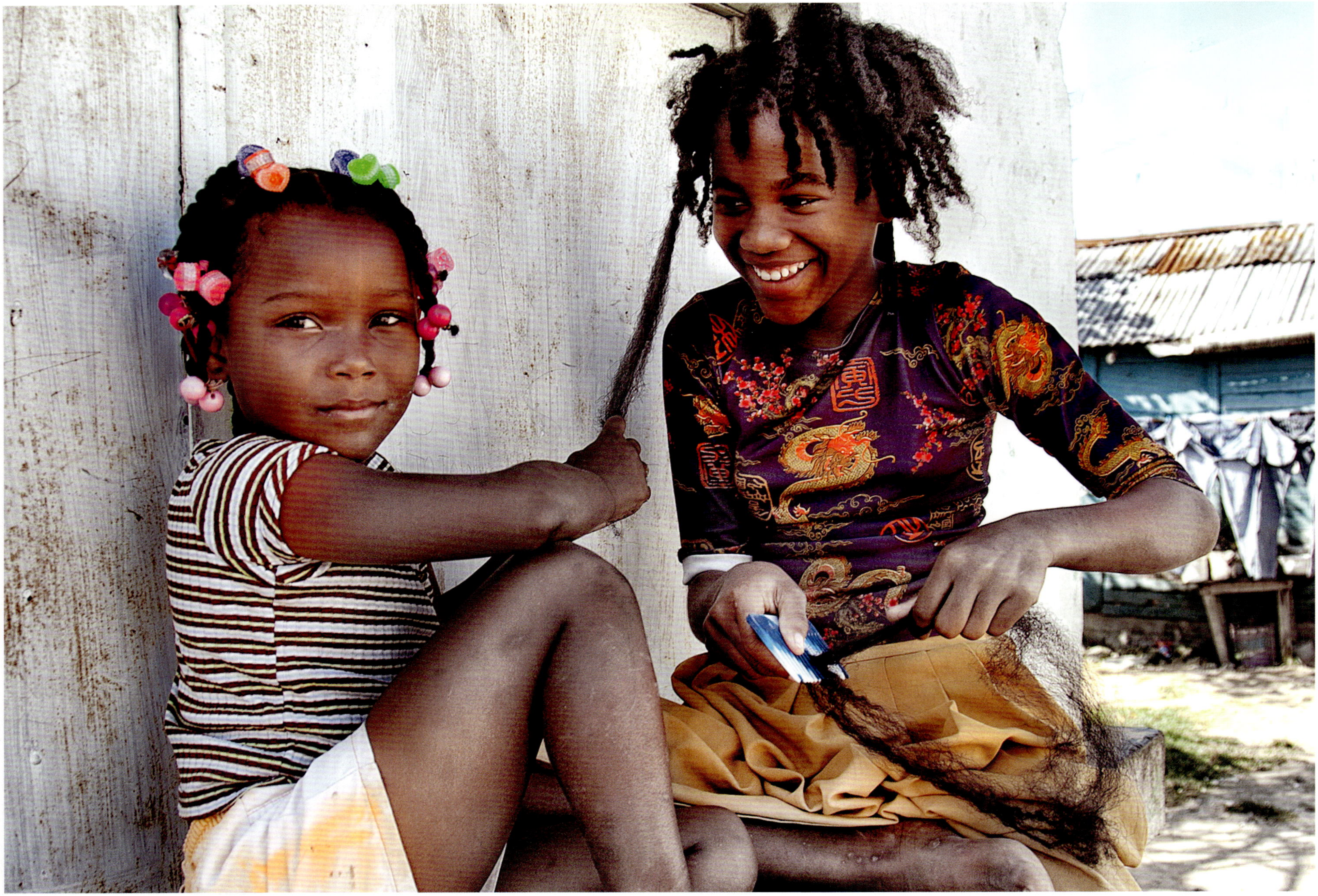

Though Dominicans tend to have curly, textured hair, the culture has long favored straight hair. Curly hair is called *pelo malo*, which translates to "bad hair," and many women feel pressured to treat it. These girls experiment with straightening.

A girl and her doll in a Sante Fe slum.

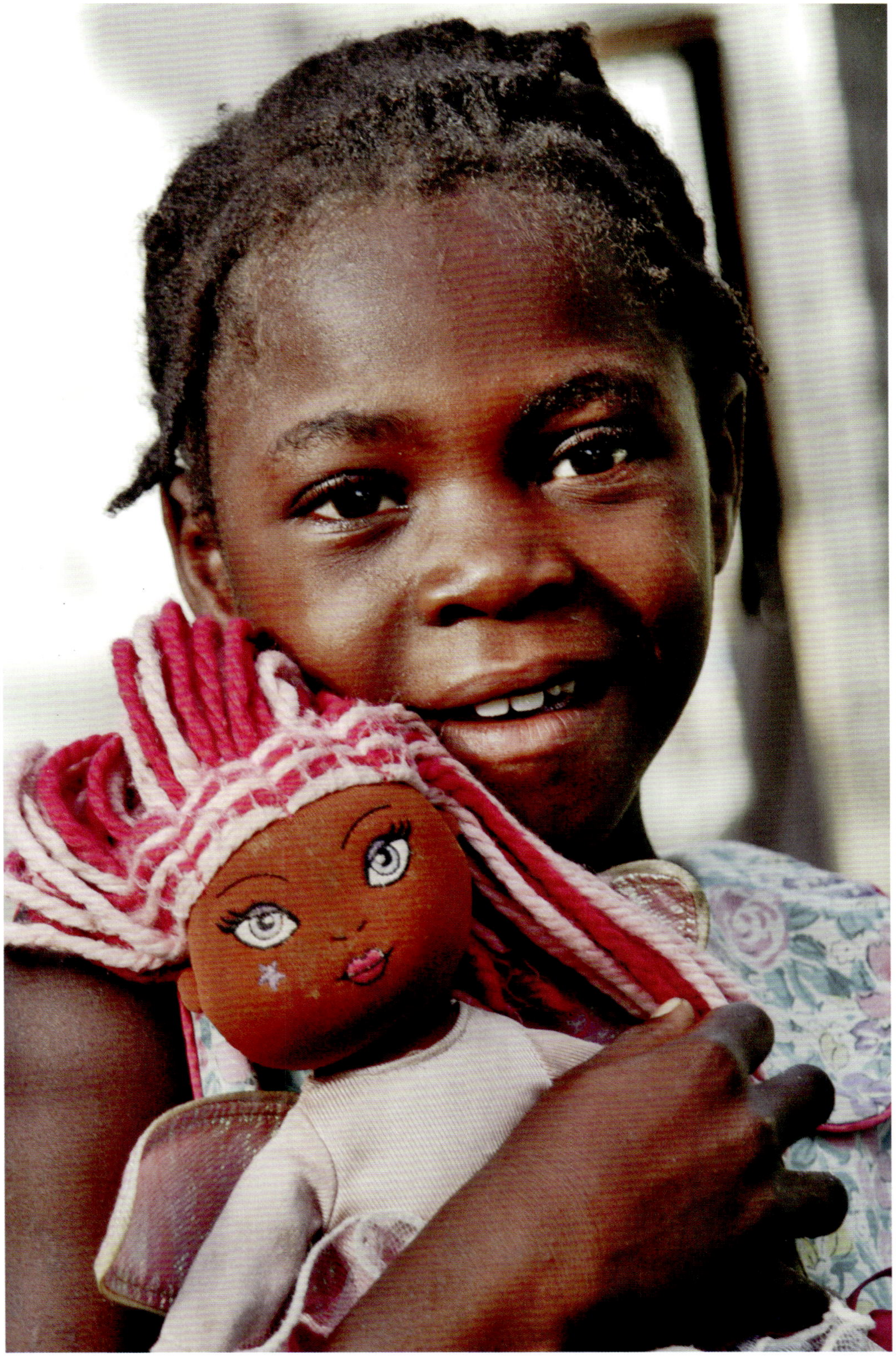

Dominican Republic / San Pedro de Macorís, San Pedro de Macorís Province

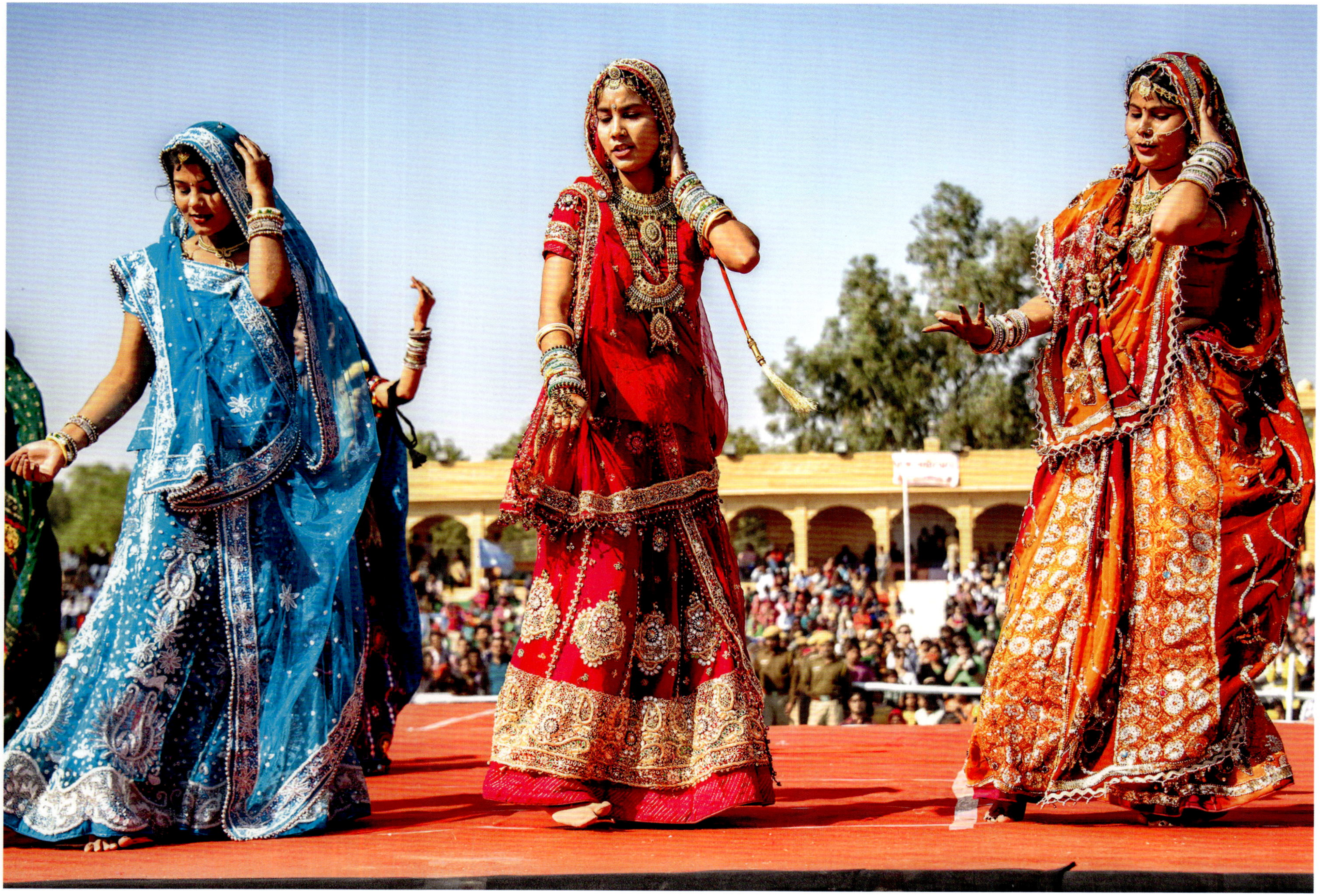

Performers at the Desert Festival in Jaisalmer. It can reach 125 degrees Fahrenheit in the summer.

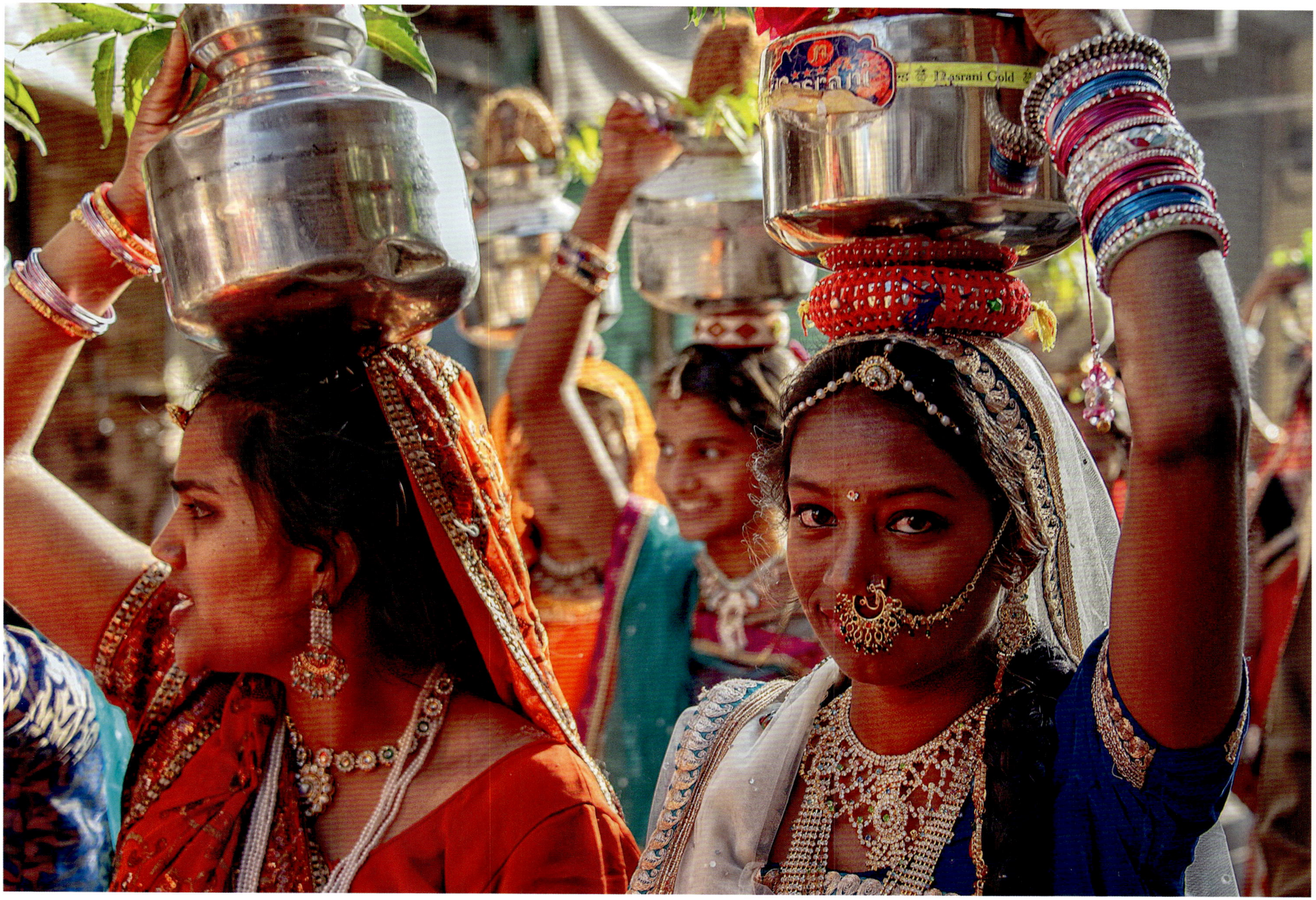

Women at the Desert Festival.

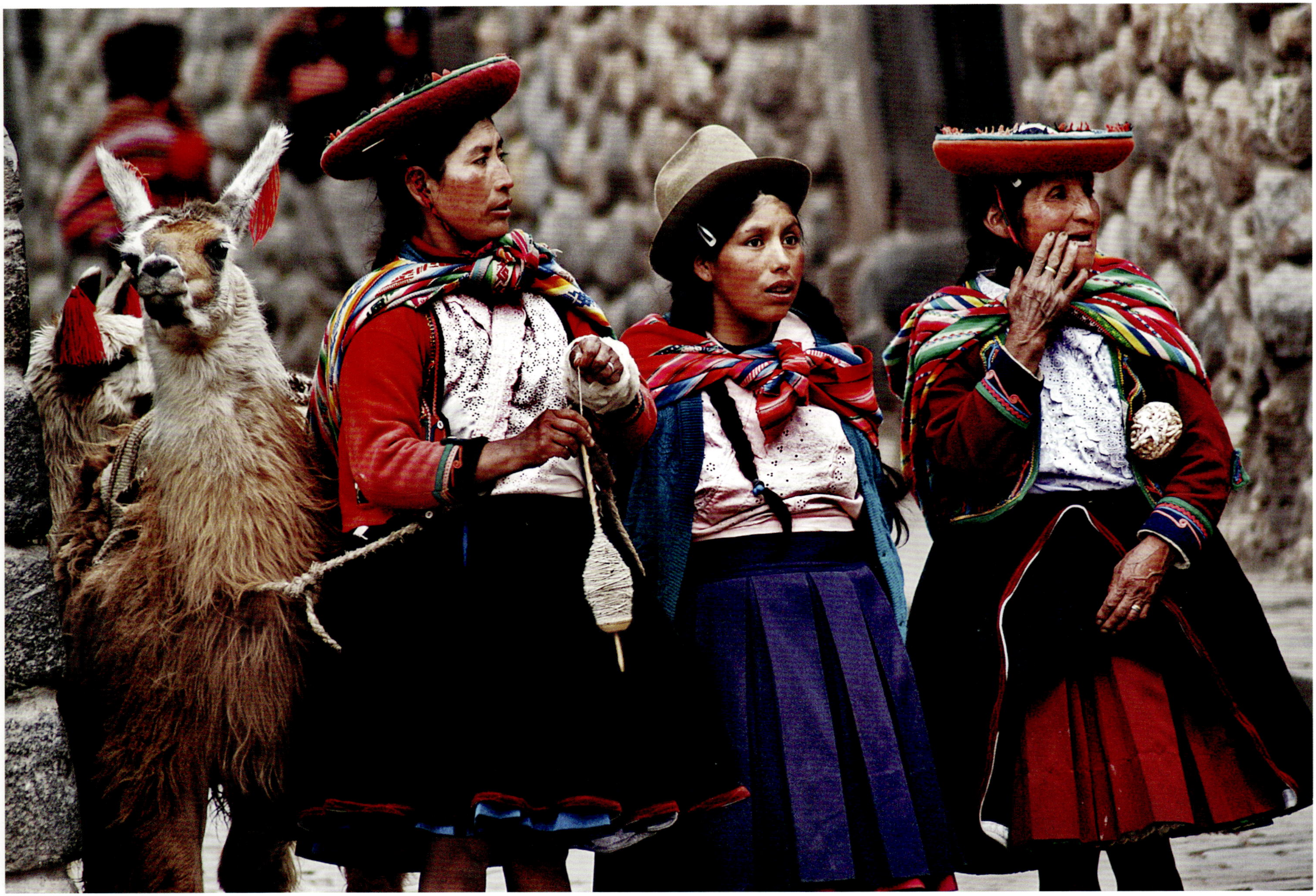

"Take a picture, mister!" This is the phrase that tourists hear while walking around the streets of Cuzco. It comes in the high and delicate voices of *cholitas*, women dressed in traditional clothing, and is accompanied by smiles as they hold their llama, alpaca, or lamb. The women offer the tourists the opportunity to take a picture of them and then hold out their hand for anything the tourists wish to hand over.

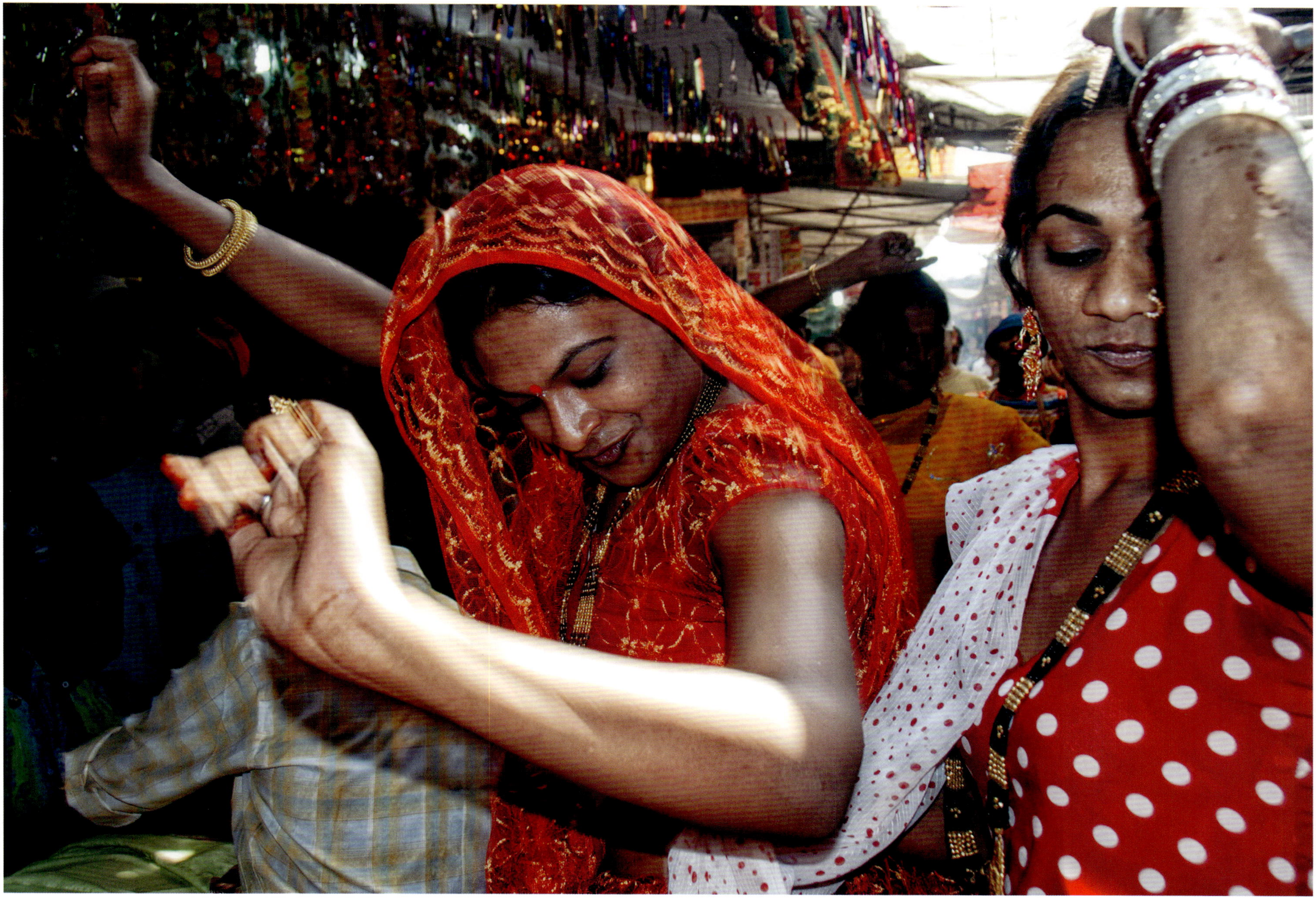

Hijras, who include transgender and intersex people, dance at the Haji Malang shrine atop the Malang Gad hill, which takes three hours to summit. Loud drums accompany the dancing, and onlookers throw money at the performers.

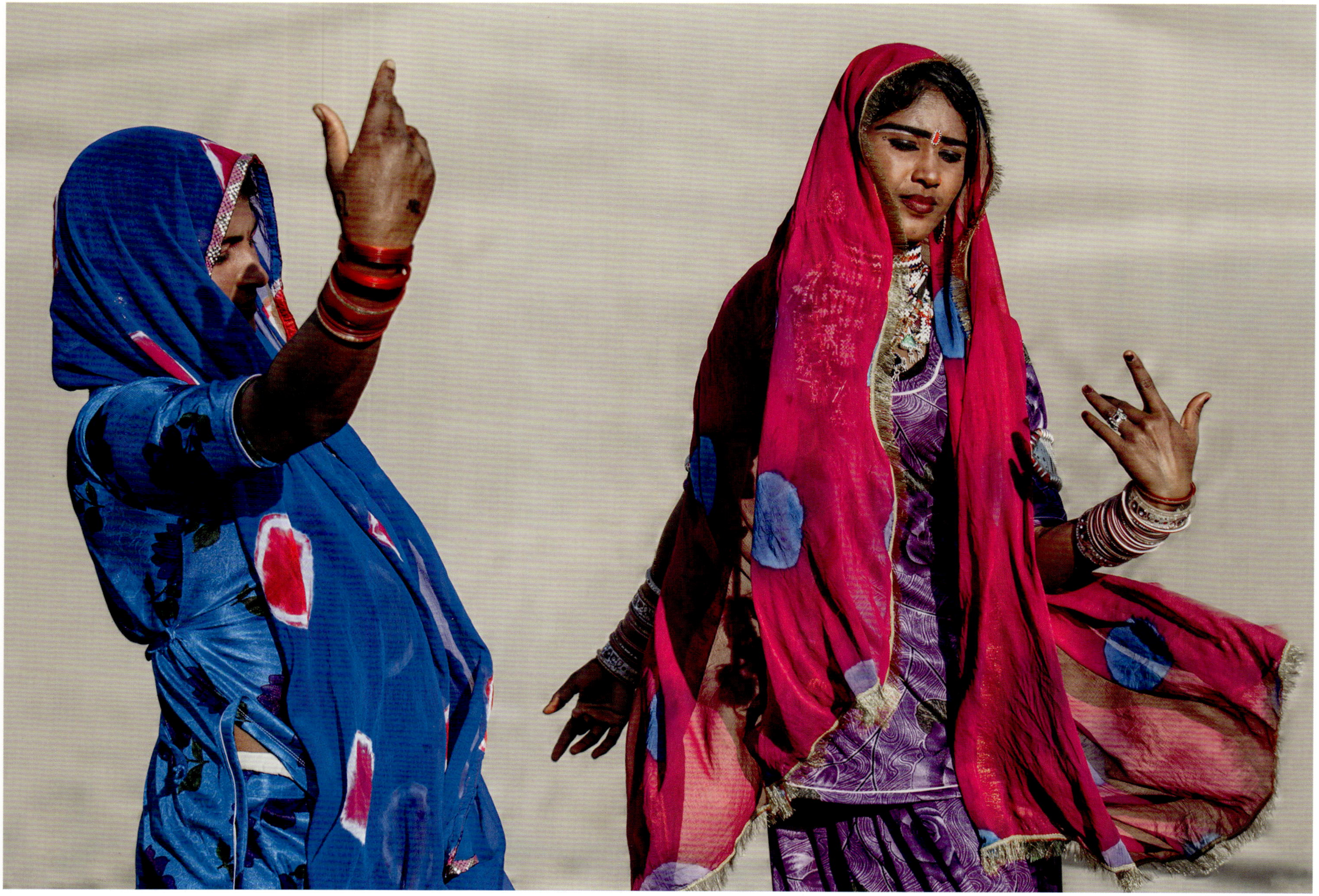

Roma perform for baksheesh in the tourist-heavy Sam Sand Dunes, located in western Rajasthan near the Pakistani border.

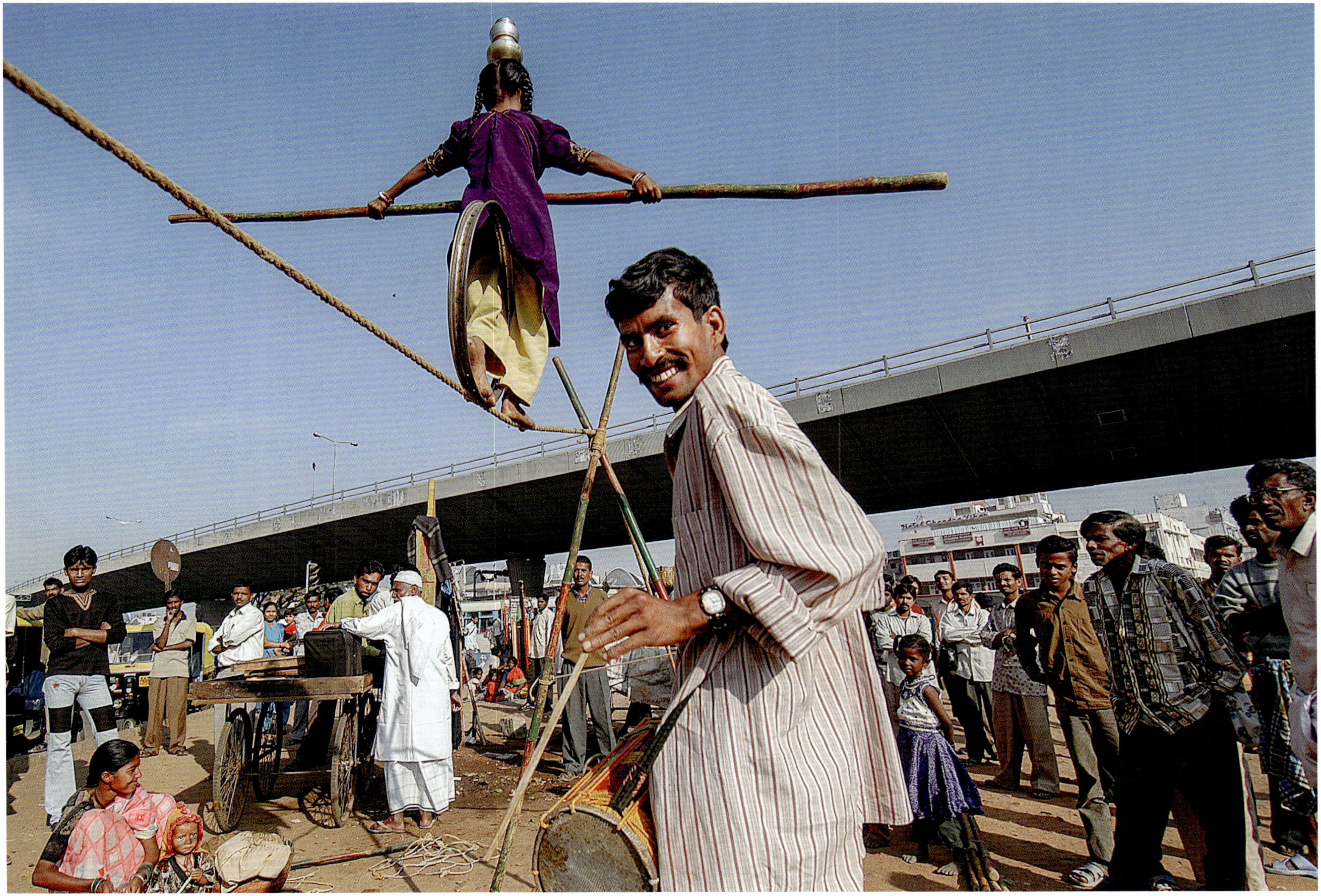

This street performance is a common type of entertainment in India. Crowds surround the act to watch; some people give money, and some don't.

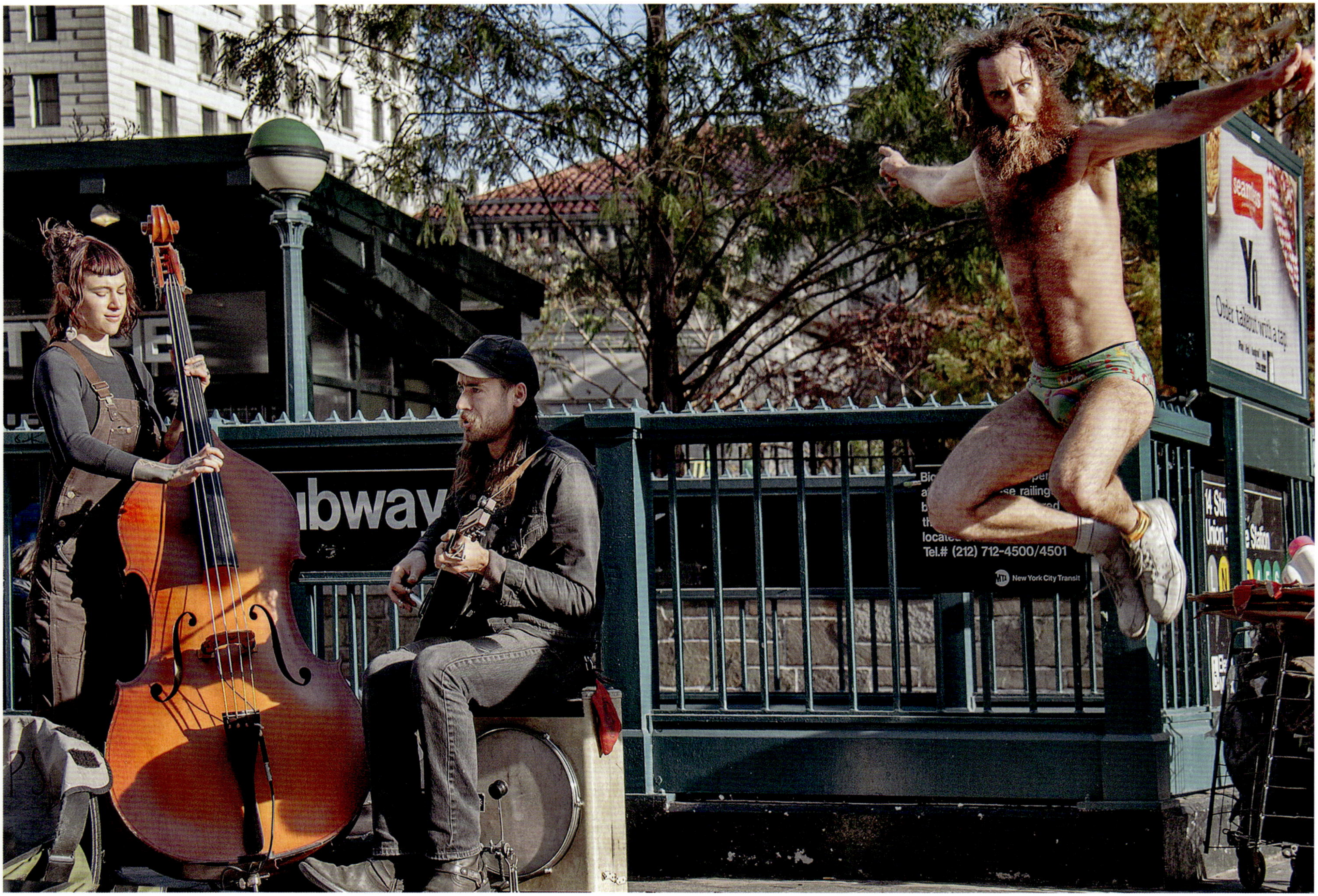

Performers outside the Union Square subway stop; one is comical (if not bordering on insane), and the others are good musicians from the South.

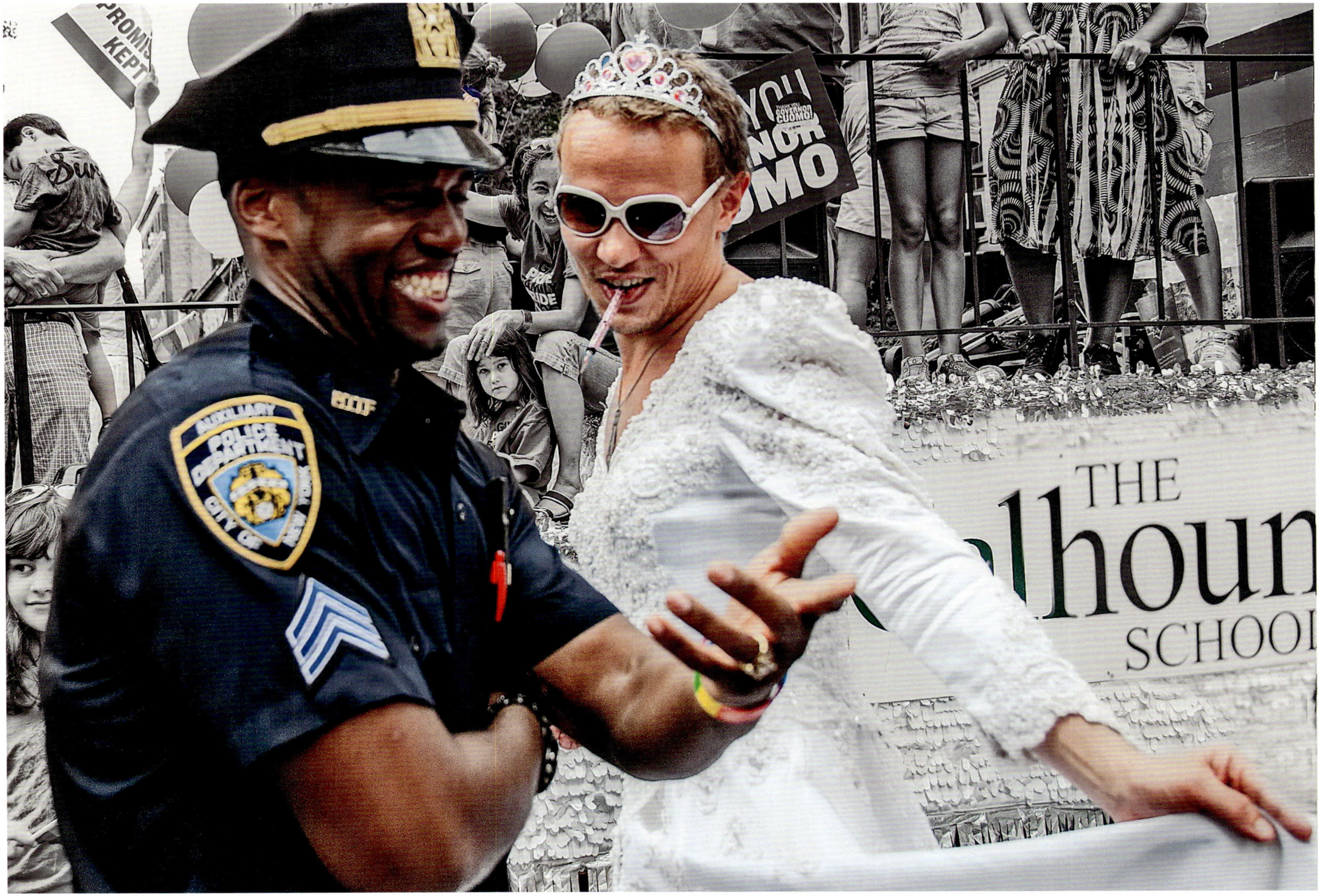

At the New York City Pride March, a cop and an attendee share a smile.

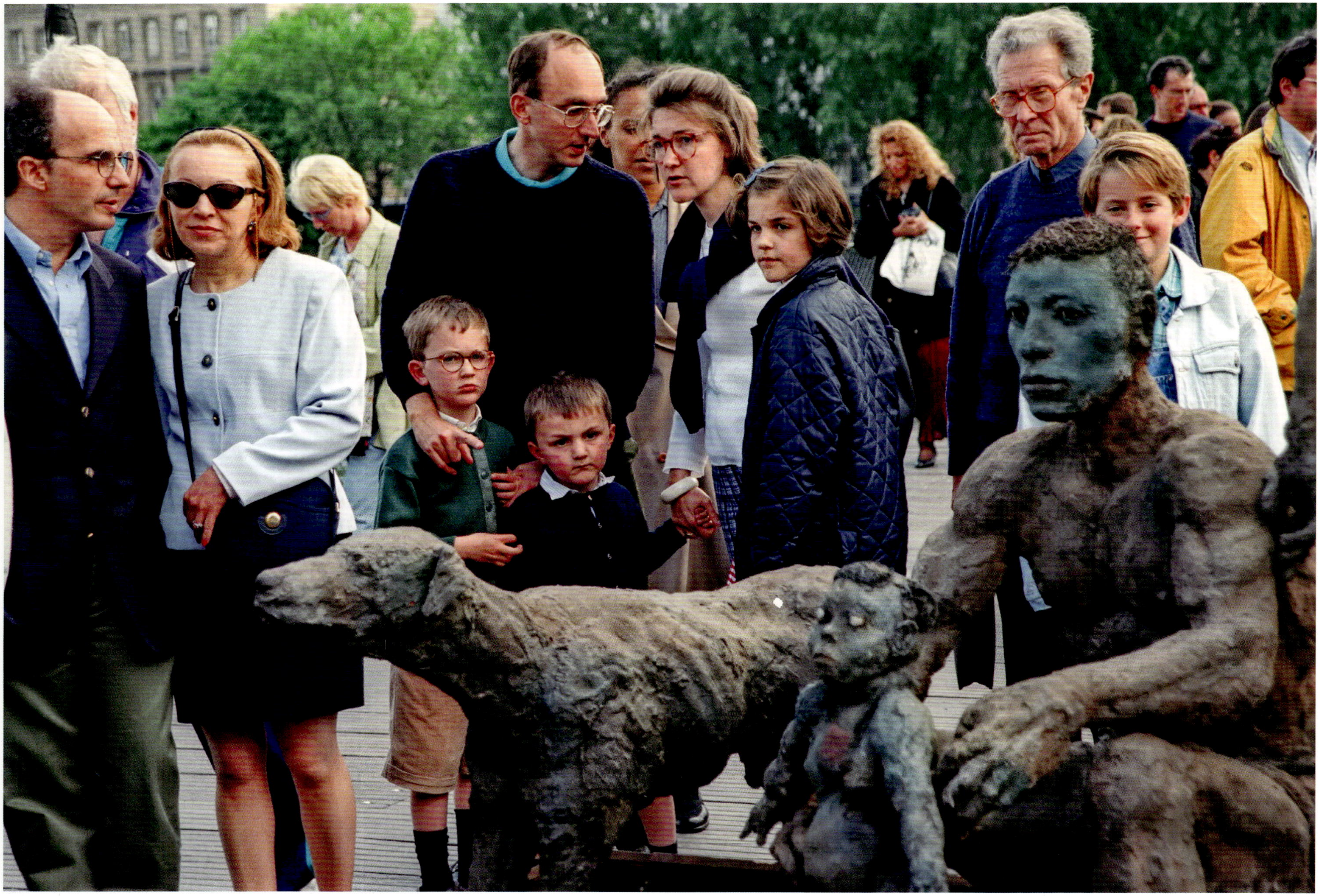

A street performer attempts to convey tribal Africa to onlookers in Paris.

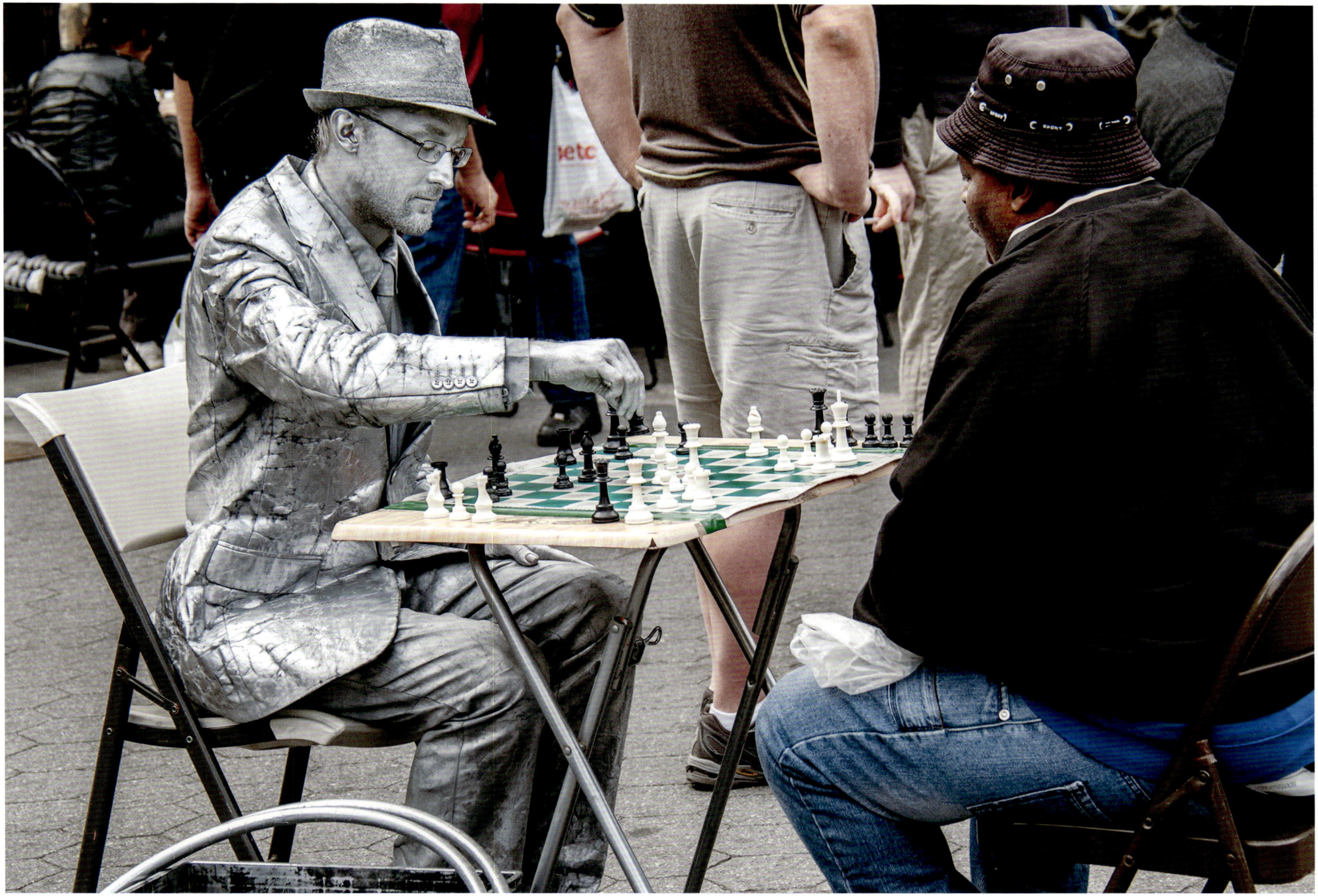

A mime plays chess in Union Square.

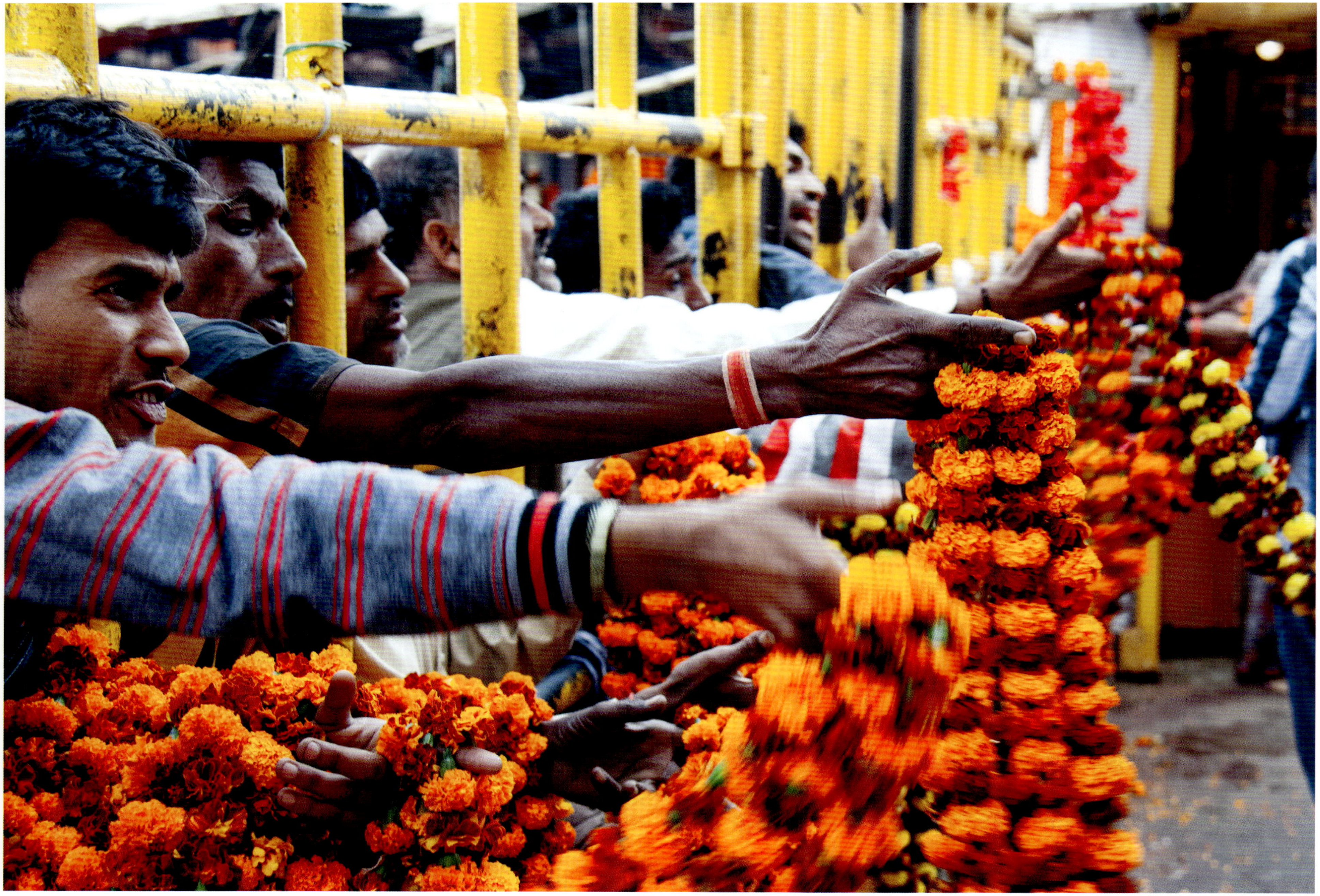

Men sell garlands made from marigolds outside of a temple in Patna.

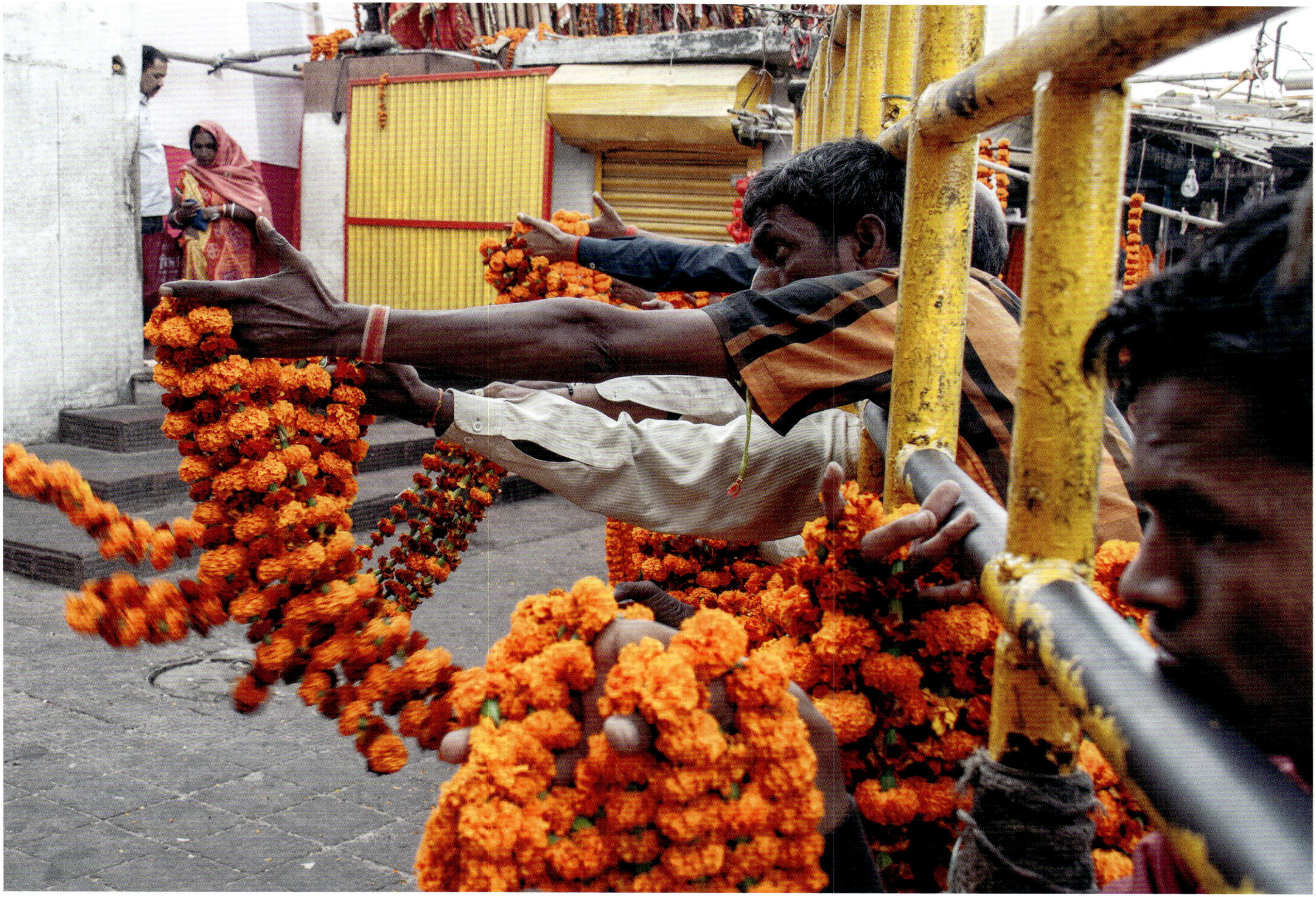

Brightly colored marigolds come from Mexico but have become ubiquitous in India, both as auspicious symbols in celebrations and for practical purposes such as insect repellent.

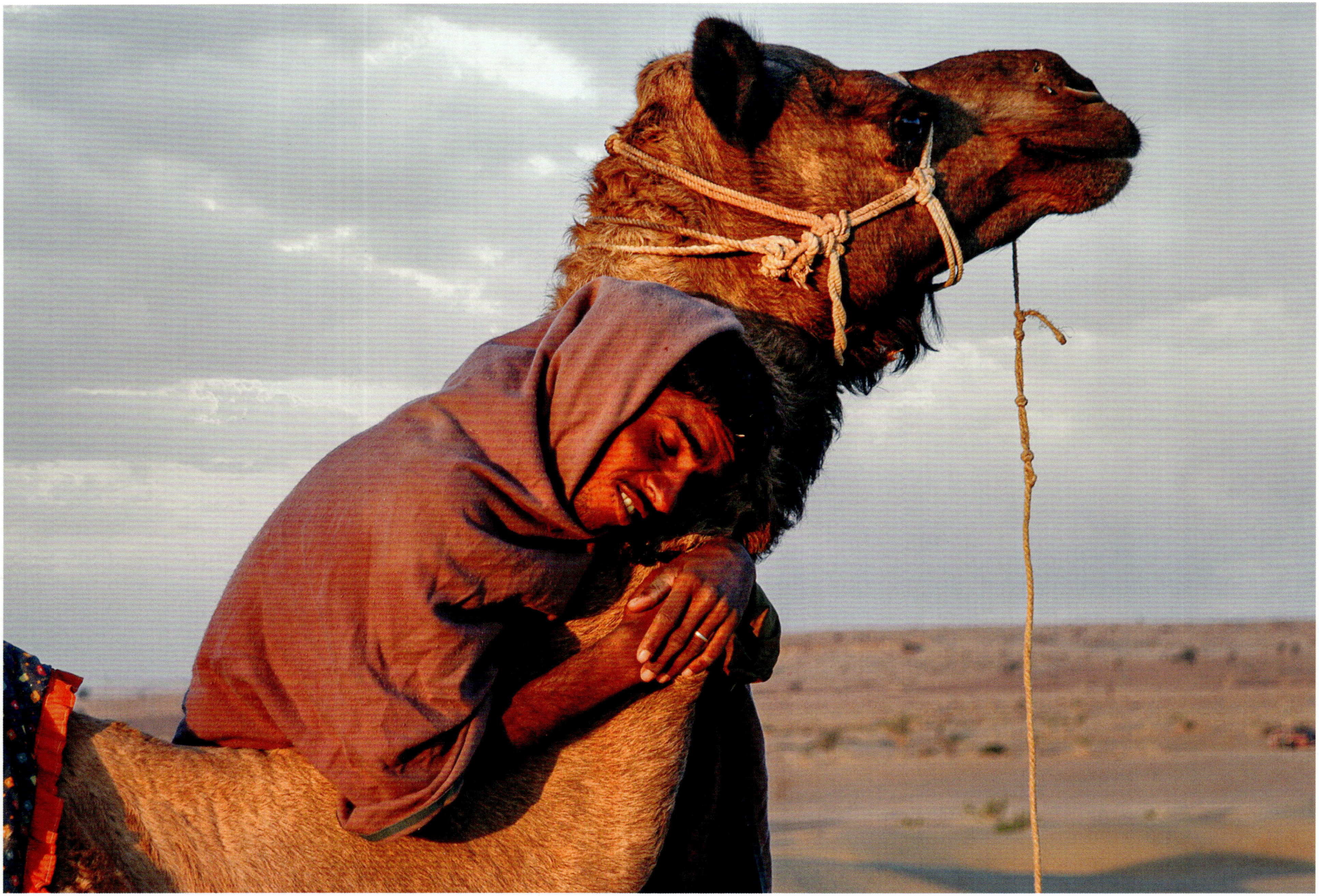

This is the end of the road before Pakistan. In the Sam Sand Dunes, a desert dune site near Jaisalmer, camel riding is offered as a tourist activity.

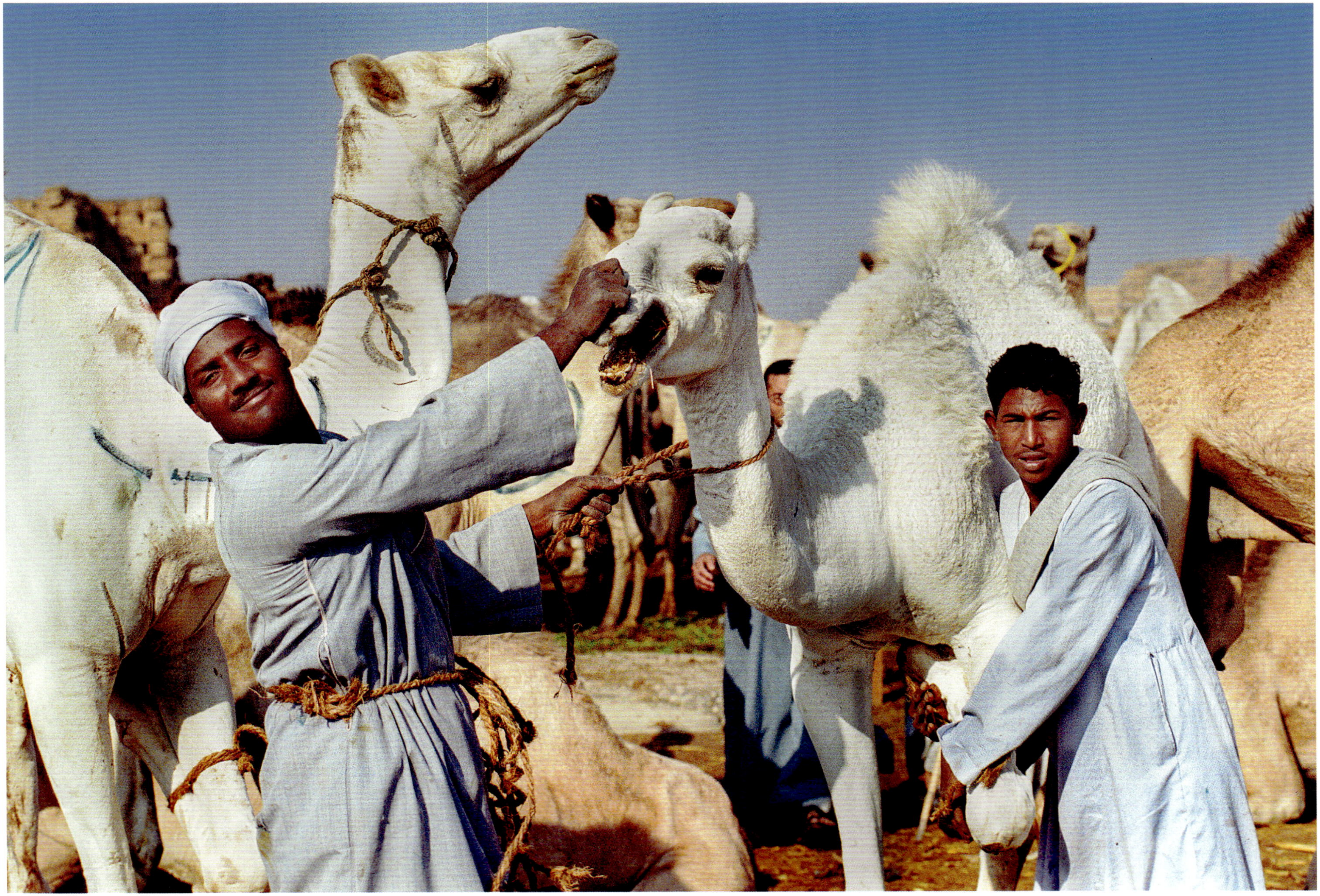

Two men at the Birqash Camel Market near Cairo where camels are bought and sold.

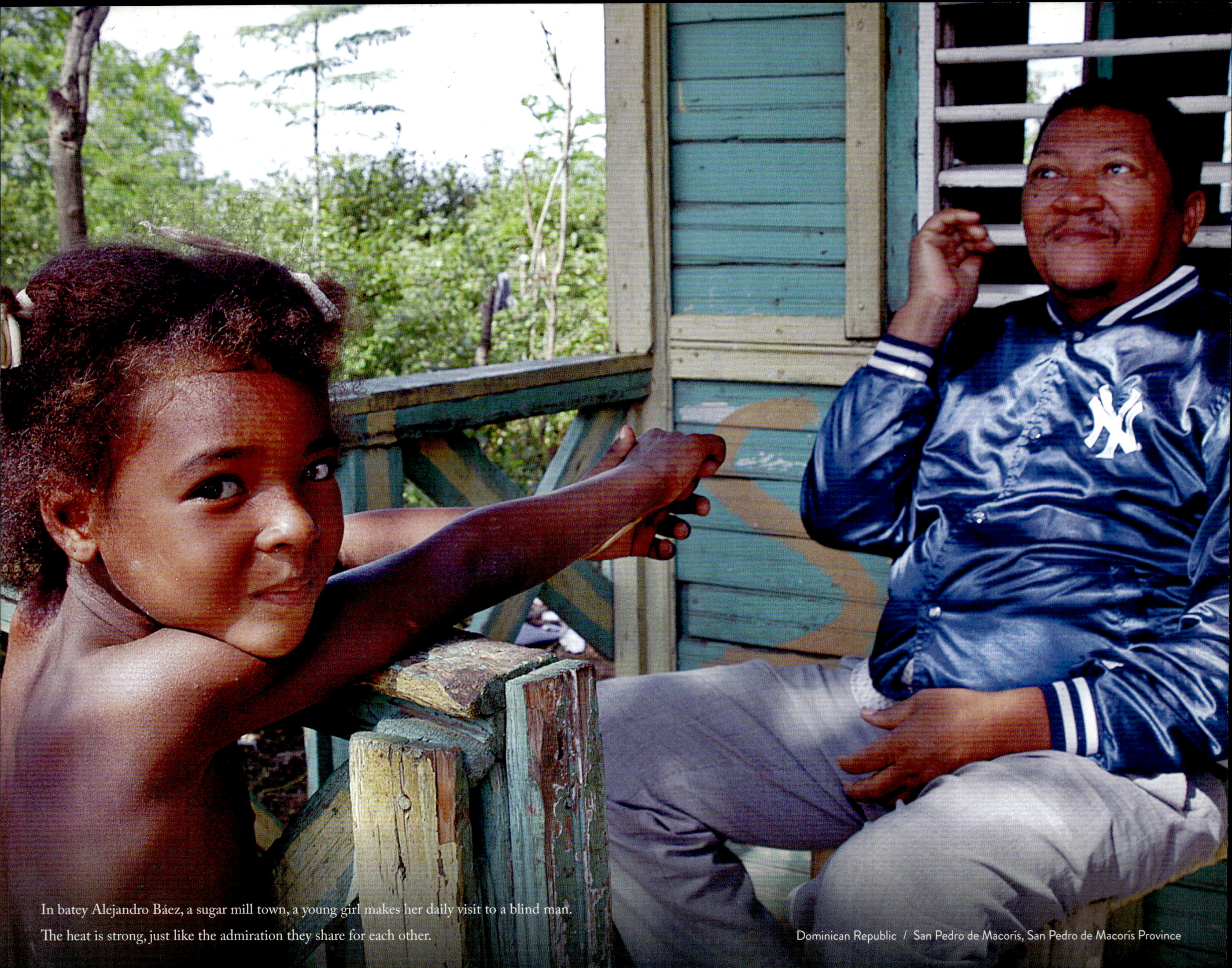

In batey Alejandro Báez, a sugar mill town, a young girl makes her daily visit to a blind man. The heat is strong, just like the admiration they share for each other.

Dominican Republic / San Pedro de Macorís, San Pedro de Macorís Province

CONNECTION

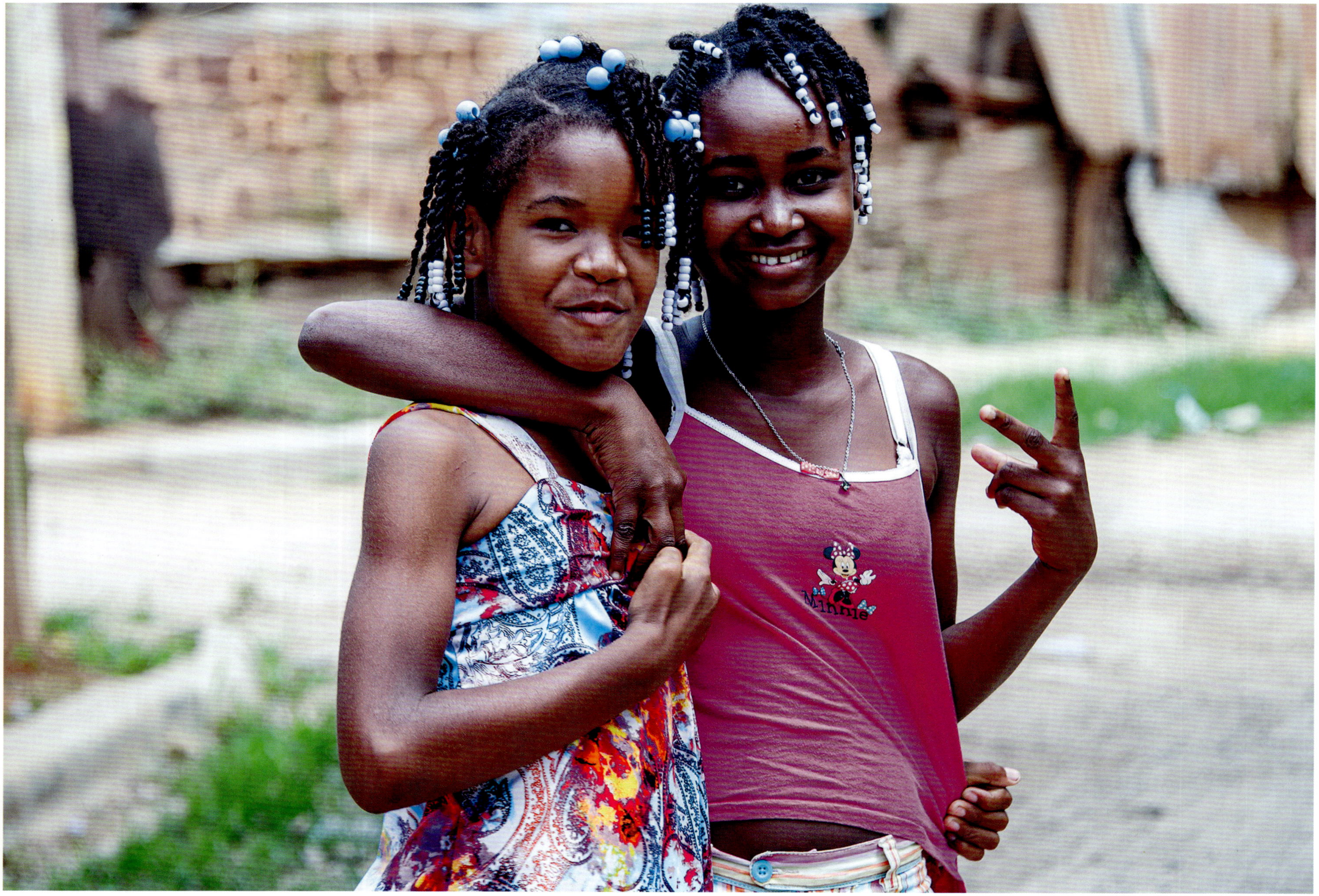

Friends smile for the camera while one flashes a peace sign.

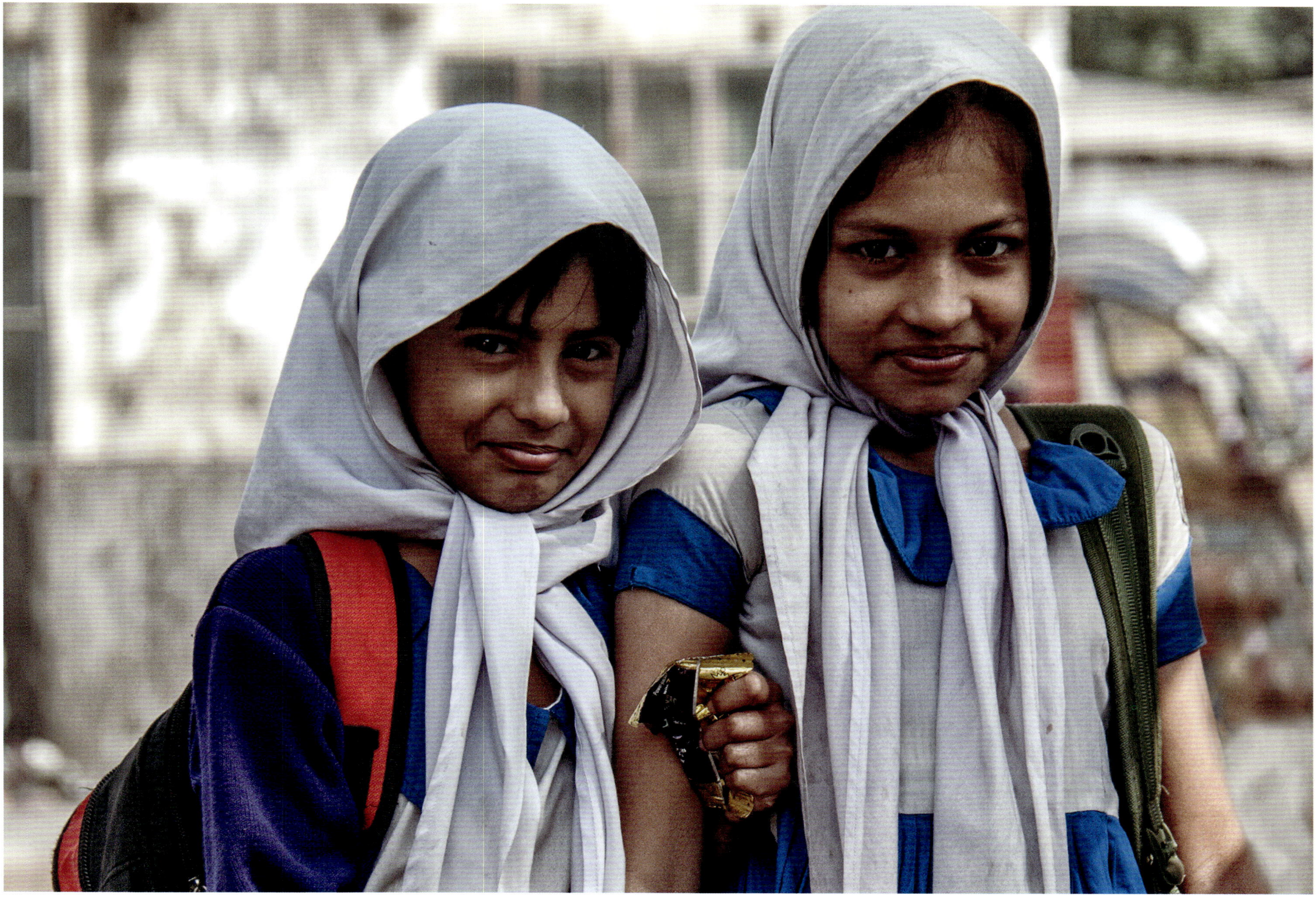

Two Bangladeshi schoolgirls. All Bangladeshi citizens must attend school for twelve years. While one out of four Bangladeshis was illiterate as of 2019, the rate has improved substantially. From 2009 to 2019, the literacy rate increased from 55.5 percent to 73.9 percent.

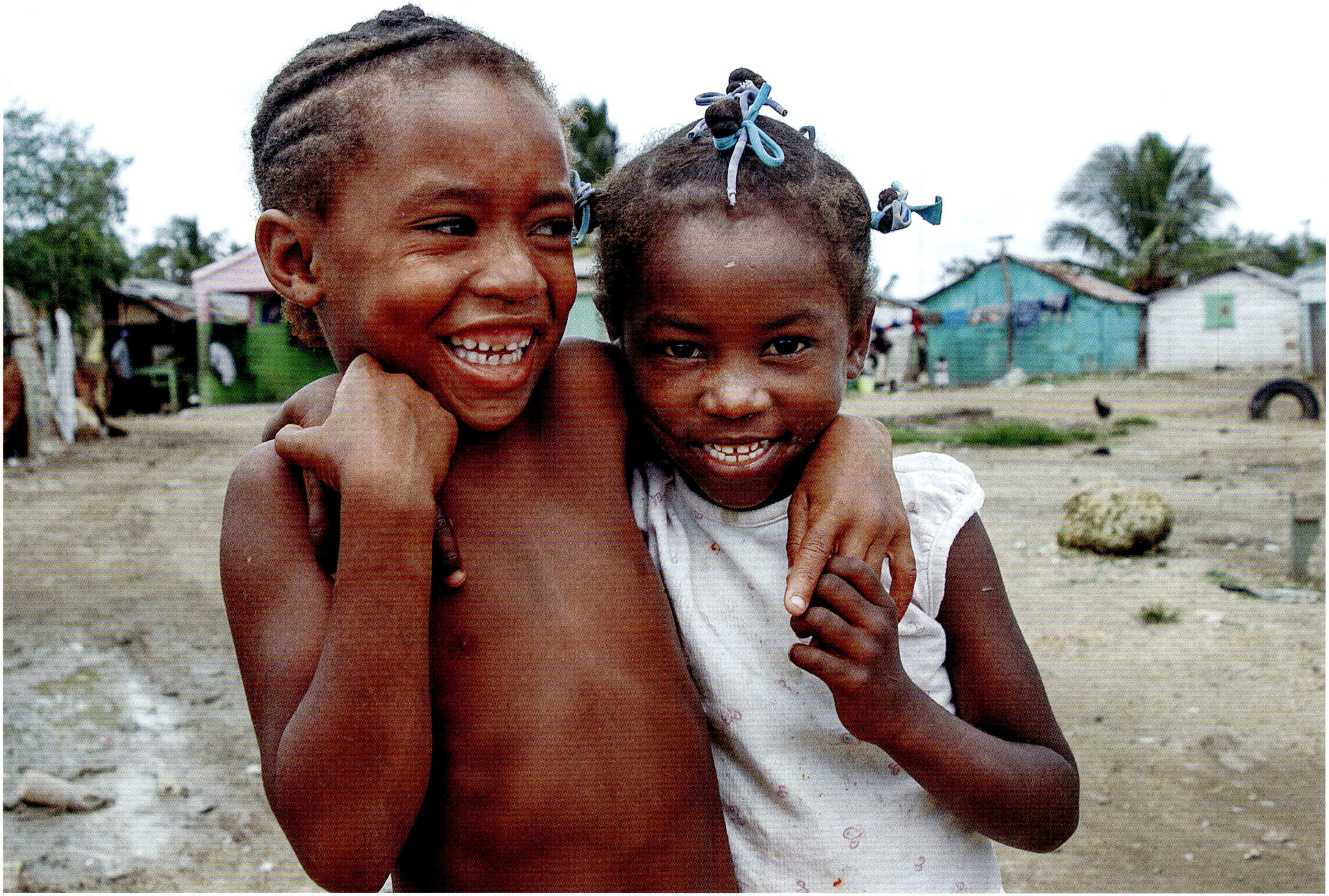

In batey Alejandro Báez, friends enjoy time together despite poverty and extreme weather.

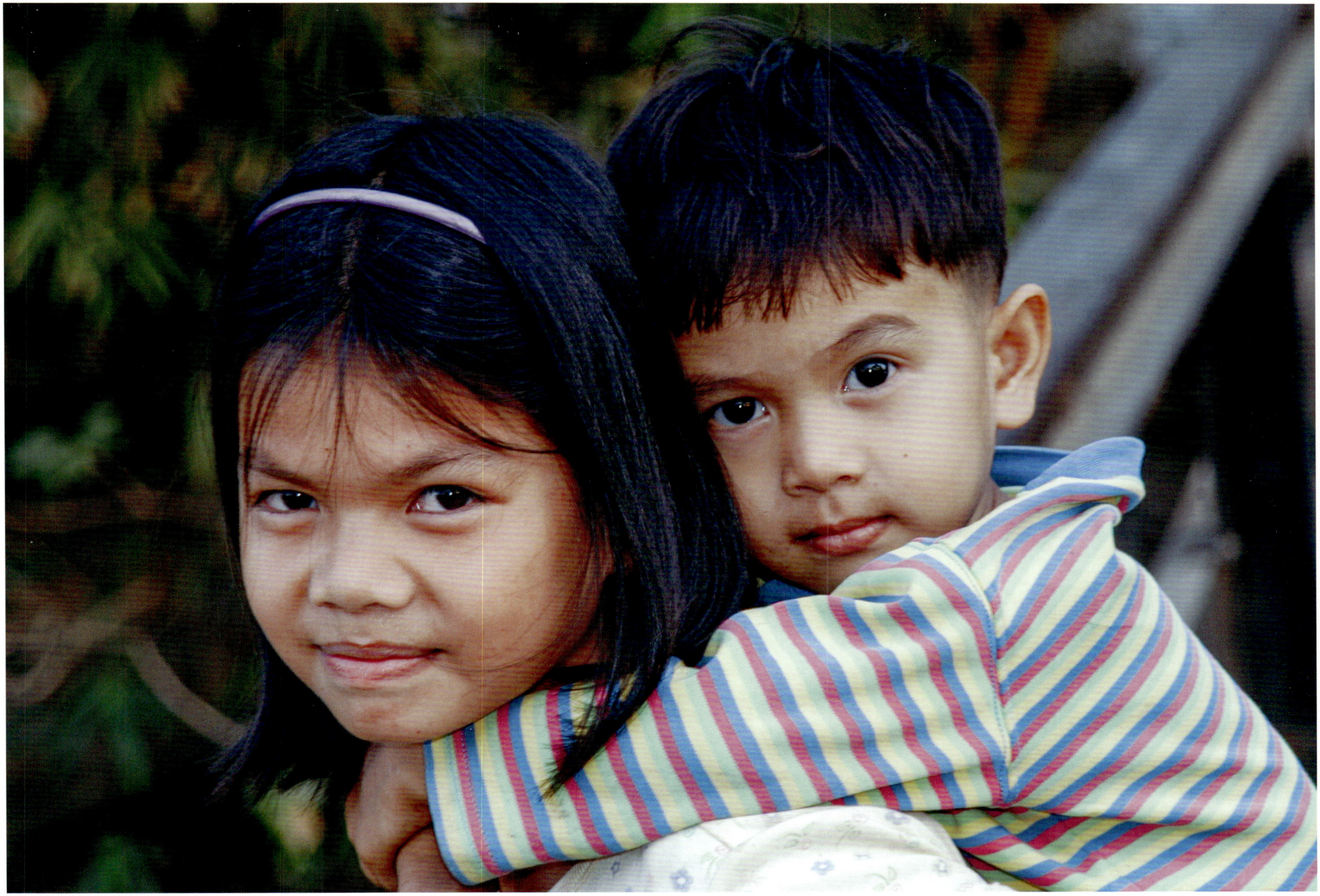

Children in Siem Reap, a city famous for its nightlife and proximity to Angkor Wat.

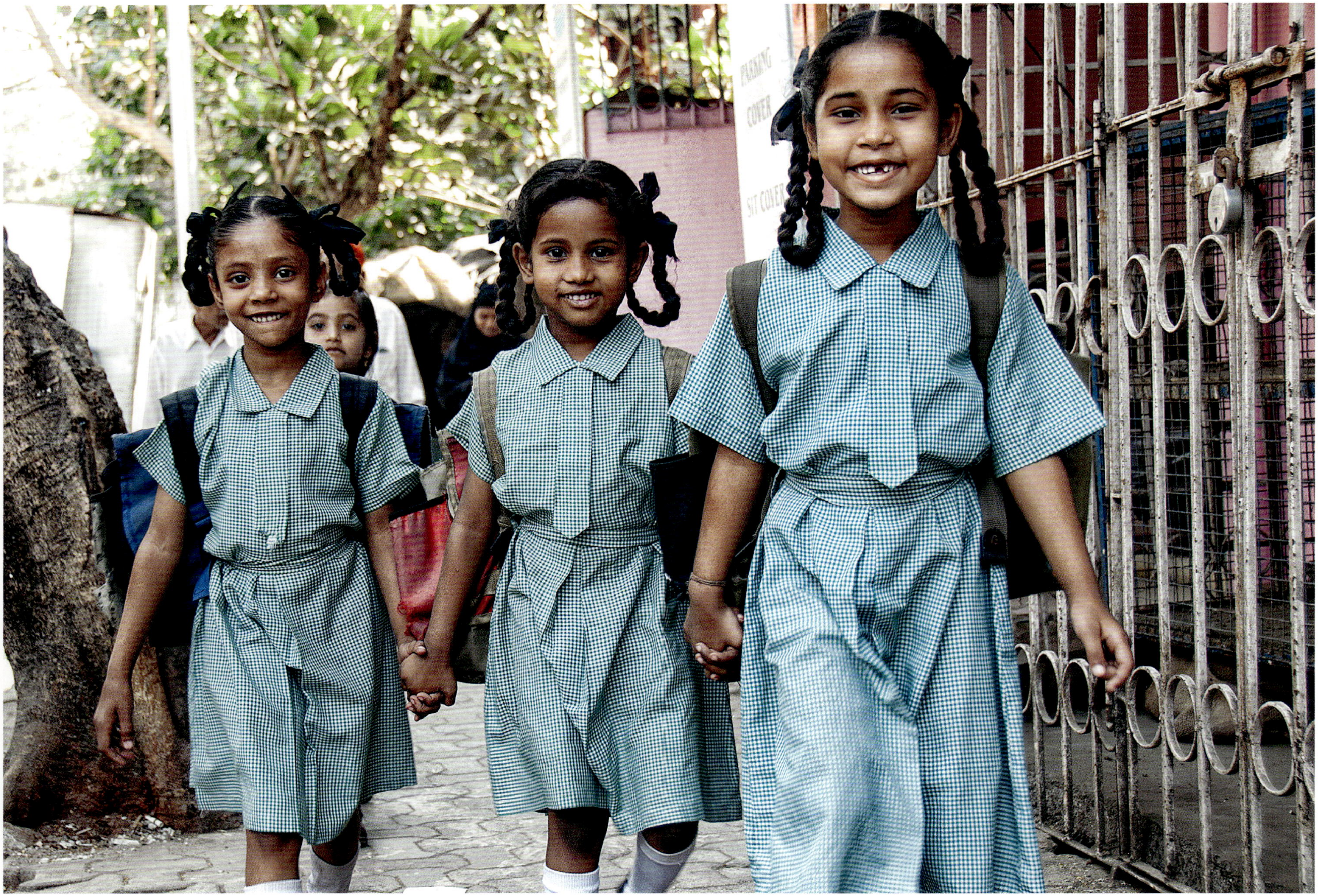

Uniformed schoolgirls on their way home in Mumbai's Mahim neighborhood.

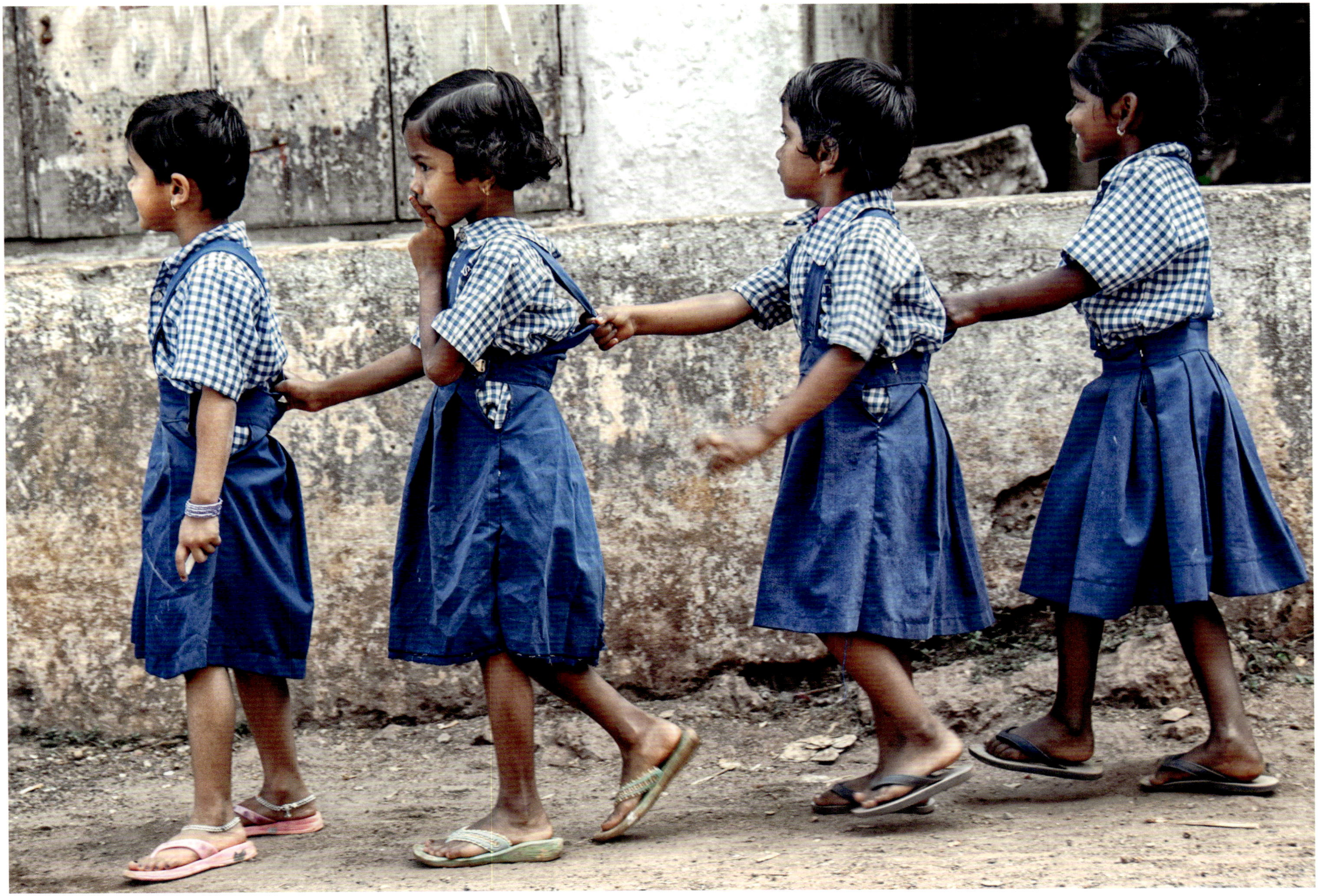

Schoolgirls in Goa, a state on the west coast of India. Goa is a former Portuguese colony known for its beaches and mix of European and Indian culture.

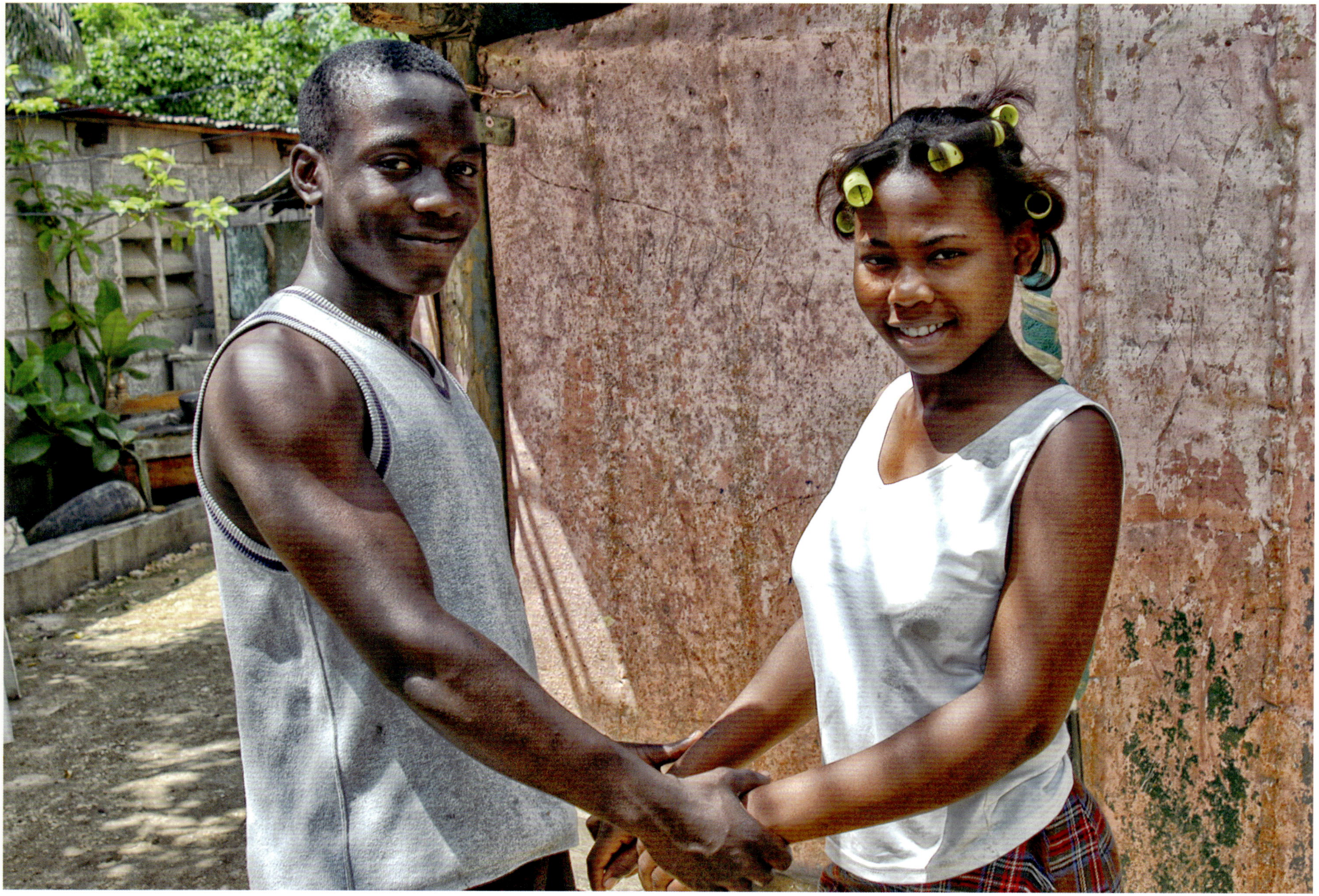

Novios (a couple) in the barrio La Filipina.

A man and woman hug. The Indian Penal Code Section 294 states that public acts of "obscenity" can be punishable by three months of imprisonment, a fine, or both. A man and a woman publicly kissing or holding hands is rarely seen in India.

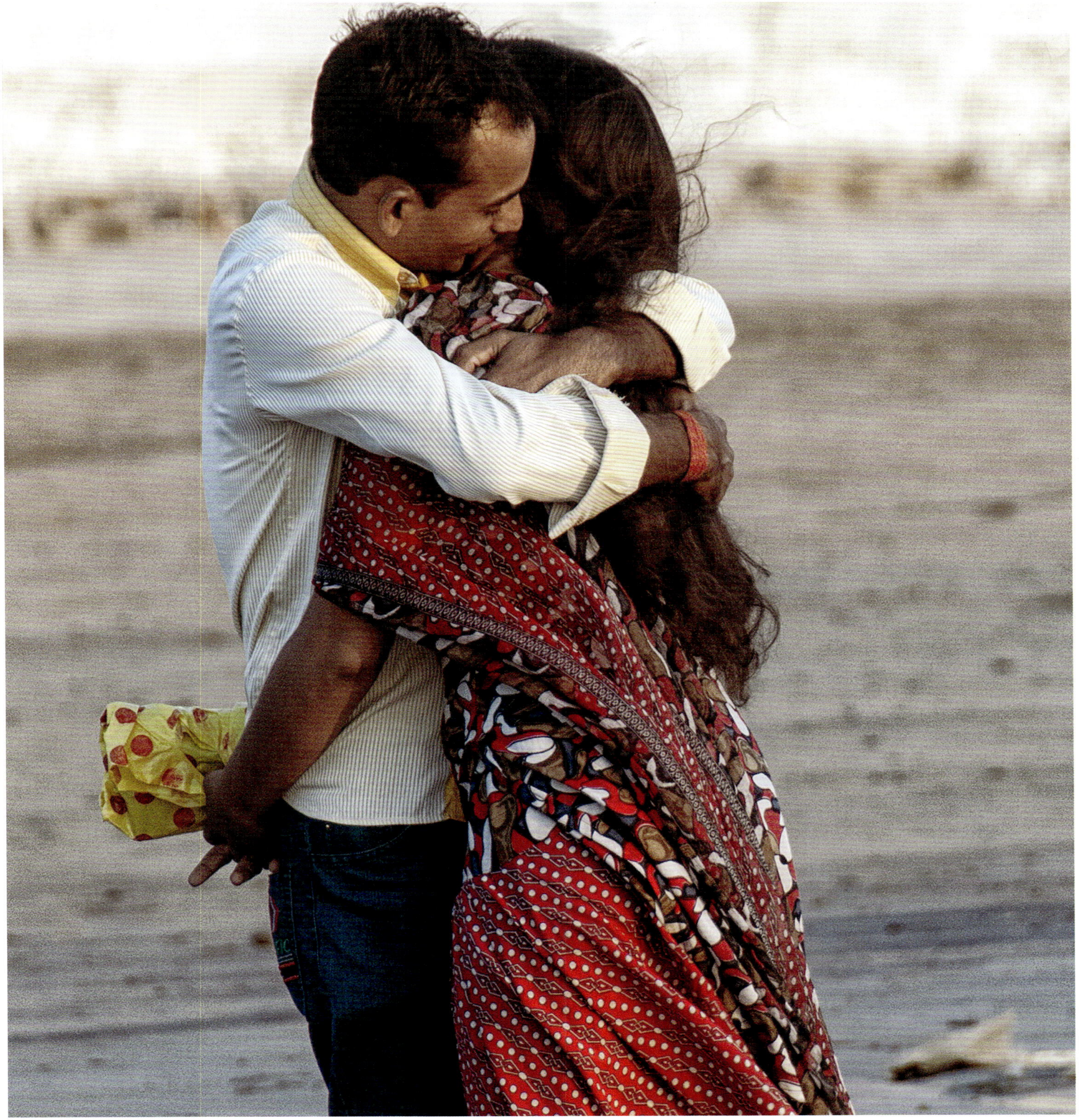

India / Mumbai, Maharashtra

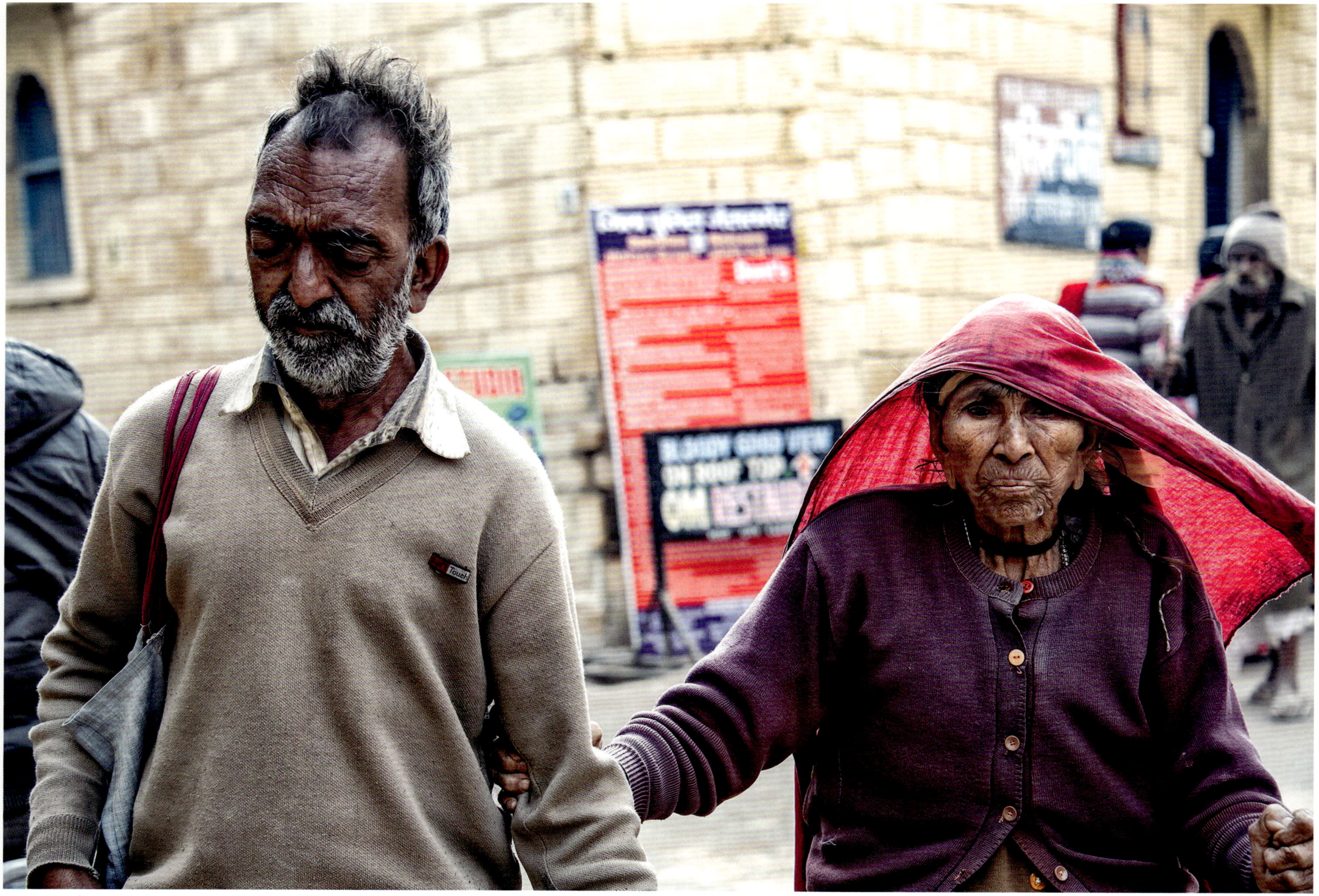

A woman holds the arm of a blind man on the streets of Aurangabad, a city in east India that is typically too off-the-grid for tourists.

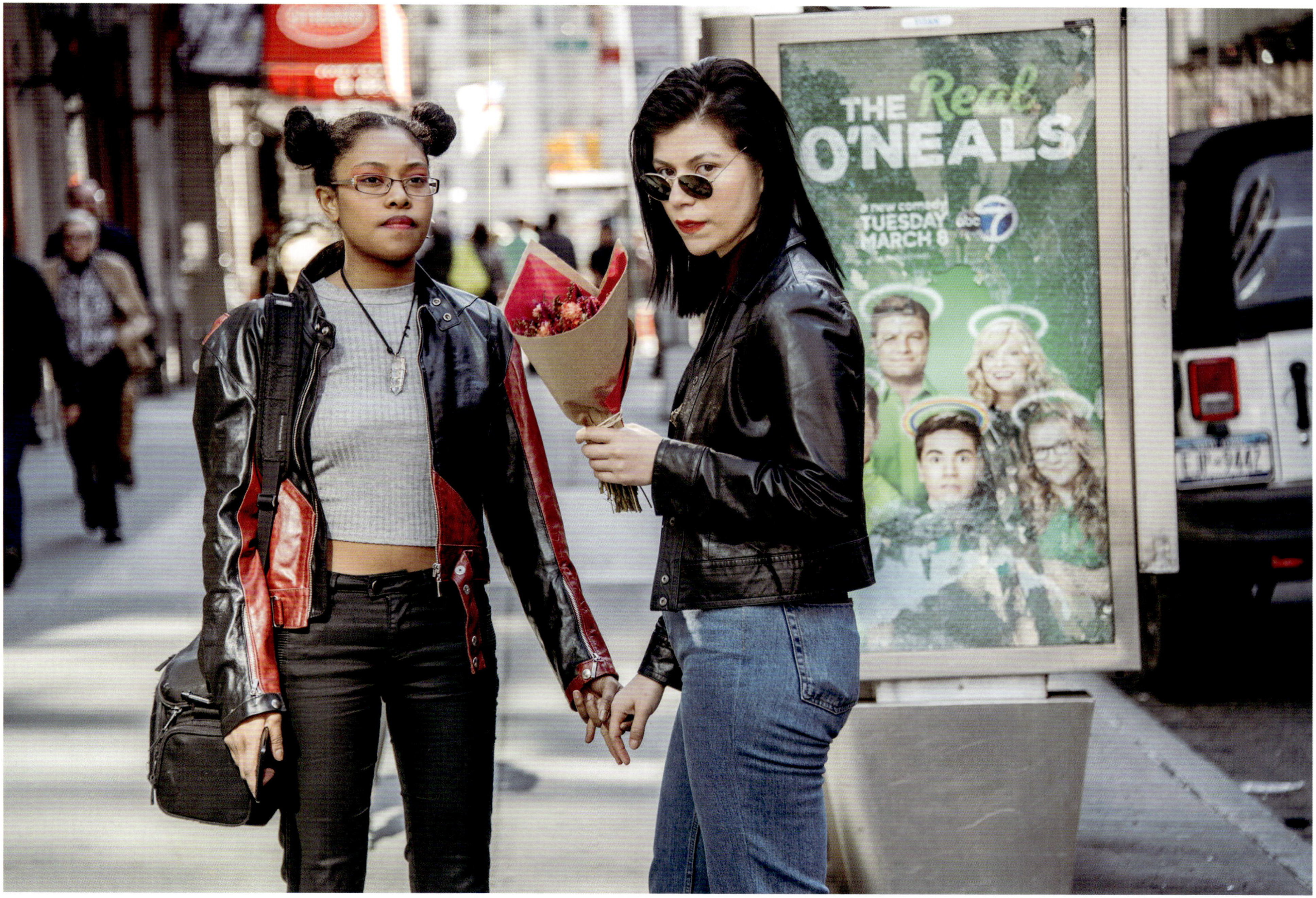

A couple enjoy a day in Manhattan's East Village.

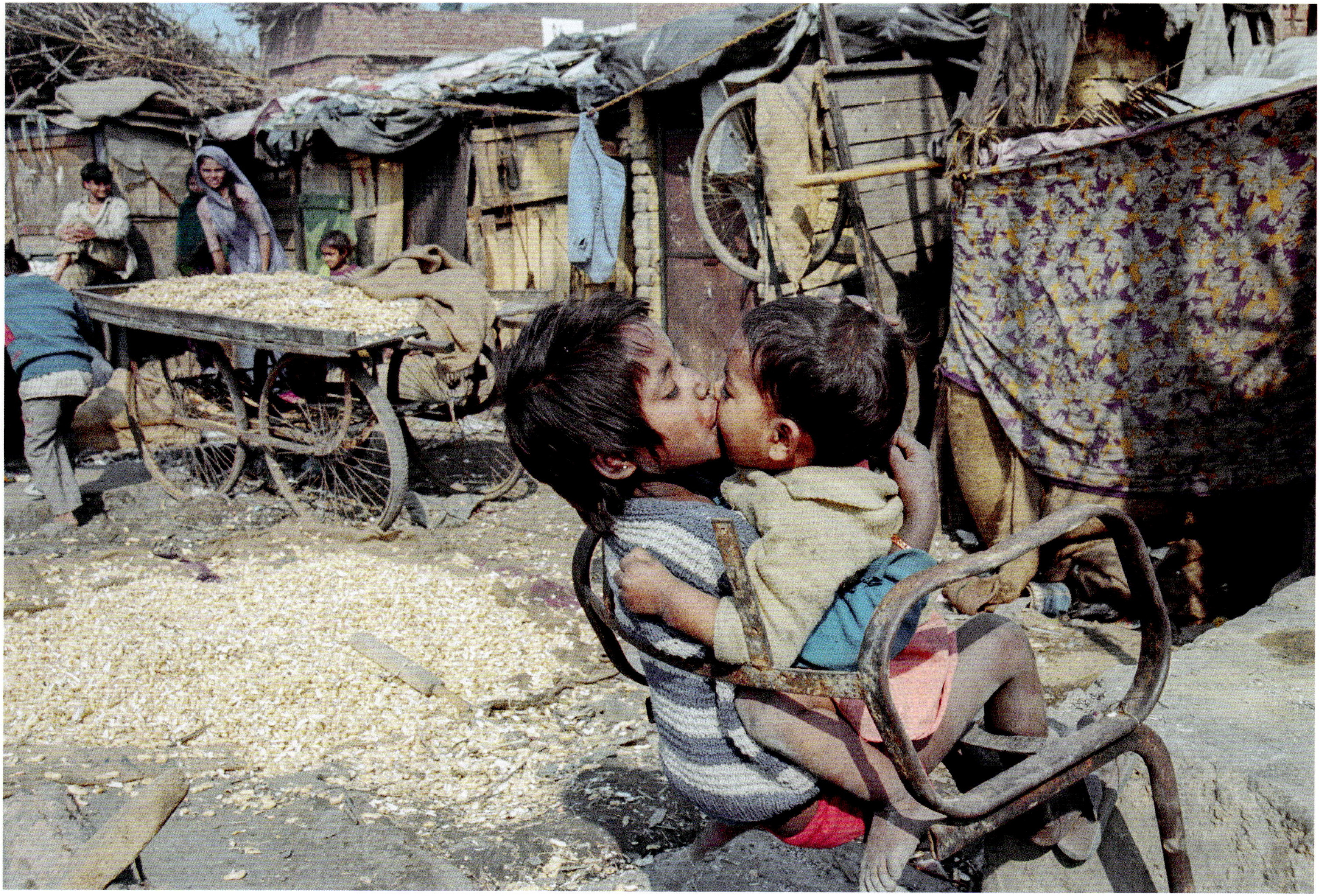

Two children find time to embrace. They, like millions of other Indians, live in poverty in Delhi slums located along miles of railroad tracks.

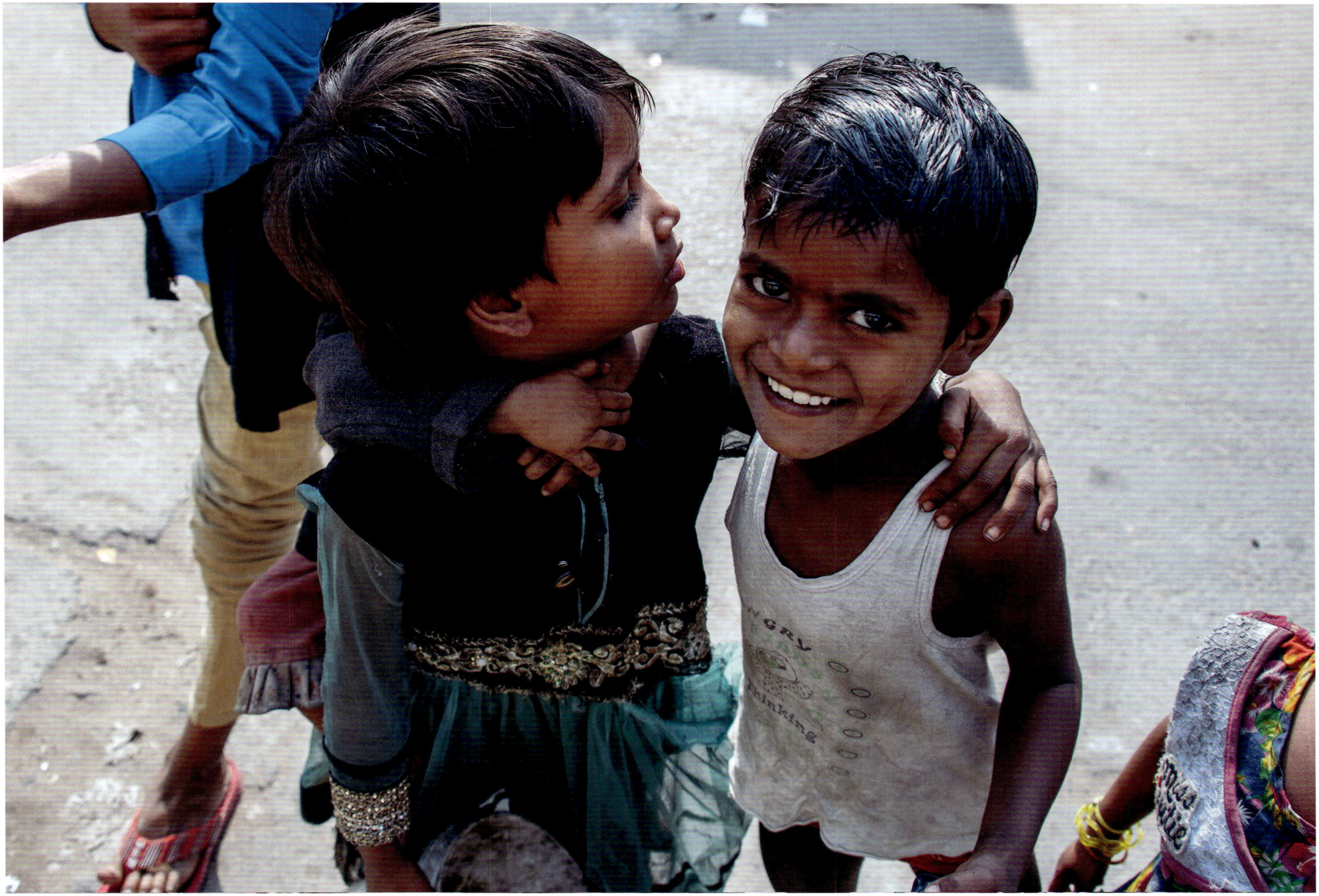

Friends hold one another.

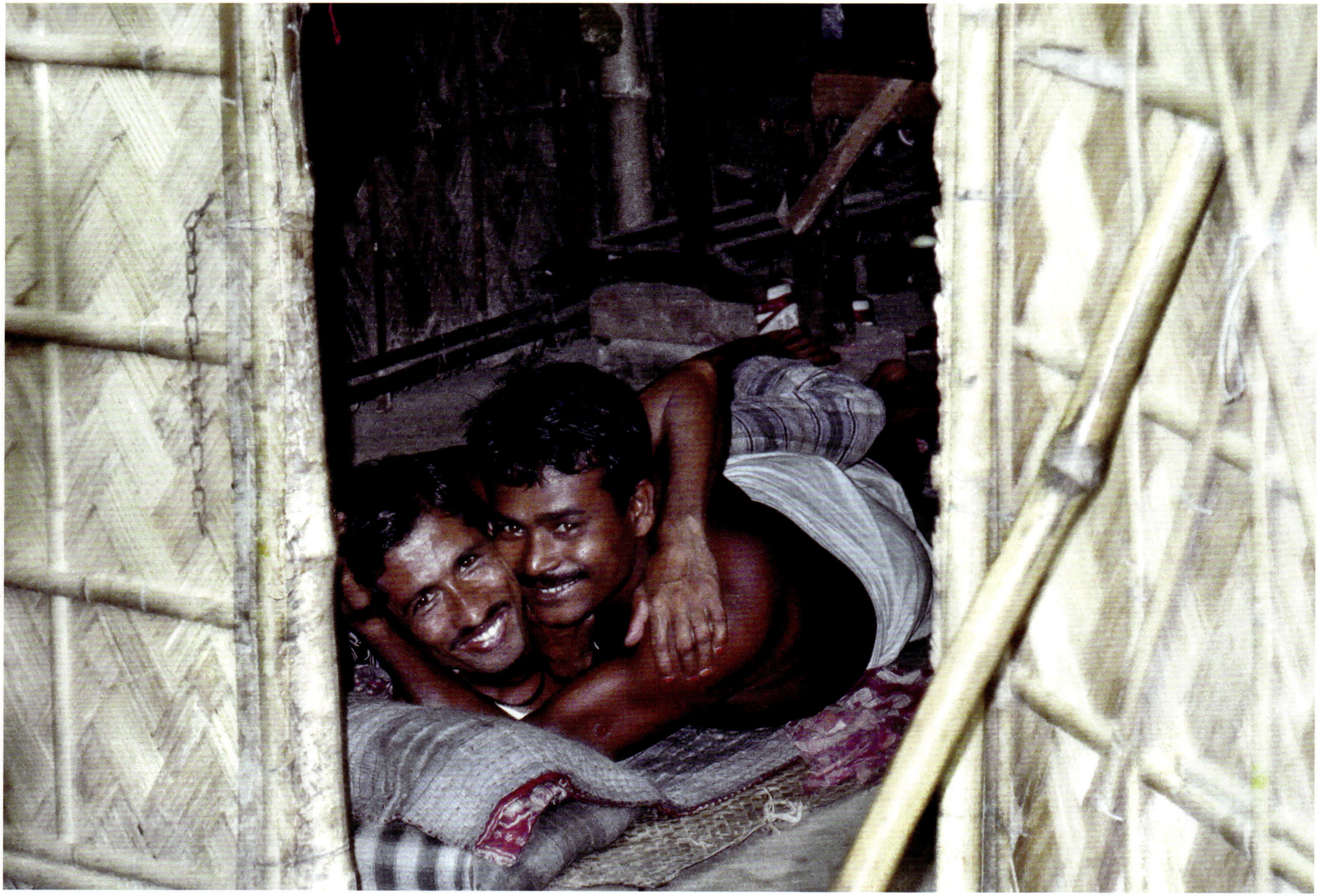

Two local men embrace.

Two women enjoy a fall day
in the East Village.

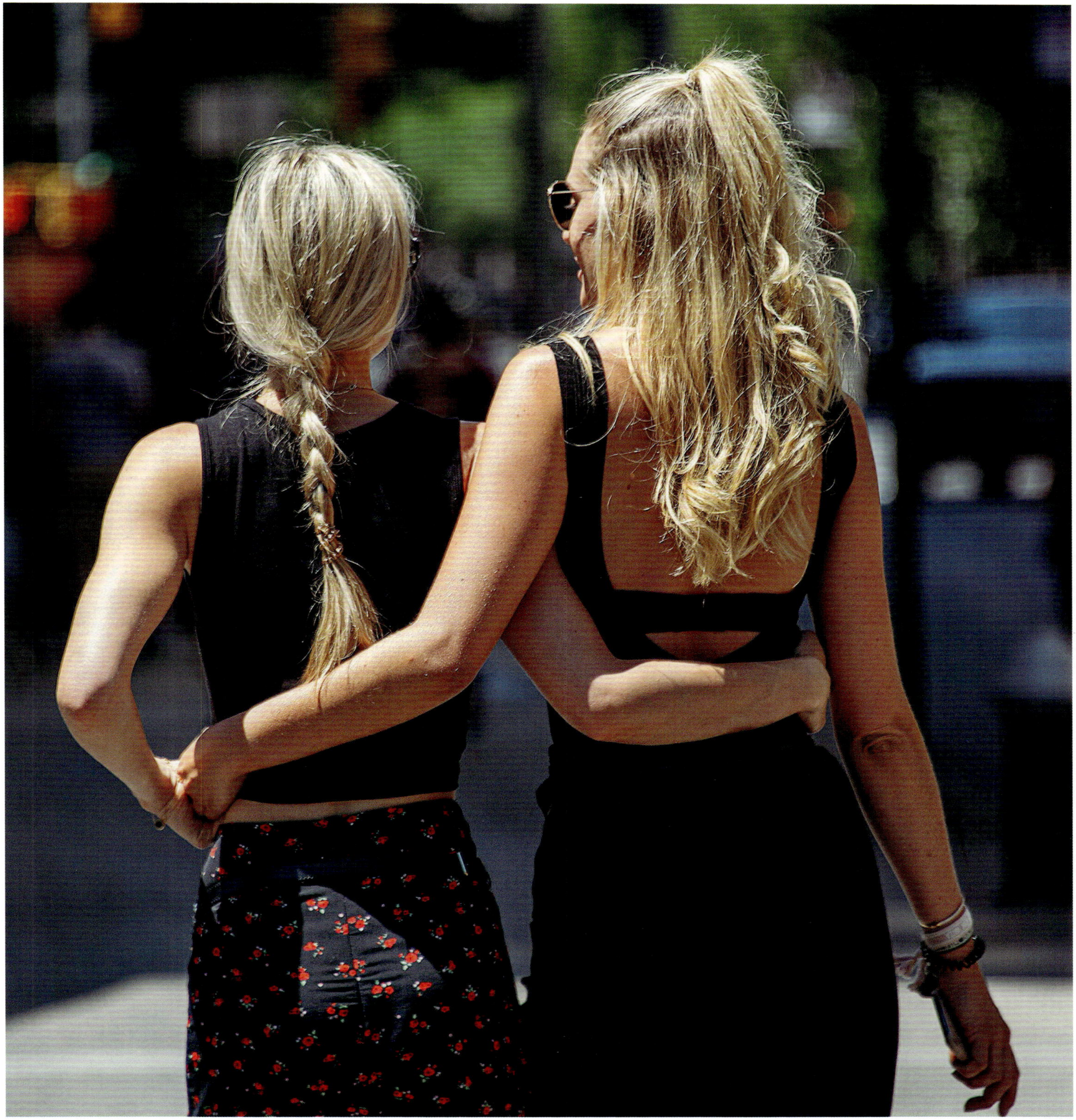

United States / New York, New York

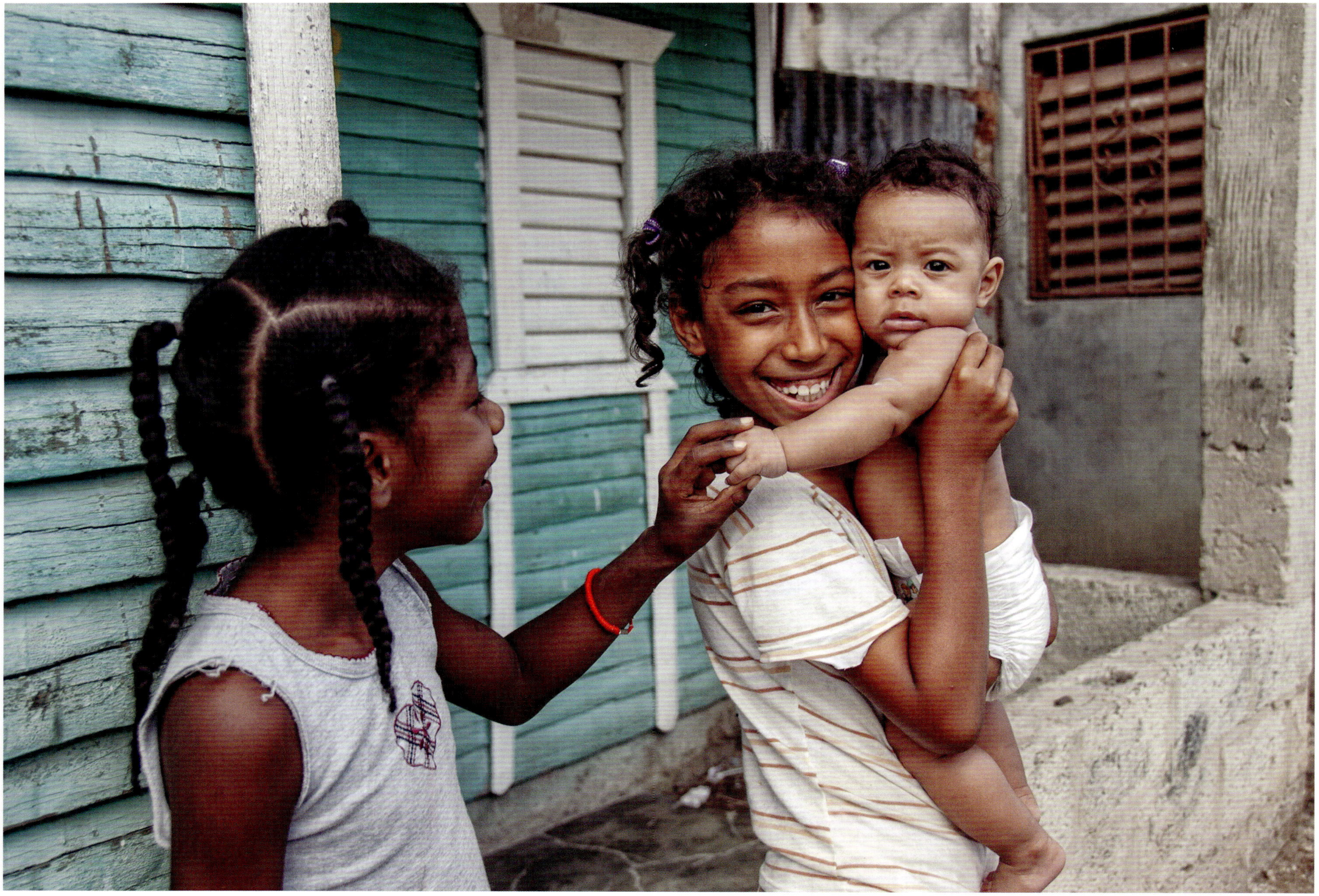

Two girls and an infant.

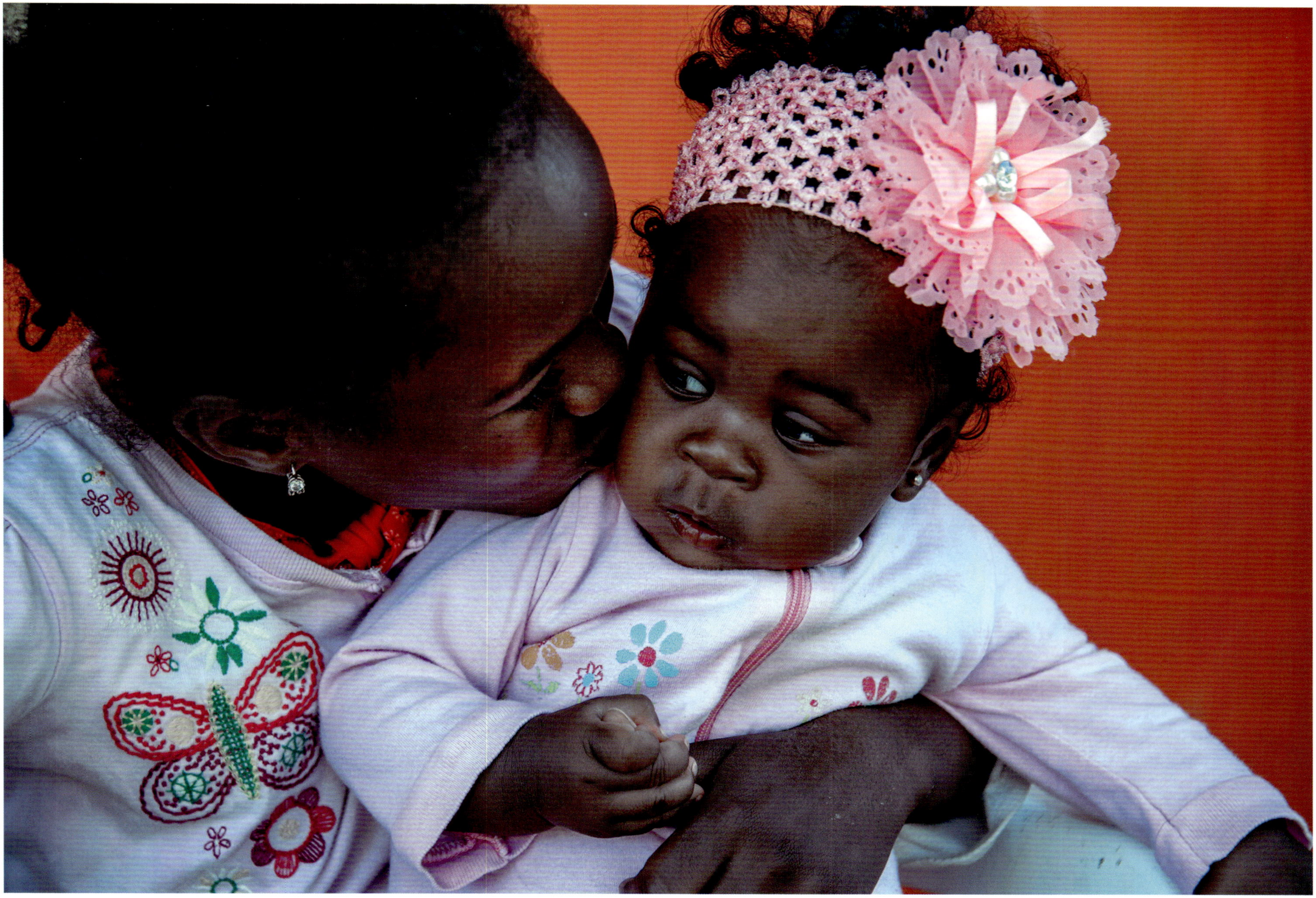

Life and love in the bateyes, the slums surrounding San Pedro de Macorís.

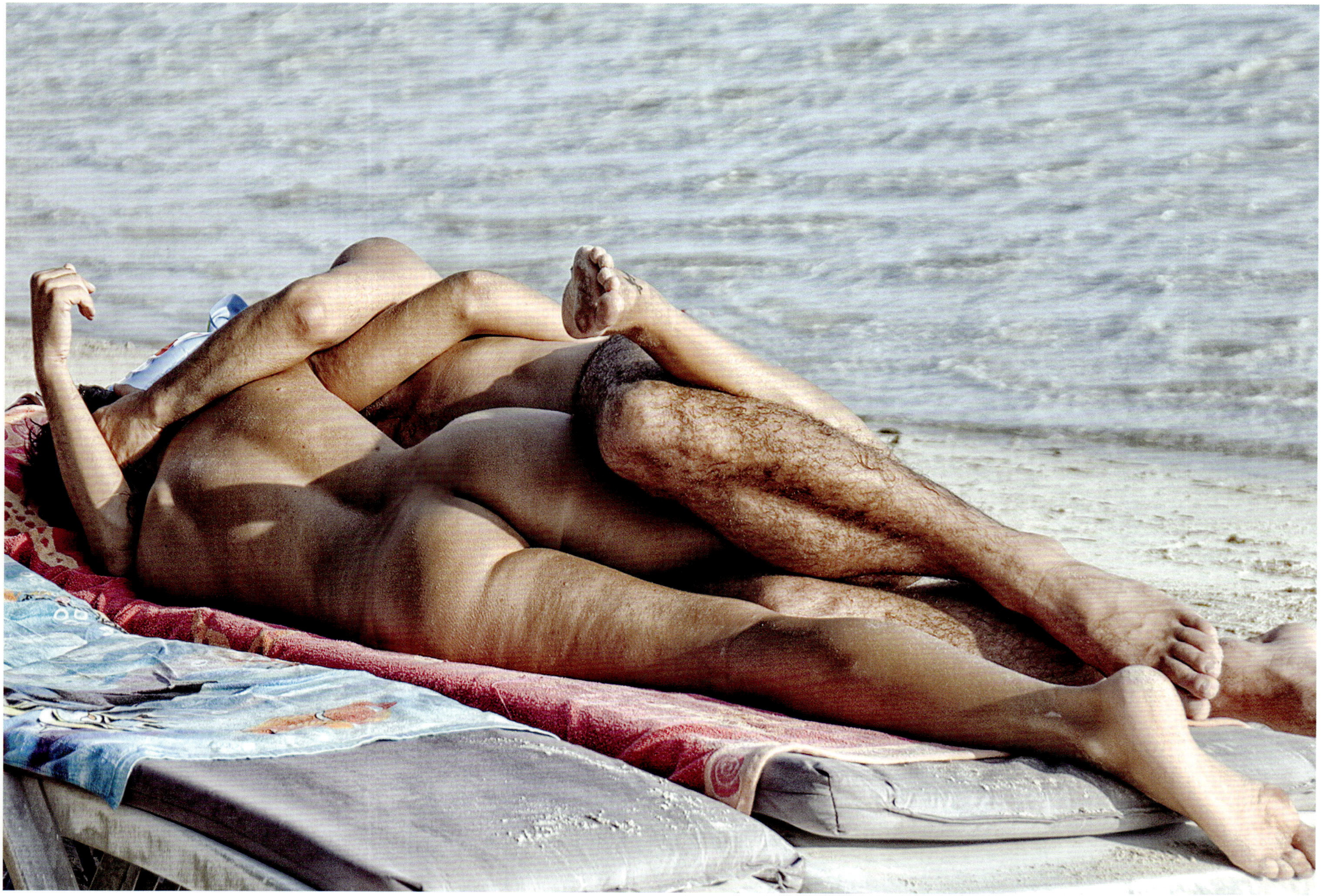

A couple enjoy time together at Boca Chica Beach.

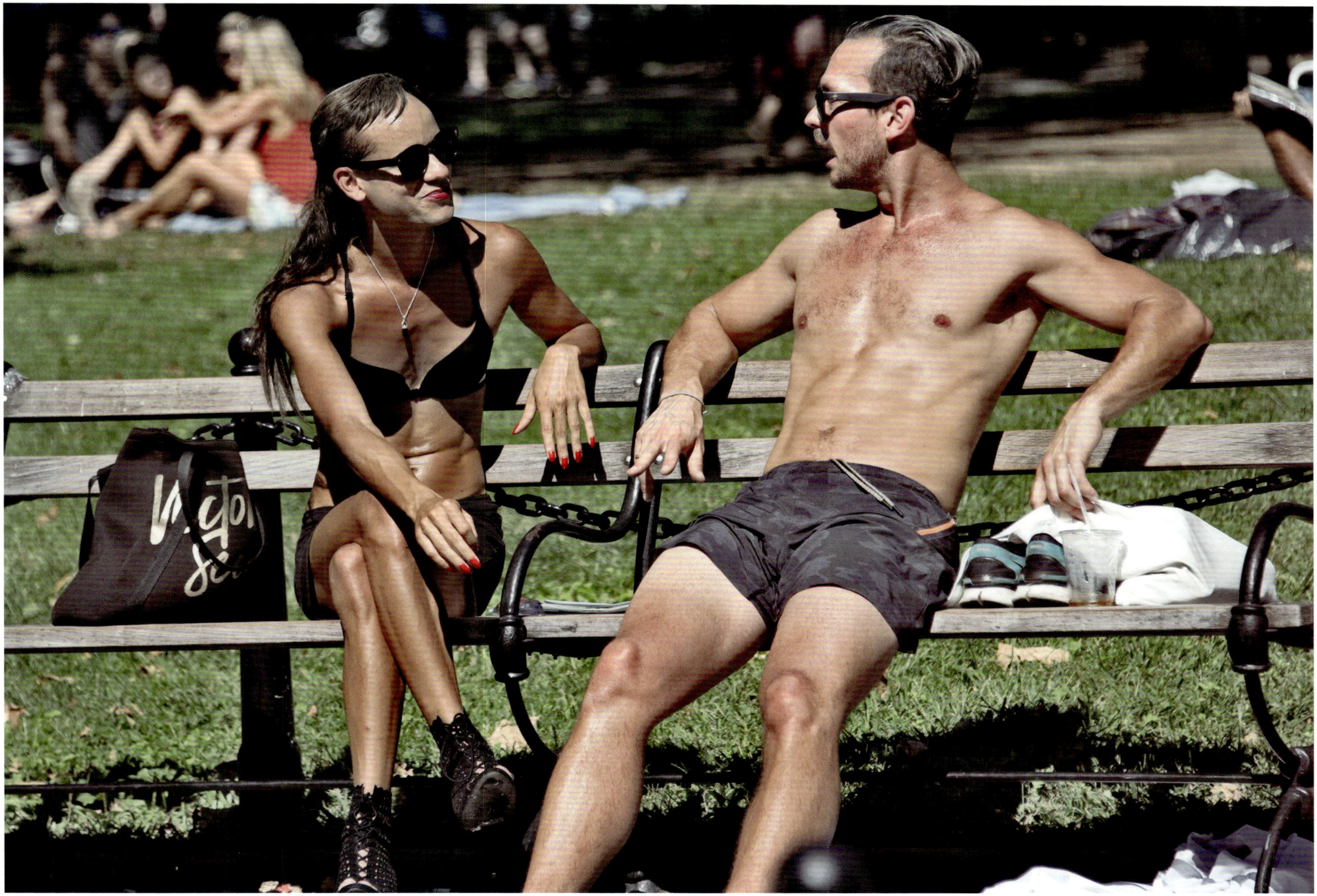

People soak up sunshine in Washington Square Park. In the summer the park has many performing artists and pigeon feeders.

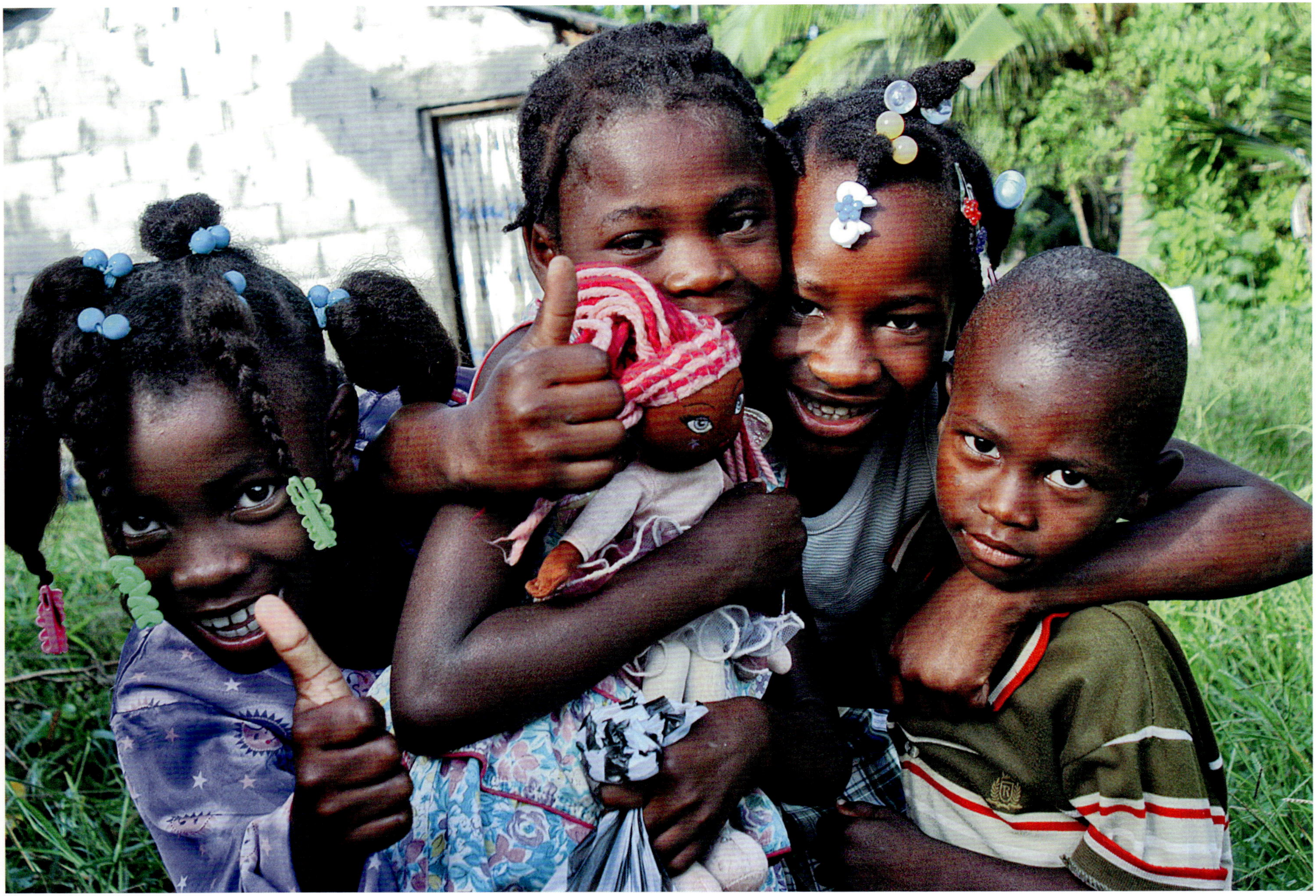

In La Filipina, local children give a thumbs-up.

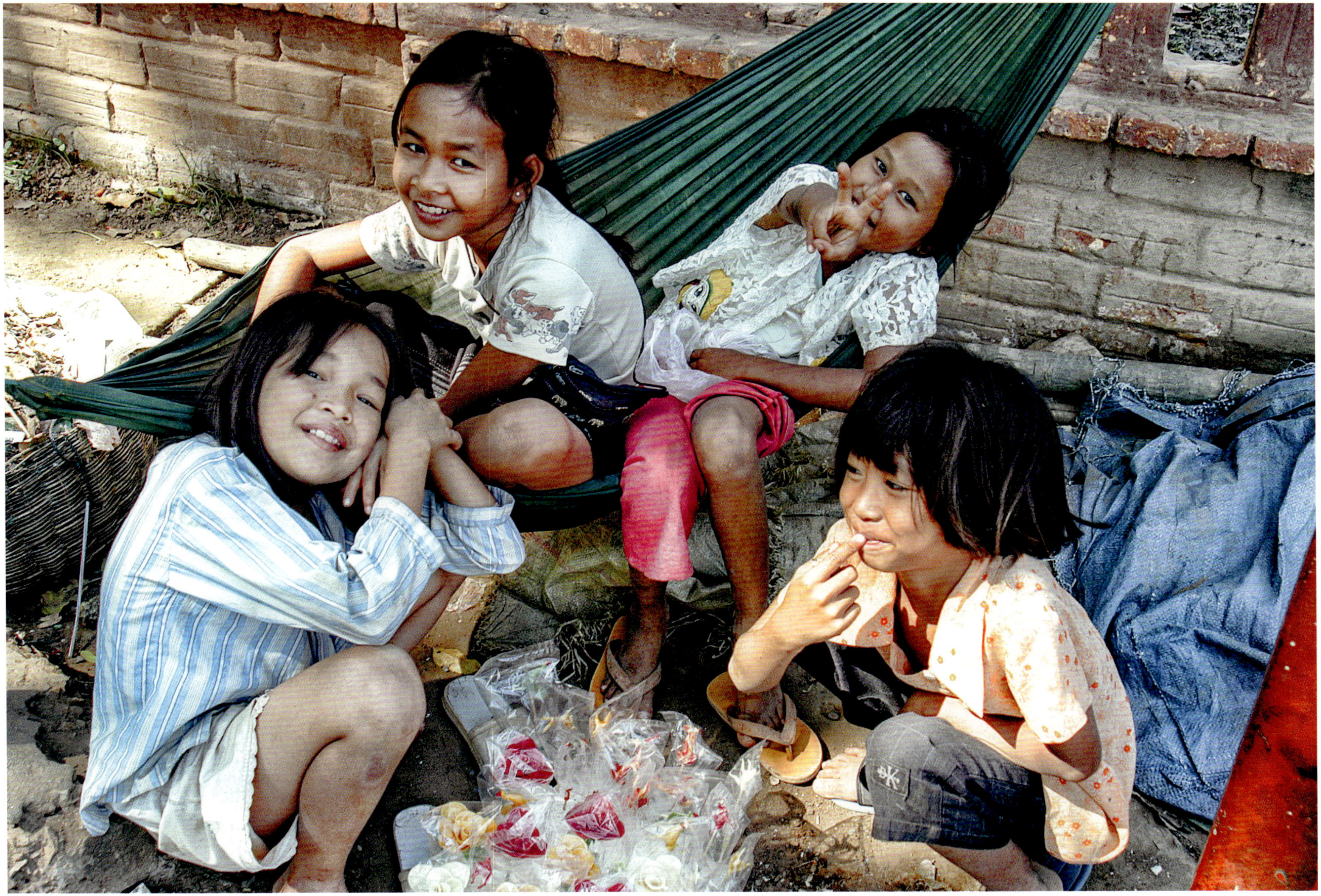

Hammocks can be found throughout Phnom Penh, even in restaurants. Here two young girls share one hammock.

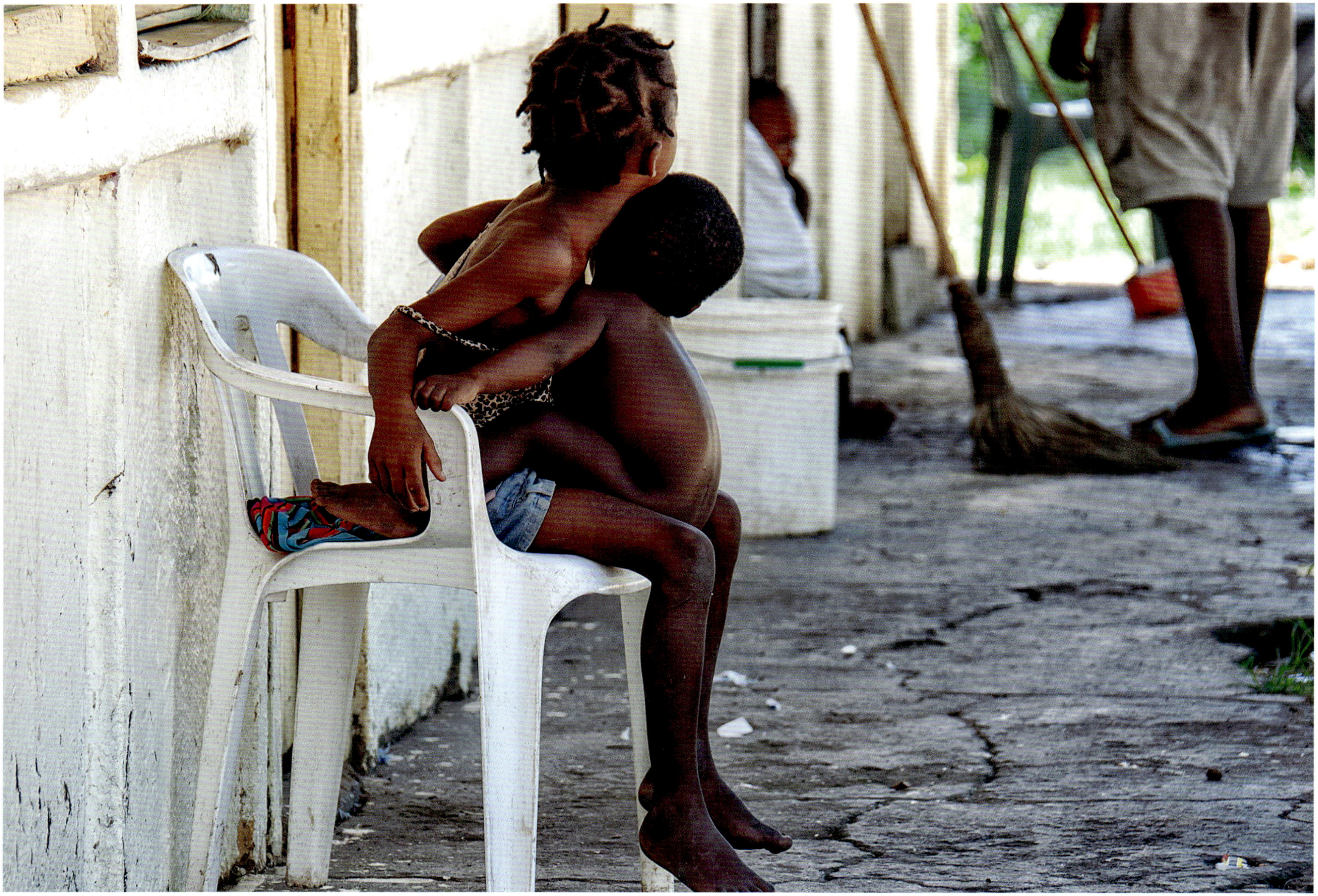

Children in batey Alejandro Báez.

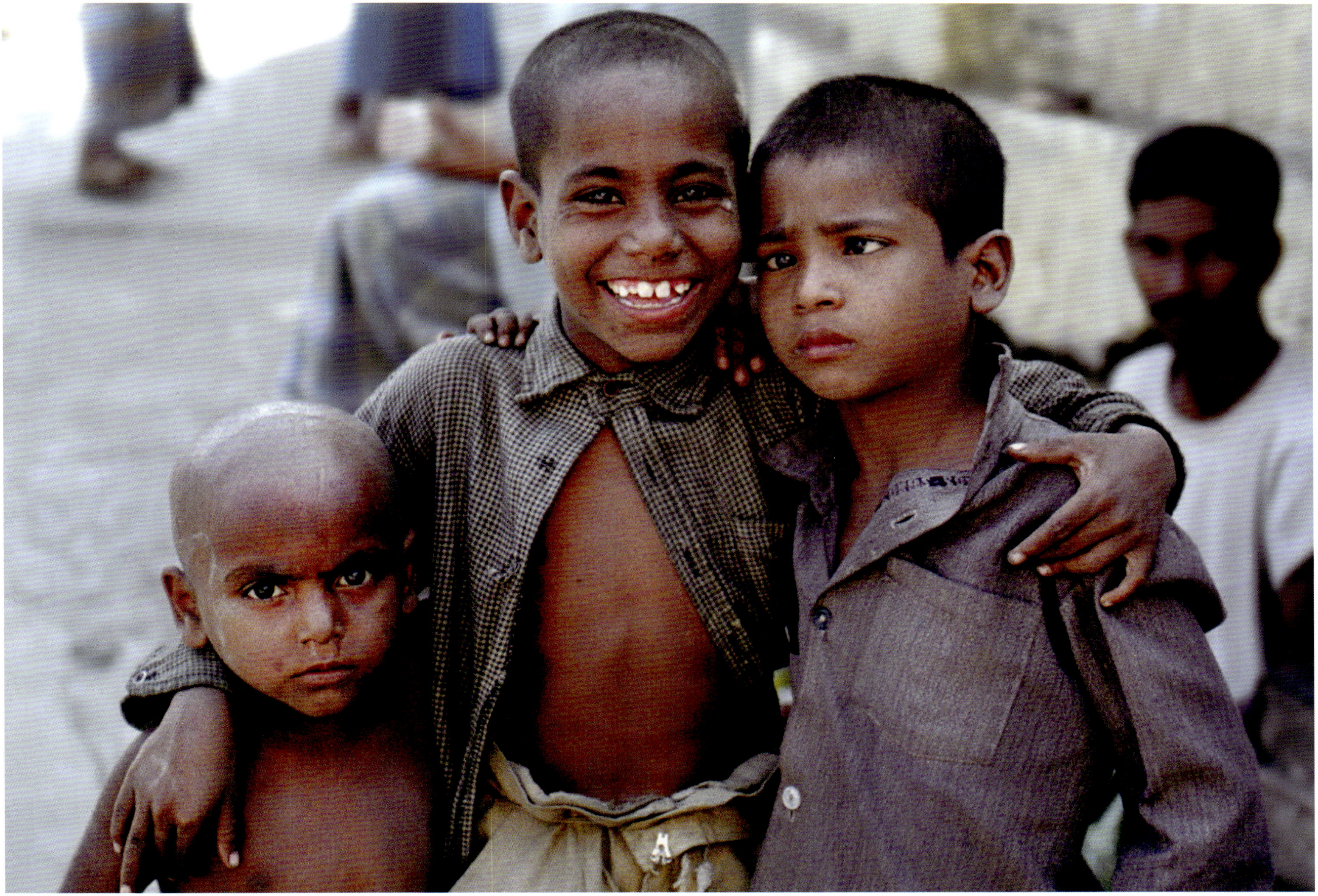

Children beg on the streets of Dhaka, but one still offers up a big smile.

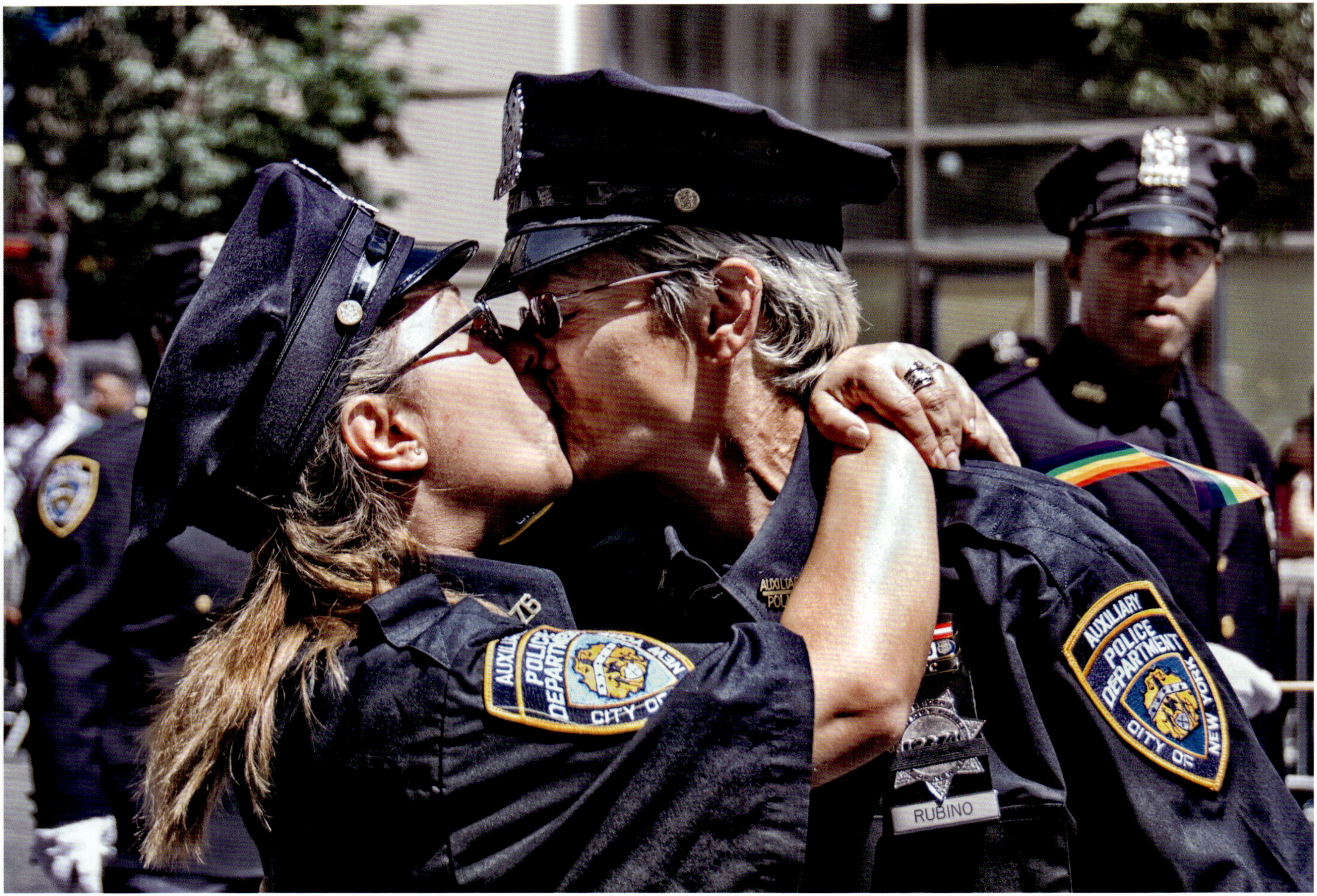

Gay New York Police Department officers share a moment of affection.

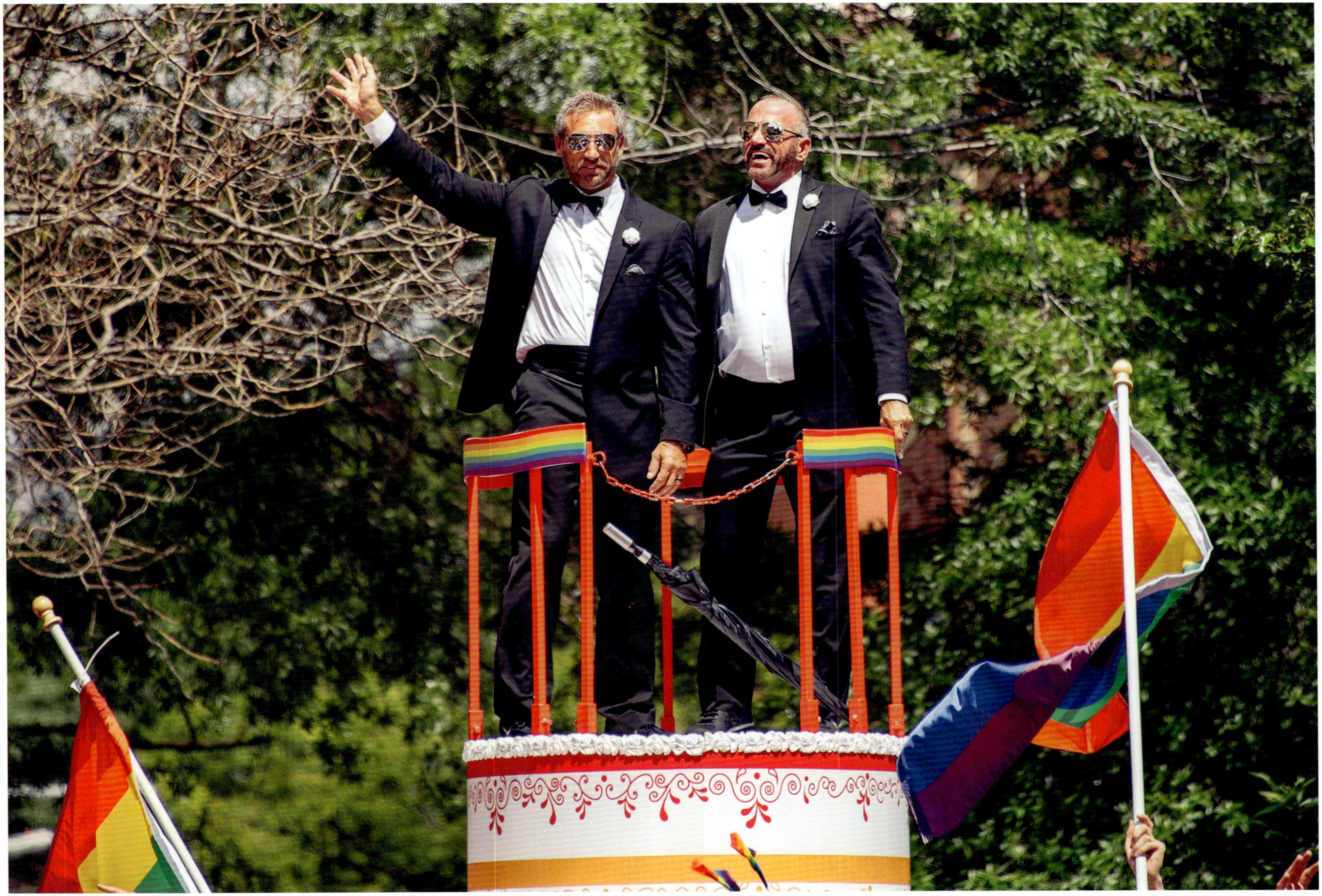

A married couple celebrate Pride Month at the Pride March in Manhattan.

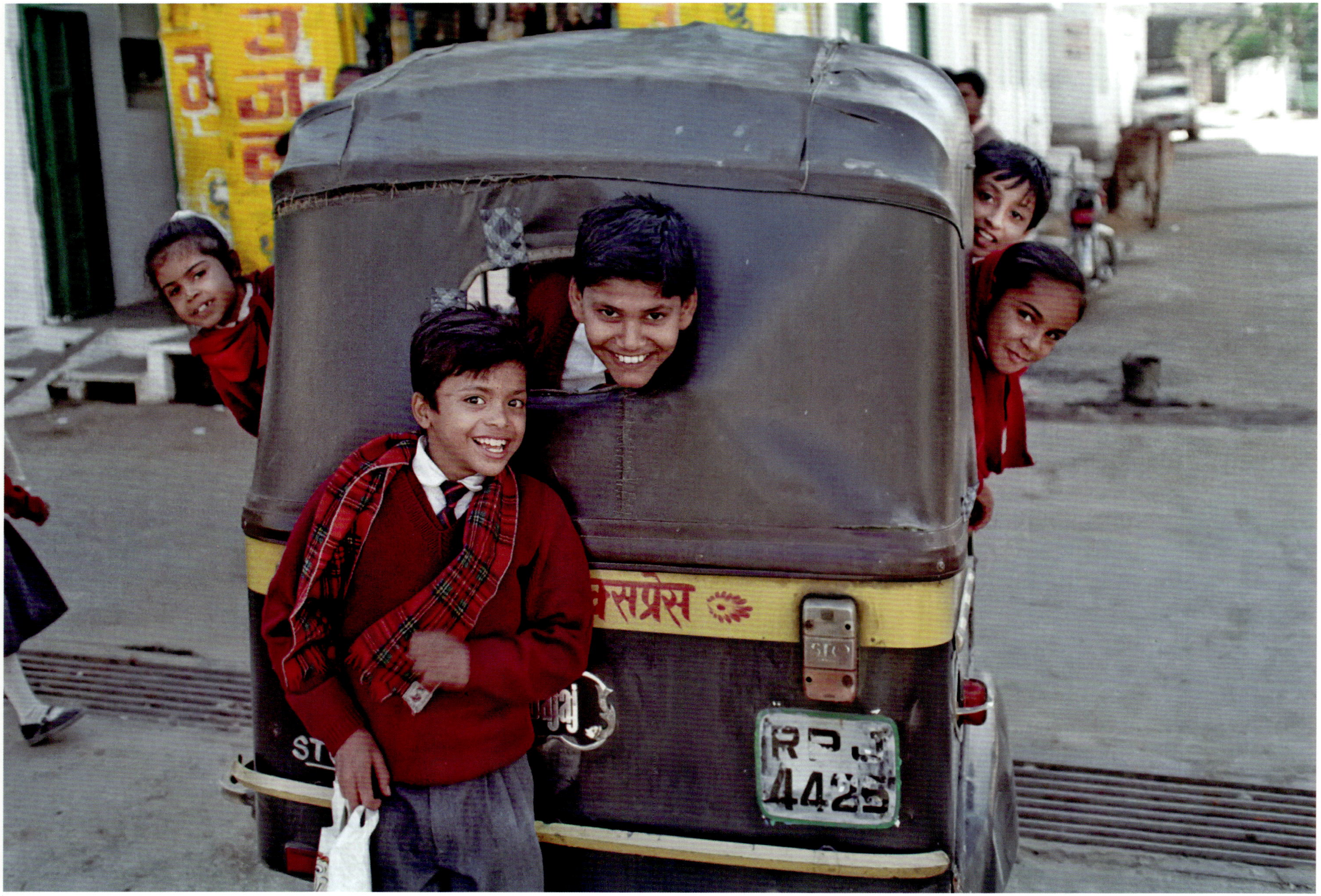

Schoolkids in a tuk-tuk.

India / Jaipur, Rajasthan

In New Delhi, India's capital, two boys offer a traditional Hindu greeting. "Namaste," sometimes spoken as "namaskar" or "namaskaram," is a customary Hindu greeting meaning "I bow to you."

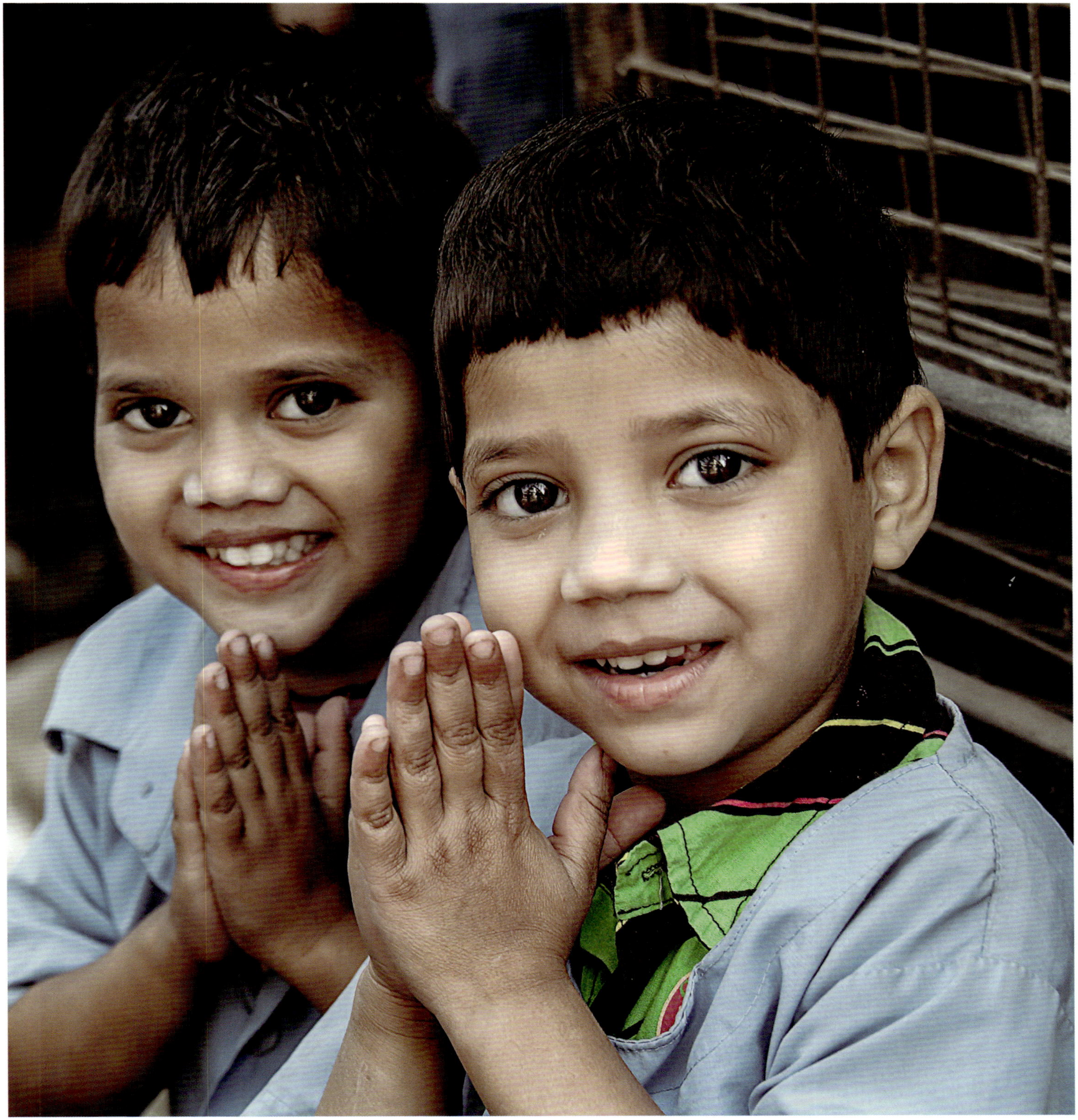

India / New Delhi, Delhi

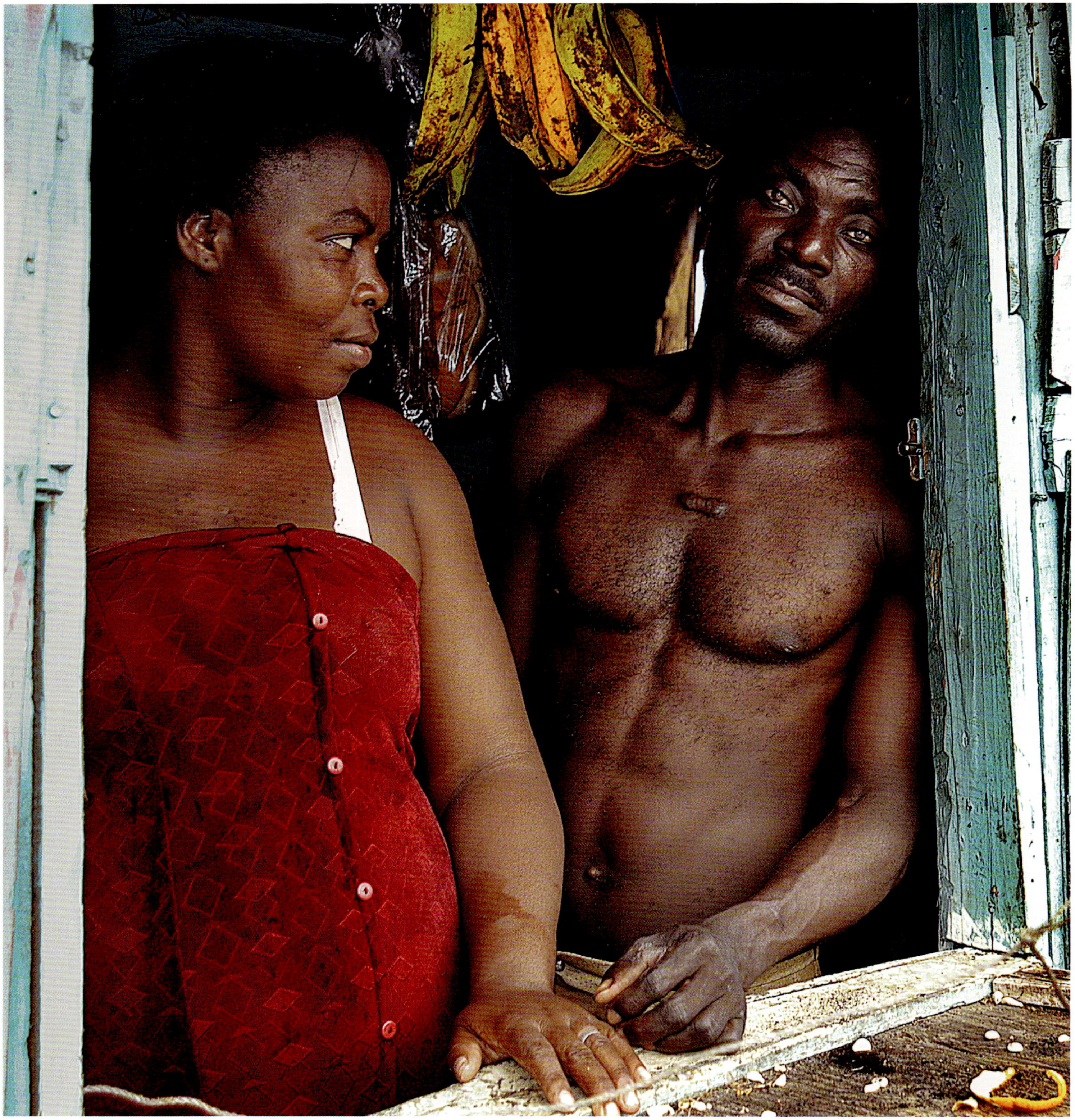

Workers at a bodega in La Filipina. The store has a low stock of vegetables, bananas, and warm drinks. Its electricity often shuts off.

Dominican Republic / San Pedro de Macorís, San Pedro de Macorís Province

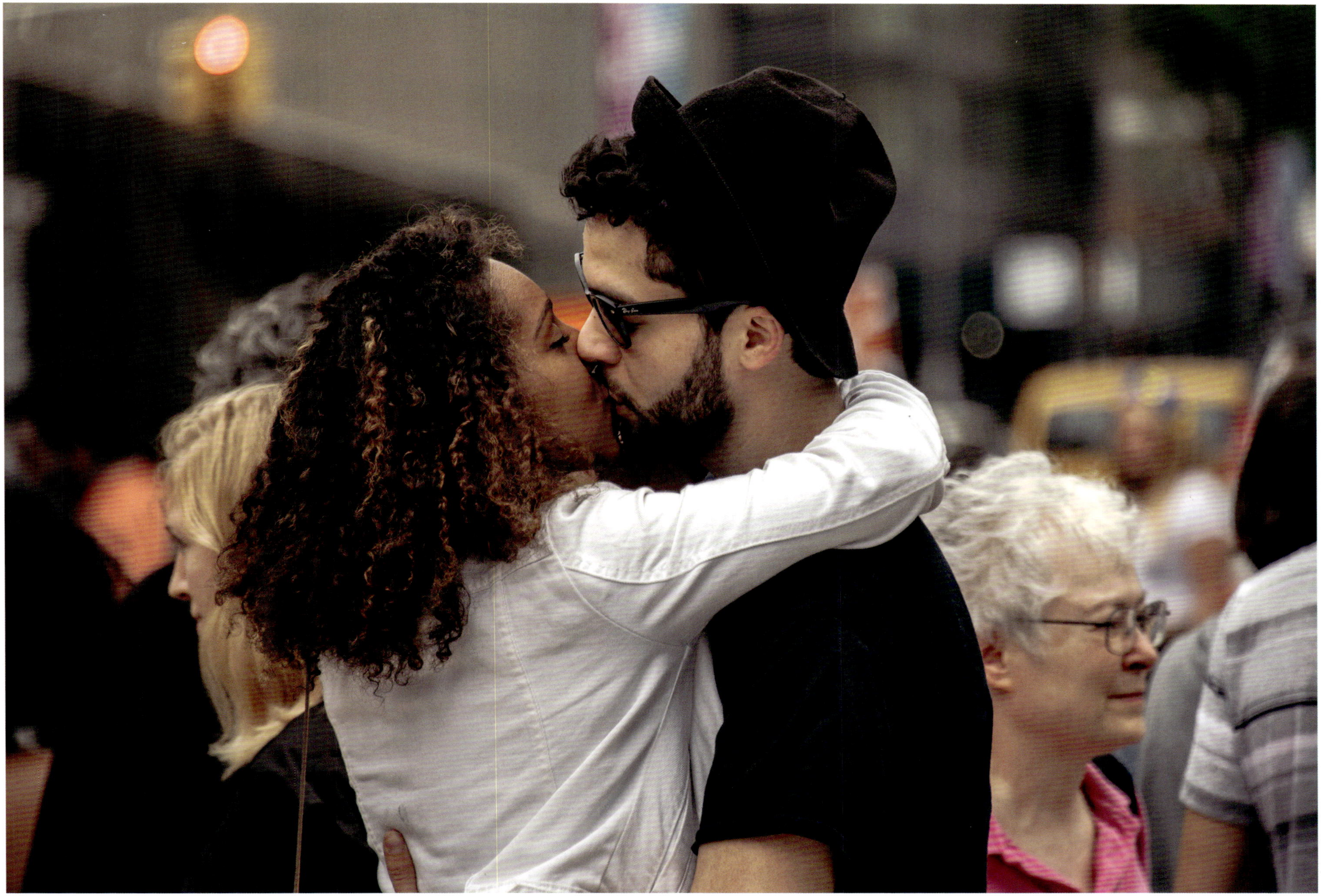

A couple kiss at Astor Place in Manhattan's East Village.

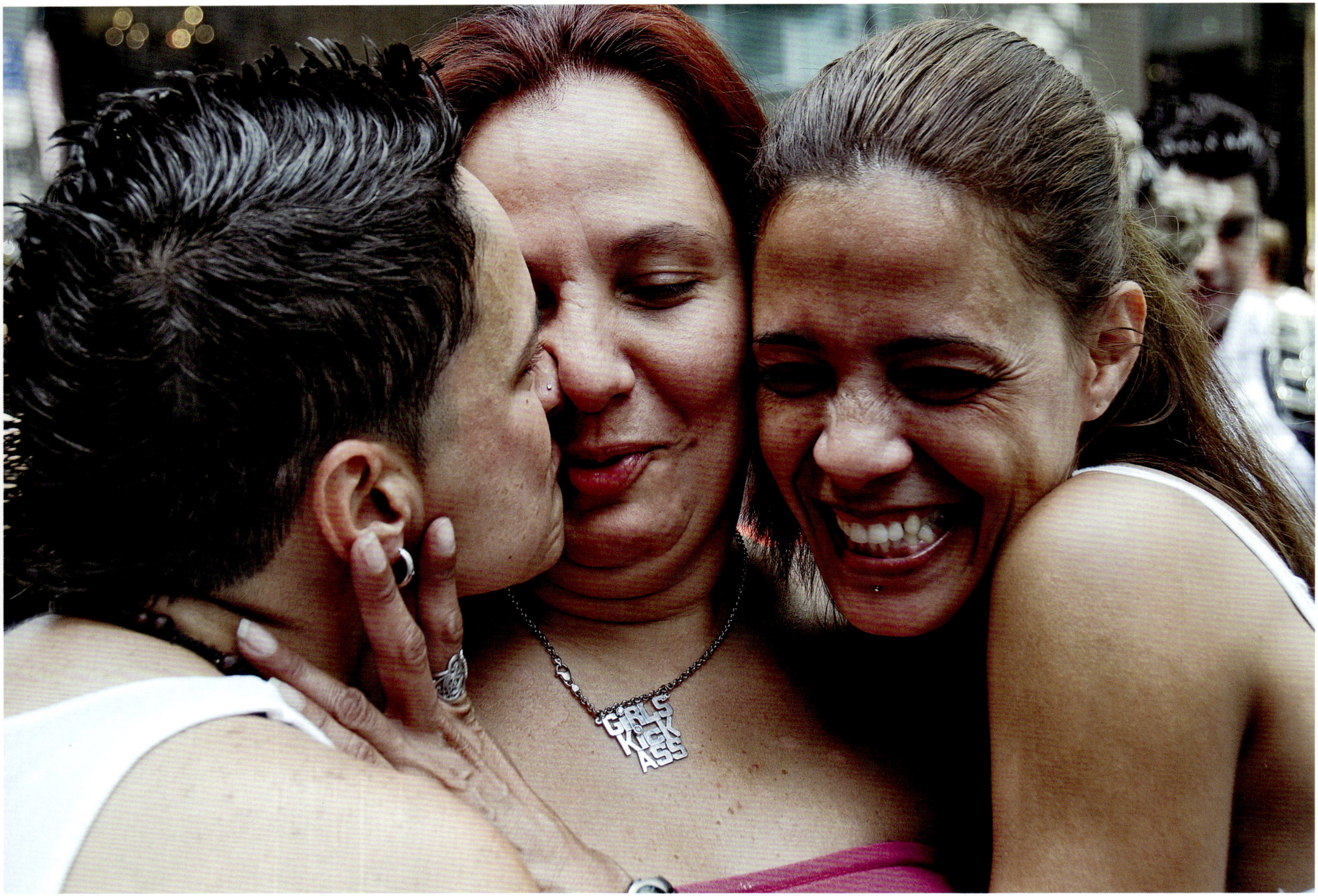

Women embrace at the New York City Pride March.

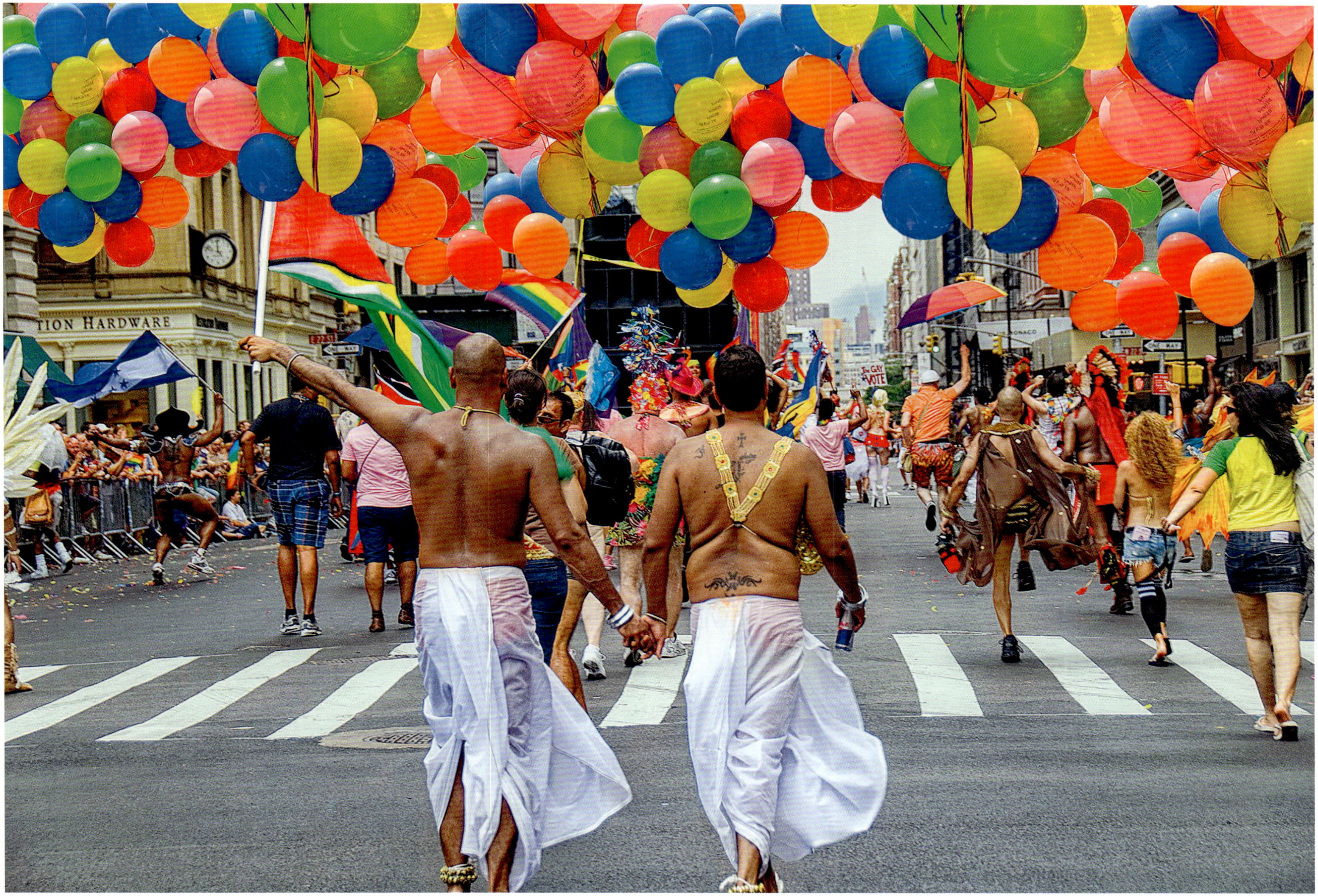

Parade-goers at the New York City Pride March walk under balloons. They are surrounded by loud music and cheers from the sidelines.

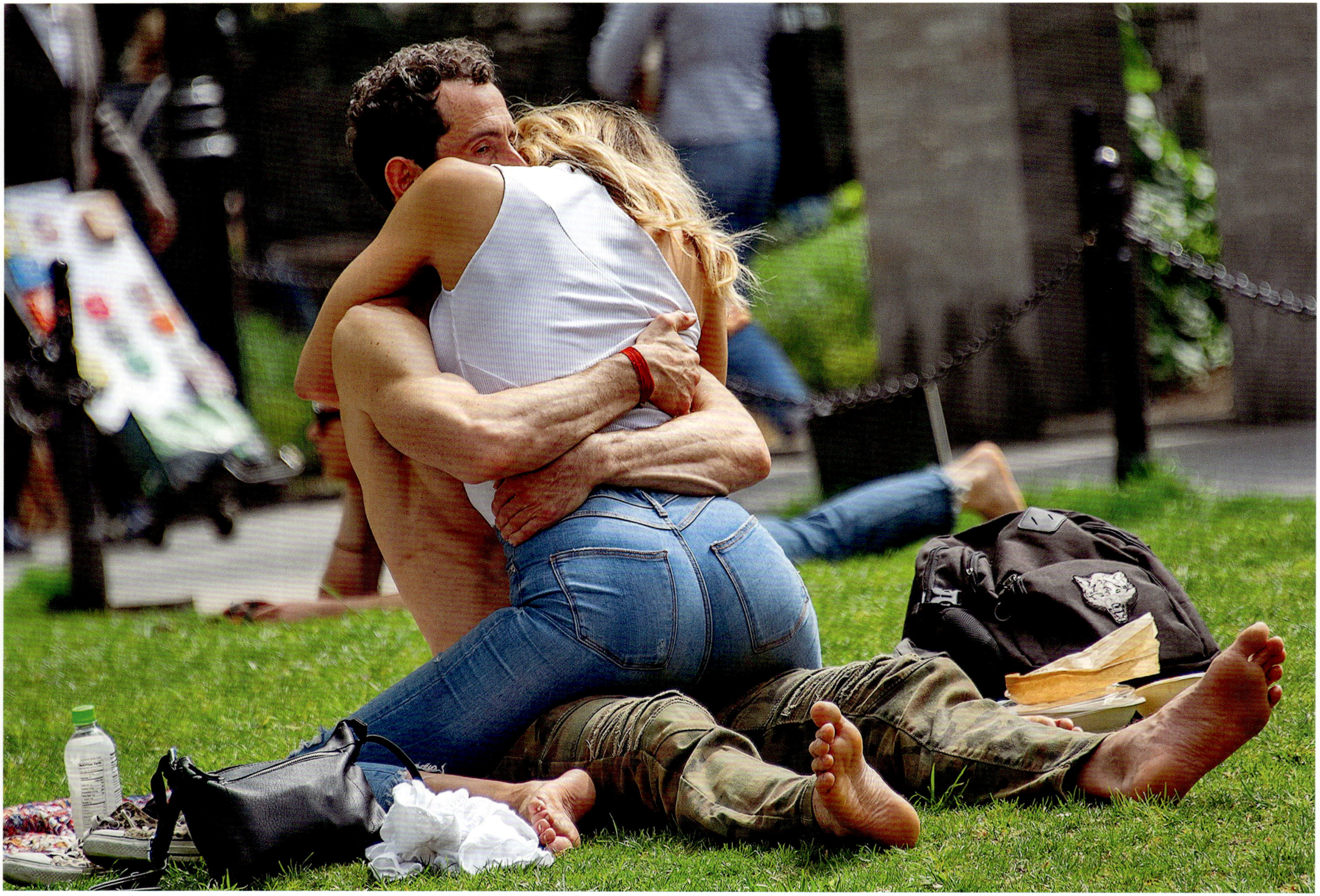

A couple in Washington Square Park.

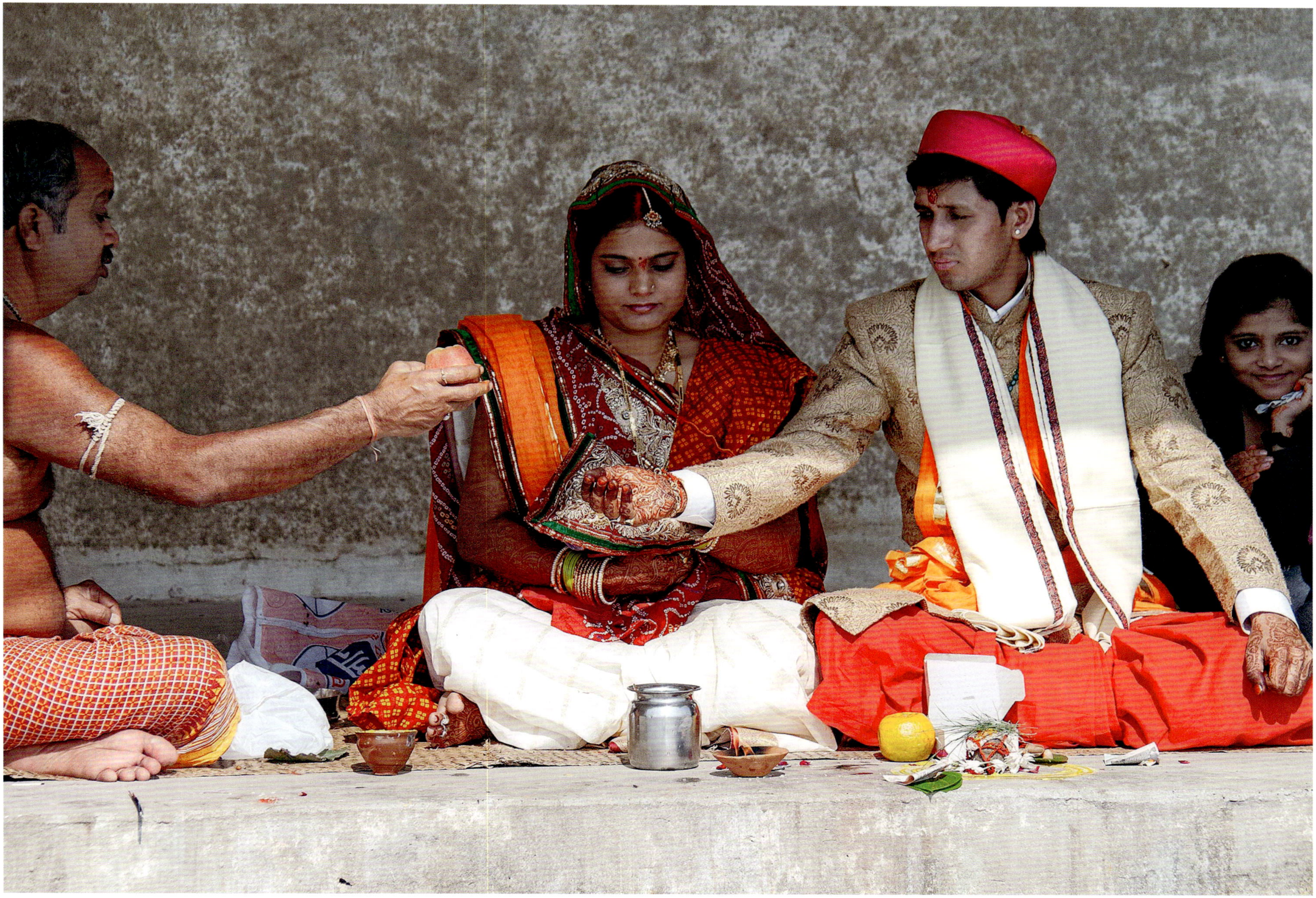

A newly married couple perform puja in the holy city of Varanasi.

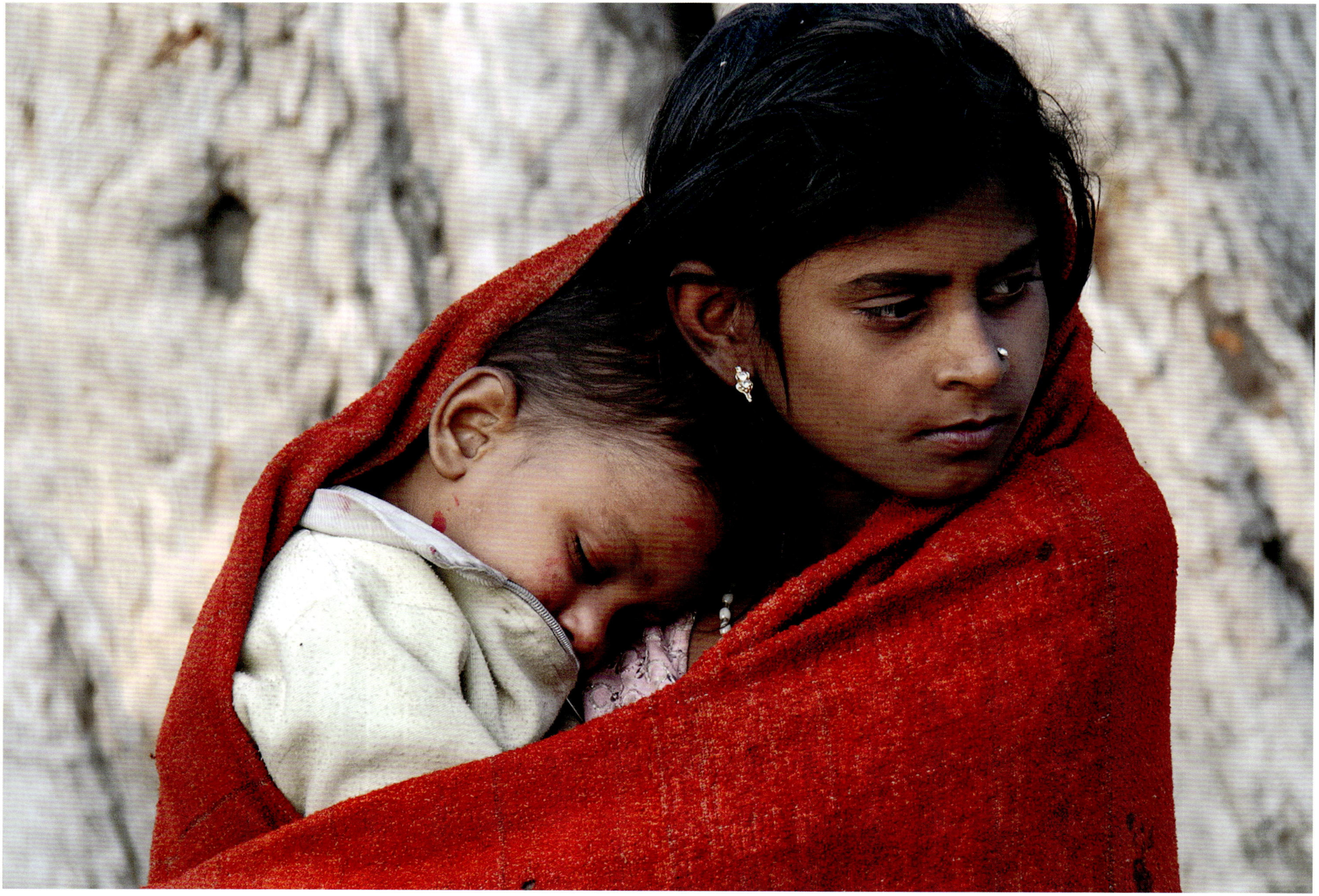

A sister holds her brother, offering protection, comfort, and love.

India / Dhanbad, Jharkhand

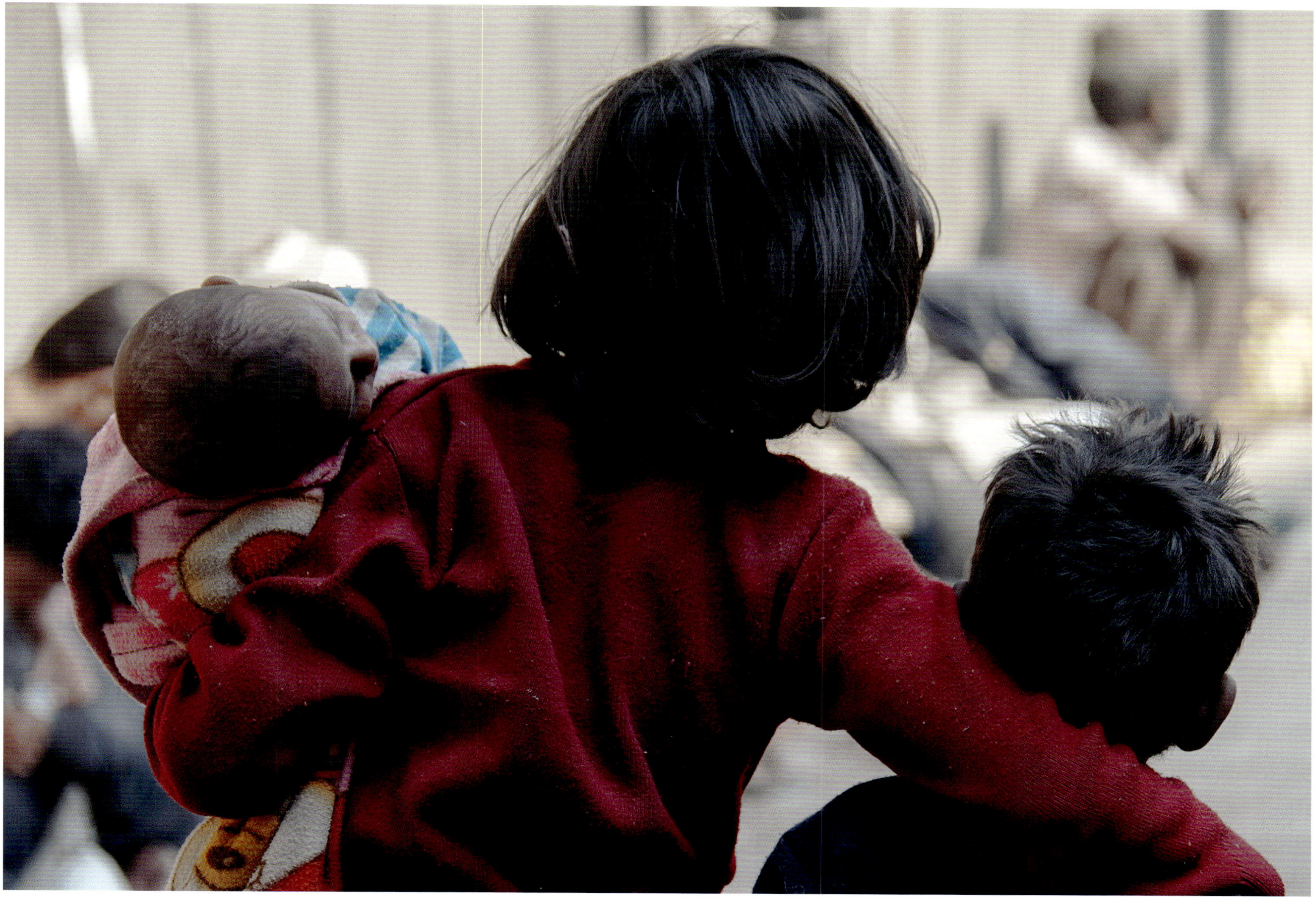

A child cares for two children even younger than herself.

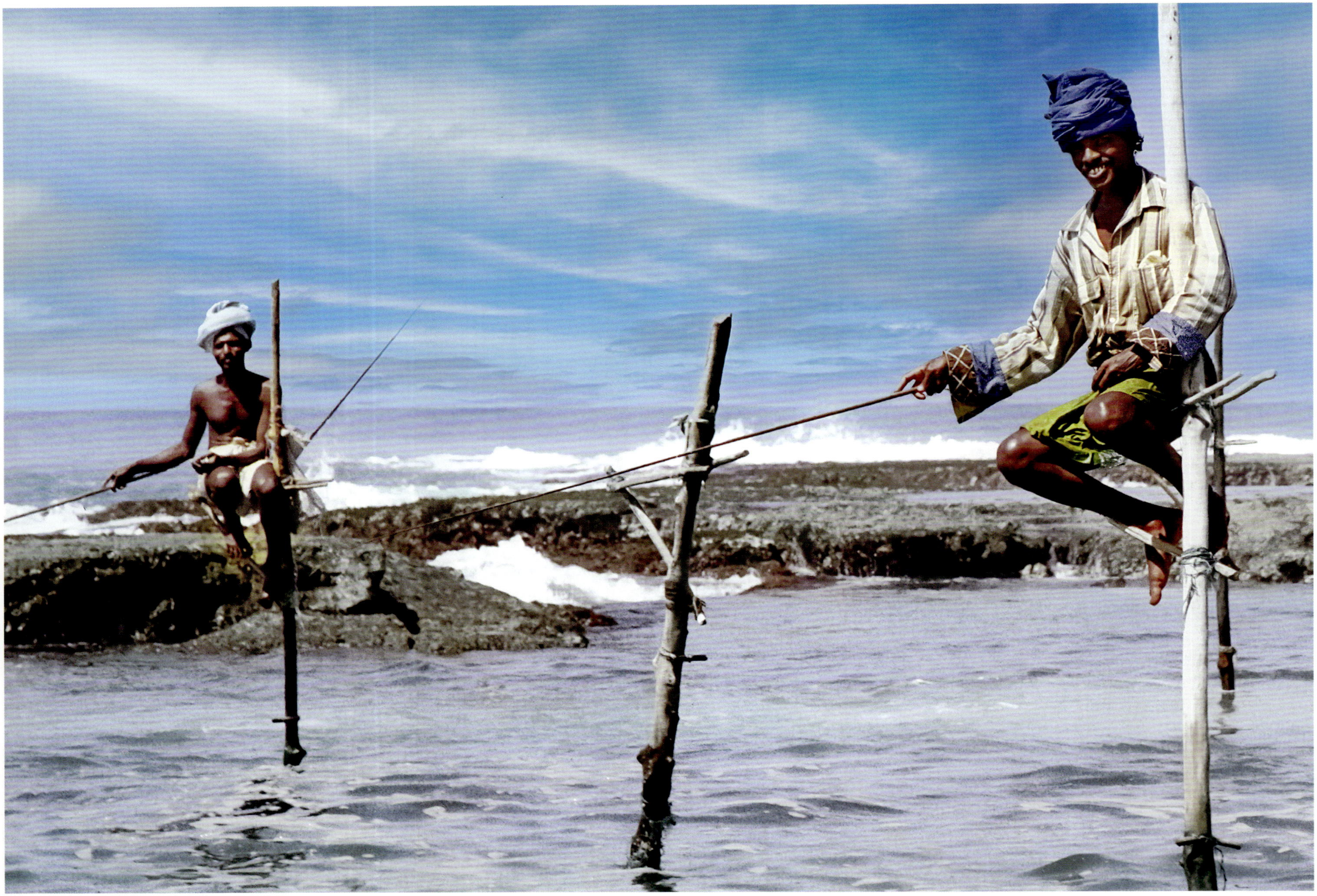

Men fish on stilts in the waters of Unawatuna in Sri Lanka. The practice orginated during World War II, when food shortages and depleted fishing spots pushed men to innovate their methods.

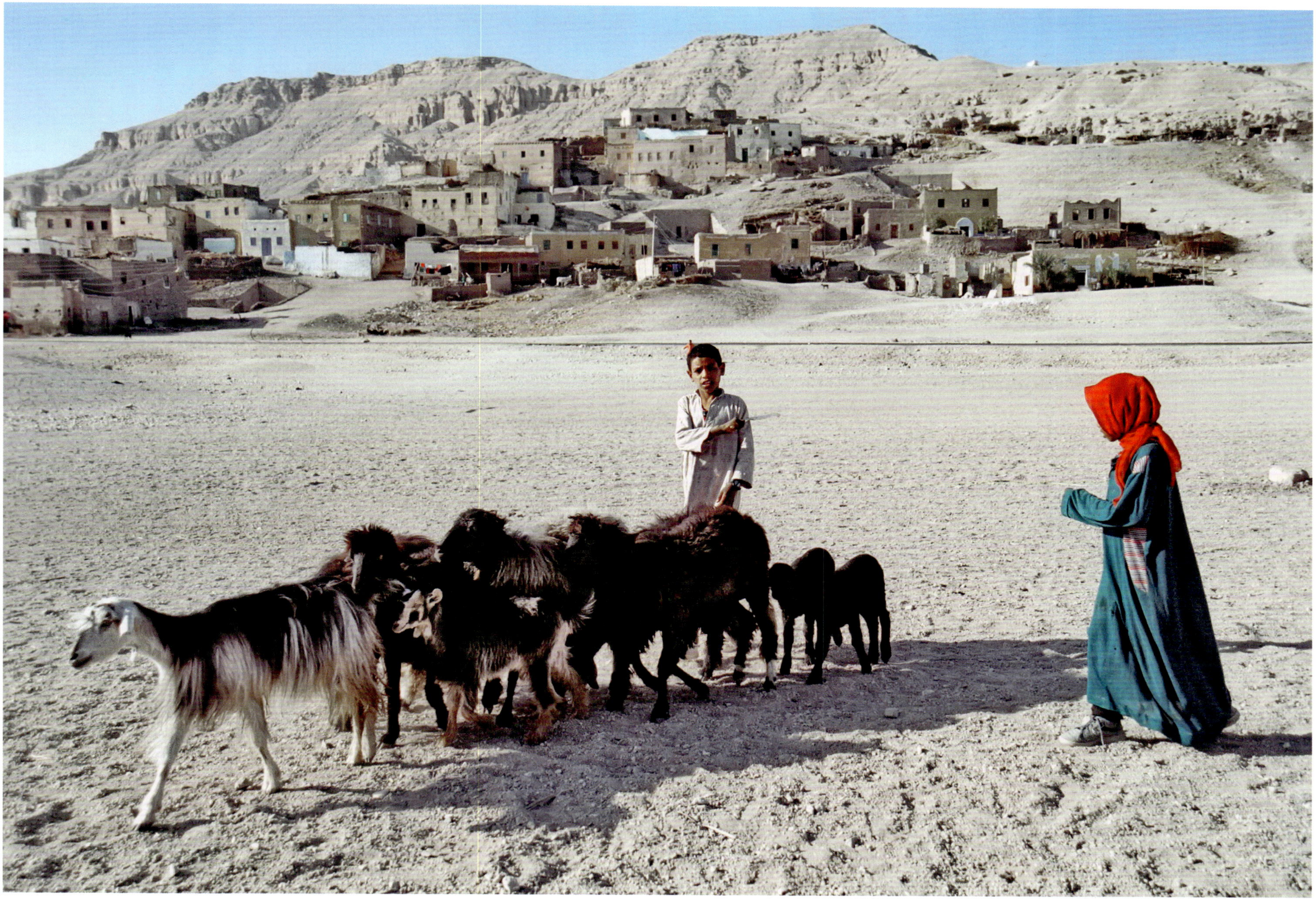

Young children tend goats. Behind them is the Valley of the Kings, with pharaohs' tombs and burial chambers.

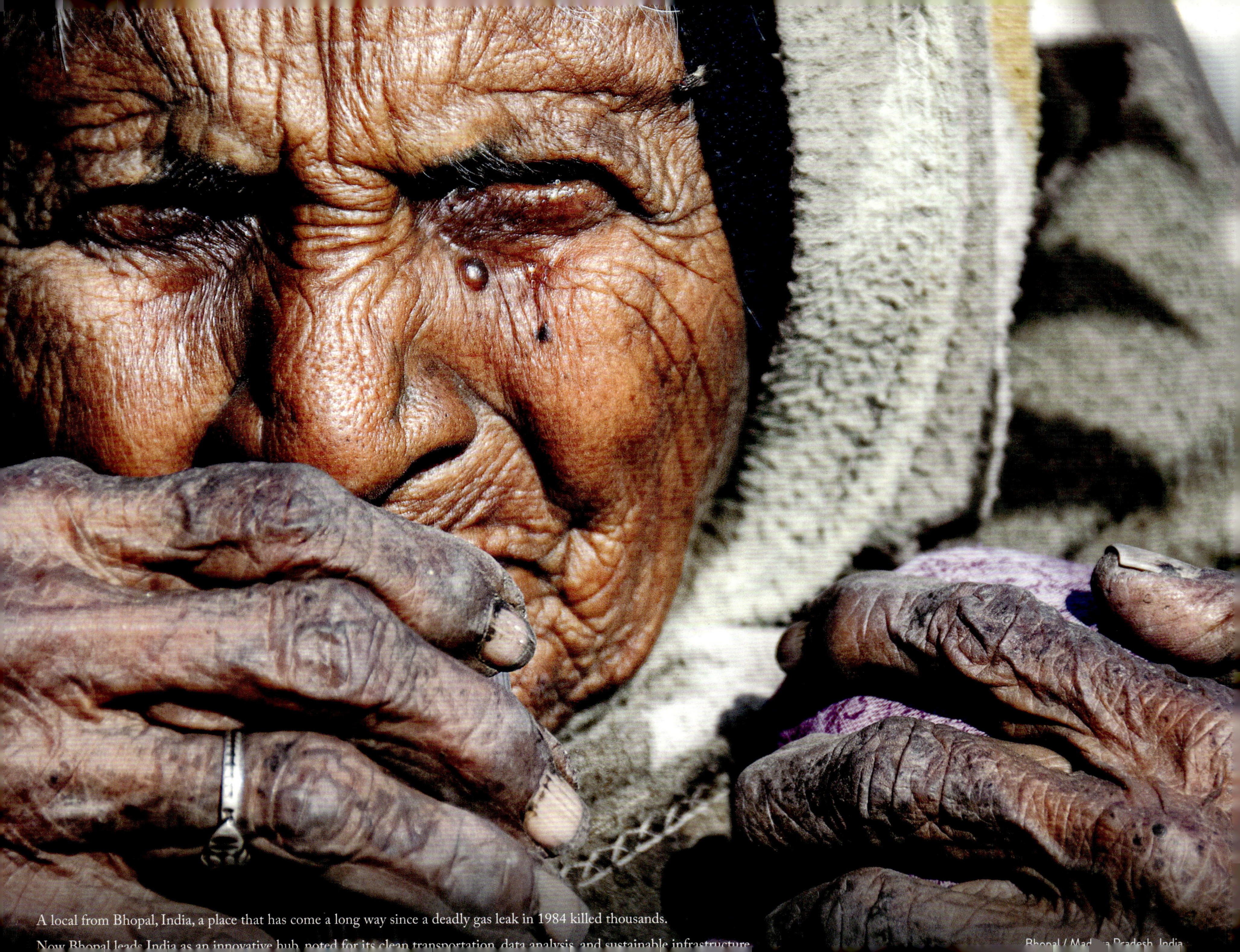

A local from Bhopal, India, a place that has come a long way since a deadly gas leak in 1984 killed thousands.
Now Bhopal leads India as an innovative hub, noted for its clean transportation, data analysis, and sustainable infrastructure.

Bhopal / Madhya Pradesh, India

RESILIENCE

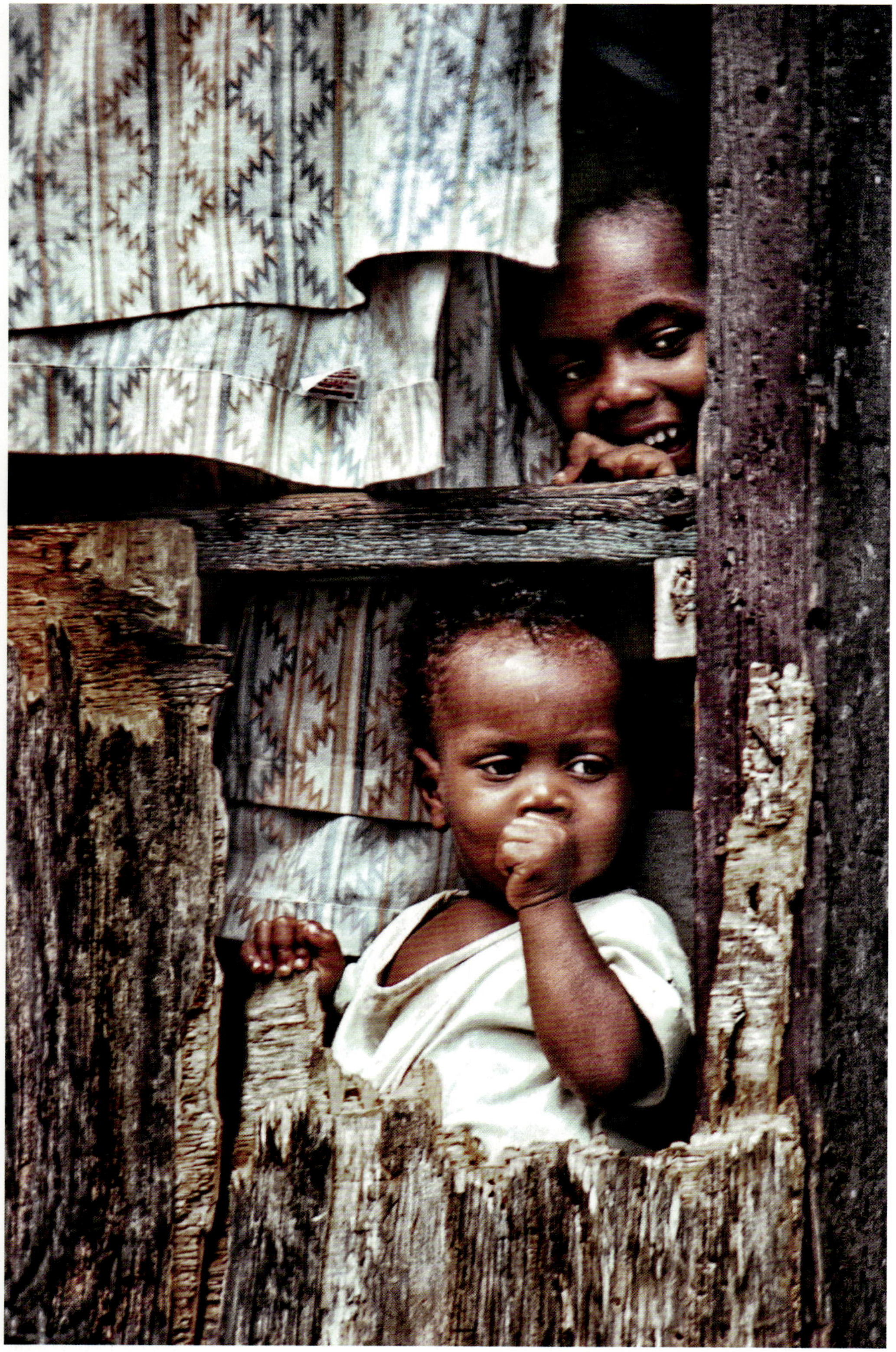

Brothers in the slums of Negril.

Children in the slums of
Ingenio Angelina.

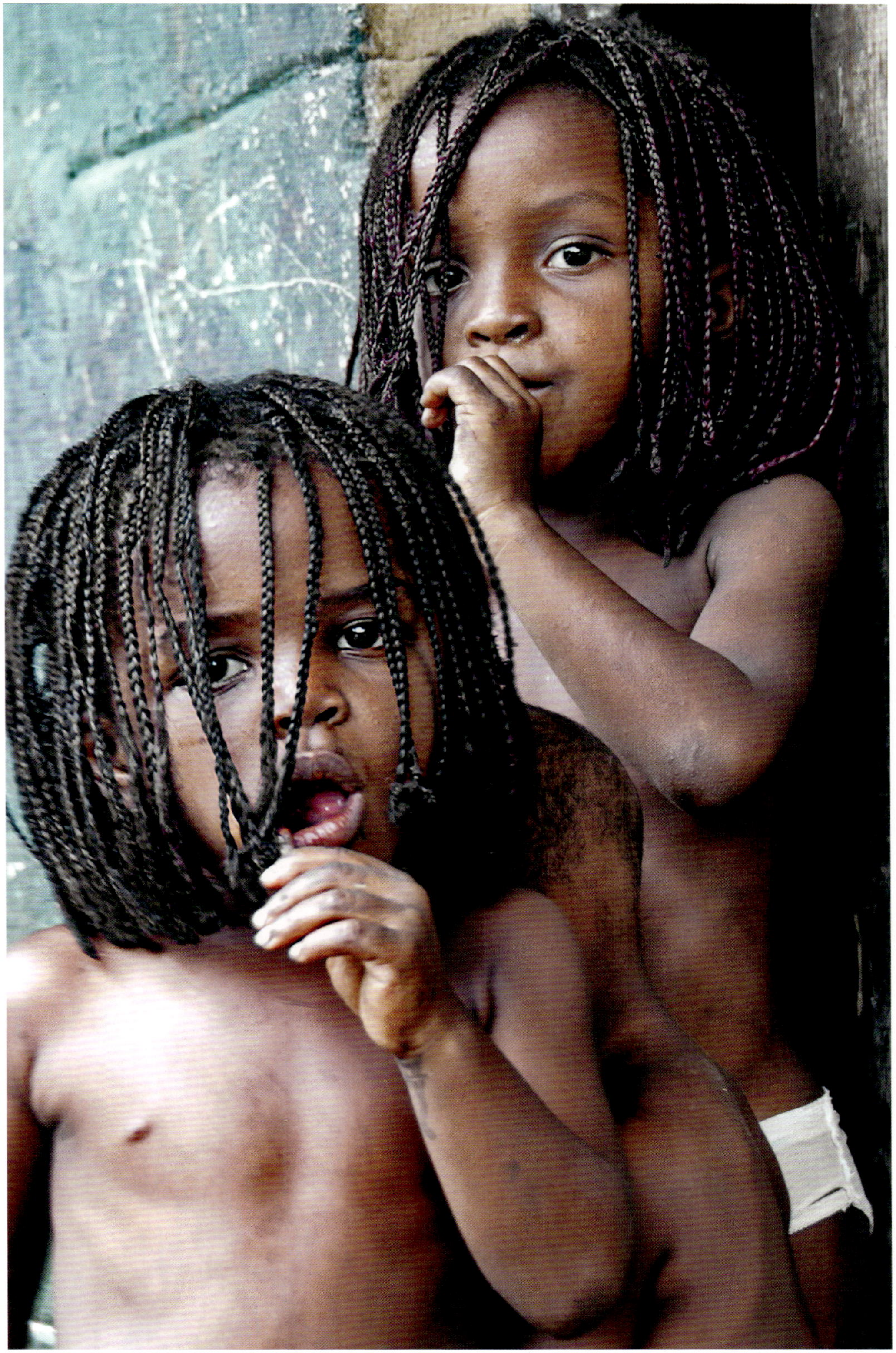

Dominican Republic / San Pedro de Macorís, San Pedro de Macorís Province

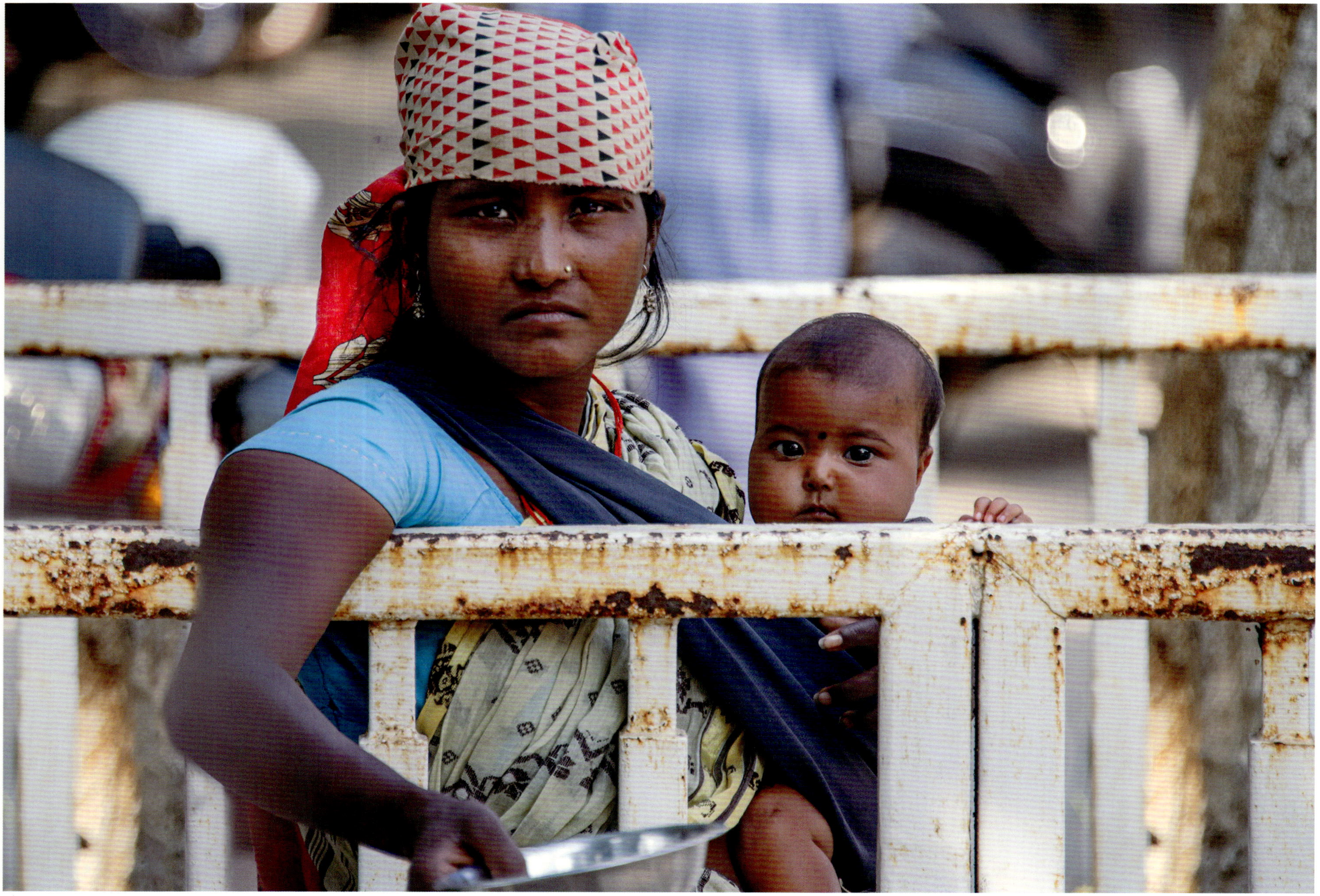

A woman carrying a child begs for money during jum'ah.

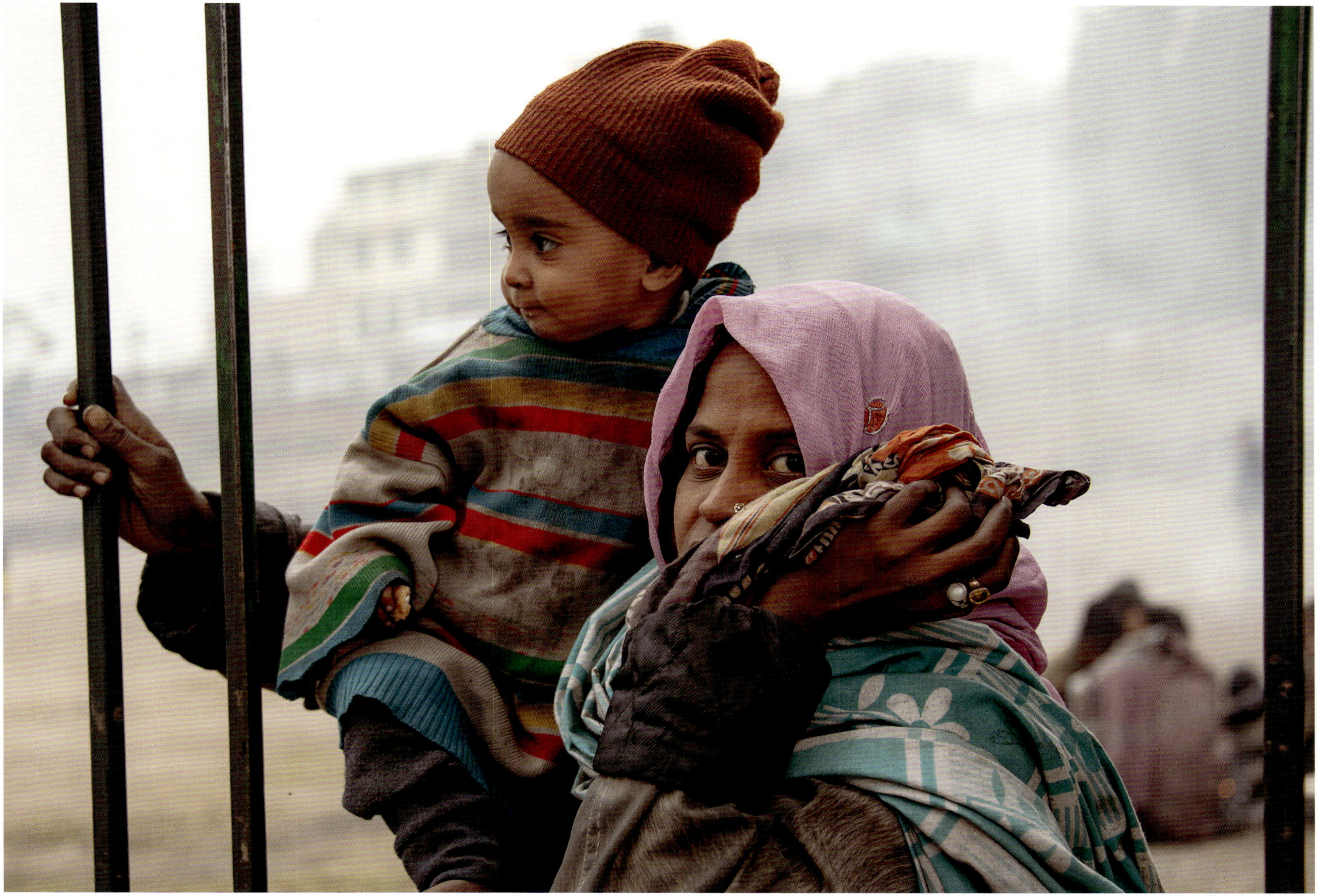

A woman and child outside the Hanuman Temple. On Tuesdays and Saturdays, it fills with Hindu devotees and the homeless, who are fed one meal.

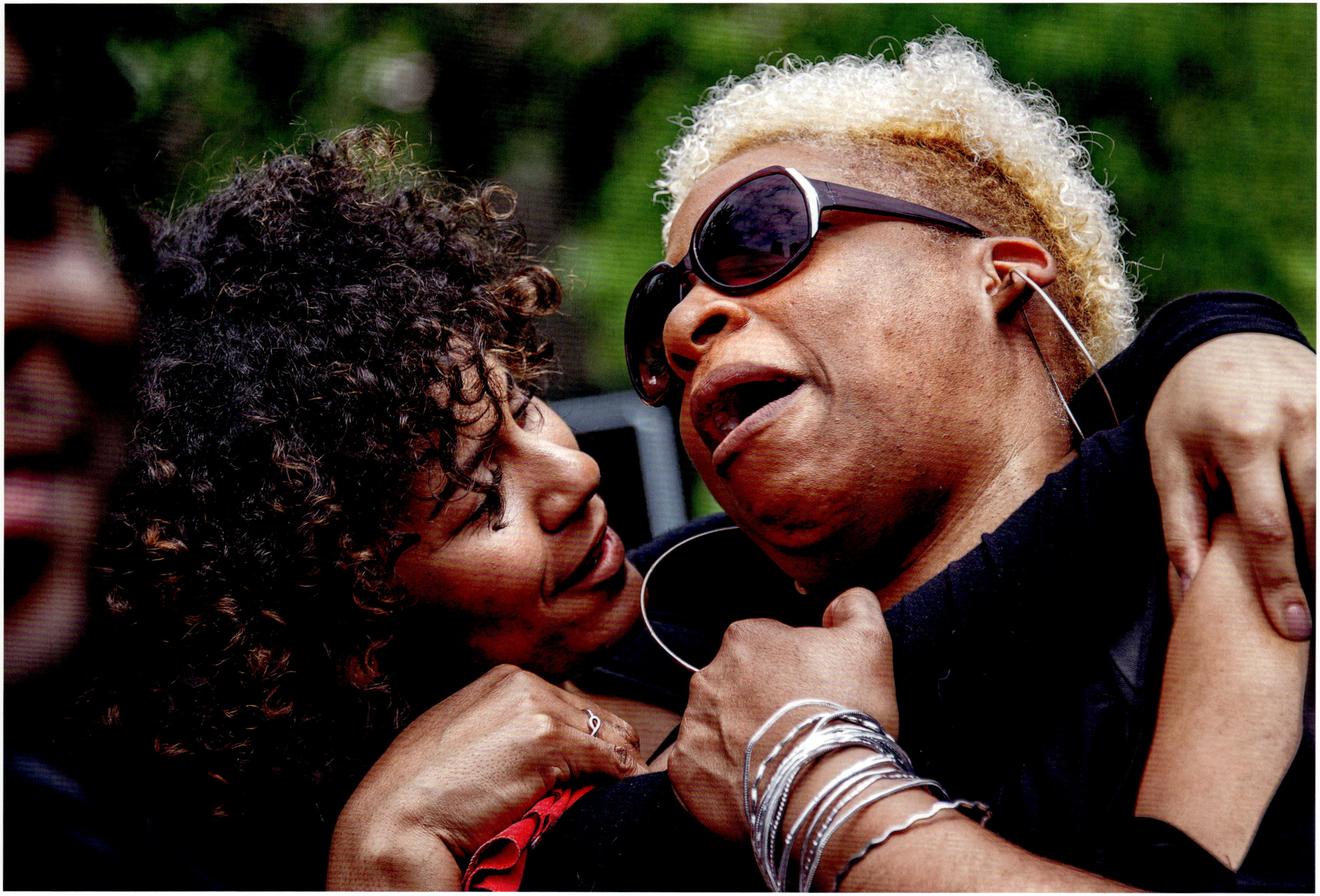

An emotional moment during an event in Union Square.

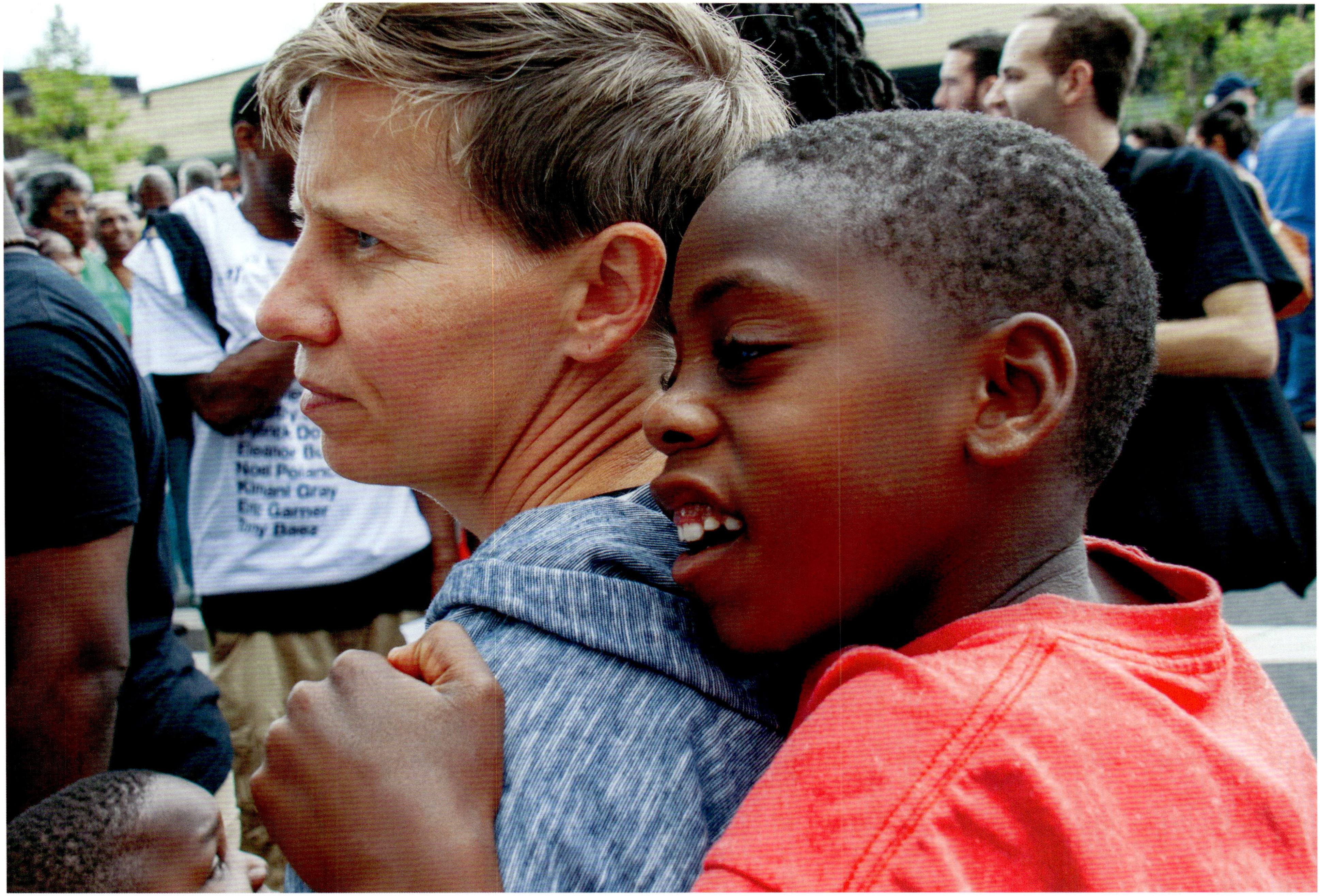

On Staten Island, New Yorkers attend a protest rally for Eric Garner, a black man who died on July 17, 2014, after Daniel Pantaleo, a New York City Police Department officer, put him in a choke hold while arresting him for selling cigarettes on the street.

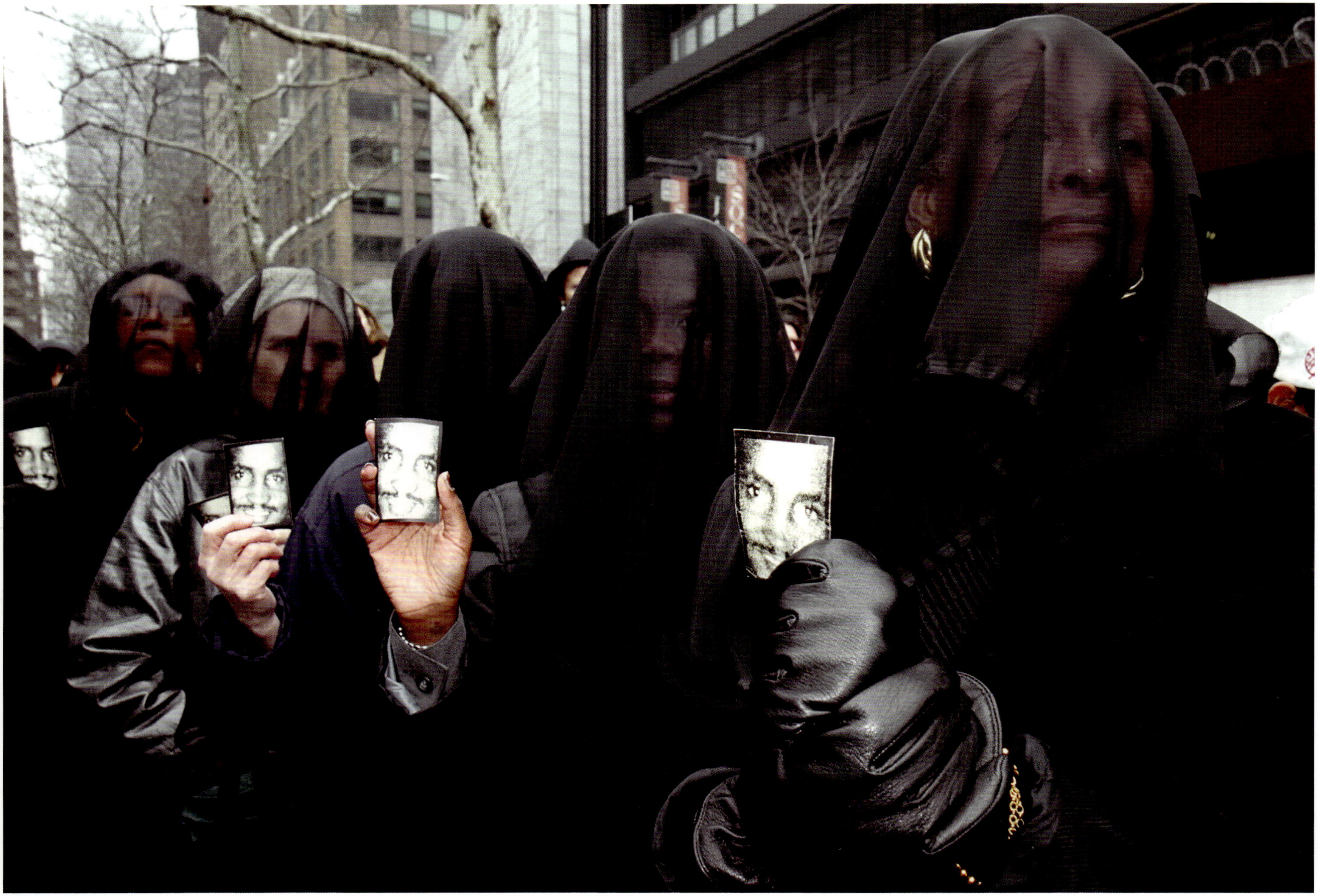

In Manhattan's Dag Hammarskjöld Plaza, near the United Nations building, women protest police brutality in the shooting death of Amadou Diallo, a twenty-three-year-old black man from Guinea. Diallo was shot at forty-one times, and hit nineteen times, by four cops who claimed that he was reaching for a firearm; Diallo had no firearm on his person, only a wallet. The cops were all acquitted.

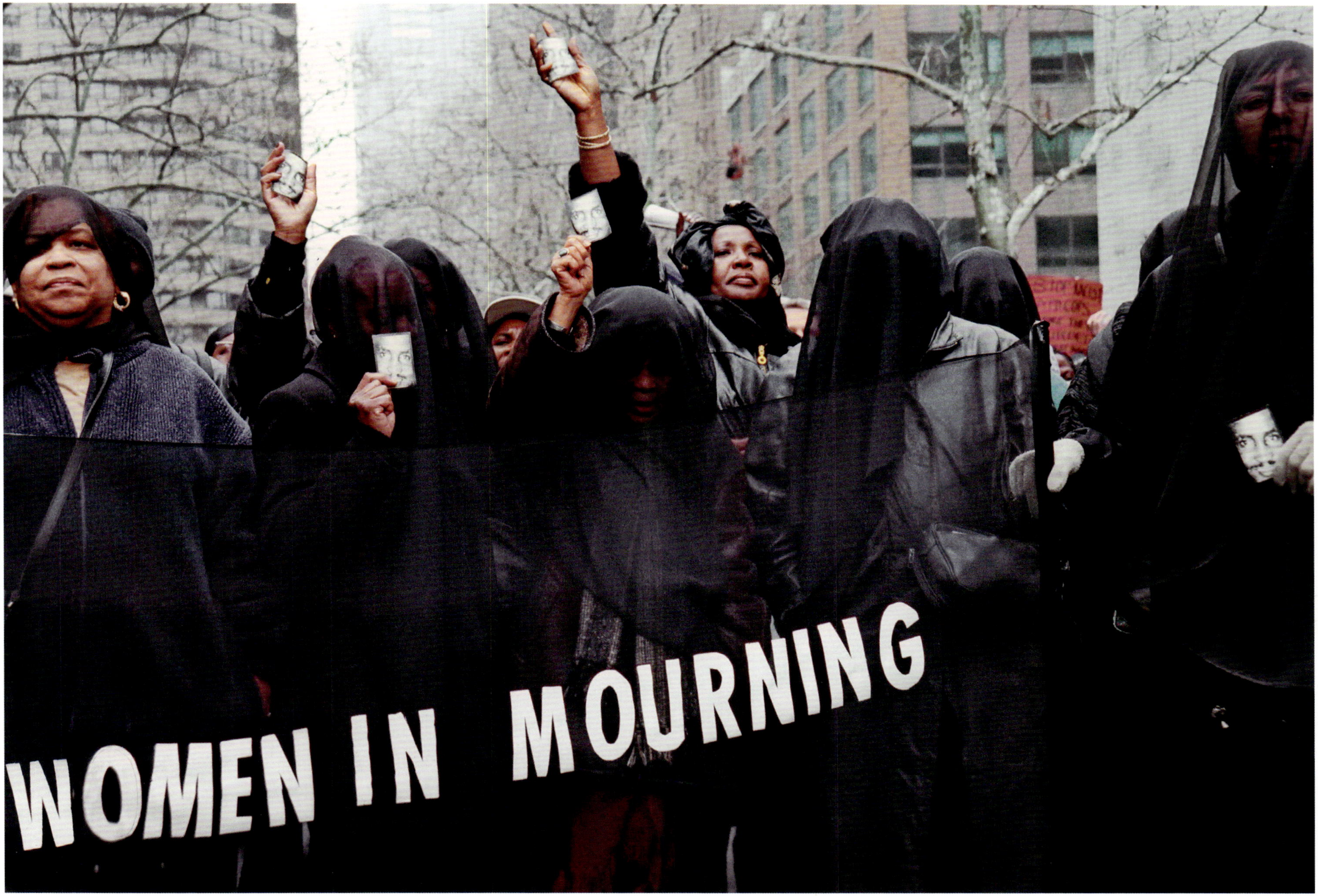

Protestors hold photos of Diallo and a sign reading Women in Mourning.

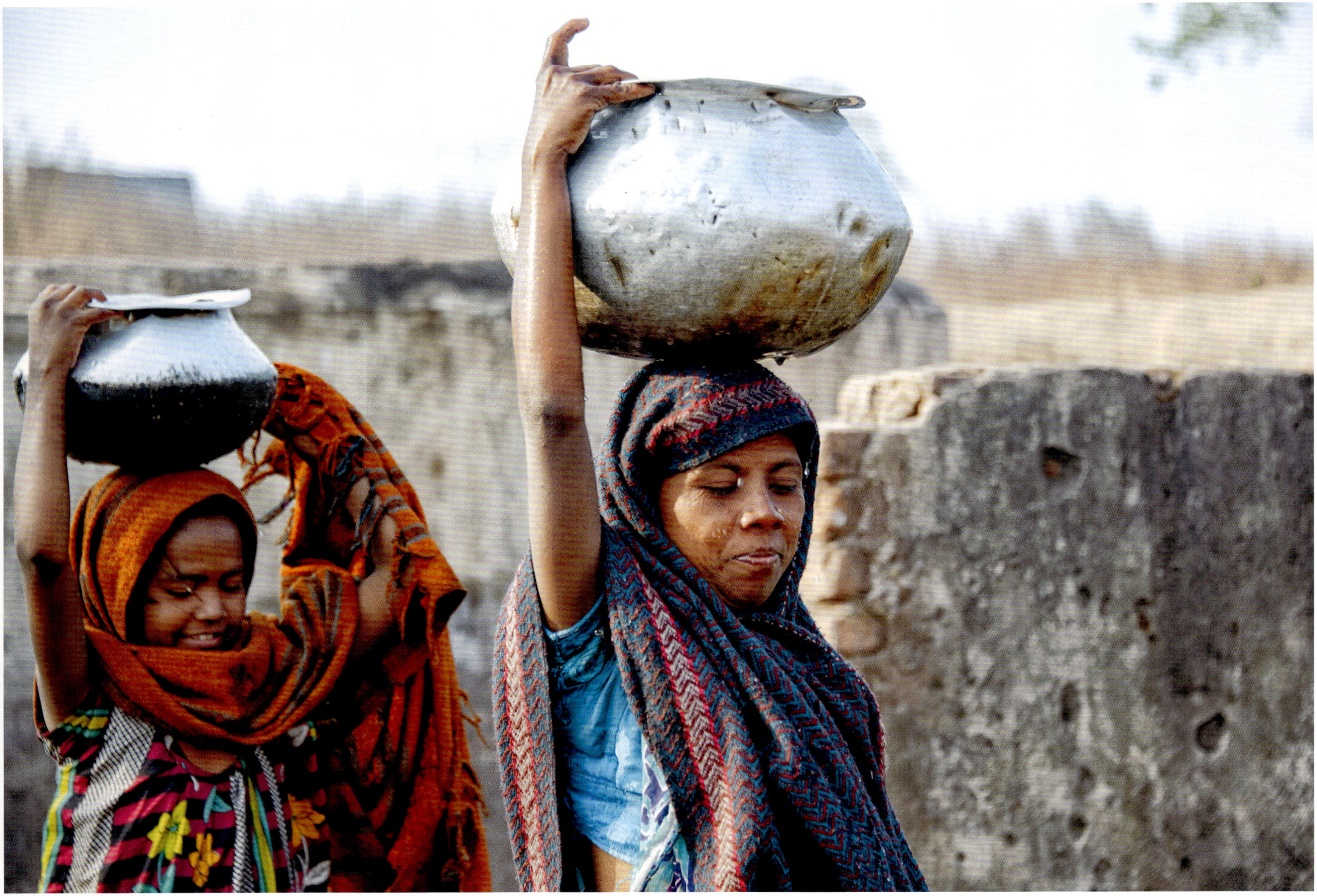

People fetch water from a well several miles from their house.

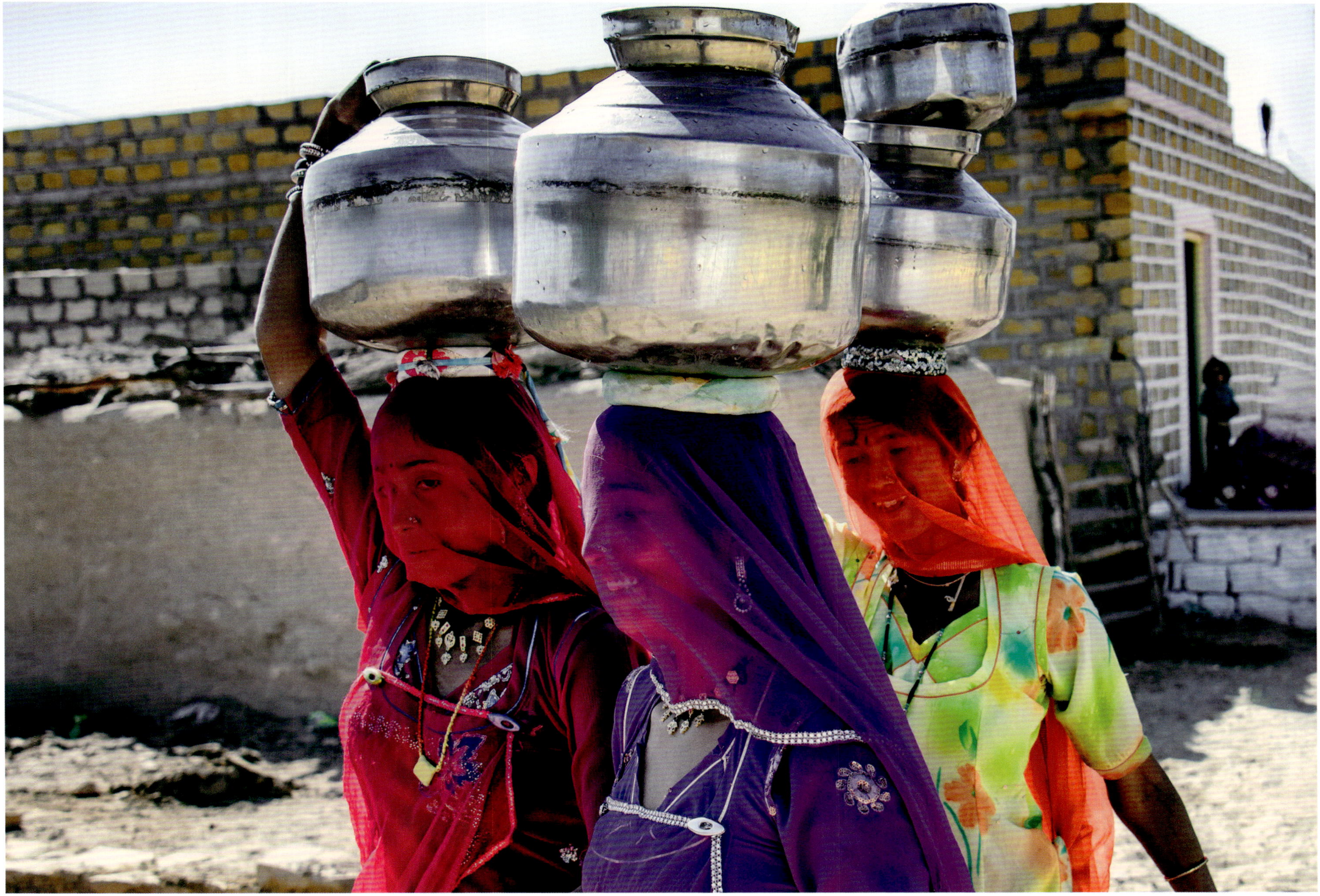

Three young women carry pots of water on their heads. In the Indian desert, water is scarce and far from homes.

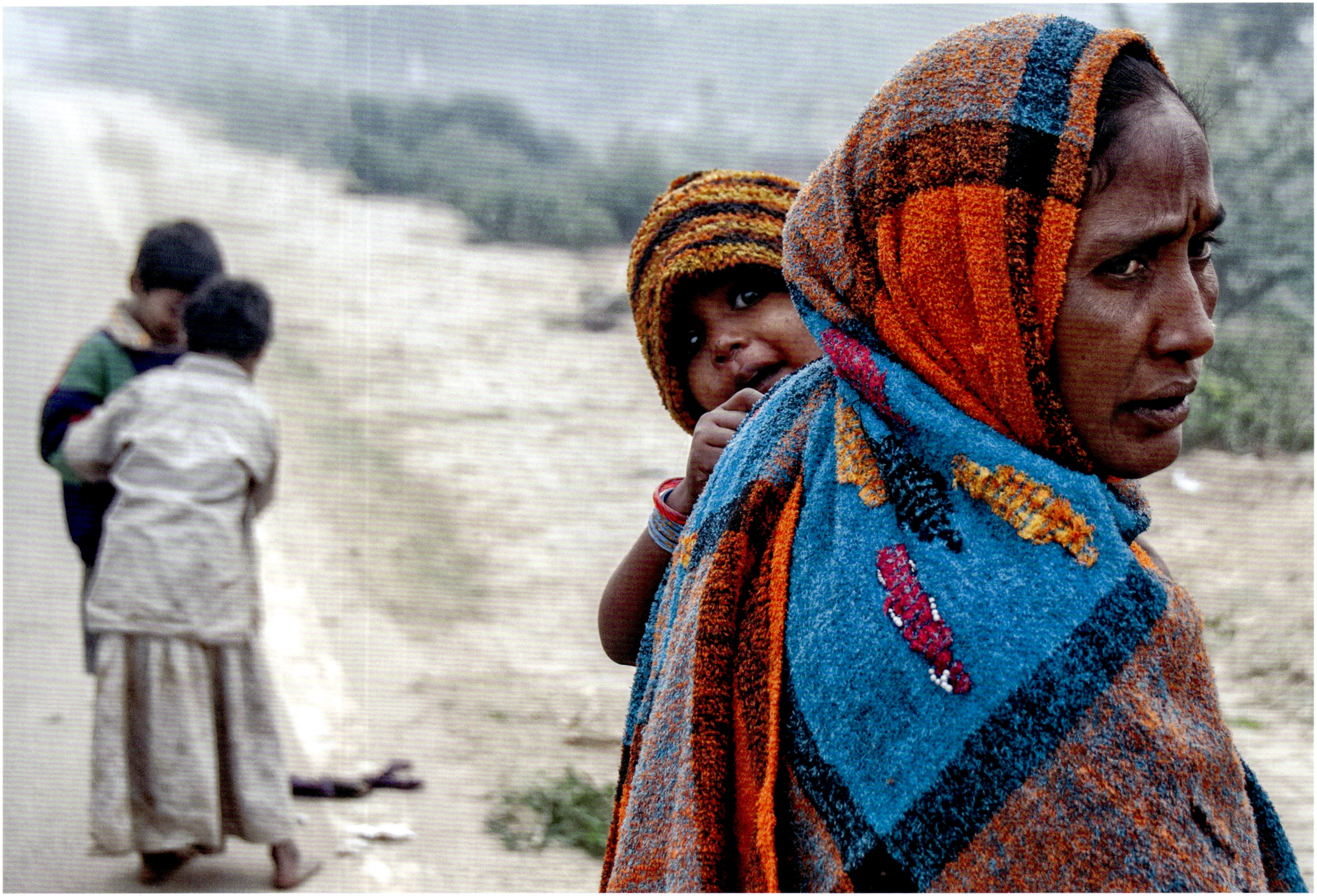

People in an area used for sourcing coal.

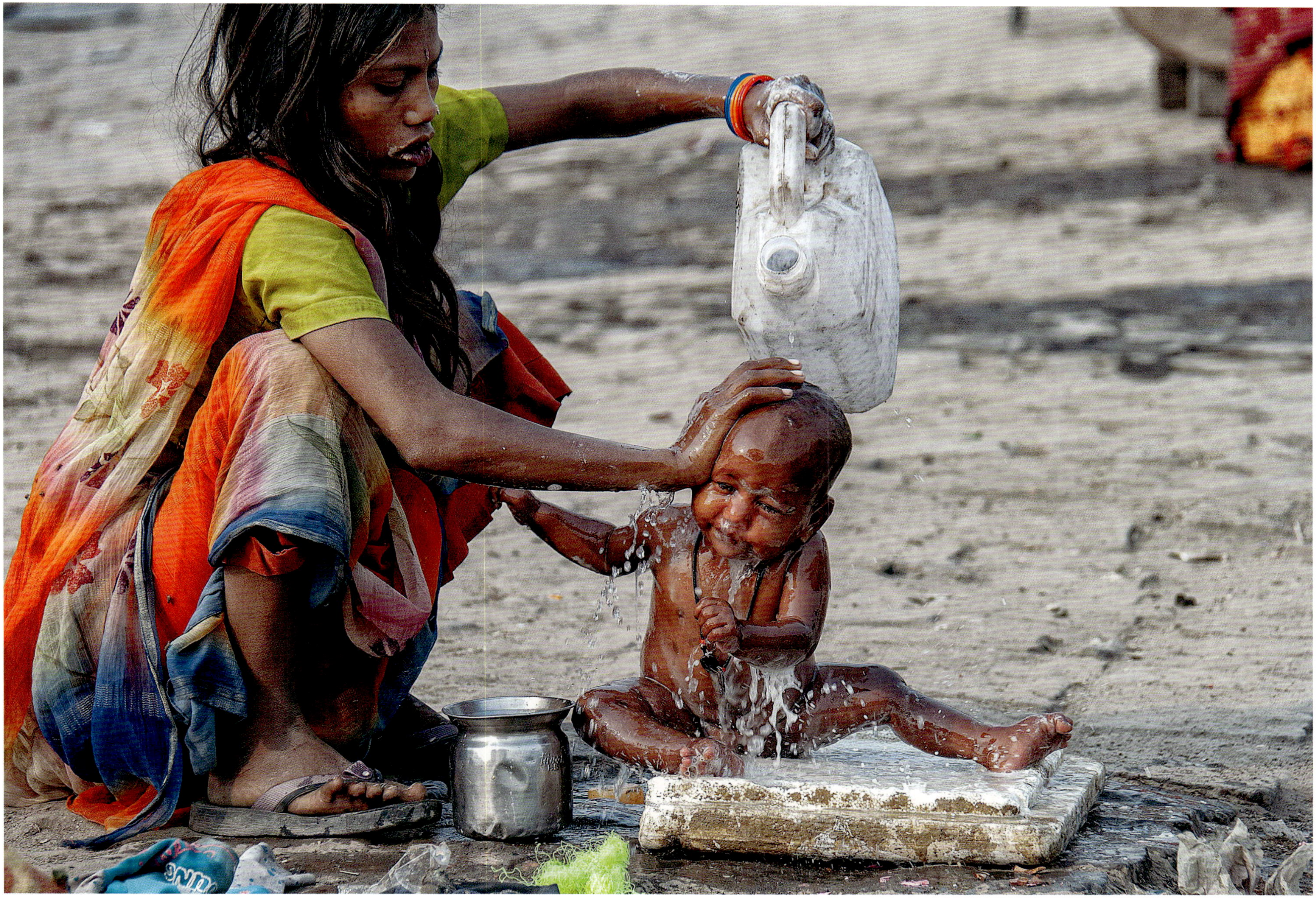

In India, daily activities like washing often take place outside. Here a child is being washed by his mother, but it is common to see men bathing outside too.

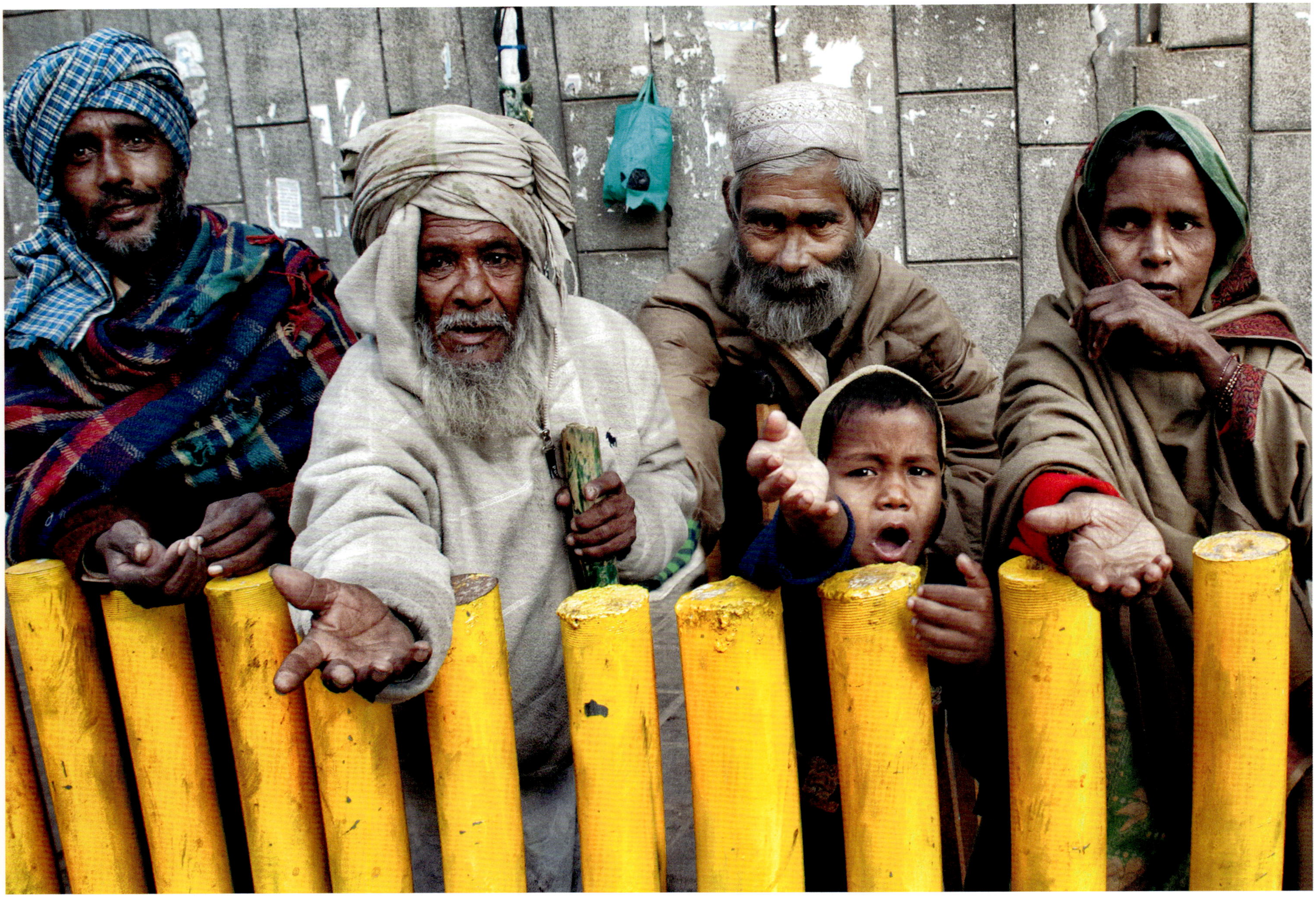

Beggars in Nizamuddin Dargah, the mausoleum of Hazrat Nizamuddin Auliya, one of the most famous Sufi saints. This dargah, or mausoleum, is one of the most popular tourist destinations in Delhi and a busy hub for Sufi pilgrims, with hundreds visiting each day.

Many women in Phnom Penh hold babies when they beg. Sometimes the children are not their own.

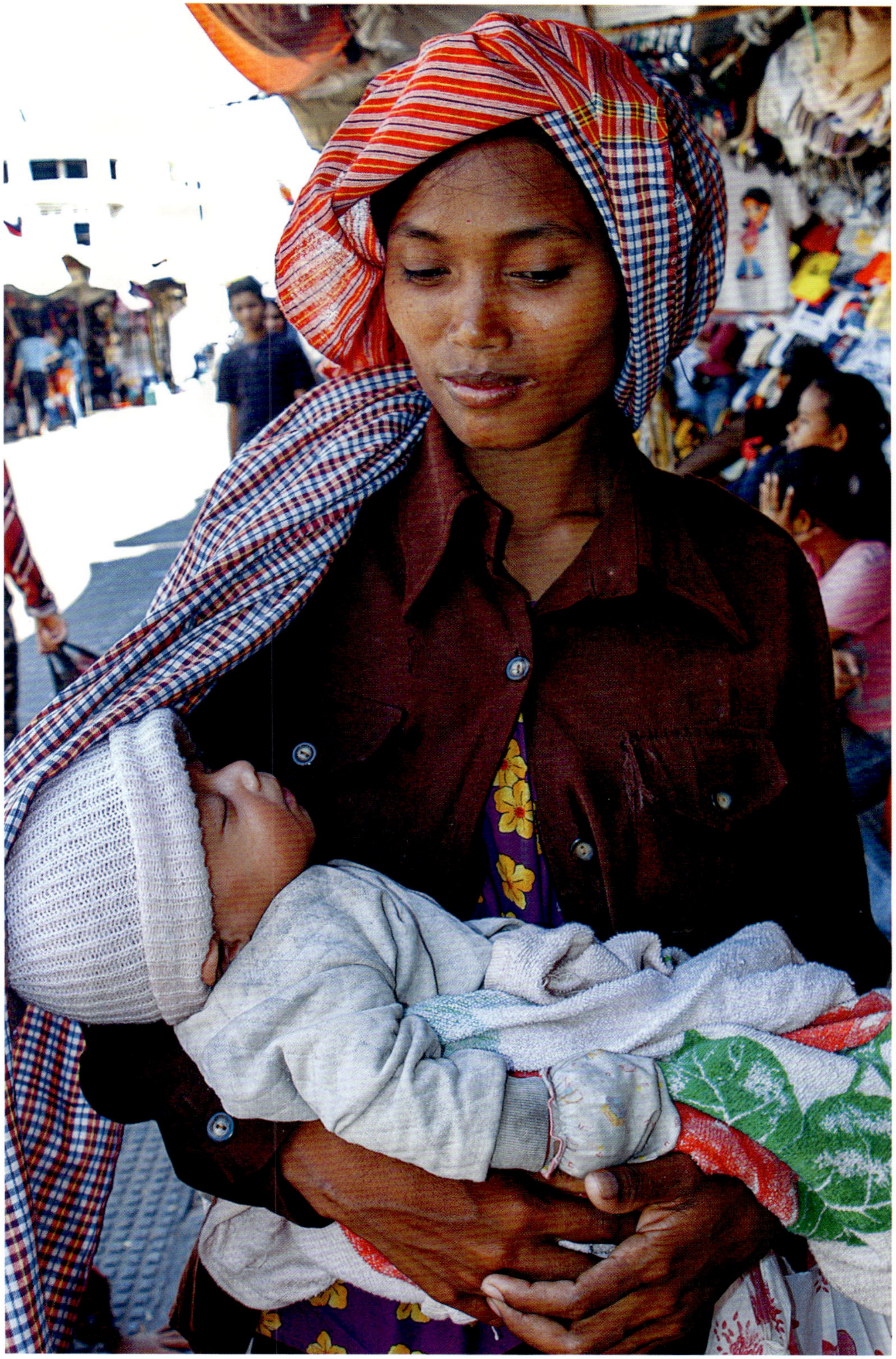

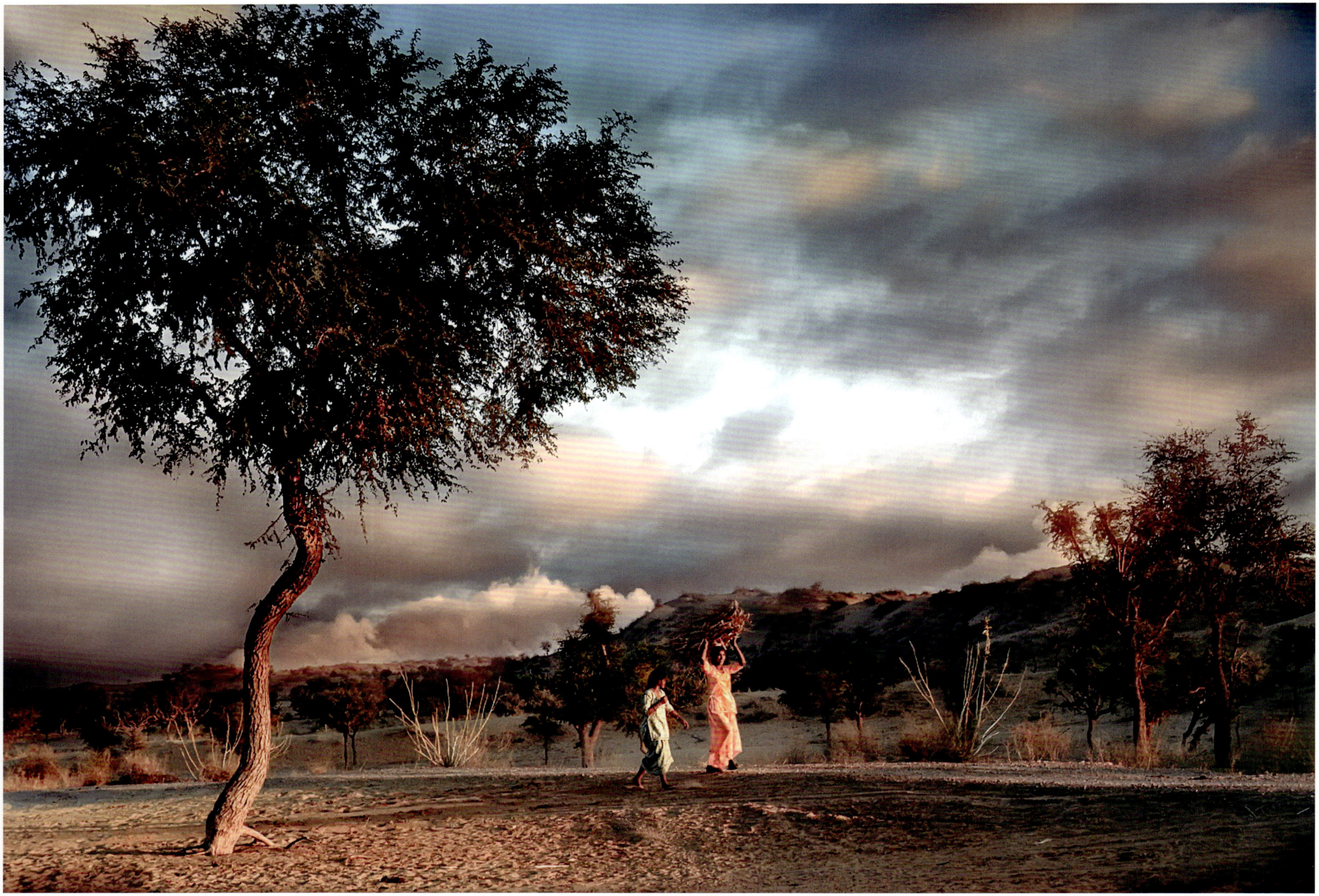

In the Thar Desert, a mother and daughter head home with branches to be used for cooking or lighting fires in the cold mornings.

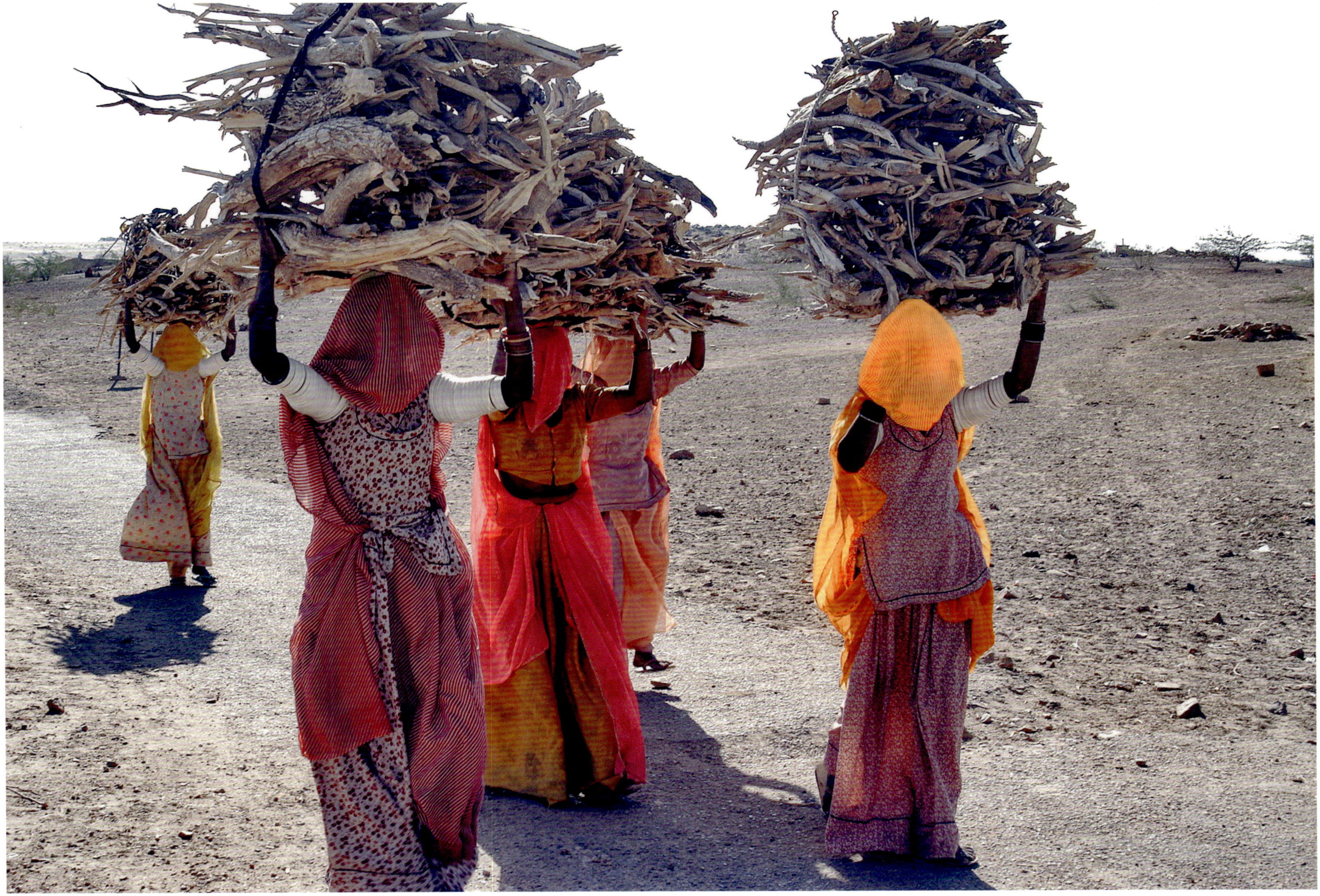

Veiled women walk in the 100-degree heat near Amar Sagar in the Thar Desert. They carry wood to use for a fire.

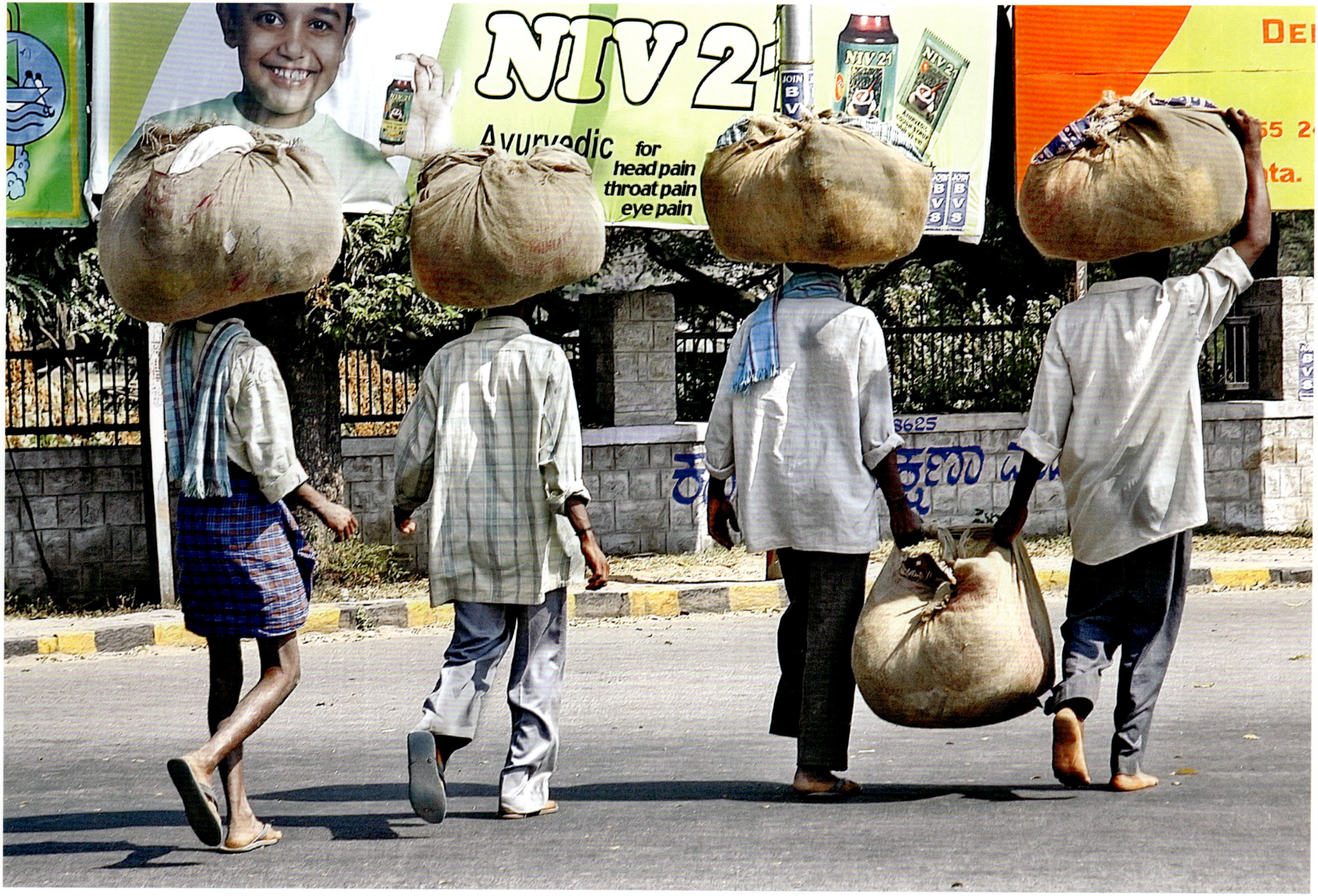

A group of men carry bushels on their heads, a common practice in India.

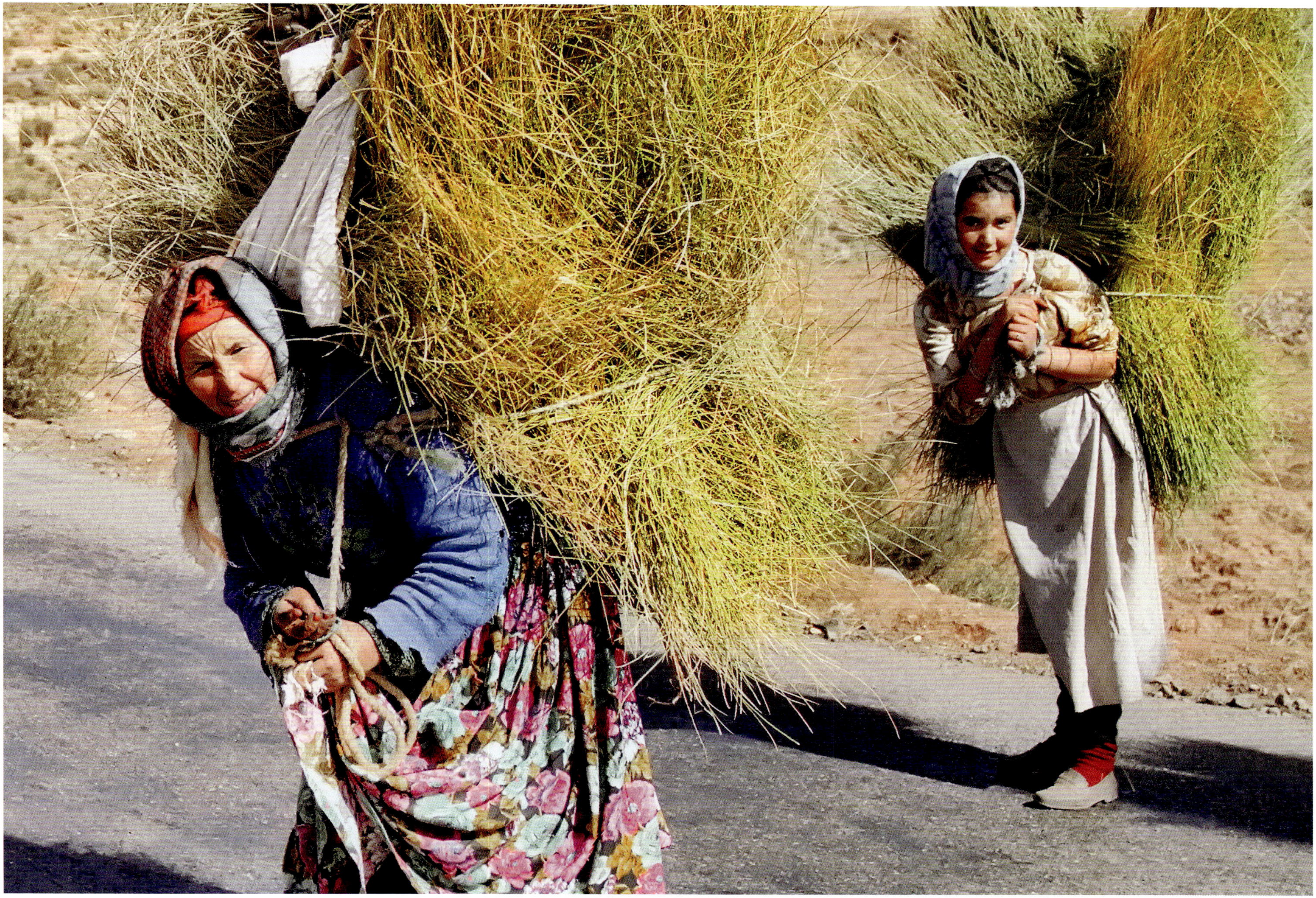

Women cross Tizi-n-Test, a small pass that connects Marrakech and Taroudant.

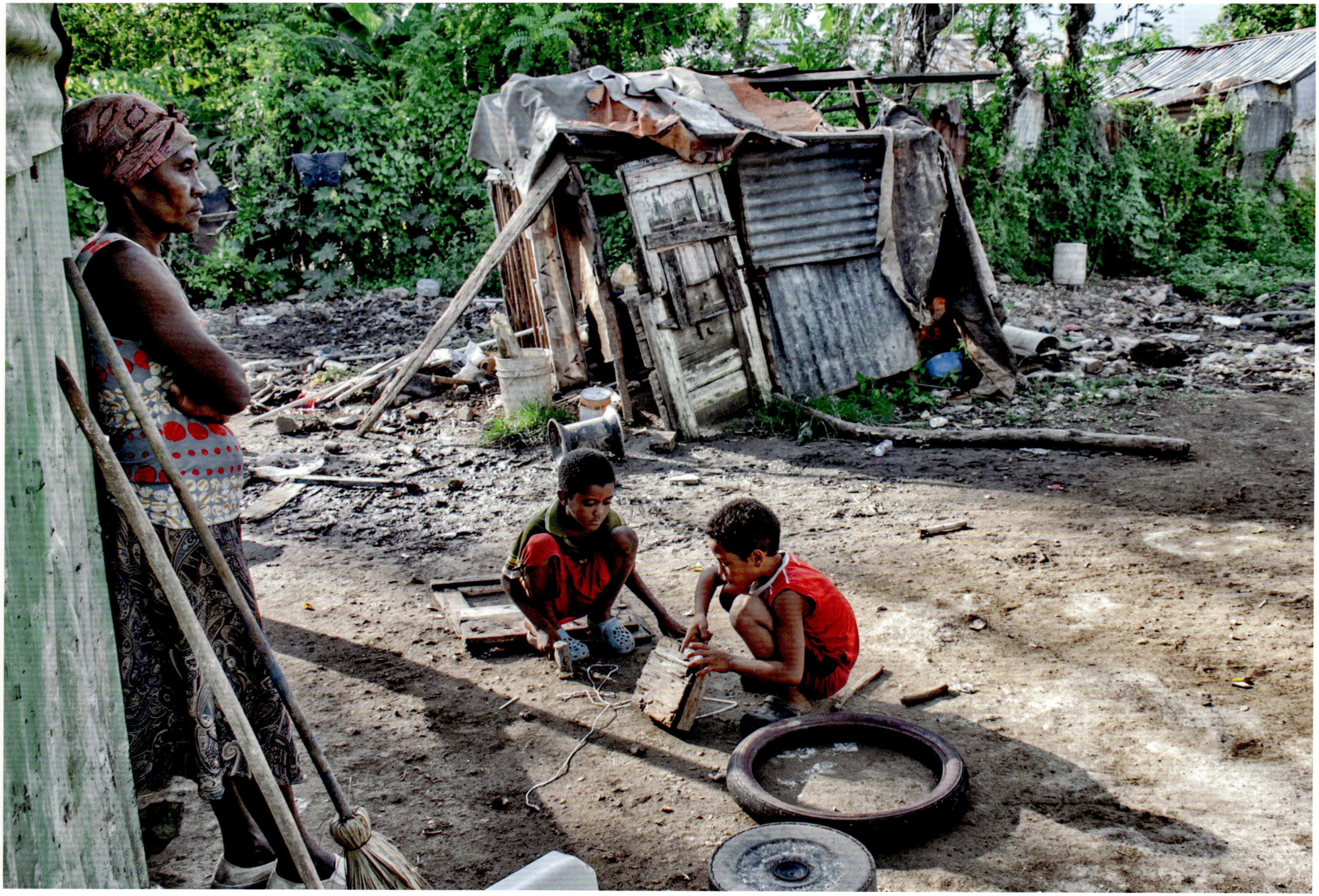

In batey Ramón Santana, a mother stands near two young boys. She has a family of seven—with one daughter of seventeen who is pregnant—and says they have no money to eat. Hunger is a common problem in the slums of San Pedro de Macorís.

Sisters: one blind, the other strong spirited, and a young boy. The women have lived in abject poverty for many decades. They are Haitians who crossed the border and live in Barahona, a western city in the Dominican Republic. The boy comes to visit them.

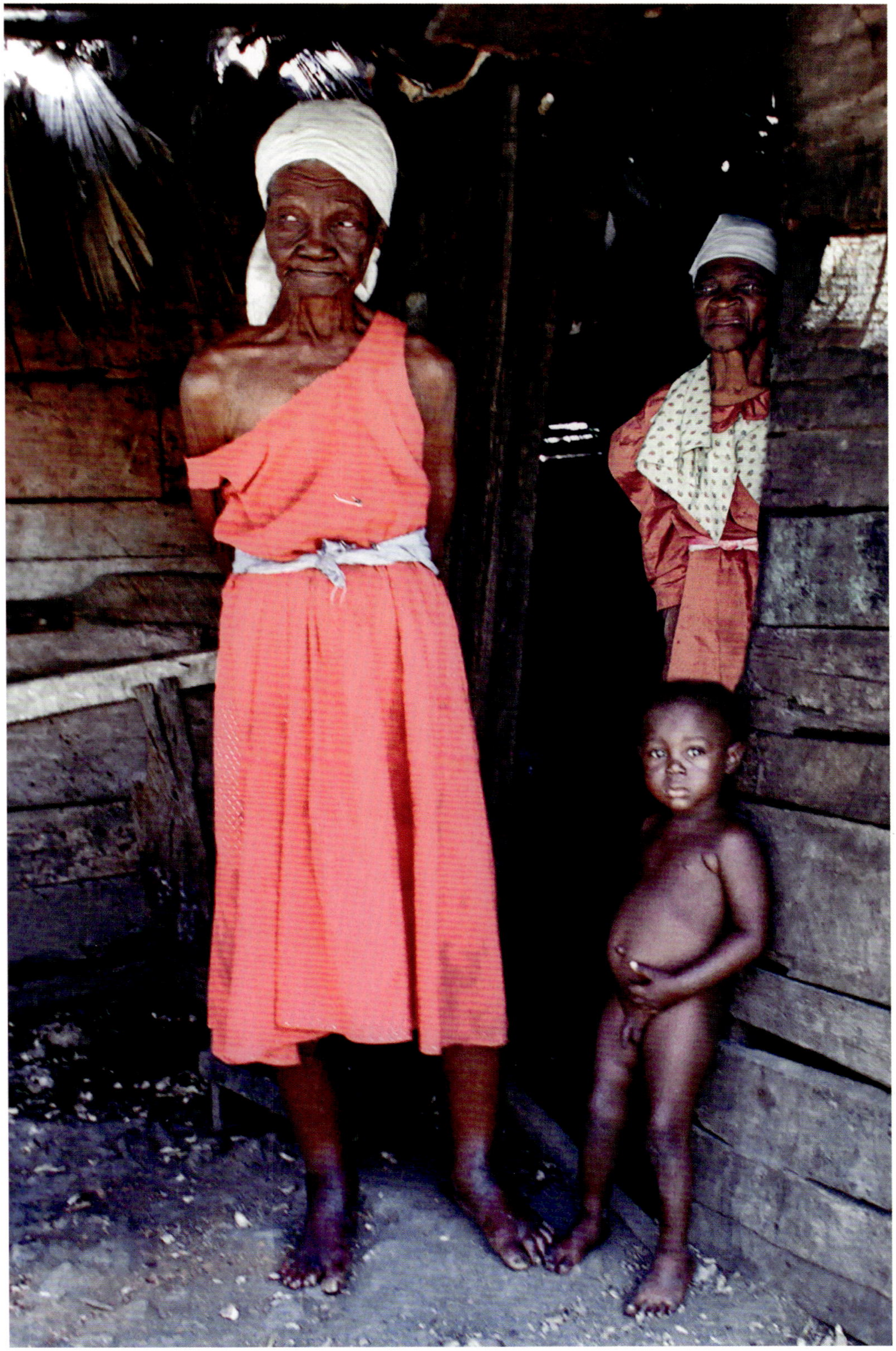

Dominican Republic / Barahona, Barahona Province

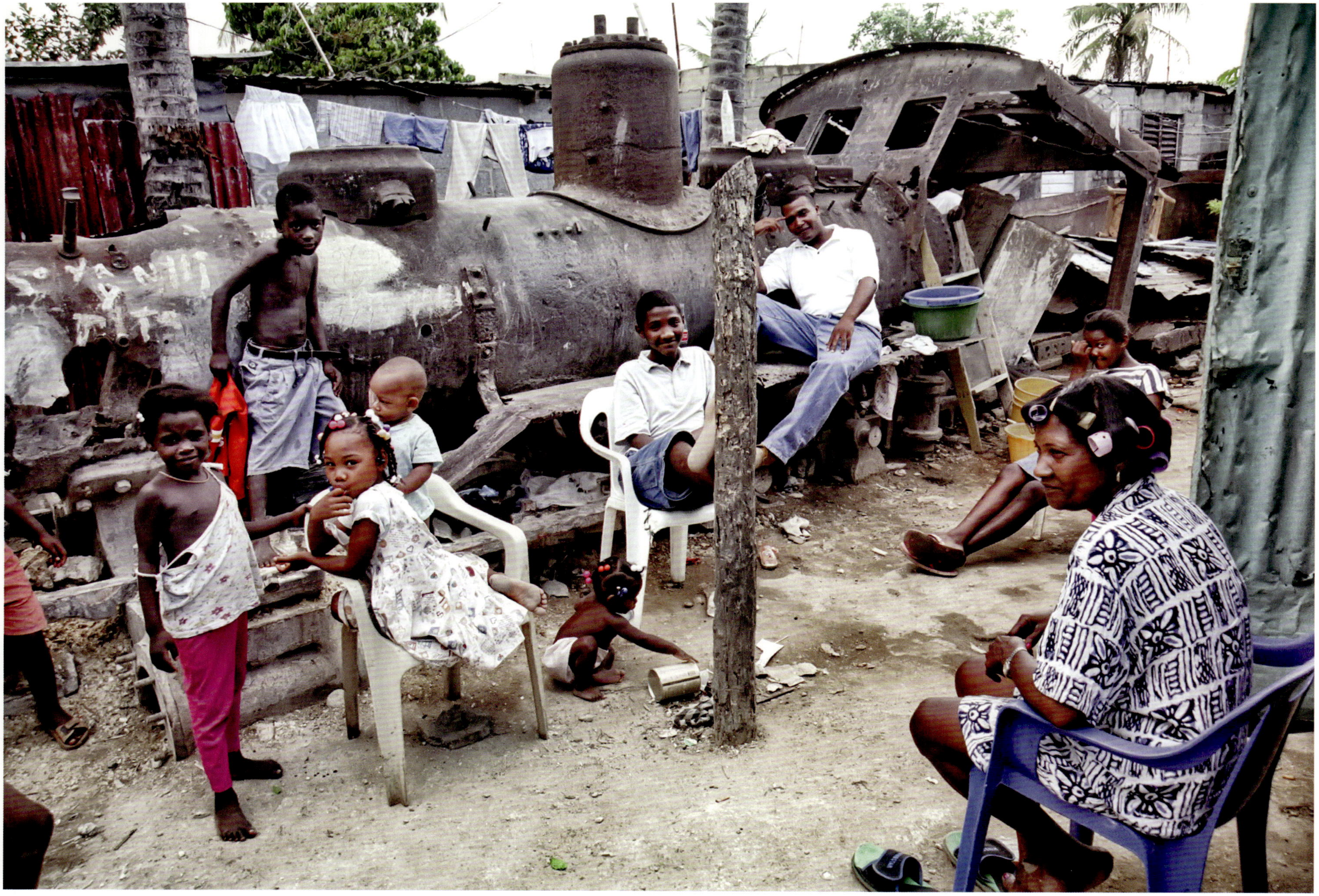

A family in Ingenio Porvenir, a town that was once home to a bustling sugar production industry. Many sugar mills were shut down by the Dominican government and have since been privatized. Cane cutters and cane workers, mostly Haitians, lost their livelihood. These people sit beside one of the many trains that carried the sugarcane to the mills, likely built in the early 1900s. The locals who live in this slum live in a rich and brutal history, but few nowadays know much about it.

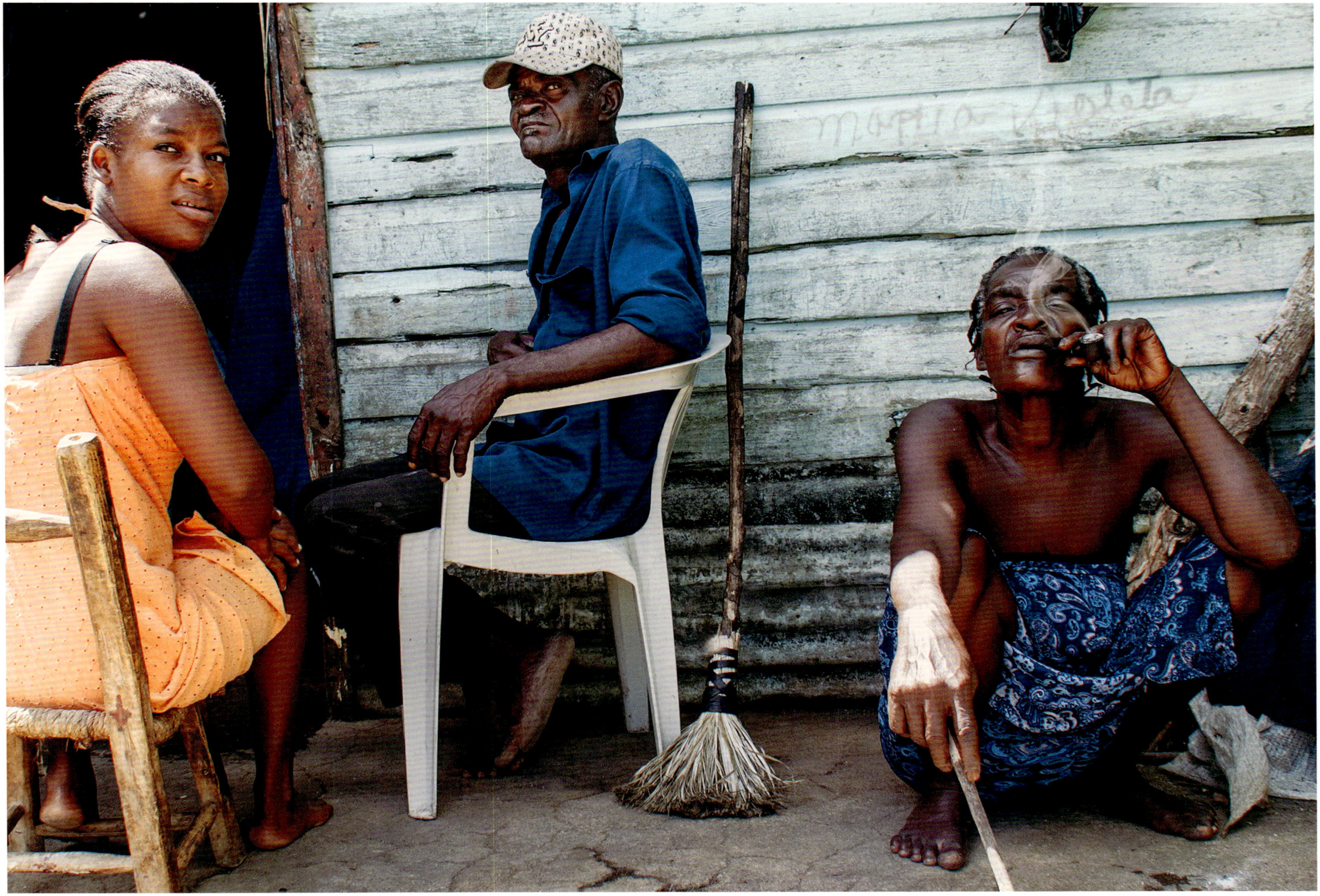

Haitian-born immigrants in the barrio La Punta Pescadora. There are many Haitian-born people living in the Dominican Republic. Recently, the Dominican government has started deporting them.

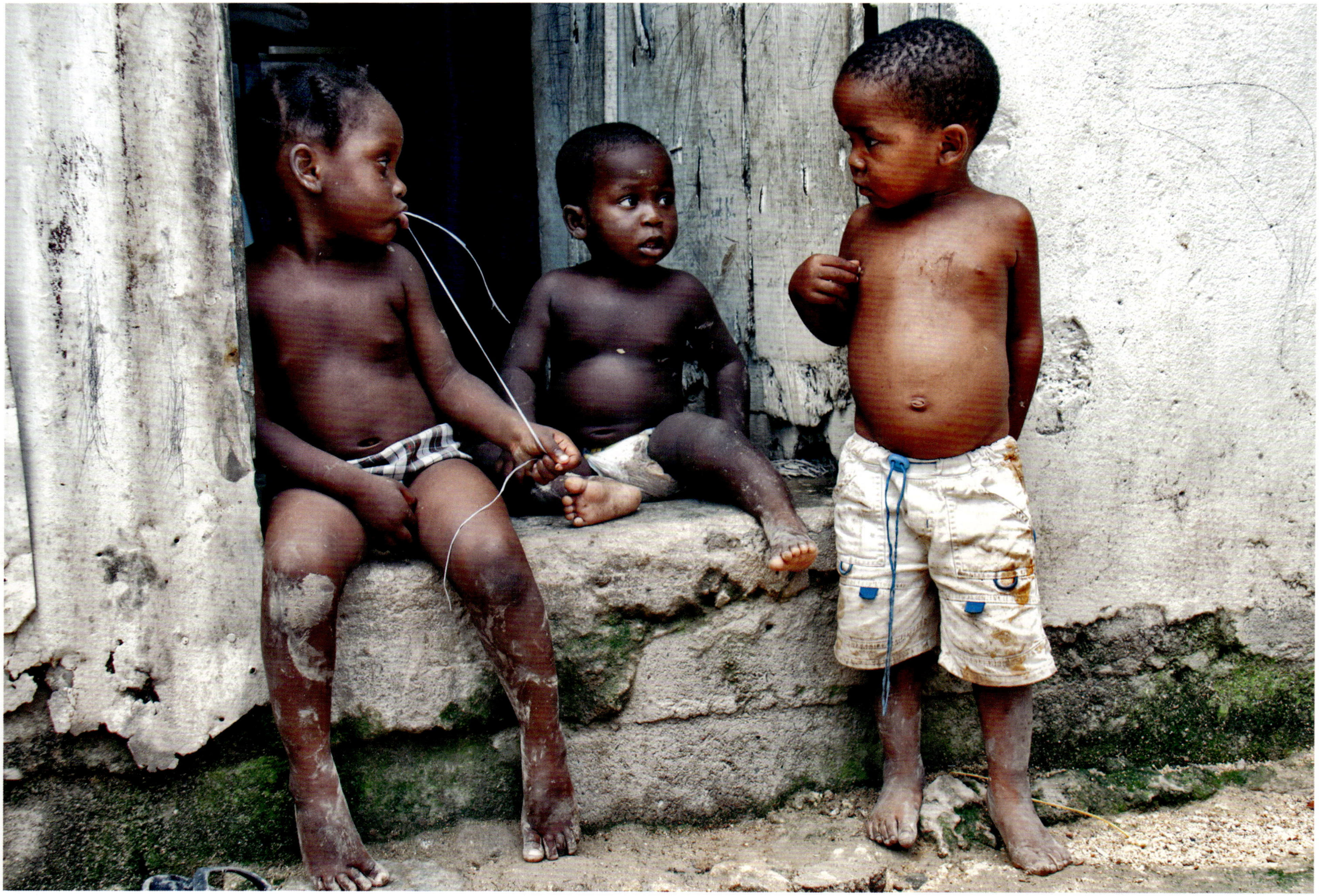

Three young children stealing some shade.

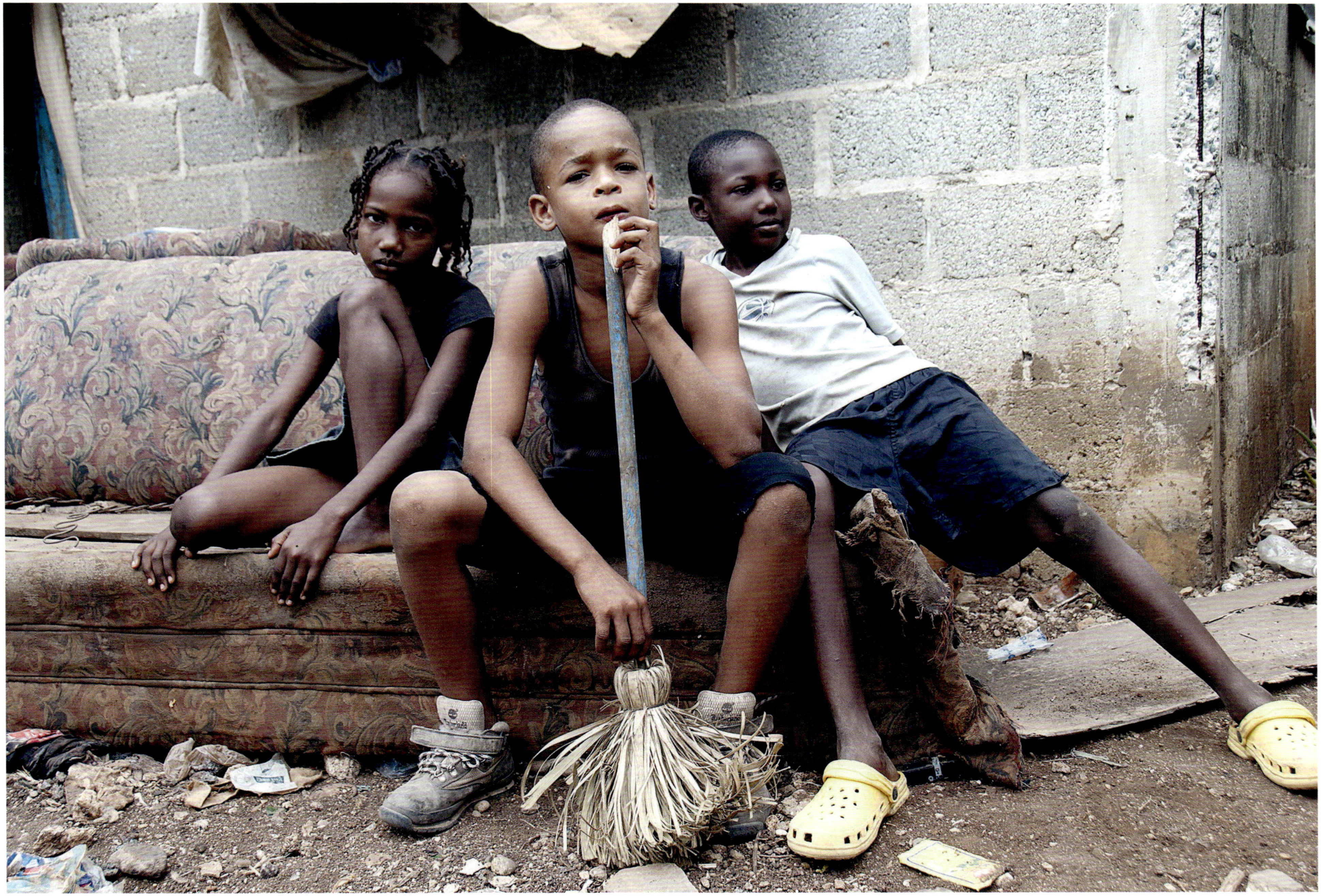

Children pose for the camera.

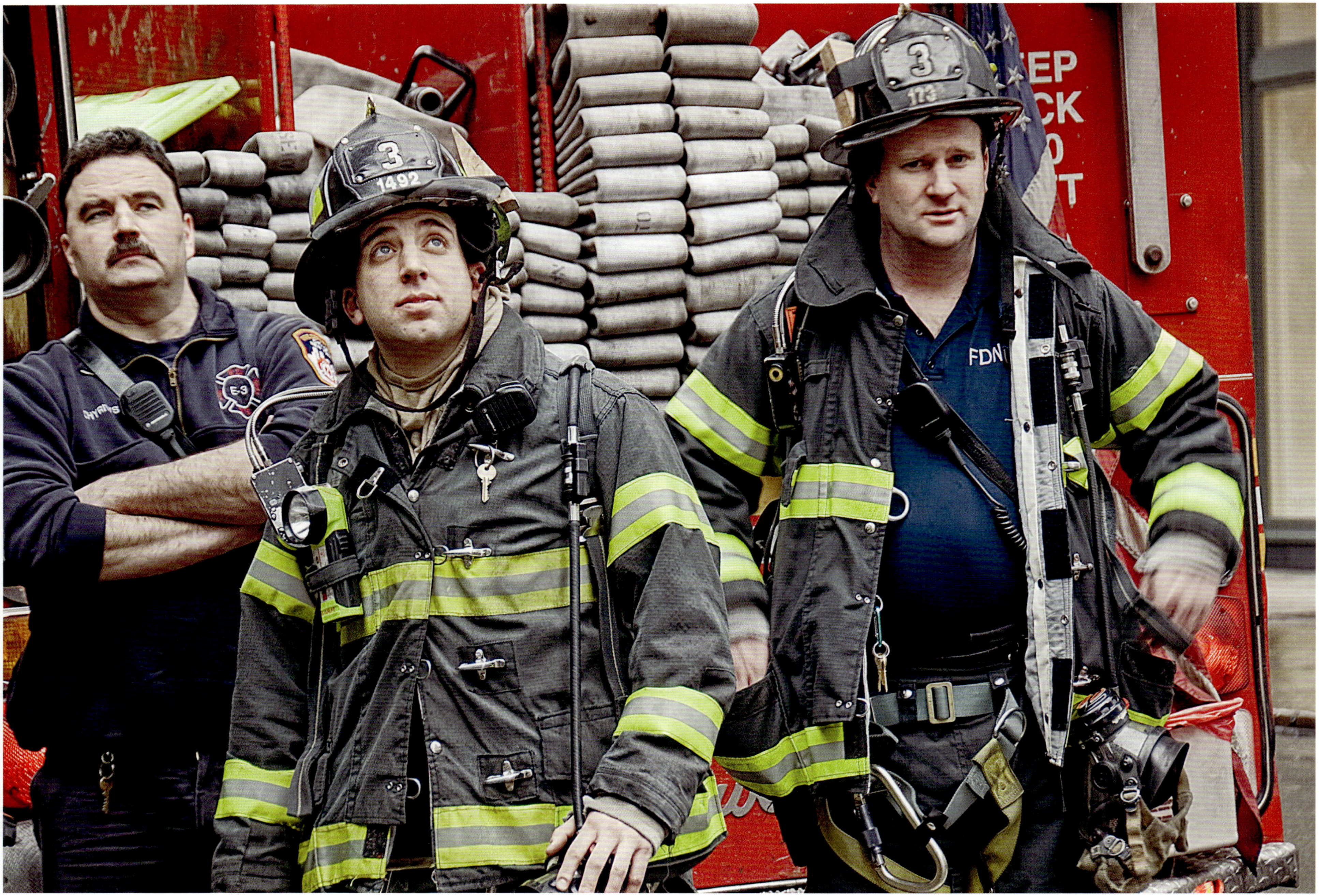

New York's bravest stand ready in the East Village.

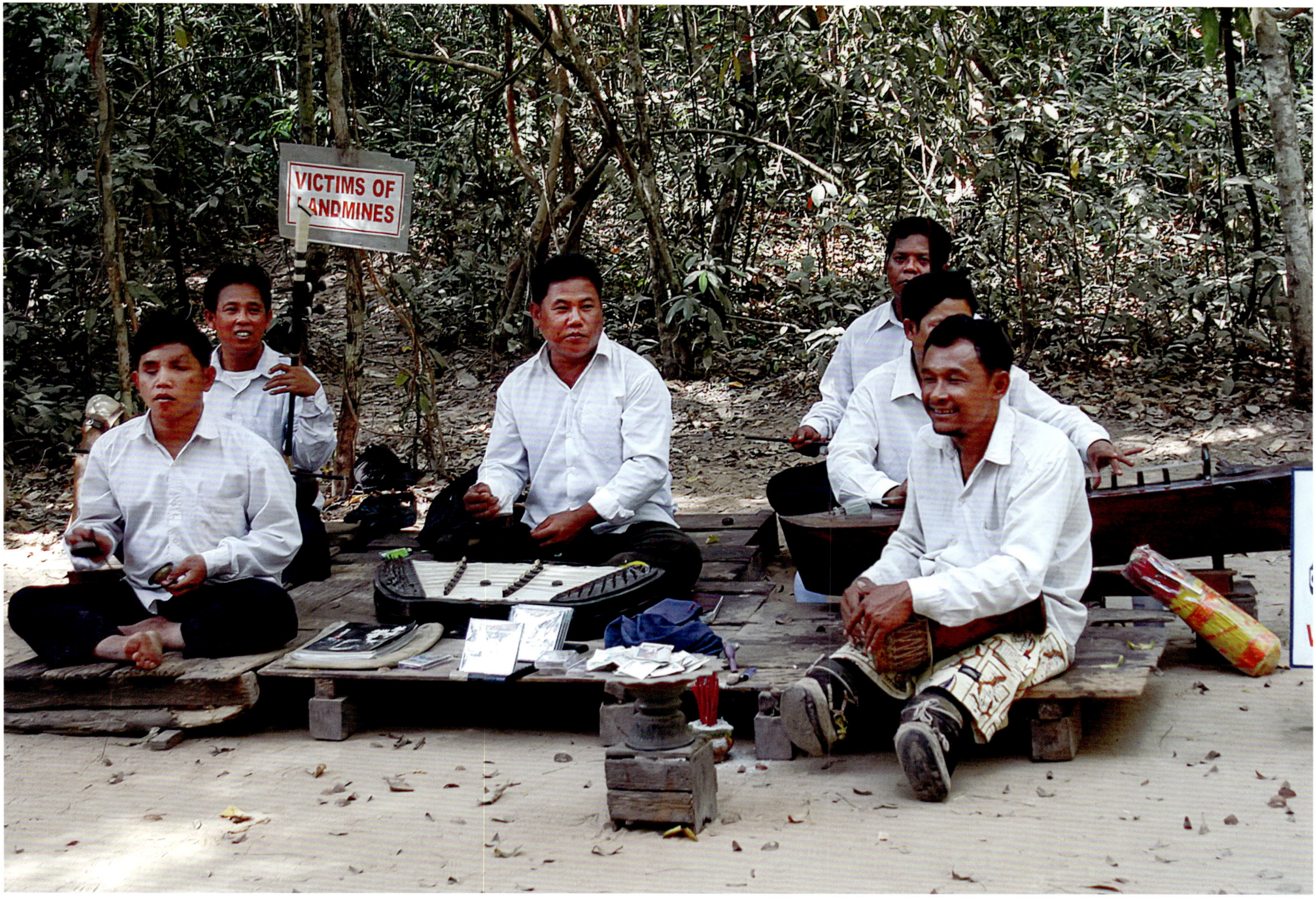

Victims of land mines play music in Siem Reap. The Khmer Rouge regime of the 1970s left Cambodia full of unexploded land mines. In the first ten months of 2019, Cambodia recorded seventy-one land-mine and unexploded-ordnance casualties, up 42 percent from the previous year.

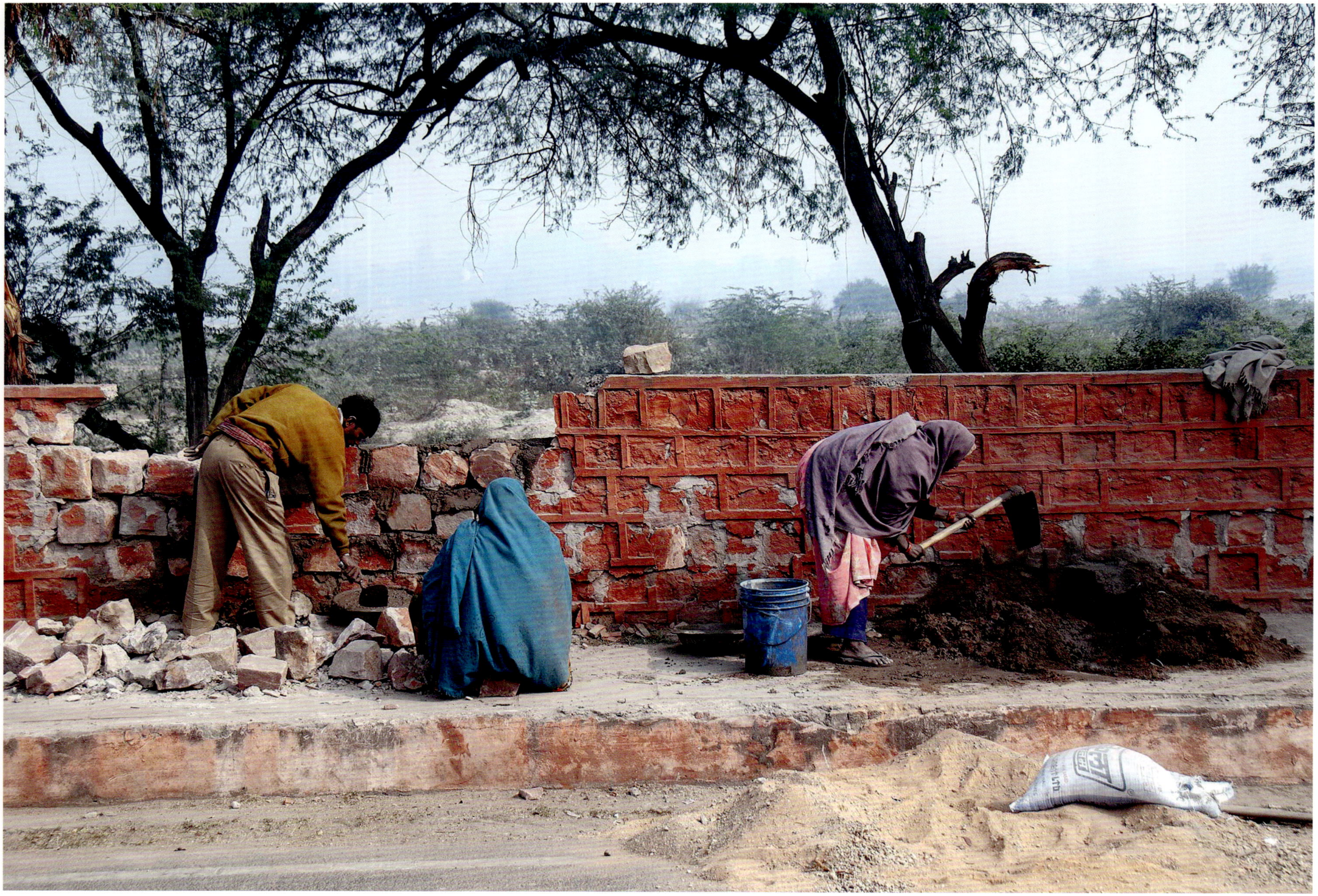

Laborers like these earn only one to two dollars a day.

Some women work very hard as
laborers, carrying bricks, cement,
or gallons of water on their heads,
and yet are paid very little.

India / Bangalore, Karnataka

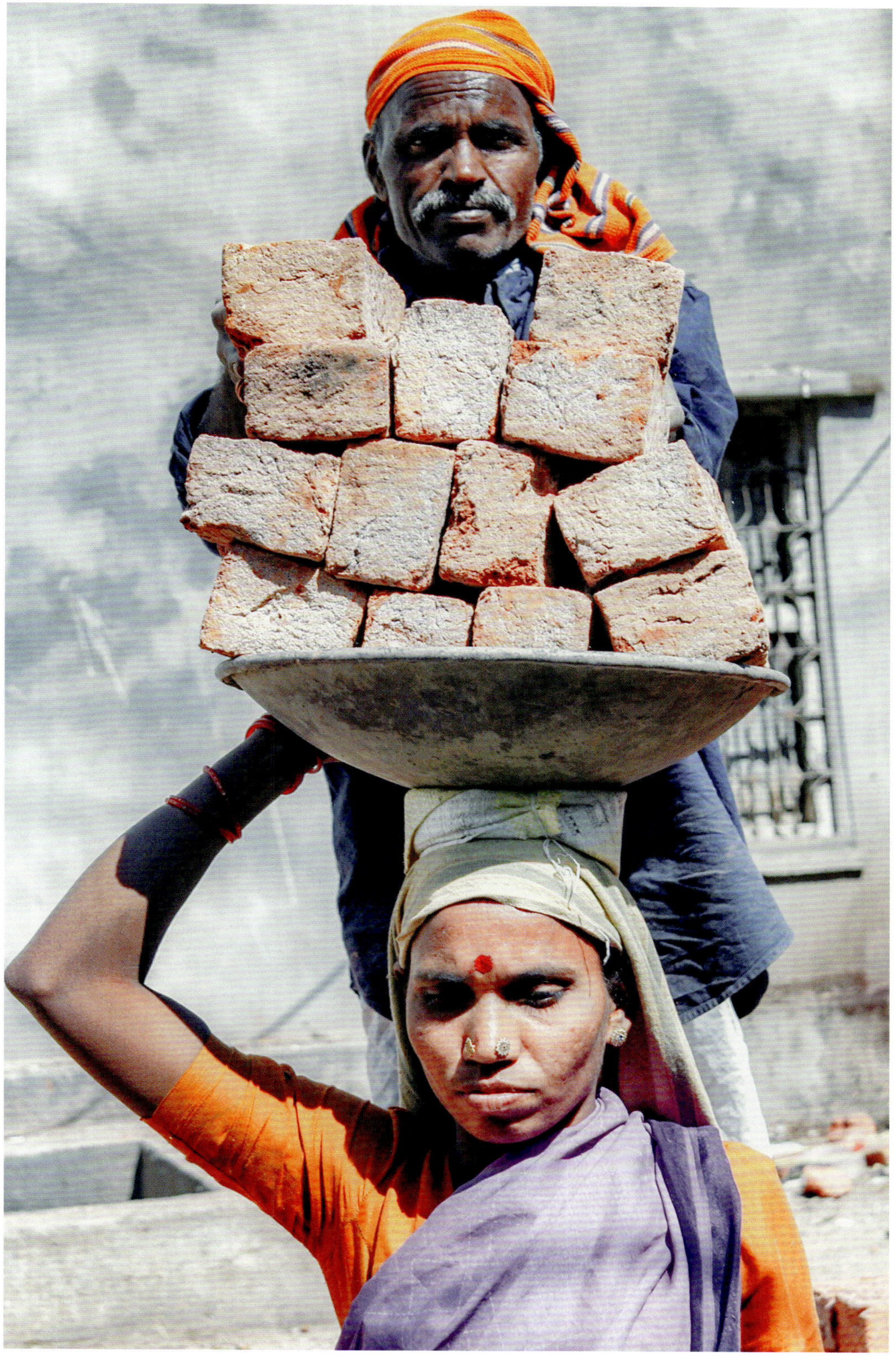

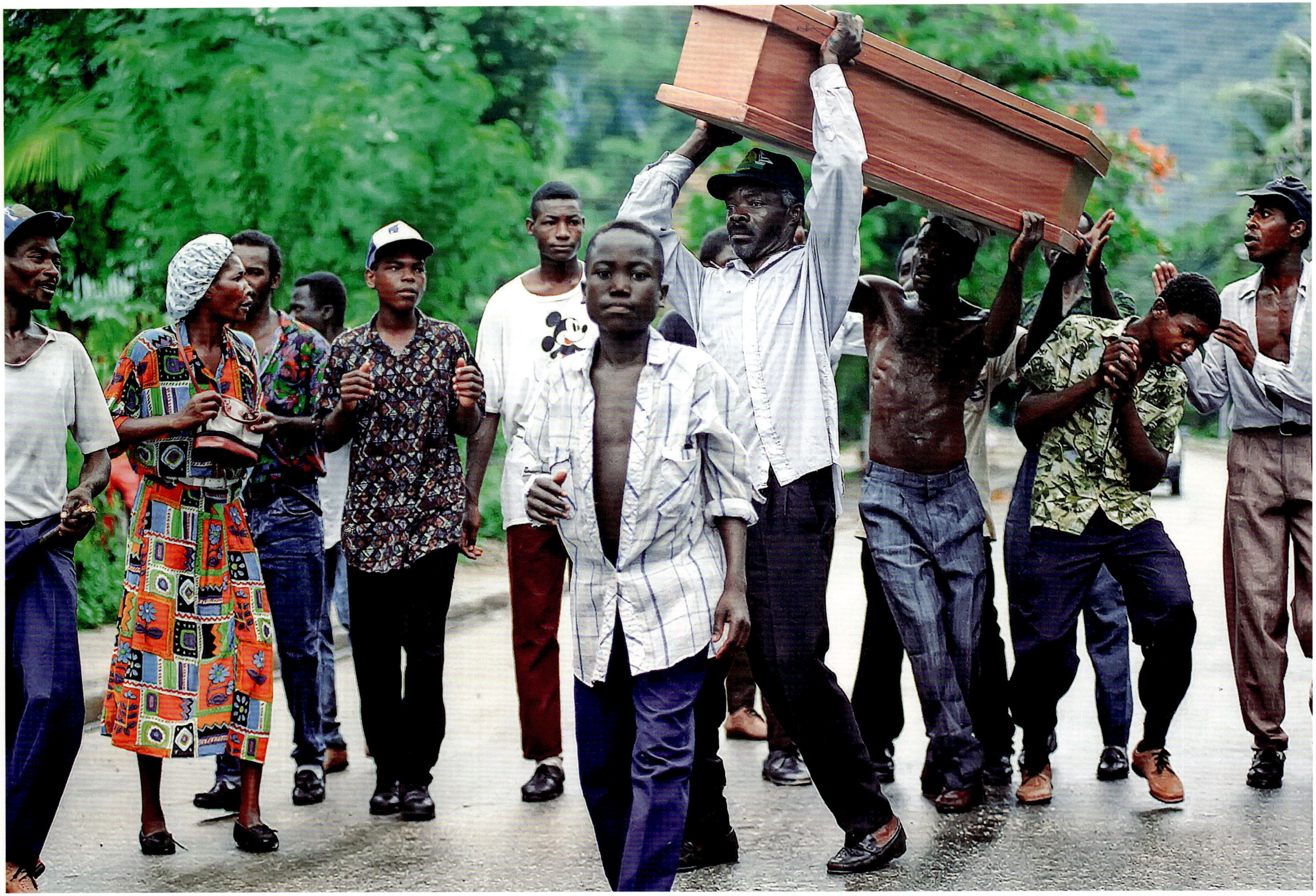

In Paraíso, near the Haitian border, a crowd of people carry the coffin of a loved one they will bury in a nearby cemetery.

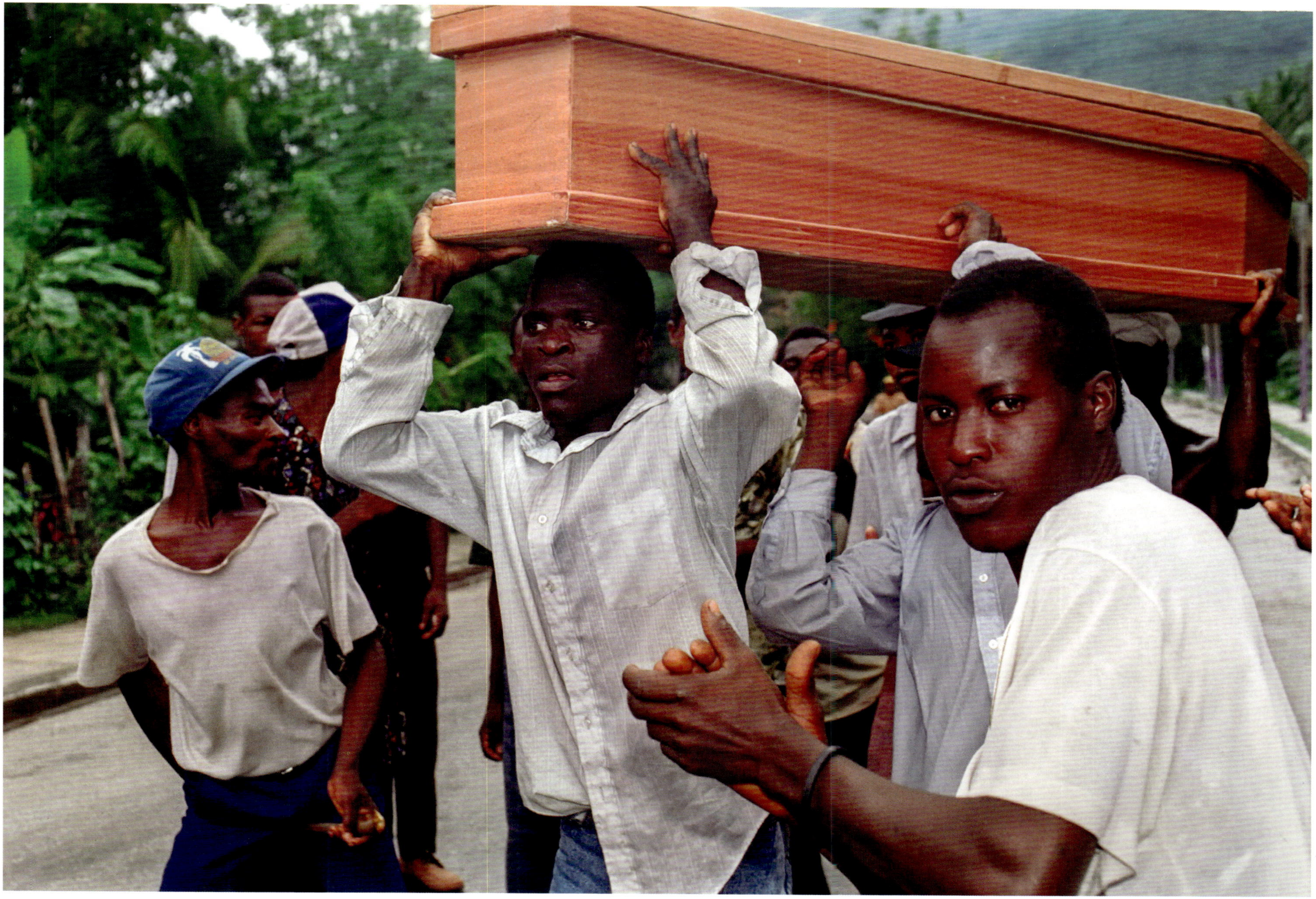

A typical Haitian burial process in the small town of Paraíso: singing anc dancing surround the pallbearers as they carry the coffin to the gravesite.

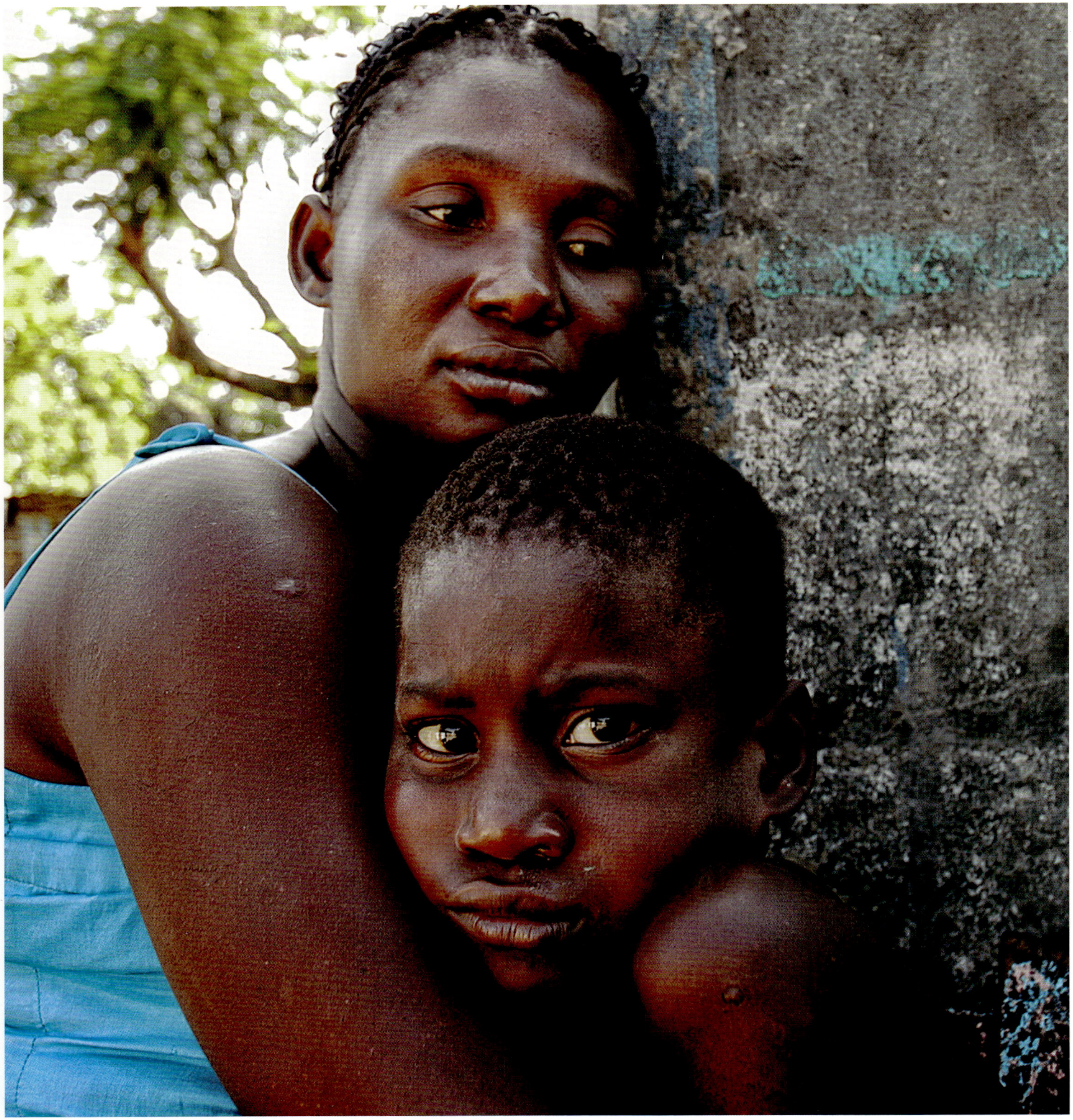

A mother clutches her son. The two live in batey Aleman, and their faces tell the story of the slums of San Pedro de Macorís.

Dominican Republic /
San Pedro de Macorís,
San Pedro de Macorís Province

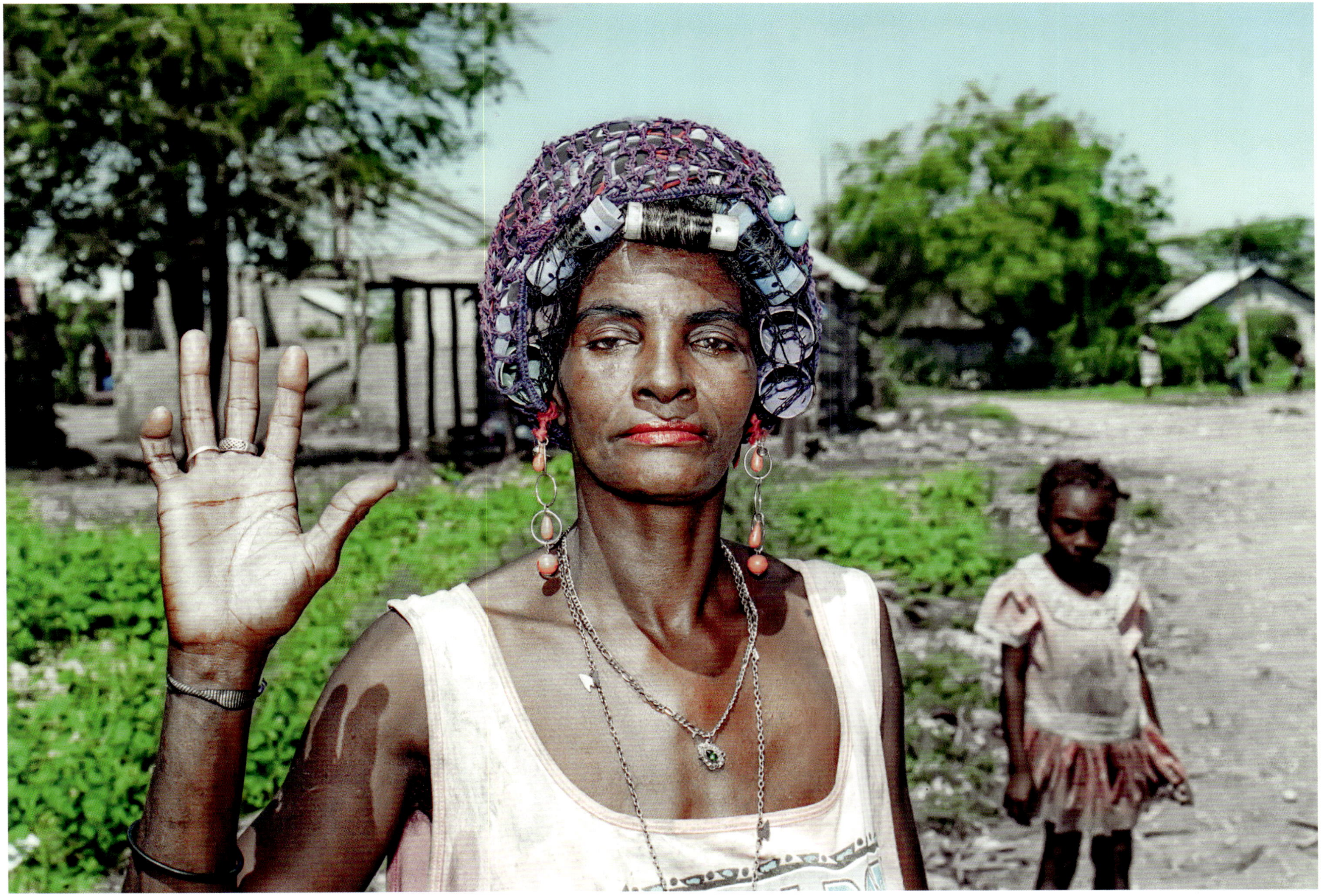

A woman and girl in the slums of Barahona, located in the southwestern portion of the Dominican Republic.

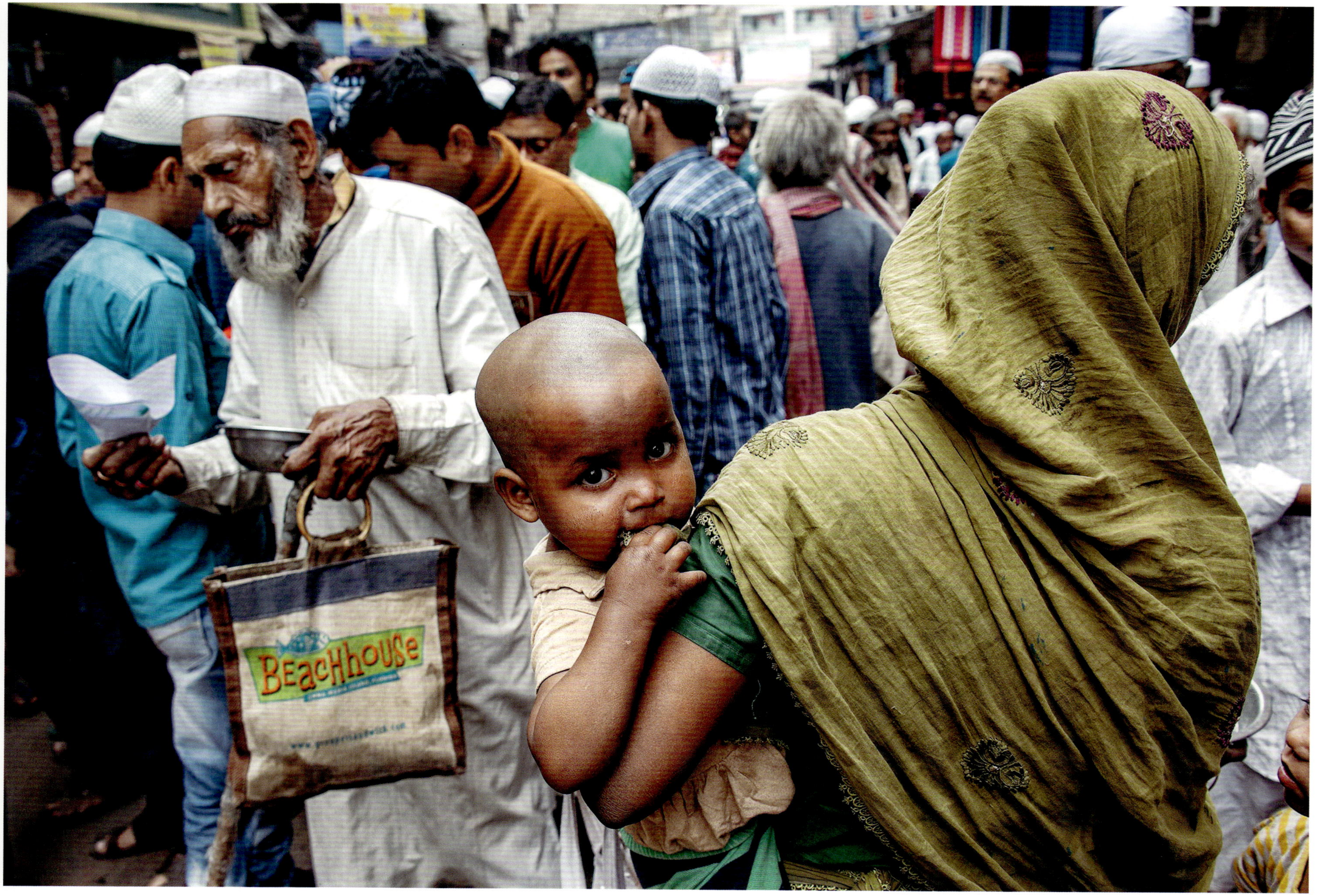

A woman holds a child as she begs.

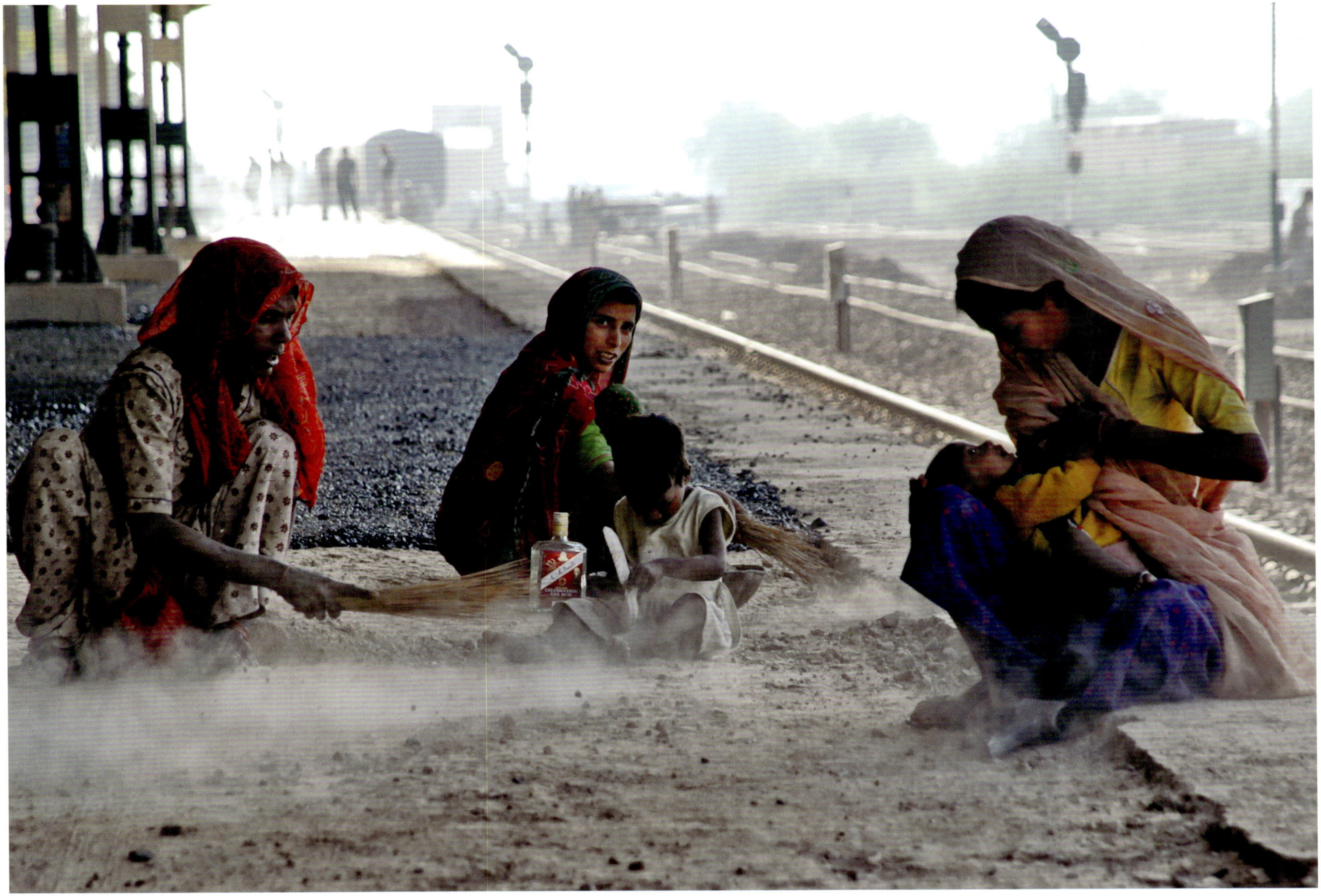

Low-paid laborers at a railroad station. One woman sweeps, creating more dust. Another breastfeeds her child.

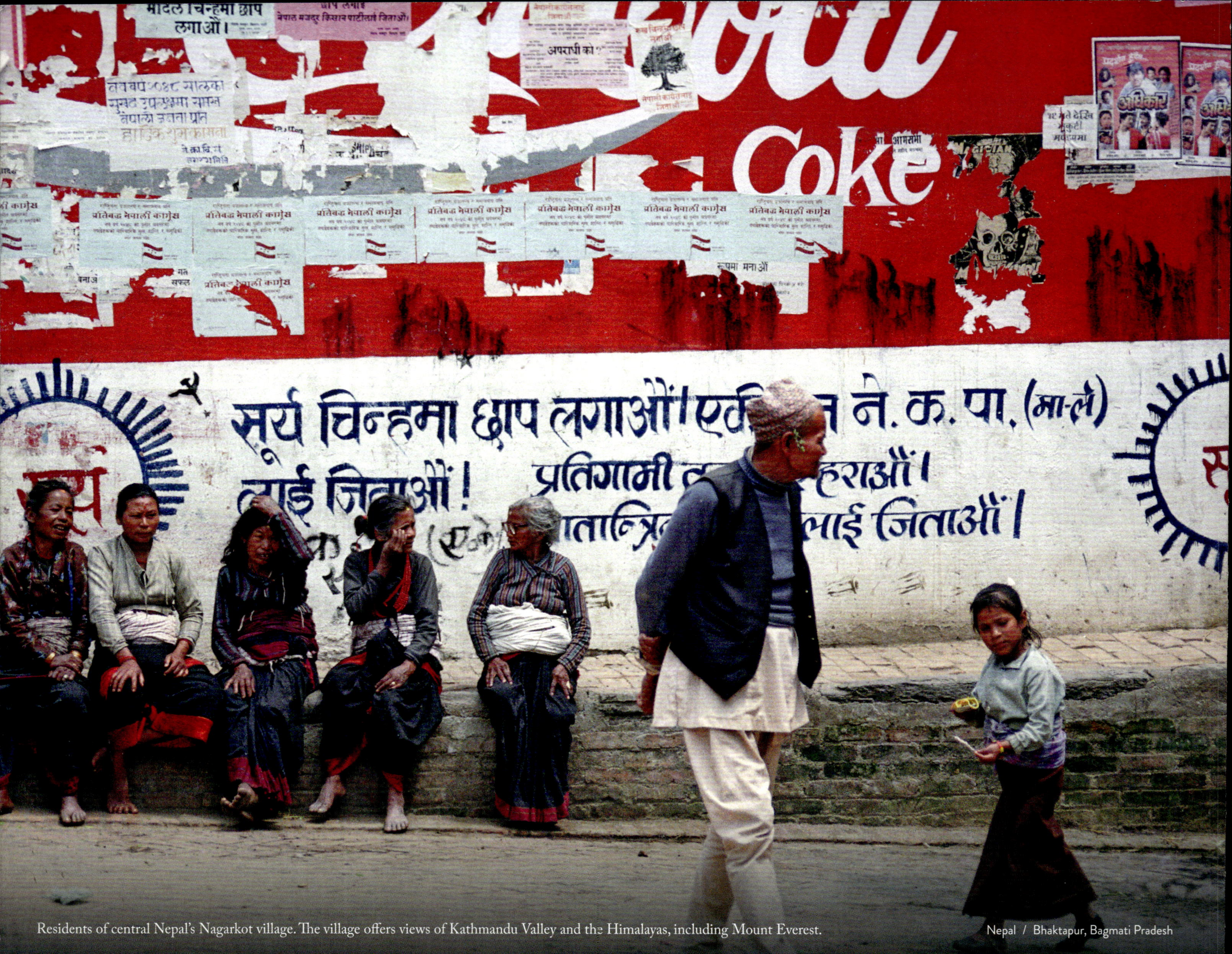

Residents of central Nepal's Nagarkot village. The village offers views of Kathmandu Valley and the Himalayas, including Mount Everest.

Nepal / Bhaktapur, Bagmati Pradesh

COMMUNITY

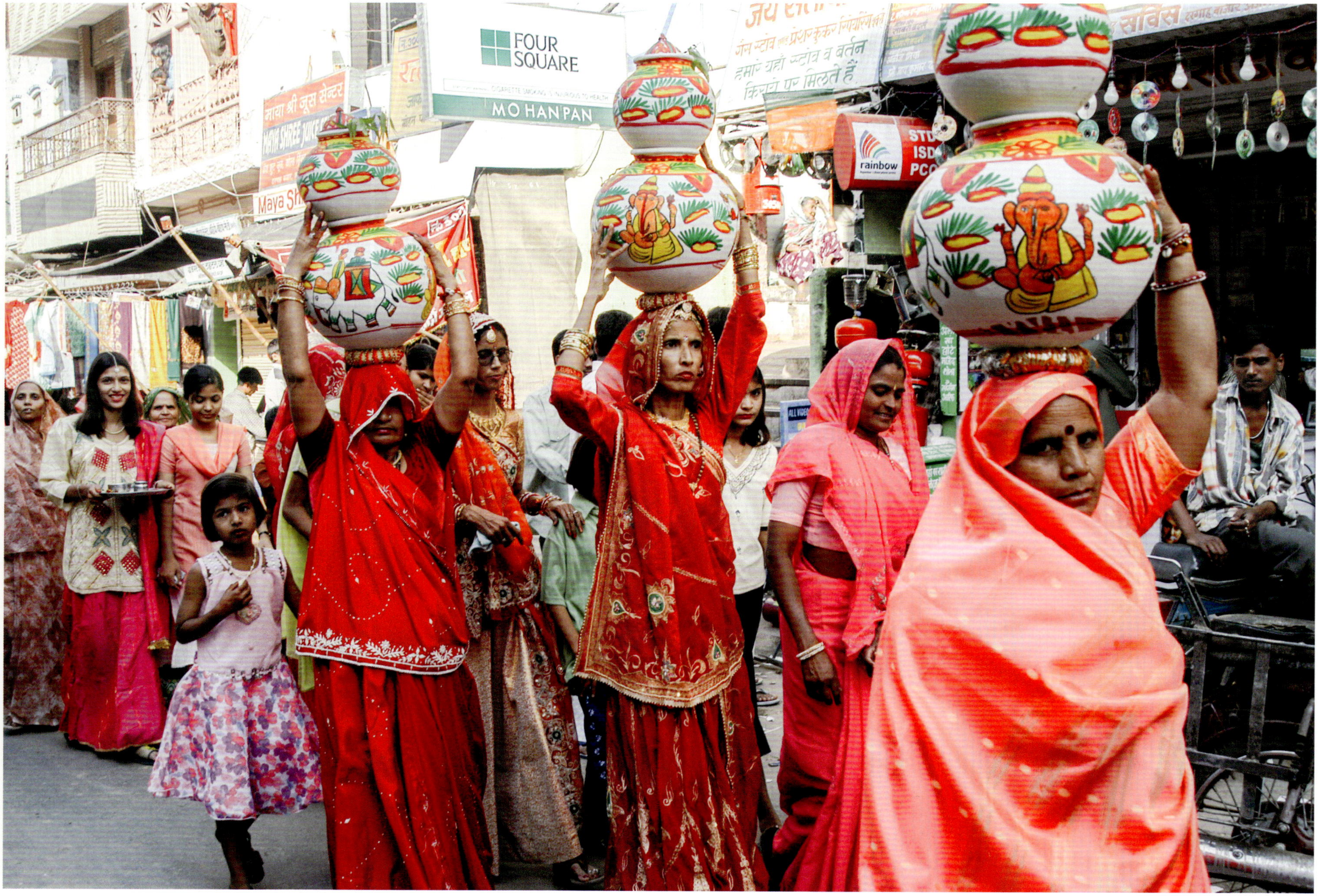

Women hold ceramic pots with painted images of Ganesh, a Hindu deity, at a wedding ceremony.

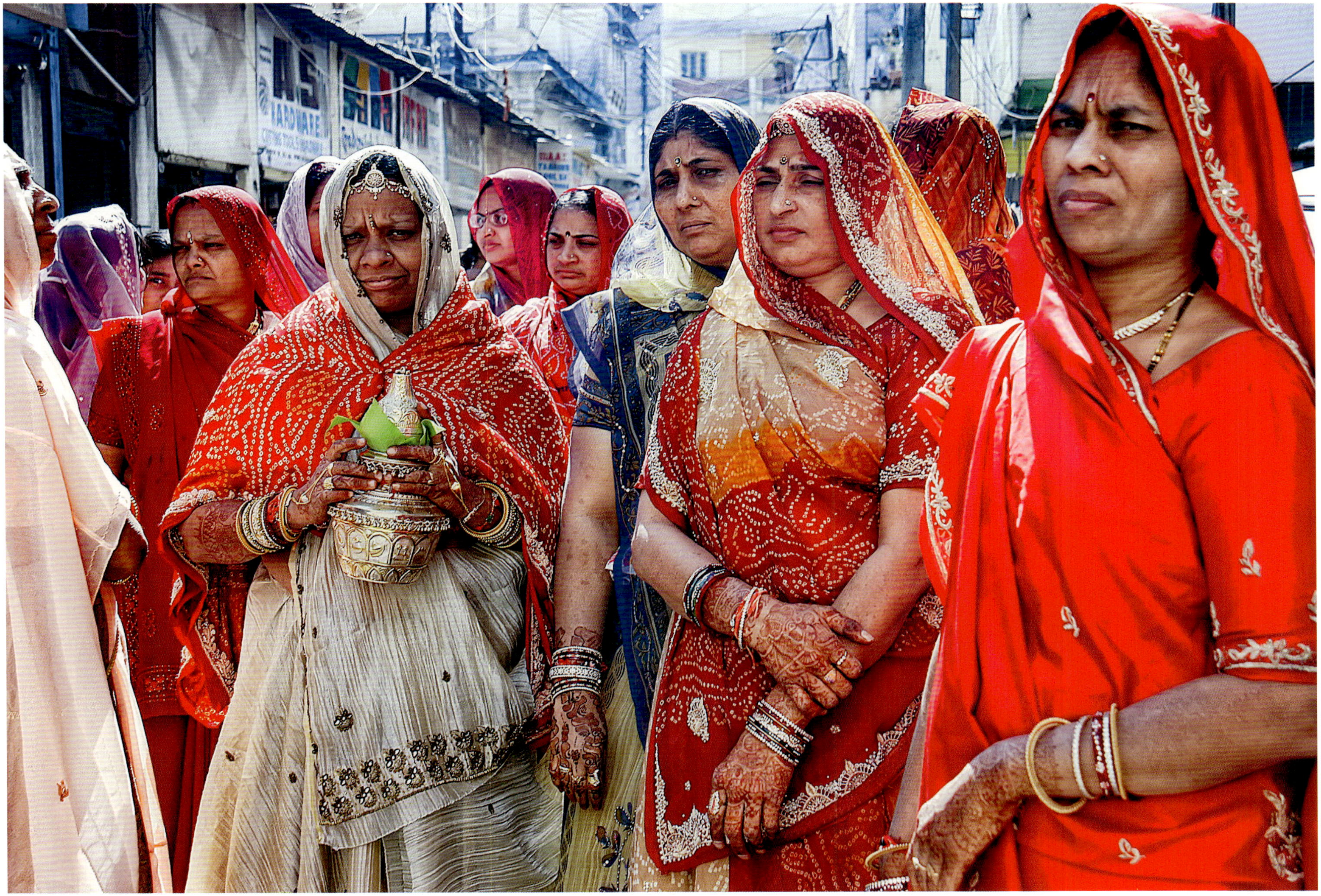

Wedding guests.

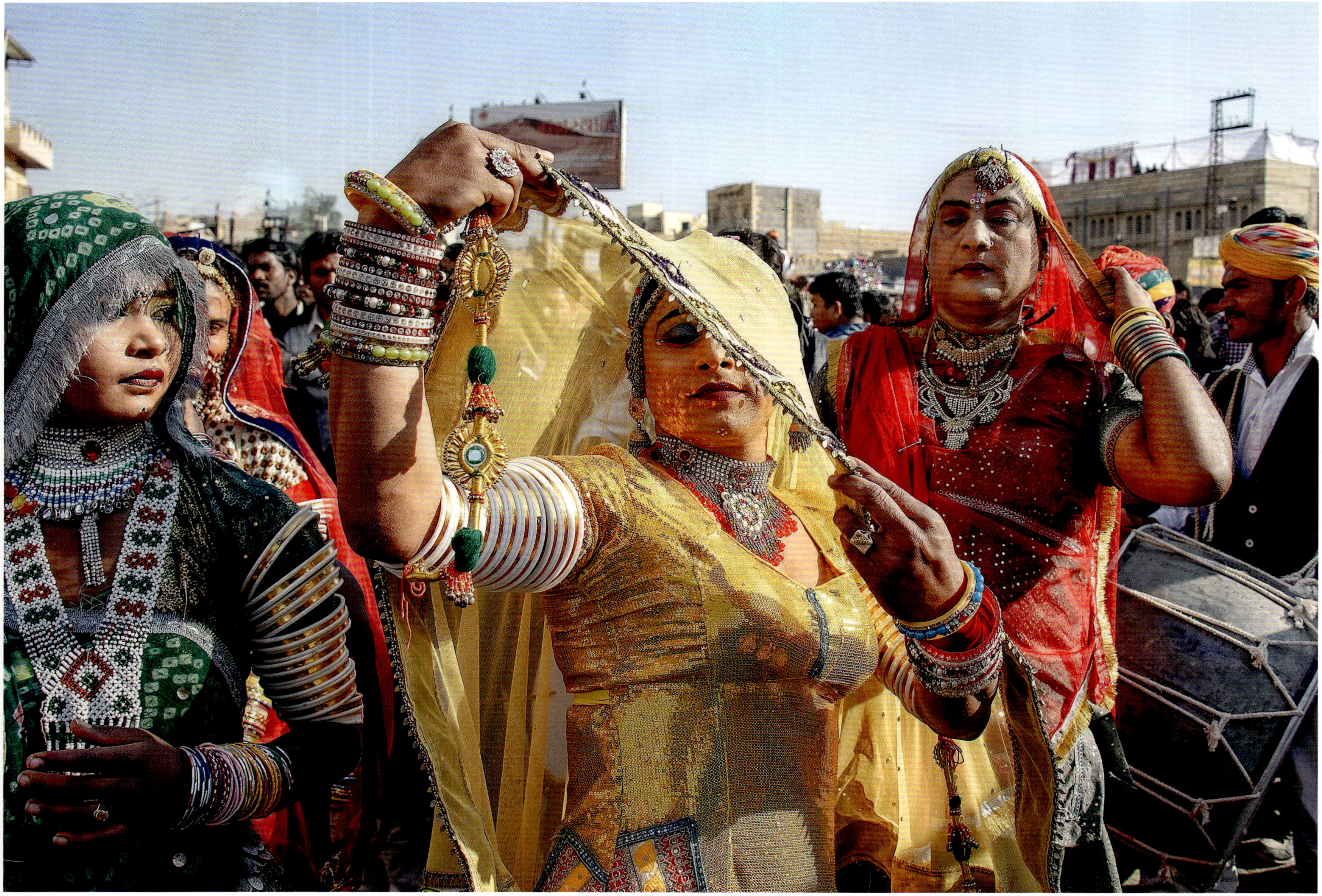

Hijras dance at the Desert Festival. Hijras are eunuchs, intersex people, or transgender people and considered a third gender in India. They are typically assigned male at birth and may or may not undergo sex reassignment surgery.

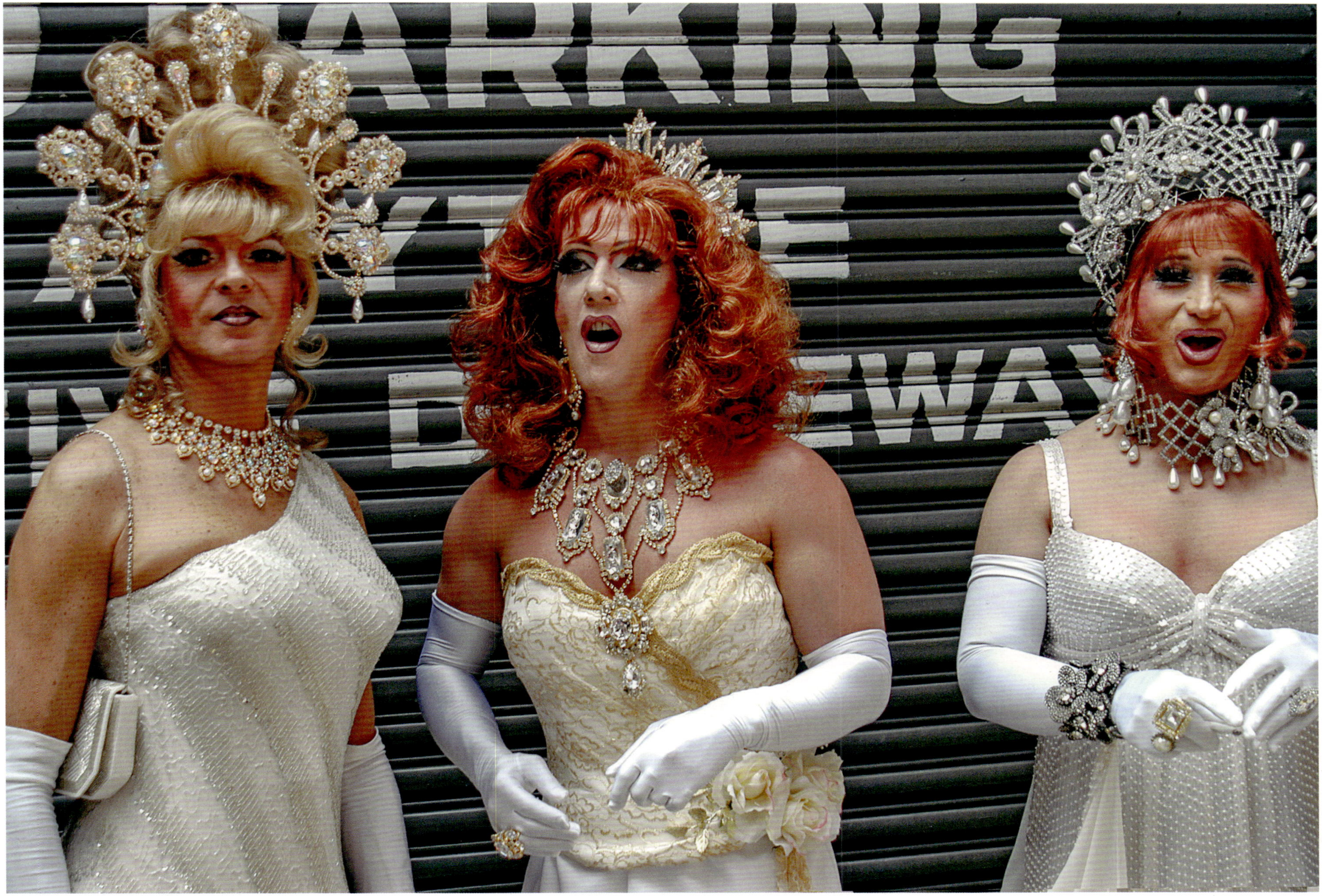

Drag performers at the New York City Pride March.

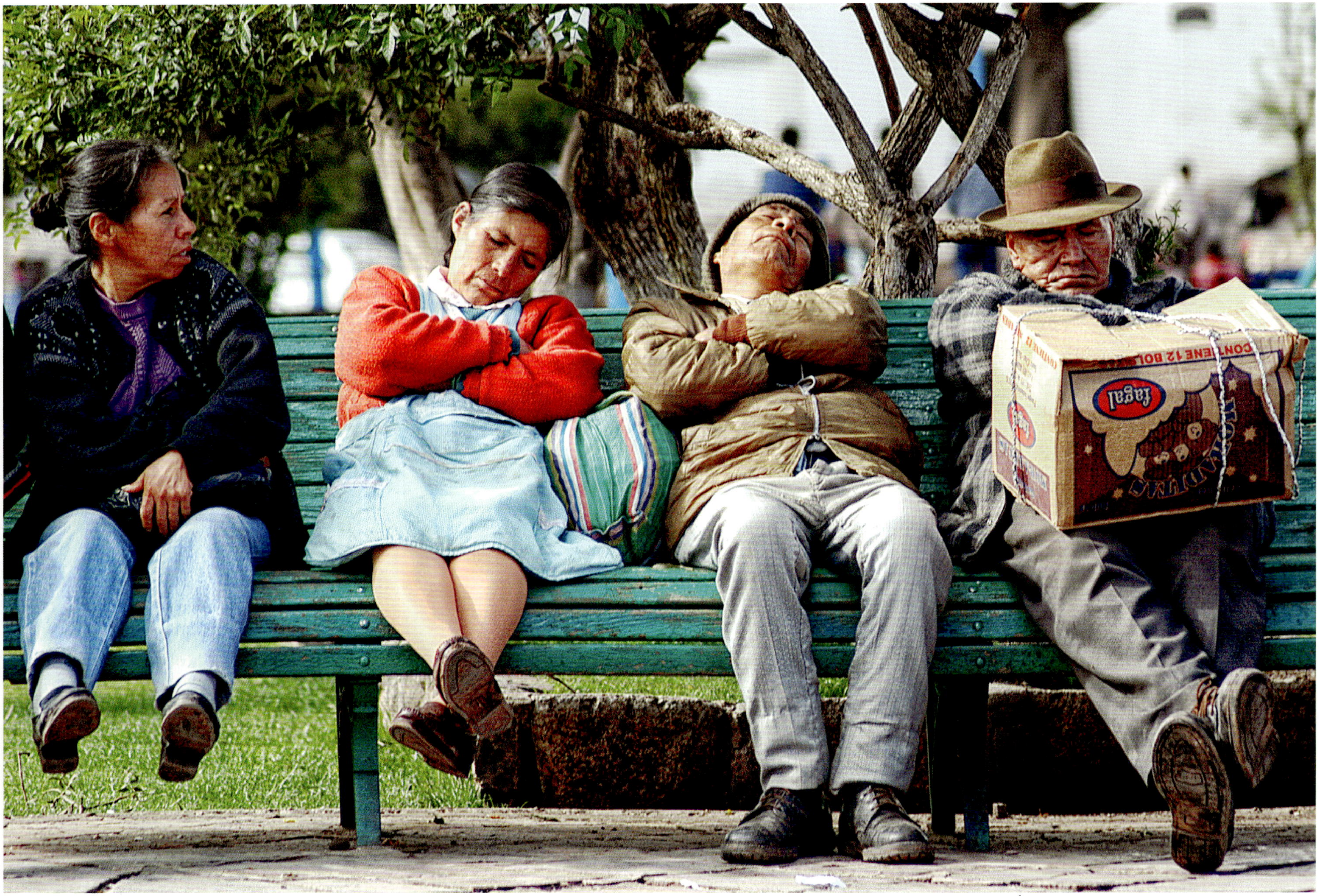

People rest on a bench in Arequipa, a colonial-era city whose historic district has been designated a UNESCO World Heritage site.

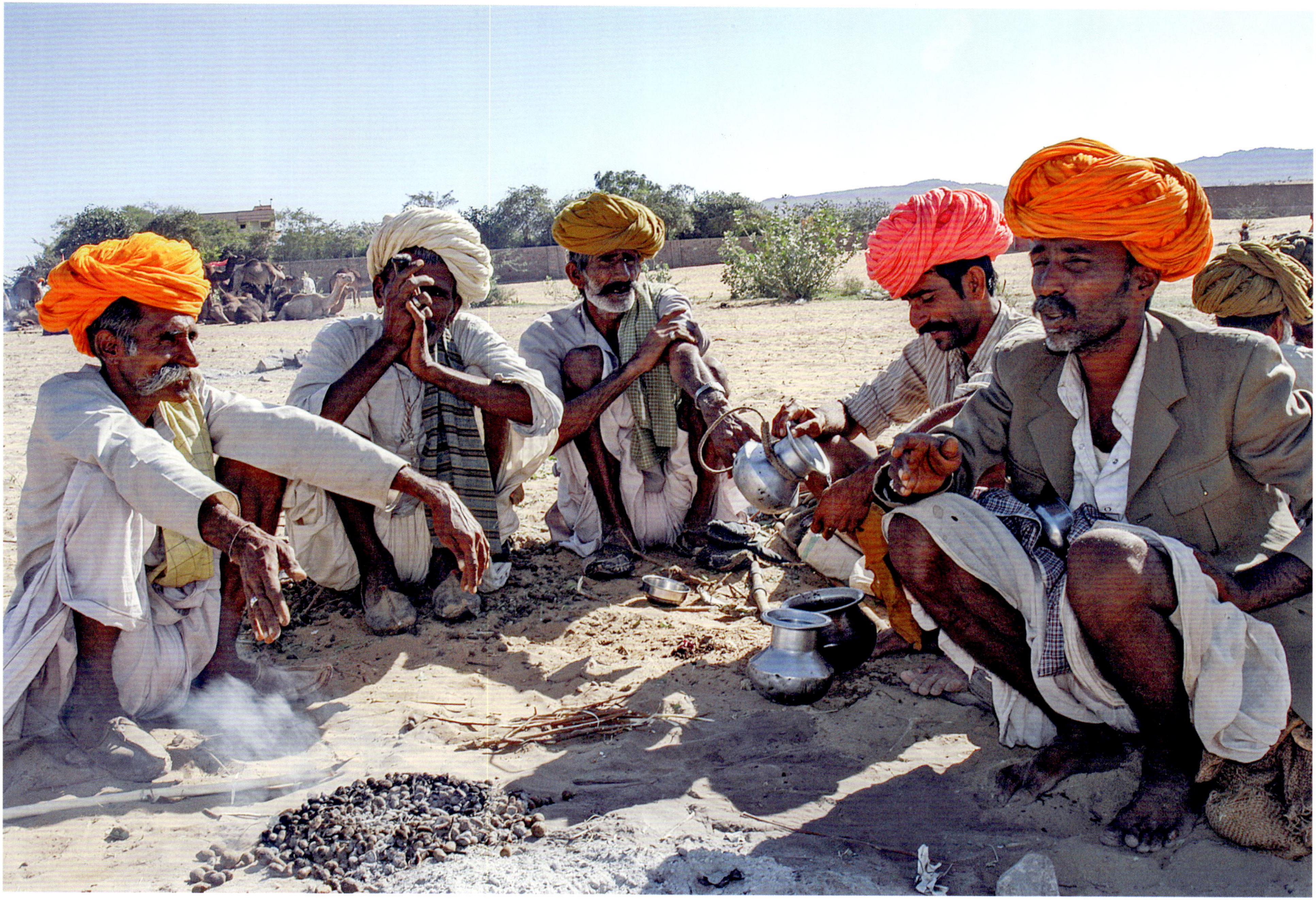

Men in Pushkar's Thar Desert, where the camel fair takes place. Pushkar is famous for its fourteenth-century temple to Brahma (the Hindu god of creation) and a place named Sunset Point, from which one can spot the whole town shimmering under the evening sun.

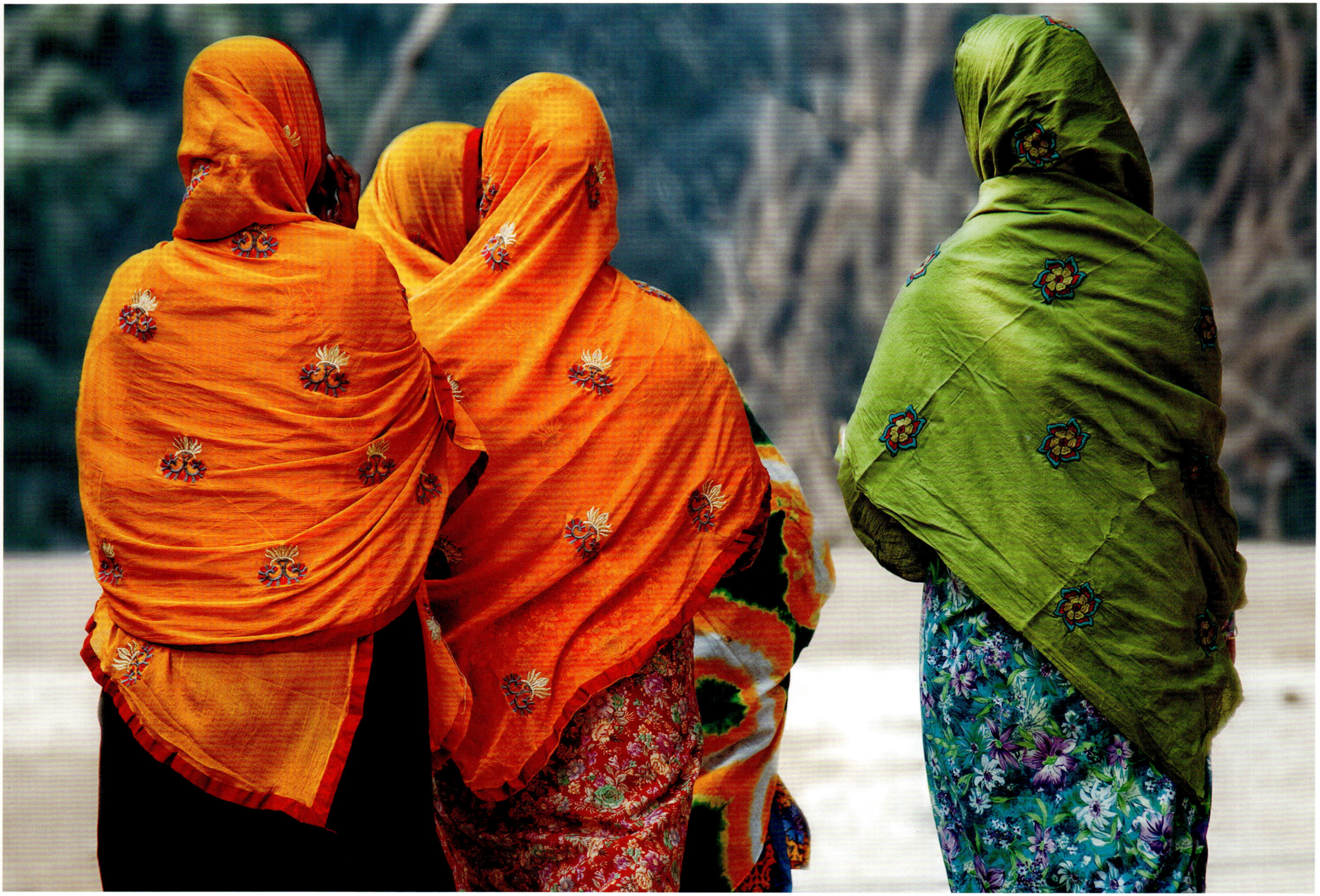

Women wear shalwar and kamiz, a traditional outfit composed of trousers (the shalwar) and a long tunic, or sari (the kameez). Younger generations have begun to adopt more Western modes of dress.

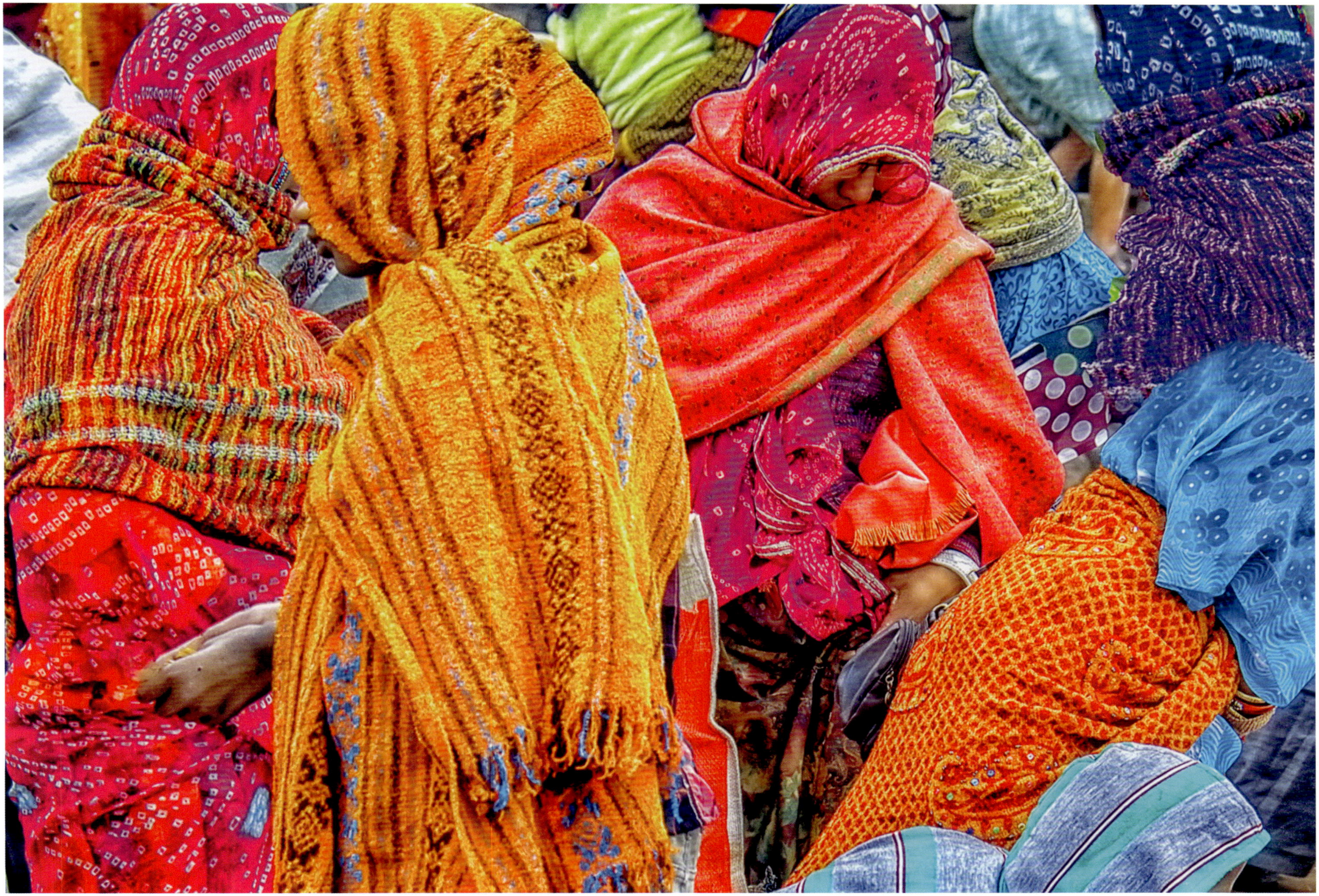

Wedding guests in beaded saris.

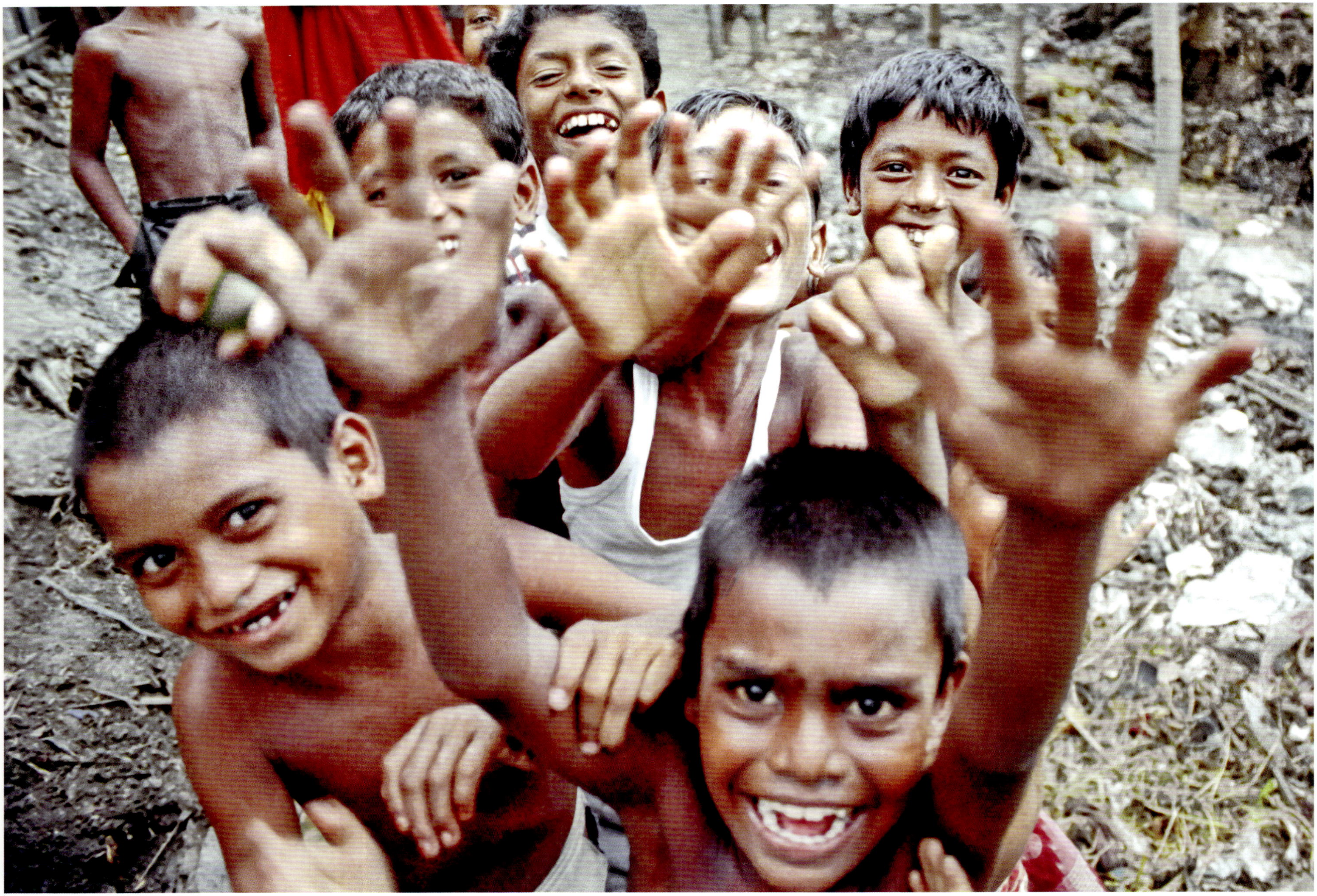

Boys in Geneva Camp, a refugee camp that was settled in Dhaka during the 1971 War of Liberation. The camp is densely populated and home to an estimated forty thousand Biharis, Urdu-speaking natives of Bihar, a state in India. Each family lives together in one small room, and there is only one latrine for every ninety families. It's no longer possible for outsiders to access the camp to photograph.

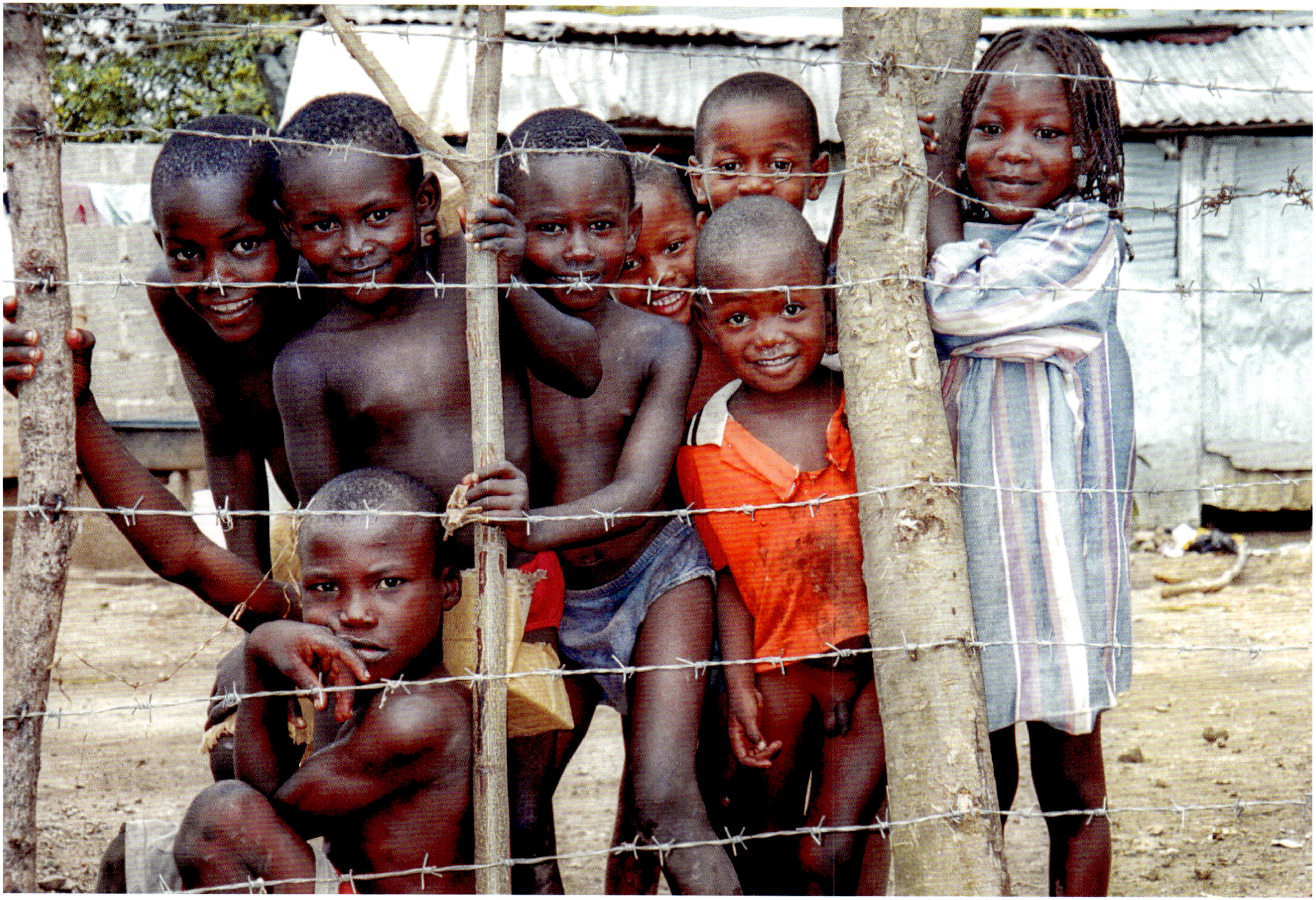

These children live in a slum but manage to keep smiles on their faces.

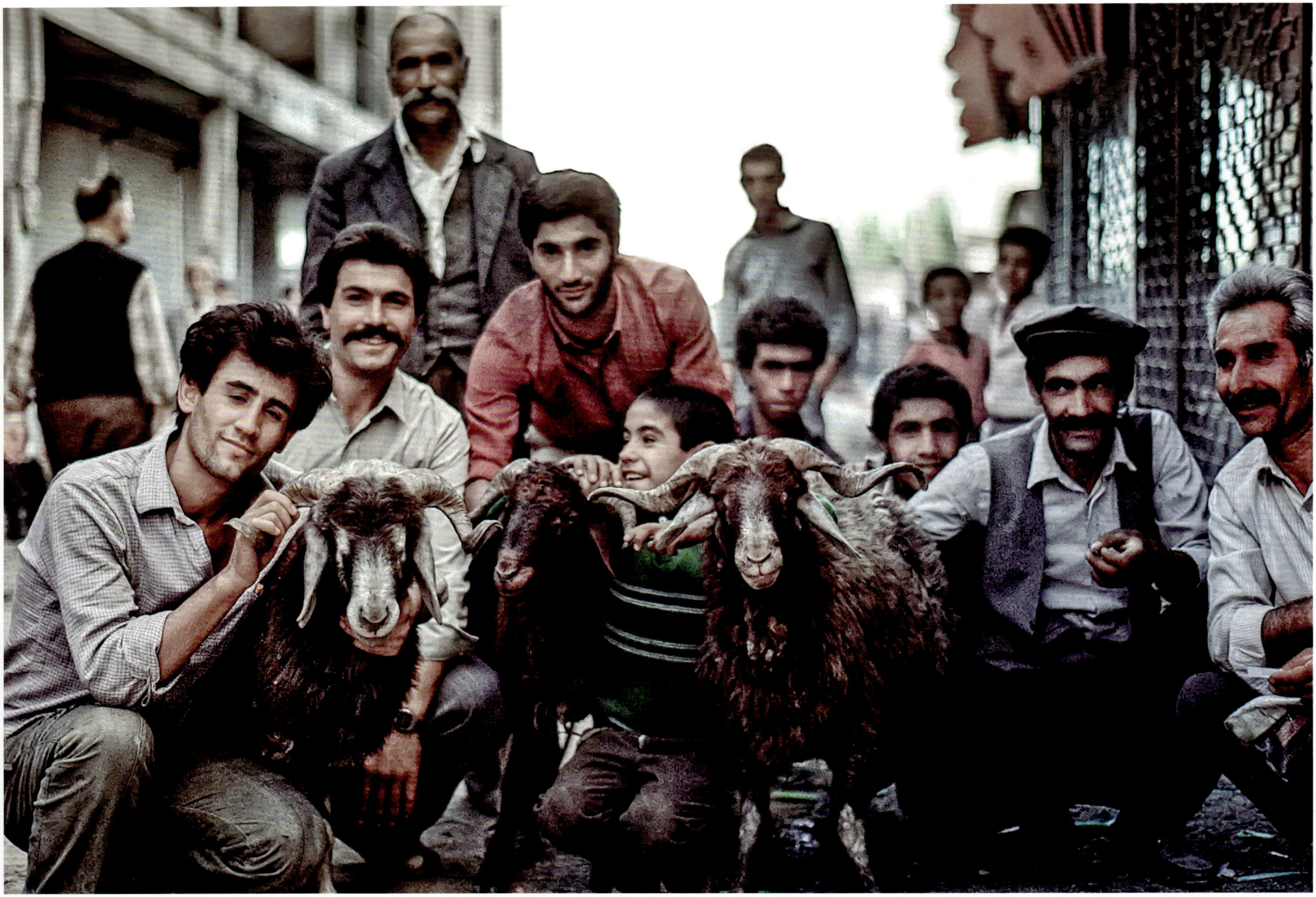

At this market, sheep are bought and sold. Malatya is a large city in eastern Anatolia; though a modern industrial town settled in 1838, it was founded near the sites of two ancient human settlements.

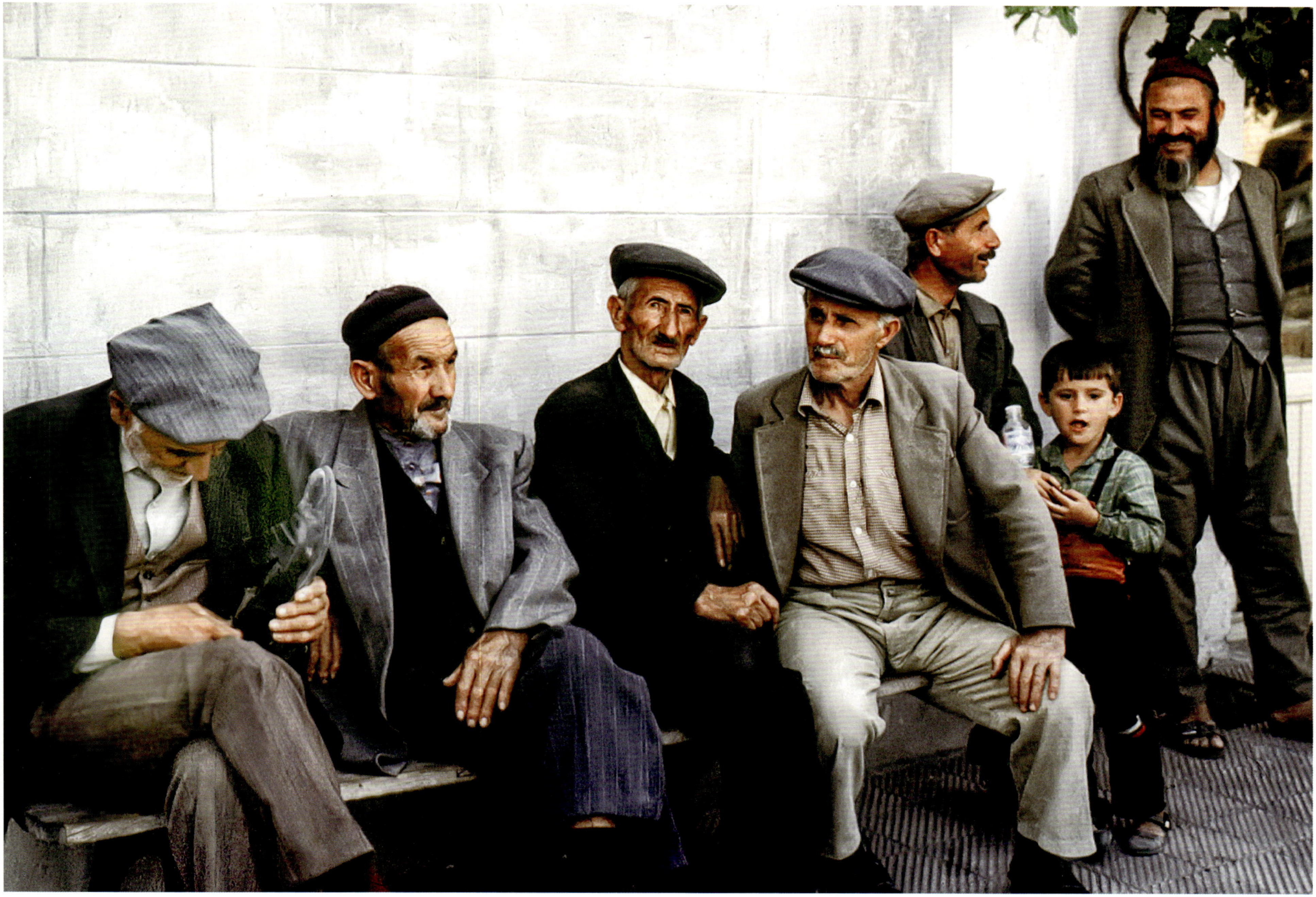

Men pose in the European section of Istanbul. Istanbul is a transcontinental city, spanning Europe in the west and Asia in the east.

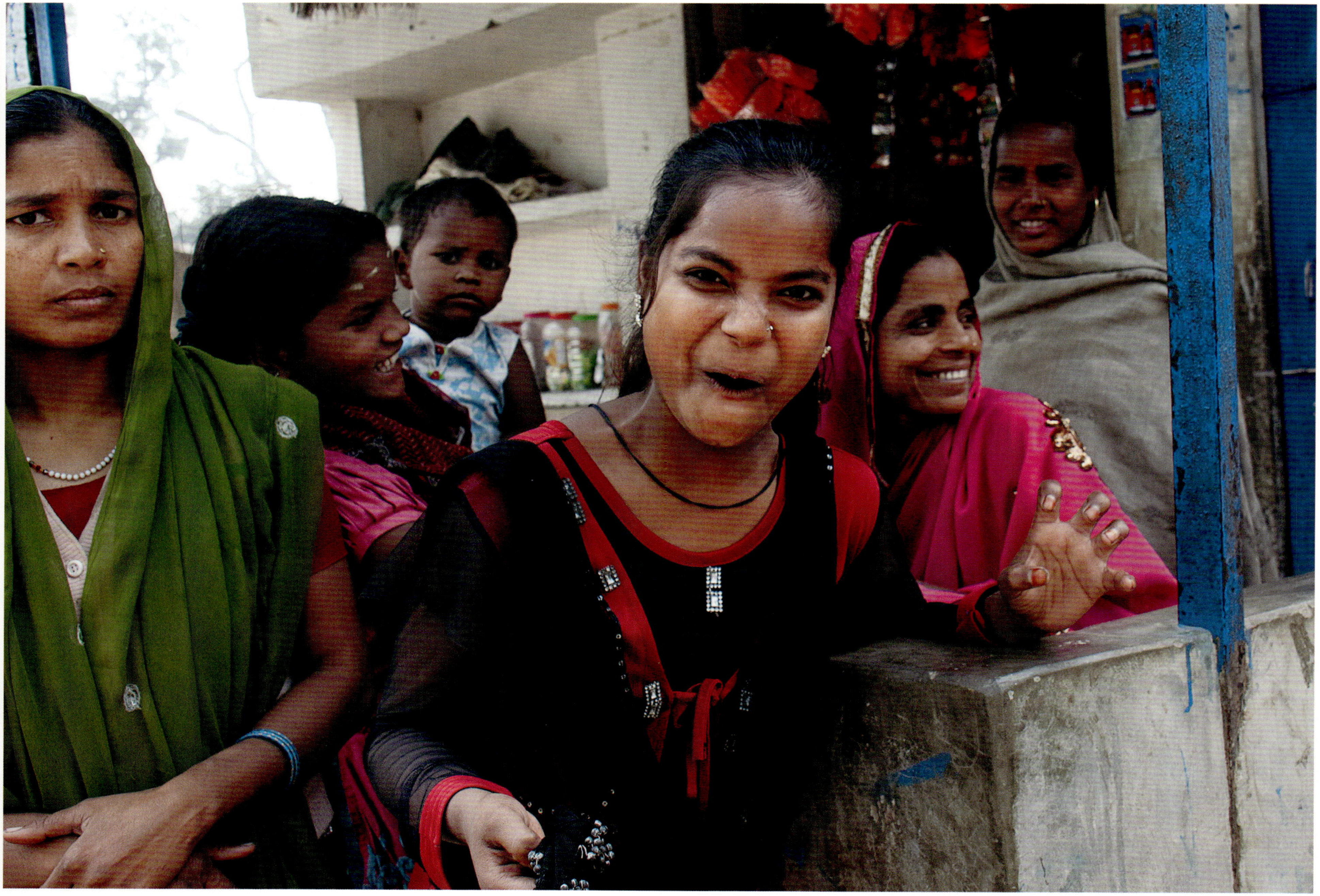

Locals in rural Bodh Gaya.

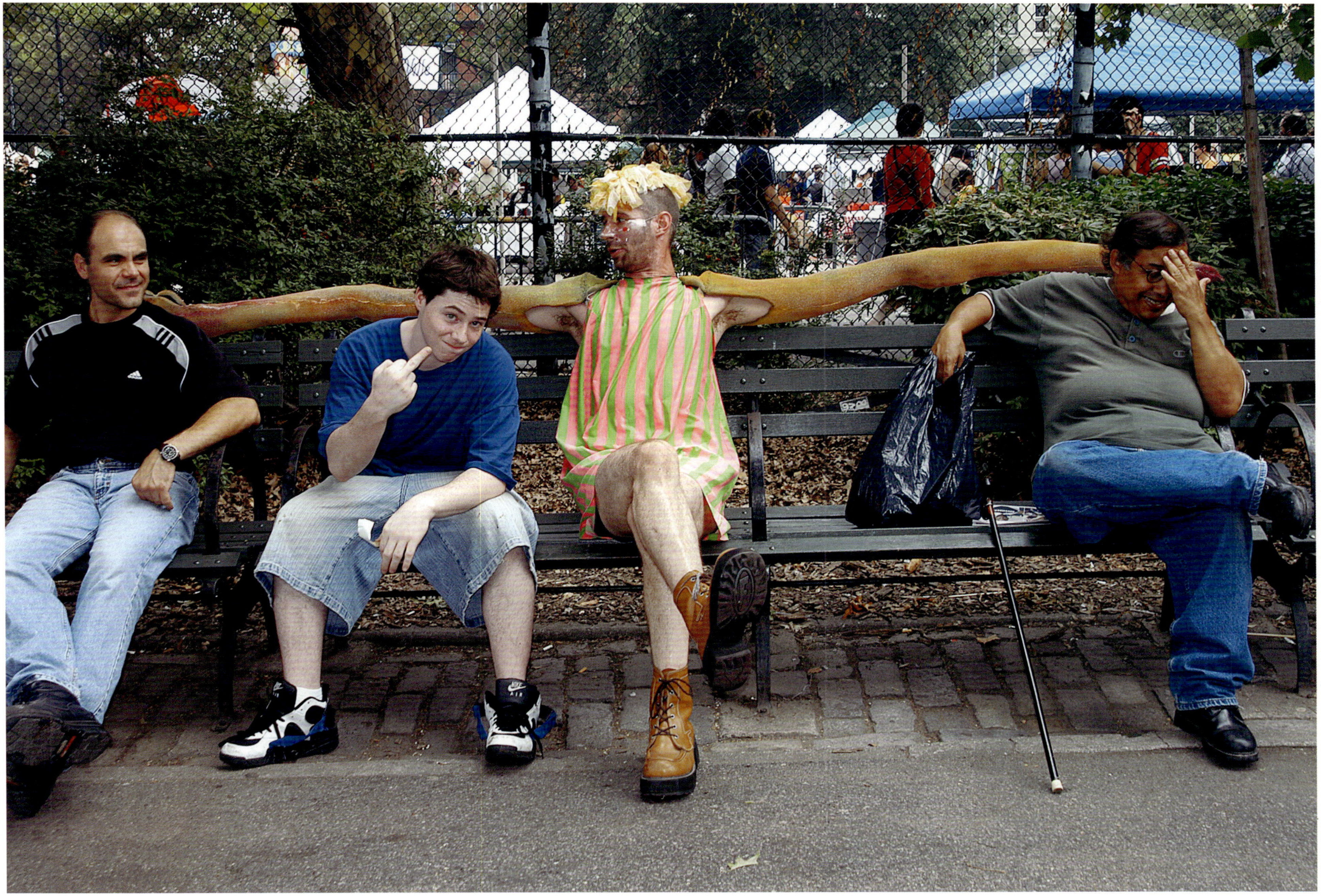

A group of men relax on a park bench in Tompkins Square Park in Manhattan's East Village.

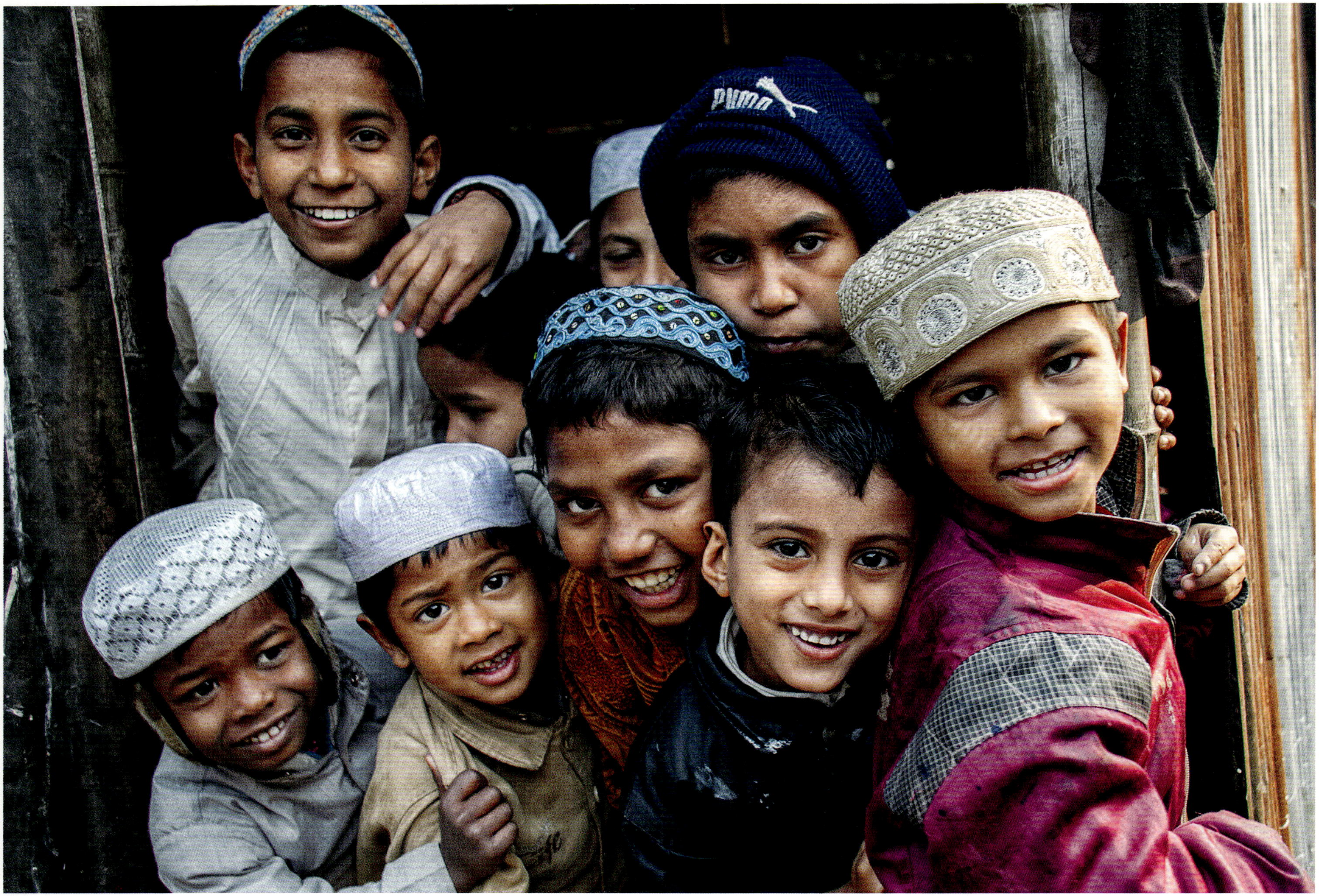

Children take a break from studying the Koran in a madrassa, a school for Islamic instruction, in a slum near Dhaka's Banani Lake.

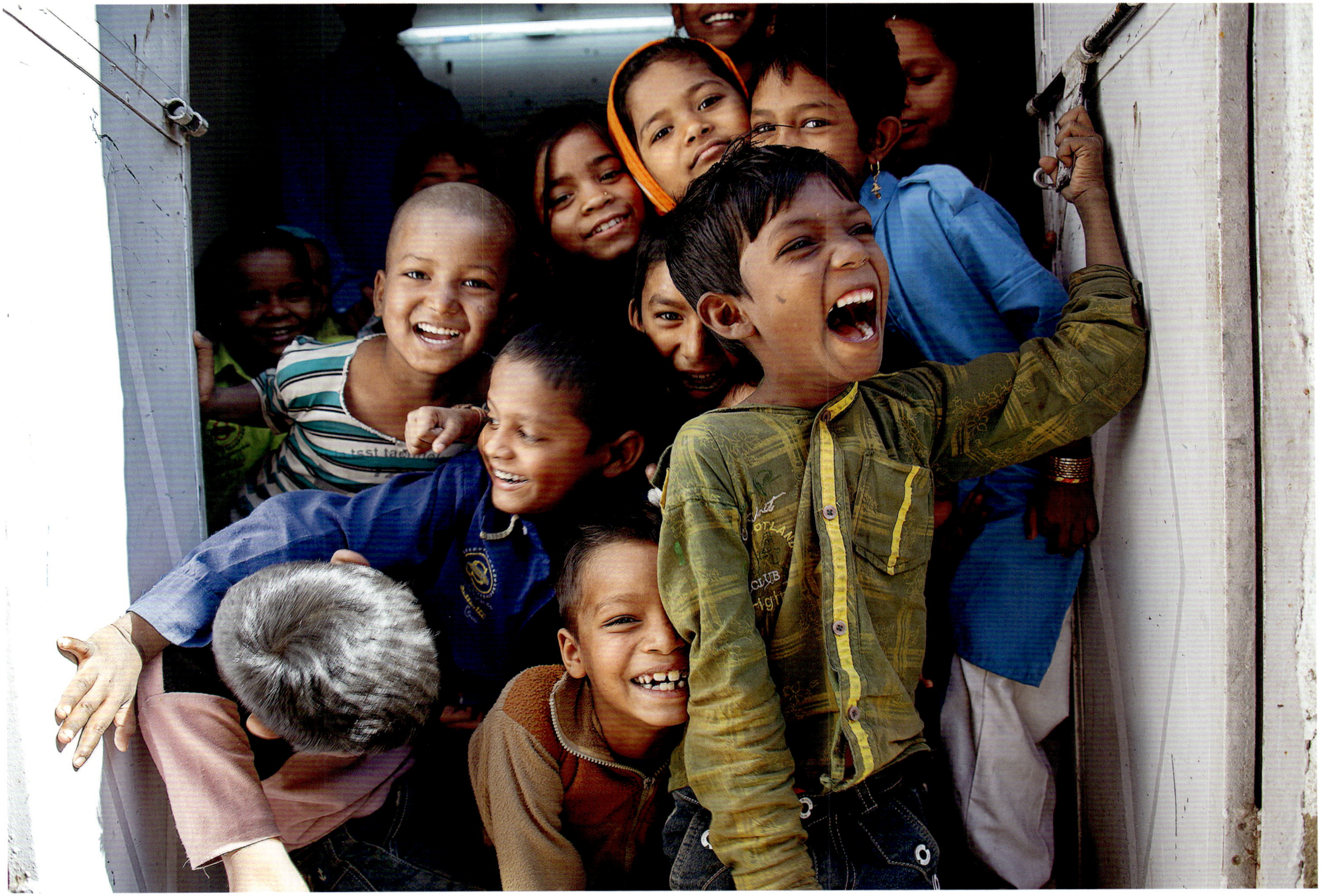

Young schoolchildren.

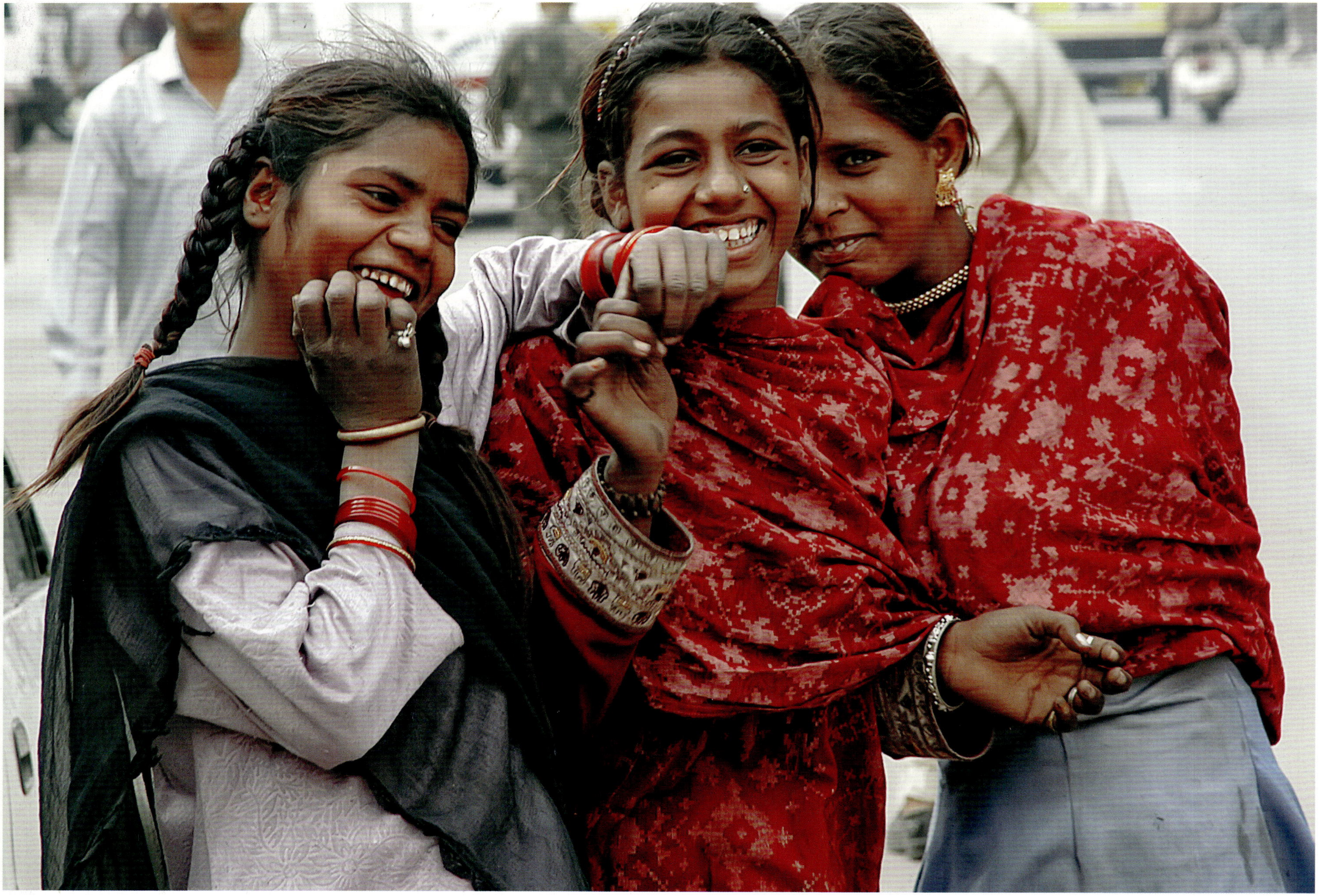

Three smiling girls in Mahim, a neighborhood in Mumbai known for its vibrant cultural diversity, educational opportunities, and accessible location.

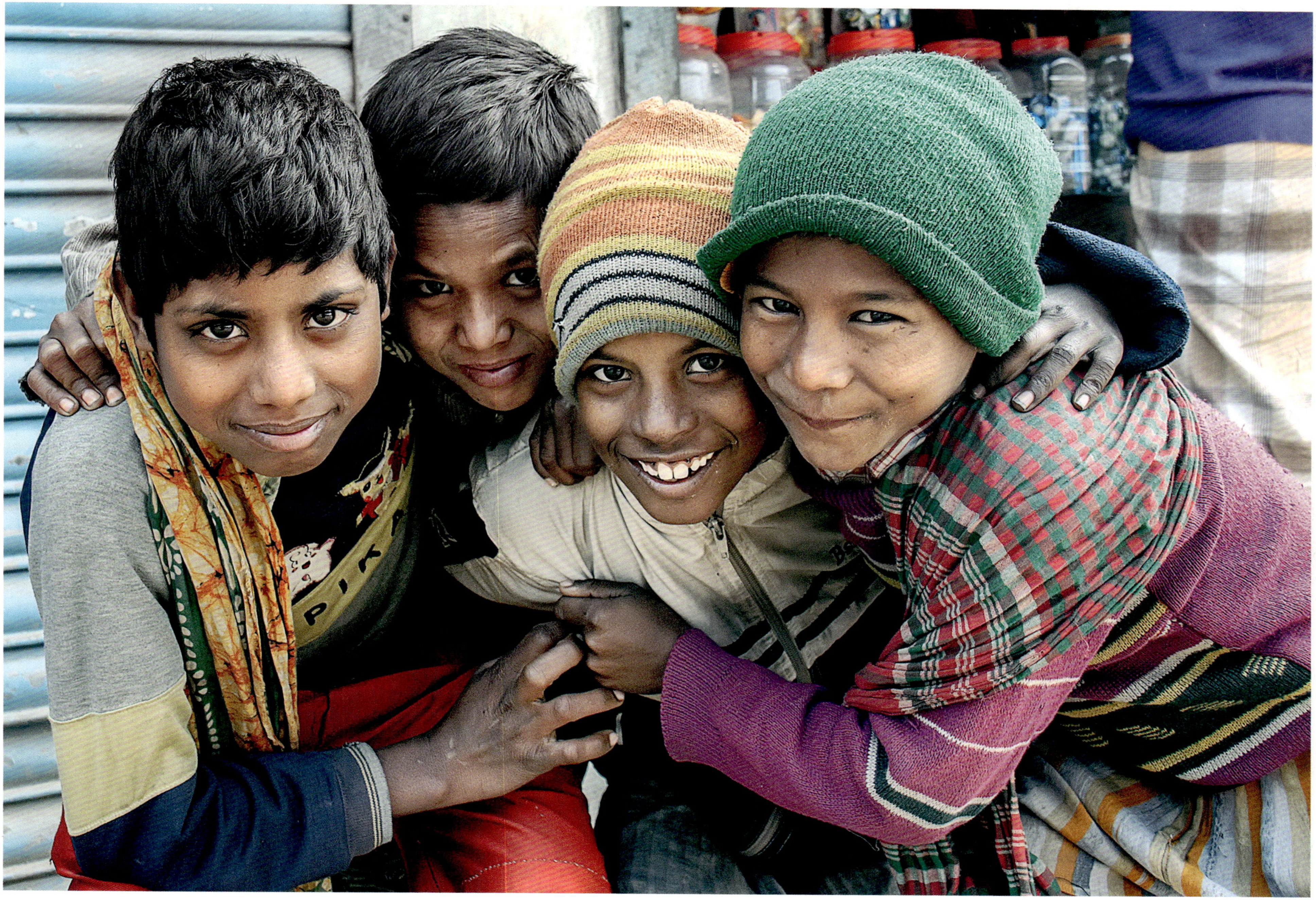

A group of children living in a Dhaka slum.

ACKNOWLEDGMENTS

My deeply felt appreciation goes to Dr. Robi Ludwig, whose motivation allowed this book to surface; Mr. Firoze Shakir, who has believed in me and supported my travels and work on the subcontinent; the people of India, Bangladesh, the Dominican Republic, and the other nations I have been blessed to travel in and through which I have gained a better understanding of the vicissitudes and commonality of humanity; Abraham Jacob Losack, who taught me the virtues of hard work; Apollo Publishers, for the opportunity to produce such an important witness to life in the developing nations and a chance to reach a wider audience; and Nikon, for making the most amazing machinery that I have grown to cherish and use in all my journeys.